The Houblon Family: Its Story and Times, Volume 1

Lady Alice Frances Lindsay Archer Houblon

THE HOUBLON FAMILY

Jacob Houblon, Fellow of Peterhouse, Cambridge.

FROM A SIGNED MINIATURE BY SAMUEL COOPER. 1664

ITS STORY AND TIMES

THE HOUBLON FAMILY

ITS STORY AND TIMES

LADY ALICE ARCHER HOUBLON

VOLUME I

Ici au milieu d'un grand Peuple
Nos Pères ont trouvés la douce hospitalité, le repos:
Nous, avec le Toit paternel,
Nous y avons trouvés La Patrie.

London
ARCHIBALD CONSTABLE
AND COMPANY, LTD.
1907

Edinburgh: T. and A. CONSTABLE, Printers to His Majesty

PREFACE

THERE are few families whose history can warrant a detailed account designed for publication, and the assumption, that any interest can be attached to such a record outside its immediate circle, demands justification. The plea which is here offered is, that the career of the Houblons affords a picture at once social and typical of their times. That the larger issues of patriotic and historic development, in the midst of which their lives were cast, have come to fill her horizon with matter scarcely within the scope of an ordinary biographical work, the author offers no apology; for this blending of the historical and biographical alone constitutes such originality and interest as her book may possess, and is the excuse for its publication. Even as in painting, the introduction of small figures gives life and proportion to the great landscapes of Salvator Rosa and Turner, the story of a family may perhaps serve to give life and *point* to that greater landscape of surrounding circumstance, in which its members lived and moved.

The narrative falls naturally into two parts, each containing the history of five generations; and while the first volume tells of the mercantile career of the Houblons, the second finds them once more *on the land*, from which they were originally drawn. From Picardy to Flanders, from Flanders to London, and from London to the Eastern Counties, has been the life-journey of this English family.

For the assistance of those persons to whom the ramifications of a somewhat intricate genealogical tree may be of interest, a paragraph pedigree has been annexed at the end of each volume, together with a skeleton chart. The individuals mentioned in the narrative, when bearing the same Christian name, are distinguished by a number immediately after it and below the line. These numbers are also given in the pedigree charts, and in the index. The two volumes are dealt with separately.

It remains for the author to tender her thanks to those who have shown an interest in these sketches of bygone days. To Mrs. Andrew Lang, who kindly undertook the pruning of an over-voluminous manu-script and the perusal of its proofs. To Mr. C. R. Ashbee, whose intimate knowledge of the industrial conditions under which the lives of the earlier genera-tions of the Houblon family were passed made his advice and criticism valuable ; and to Miss Lena Diver, without whose patient and intelligent searches among the musty treasures of the Record Office and elsewhere, the narrative, as it is here presented, would have been impossible to the author.

ARMS OF LINDSAY

CONTENTS

LIST OF ILLUSTRATIONS

THE HOUBLON FAMILY

CHAPTER I

'DES HOUBELON; DE PICARDIE'

'With my staff I passed over this Jordan, and now I am become two bands.'—GENESIS xxxii. 10.

THE Houblon family is of French origin. That its earliest known ancestor was of 'gentle' birth and originally came from Picardy there is no doubt, though we have not been able to discover the whereabouts of the fief in that great Province which gave their name to the seigneurial family. A scion of the stock of des Houblon—or des Houbelon, as it was formerly spelt—found his way to Lille near the close of the fifteenth century. His move there would have been both easy and natural, for not only was the language of the northern French and Belgic provinces the same, but the so-called Picardian Jurisdiction prevailed over both, facilitating the migration of families and individuals from one part of the country to another.

The younger sons of Picardy's *noblesse* were proverbially adventurous and enterprising. They were often men of the sword; knights errant; and they frequently travelled, not only over France and the Netherlands into Spain and Italy, but across the seas into Scotland. A close alliance existed in those days between France and the latter country. The French were reluctant—as they still are—to speak any tongue but their own;

but a Scottish gentleman thought ill of himself if he did not converse in the French language with ease. Much romance has been attached to the Scots in France, to the bold gentlemen archers of the astute and treacherous Louis XI., and to those chivalrous knights of whom Froissart and Monstrelet have told many a gallant story; but of the French who went to Scotland, and there were many who did so, no one has written or sung. One of Scotland's best families is descended from a noble youth whose energies and ambitions had found no scope for fortune in his native land. Originally it was *nulle terre sans Seigneur*,[1] later it came to be *nulle Seigneur sans terre*; so, wise in their generation, the cadet *gentilshommes* of Picardy and Normandy, like our own younger sons of peers, were content to take their place among the commons *sans terre* and distinctive title, and find their fortune at a distance from home. In this wise it came to pass that, like Ronsard, the sixteenth-century French poet who shared his pilgrimage, Jehan des Houbelon took ship in the service of the fair child-Queen of James V. of Scotland, when she sailed with him away

1537 to Scotland in the year 1537. In order to go with Magdalene de Valois, daughter of Francis I. of France, Brantôme tells us that 'Monsieur de Ronsard left his service as page to the Duke of Orleans, who gave him to her; and he went to see the world.'[2]

Miss Strickland has told the romantic story of James V. and his wooing with great charm, also of the tragic end of the 'pleasant Magdalen—the flower of France,' as she was called by the Scottish King's Herald.[3] She brought many ladies and gentlemen in her train from France, some of whom probably came, as did de

---

[1] *Mémoires de la Société d'archéologie de la Somme*, ii. 302.
[2] Brantôme, *Lives of the Princesses of France of His Times;* apud *Queens of Scotland.* Strickland, pp. 502-3.
[3] *The Deploration of the Death of Queen Magdalene*, by Sir David Lindsay, Lord Lyon of Scotland. 1537.

Ronsard, to 'see the world.' They apparently did not like Holyrood—beautiful as it was—so well as France; while James and his bride were for the time so absorbed in each other's society as to make life *triste* at the Court.[1] So after the fragile seventeen - year - old Queen had succumbed to rapid consumption, her attendants mostly returned home. Jehan des Houbelon, however, chose to stay and adopt the country for his own.

Although he settled down as a merchant in Edinburgh and later became a zealous protestant, he had had as yet no time to develop these virtues when, the year following his arrival in the north, we find him in London. The object of this visit may have been still further to 'see the world'; or perhaps it was made for the purpose of establishing a mercantile connection in that city. His name occurs under the form of von Hoblyn, a mode of spelling it very common in early times, and representing the effort of the English scribe to render into English the sound of the name as pronounced in the foreign way. The prefix *von* to him who wrote it (rather than *de* or *des*) would have been unimportant, either being foreign and belonging to a foreigner.

In 1538 Thomas Lord Cromwell was at the height **1538** of his power, though but two years later saw an end to his career. The work of suppressing the monasteries, and later the abjuration of papal claims, was fruitful of future advantage, but it was done at great cost, for the opposition was powerful and determined. Henry VIII. supported Cromwell and his measures unflinchingly; but when the task was accomplished he nevertheless threw over his man.

The last and greatest of the oaks felled by Cromwell in clearing the ground were the King's cousins; and among the mass of documents which bear witness to the tireless

---

[1] *Lives of the Queens*, etc.

espionage by which he netted the opponents who sought
to stay him, is the one in which the name of von Hoblyn
occurs.

In this document we find Cromwell's spies bearing
witness to things spoken or done that could be twisted
into the crime of high treason which it was desired to
bring up against the Marquis of Exeter. Cromwell had
found him in his path, and struck, regardless of his royal
lineage. The evidence, if true, shows that Exeter aimed
high. A man, named in the document Qymparel, was
the marquis's servant. Peter Corringdon was a spy;
while a Richard Kendal was also in the plot, engaging
men to act in the coming 'business' in the service of
Exeter. 'For,' said Qymparel, his master 'was Heir
apparent, and in case the King should die or marry, the
Marquis should be King.' For this reason 'he desired
one Richard Harrys that he be retained to Kendal for
the Marquis.' Peter Corringdon the spy then goes
on to retail another point in the evidence. 'Richard
Kendal said to von Hoblyn (tenant to Gilbert Becket
and another) that he, Kendal, must shortly make (or
engage) a hundreth men. For this reason, after supper
he must entertayn them.'[1] It would appear that the
supper took place, and that some at least of the
individuals mentioned in Corringdon's evidence took
service with Kendal. Whether 'von Hoblyn' joined
in the plot or was engaged among the 'hundred men,'
we know not; but it is at least clear that he was
still in sympathy with those who desired to preserve
the *status quo*, in respect of things temporal and
ecclesiastic.

When Exeter paid the penalty of his ambition and
claims,—not least of which was the threat as to the
marriage with Anne Boleyn,—Montacute, his cousin
and the Countess of Salisbury's son, fell likewise; and

---

[1] *Letters and Papers*, 30 Henry VIII., 140, No. 961.

soon afterwards the Countess herself. She was a Tudor, and niece to Edward IV.; but all three 'were executed.'[1]

Jean des Houbelon married a Scottish lady named Elizabeth or Bessie Cumming, and soon translated his name into Hope. 'They had their name from the plant,' remarked an old chronicler of the family, 'and not from *esperance*, the virtue in the mind.'[2] Though the commonly accepted explanation of the change from Houbelon to Hope is in the fact that the plant which is *houblon* in French is *hop* in English, and that, in common with many other strangers in a new country, the Houbelons adopted the English equivalent for their name;—it is equally possible, in the present instance, that it was simply an abbreviation. *P* and *b* are commonly interchangeable, and Houbelon needed but to be Houpelon, or Houpe only. The old family mansion of the Hopes in the Cowgate of Edinburgh, built in 1616, had indeed this legend carved over its doorway:

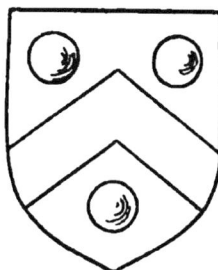

1616

ARMS OF HOPE.

At Hospes Humo.

i.e. 'I am a stranger on earth'; and though intended by the good man who wrote it, as a profession of faith in the divine origin of man, and his own ultimate hope of attaining to its realisation, the words yet contain the same letters as make up his own name: Thomas Houpe.[3] Nevertheless, in the time of this Sir Thomas Hope, the first comer's great-grandson, the family patronymic was sufficiently well established to admit of his making punning allusions to his '*hopes*

---

[1] See for interesting account of Cromwell and his work, Green's *Short History of the English People.*
[2] *The Coltness Collections. Printed for the Maitland Club. Being Memorials of the Stewarts of Allanton, Coltness, and Goodtrees.* By Sir Archibald Stewart Denham, pp. 14, 15.
[3] *Traditions of Edinburgh*, by Robert Chambers, 1868.

anent his sons,' in presenting petitions to the King's Majesty in respect of them. Sir Thomas Hope was high in the King's favour, notwithstanding his strong presbyterian sympathies. He was created a Baronet by Charles I. in 1628, and at the same time Lord Advocate of Scotland, which he continued to be till his death in 1645.[1]

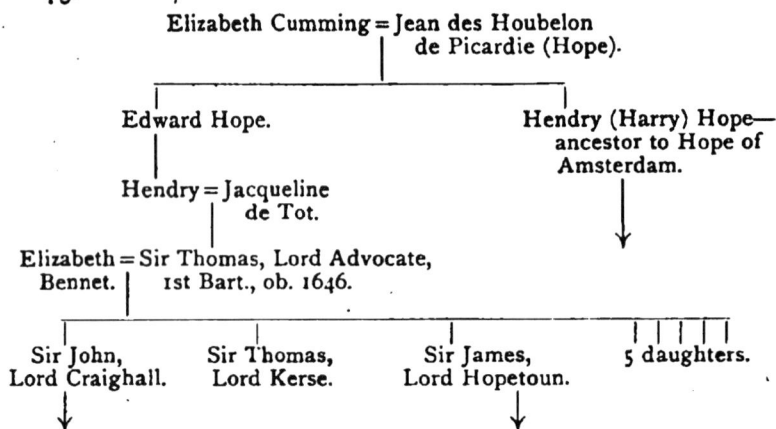

Elizabeth Cumming = Jean des Houbelon de Picardie (Hope).

Edward Hope.

Hendry (Harry) Hope— ancestor to Hope of Amsterdam.

Hendry = Jacqueline de Tot.

Elizabeth = Sir Thomas, Lord Advocate, Bennet. | 1st Bart., ob. 1646.

Sir John, Lord Craighall.

Sir Thomas, Lord Kerse.

Sir James, Lord Hopetoun.

5 daughters.

Their French origin made the early Hopes of Scotland ambitious their children should 'get a grip of that language '; and so the young men went to France and at the same time advanced their business as merchants, for though the Lord Advocate Hope was the first of many great lawyers of his race, trade had in the first

[1] Sir Thomas Hope, Lord High Commissioner to the General Assembly which met at Edinburgh, 2 Aug. 1643, was the only Commoner who ever filled that great office. He was also Commissioner for managing the Exchequer in 1645, and died the following year 1646. Three of his sons were Lords of Session, likewise several of his grandsons. It would appear that officious genealogists were desirous of tracing a more illustrious descent for one of the Lord Advocate's sons—Lord Hopetoun. In this connection Sir Archibald Stewart Denham, himself descended from a daughter of Sir Thomas, remarks in reference to the French origin of the family : 'This is our Familie tradition of the Hopes, however fictitious genealogies may be invented to flatter a noble overgrown rich family as is now earl Hopton's' (sic). See Memorials of the Stewarts of Allanton, Coltness, and Goodtrees, by Sir A. S. Denham. This allusion probably refers to the suggestion that the Hope family had their ancestor in John de Hope, one of the free barons who submitted to Edward I. when he invaded Scotland in 1496. See The Ancient and Modern State of the Parish of Cramond, by J. P. Wood, p. 132.

instance made the fortunes of the family. The story of his 'guidschir from whom he was in the degree of third in descent' is told in his diary, and has likewise been handed down the generations to his descendants.[1] Truly the Picardy youth must have had some good stuff in him; for while he produced a race of great lawyers on the one part,[2] on the other he and his Bessie were the progenitors of another distinguished family. Harry Hope, likewise his descendant, having married a daughter of his cousin the Lord Advocate, became the founder of the famous banking house of Hope of Amsterdam. 'A house,' we are told, 'for extent of commerce and solidity of credit long considered superior without exception to any private company in the world.'[3]

But when Jehan des Houbelon came to Scotland in Queen Magdalene's suite, his kinsman of the same name had already been established for a generation in French Flanders; and we shall presently see how many other families also made their way to the neighbouring Provinces of the Netherlands in these early times. A tradition has come down to us as to the arms of the French seigneurial family of des Houbelon which Burke gives as: 'Azure Three Fishes naiant propper, the Crest a dexter hand holding up a book expanded propper.'[4] If this be so, the Scottish Hopes likewise bore these arms in Picardy.

ARMS OF
DES HOUBELON.

---

[1] *Diary*, published by the Bannatyne Club, 1843. The Lord Advocate Hope's letters have been published in the *Miscellany* of the Scottish History Society, vol. i.

[2] The head of the Hope family in Scotland is Sir Alexander, 15th Baronet, of Pinkie House, Midlothian, who is descended from the King's Advocate's eldest son. From a younger son, the Earls of Hopetoun (now Marquesses of Linlithgow) are descended.

[3] Robert Chambers. *Biographical Dictionary of Eminent Scotsmen*, ii. 285-6. Ed. Rev. Thos. Thomson.

[4] Burke's *General Armory*.

It has been suggested that the name of a certain village called Houpelin, situated on the river Lys and near to Lille, might warrant the assumption that they belonged to the noblesse of the province of Lille and that they took their patronymic from that fief.[1] The names are so alike that this might well have been, the letters *p* and *b*, as we have already observed, being interchangeable, the same being the case with regard to the terminations *on* and *in*. Though we do indeed find a member of the family, who emigrated to America out of England in the seventeenth century, spelling his name Houpleine, there is nothing further than this to give colour to the idea; while, at any rate, we have distinct evidence that the earliest member of the family of whom we have found any trace in Flanders lived not in the village of Houpelin but in that of Fives.[2] That the Flemish Houbelons, as well as the Hopes of Scotland, came from Picardy there is much circumstantial evidence to show. How long the first of the name may have inhabited the Chatellenie of Lille before we come across him it is impossible to determine, but suffice it to say that he adopted the country and people as his own, identified himself with the political and industrial conditions which he found in being, and settled down as a native of Walloon or French Flanders, unconscious that he and his children were but 'sojourners in a strange land,' to be exchanged by and by for one over the seas. It is probable that the first emigration was prompted, at any rate in part, by the same considerations as the second; religious reform may have induced a change of abode in both.

In France the fifteenth century already saw a great change in respect of religious feeling. A vast number

---

[1] See *La Marche de Lille.* An escutcheon in this MS. bears the word 'Houpelin' written across it. (British Museum.)

[2] 'Fives veut dire Cinq Sources.' See Lewez, *Histoire particulière des Provinces Belges*, iii. 107.

of people in the northern provinces were imbued with principles strongly at variance with the accepted dogmas of the Roman Church. Direct persecution was indeed hardly yet systematised in France; but those professing the new tenets, in whatever form, generally had their minds awakened and liberated, by their attitude of independence from the ancient trammels of thought and action. Thus, even the old were enabled to form new projects of life, and to take steps which involved a complete revolution of the conditions in which they had been wont to exist. Awakening came with the New Learning, enterprise followed with the Reformation, and the Houbelons, and such as they, felt the influence of both to the core. In this manner the same spirit of freedom and emancipation of mind which inspired the one *gentil-homme de Picardie* to 'see the world' in Scotland, had already drawn the other to Flanders, and while John of the north had wit to use his situation to increase his fortune by trading with his old country, the Jehan who went to Flanders was as ready to adapt himself to his new surroundings as his kinsman. Both likewise early espoused the tenets of the Reformation. Edward Hope, the son of John, was 'one of the most considerable inhabitants of Edinburgh in the reign of Queen Mary'; and not only was he 'one of the Commissioners for that metropolis to the Parliament,' but he was likewise 'a great promoter of the Reformation[1] and was chosen a member of the first Protestant General Assemblie.'[2] We shall presently see how their love for truth and the liberty to think and act in harmony with it, was to colour the lives of the Houbelons of Flanders.

Though noble birth did not then preclude the younger members of a seigneurial house from any profession

[1] *Peerage of Scotland,* 1813, by Sir Robert Douglas (ref. Calderwood, *Church History*, MS.).
[2] *The Ancient and Modern State of the Parish of Cramond,* by J. P. Wood.

other than a military one—for trade was honoured and
its privileges cultivated—it would appear that it was
generally at a distance from home that the young men
found scope for their industrial energies.   Hence the
migration into the teeming cities of the democratic
Netherlands.   But while they frequently became crafts-
men, and worked their way up in the social and industrial scale from humble beginnings, it was another
matter in respect of their family alliances; and for many
generations the registers, so carefully kept by the protestant communities whether at home or afterwards in
England, reveal that *like married like* in respect of
gentle or plebeian origin, and this rule was kept with
regard to the Houbelons both in Flanders and in Scotland.   While John of the north married a lady of the
Scottish house of Cumming, when his grandson took
to himself a French wife, she was of the same degree
and birth as had been his ancestor ere he forsook
Picardy for his northern home.   It was in his capacity
of a merchant that Henry Hope was wont occasionally
to visit Paris; and once when he went there to bring
home the silks and velvets, and gold and silver lace, that
the Scots—poor as they were supposed to be—must
needs have, he met Jacqueline de Tot, whom he made
his wife.   Later she became the mother of the Lord
Advocate, Sir Thomas Hope.

Having seen the beginnings of the fortunes of the
Hopes of Scotland, and recognised the success which
was to mark their careers in jurisprudence, we will
proceed to the history of their Flemish kinsmen, the
circumstances of whose lives and surroundings are exclusively to concern us in this book.   Meanwhile, as
much of the interest attaching to the history of a family
depends upon the country which it inhabits, we may
perhaps be allowed a few words about the Netherlands,
and French Flanders in particular.

The great fief of Flanders was the most ancient of the feudatory states of France. In that part of it that lies on the borders of France proper, was situated the domain of the Walloons. This domain comprised the provinces of Hainault, Namur, Liége, and Luxemburg, besides part of Brabant. And here the French language was spoken as well as the ancient Walloon dialect, said to be derived from the *langue d'Oïl* or northern French, and to this day much resembling in idiom the patois of the French provinces of Picardy and Lorraine.[1]

In Teutonic Flanders, so-called, lying between the seacoast and the Scheldt, and the rivers Lys and Aa, the language spoken was Flemish, and the country resembled parts of Holland in that it was flat and very populous. Walloon Flanders (except for its thriving cities) was in those days but thinly populated, being wild and picturesque, abounding in quick-flowing rivers and thick forests. The character of the peoples likewise differed, as much as did the features of the country and language. The chief towns of Walloon Flanders comprised Lille, Tournay, Courtrai, Douay, Orchies, etc., while those of the Teutonic states included the important and rich cities of Ghent and Bruges, besides Ypres, Ostend, Nieuport, Dunkirk, and others. In all alike the mainspring of existence was busy, thriving, intelligent industry. An almost unbroken record of these qualities distinguished the Flemish peoples throughout many centuries, a record only blemished by a civic pride and intolerance that seems inseparable from the burgher life of the Middle Ages.

Under a long line of Flemish princes the country had waxed prosperous and powerful till, by the marriage of the heiress of the last of its Counts with the Duke of

[1] See *Mémoires de la Société des Antiquaires de Picardie*. Amiens, 1837-9.

Burgundy, brother of Philip of Valois, the two states were united in one.   Later still, Flanders together with the whole of the northern provinces known as the Low Countries, passed, through the marriage of Mary of Burgundy with Maximilian, the Emperor's son, into the hands of the Hapsburgs; French Flanders was thus for a time severed from the old tie to France, and found in them, cold and haughty suzerains.

At the date of the union of the provinces of the Netherlands with Spain under the Hapsburgs, the inhabitants were a bold and free people.   The great merchants and *bourgeoisie*, while they prized the refinements of luxury and taste beyond any other people of their time, were also imbued with a spirit of freedom which had known how to defy authority successfully when those liberties were unjustly infringed.   Motley's book on the revolt of the Netherlands thus describes them: 'There was life, movement, bustling activity everywhere.   An energetic population swarmed in all the flourishing cities which dotted the face of a contracted and highly cultivated country.   Their ships were carriers of the world.   Their merchants, if invaded in their rights, engaged in vigorous warfare with their own funds and their own frigates; their fabrics were prized over the whole earth; their burghers possessed the wealth of princes, lived in royal luxury, and exercised vast political influence; their love of liberty was their predominant passion.'[1]   The Spaniard, arrogant, narrow, and bigoted, was incapable either of understanding or sympathising with this spirit of civic freedom in the provinces, or with the progressive ethical development which had resulted from the free exercise of thought and action throughout many generations.   On the other hand, the people of the Netherlands were unable to appreciate the splendid prestige of race and military

[1] J. L. Motley, *Rise of the Dutch Republic.*

enterprise which had made the Spaniards the then rulers of the world. Intensely commercial, the people had exchanged ideas as well as commodities with other nations. 'Truth was imported as freely as less precious merchandise, and the prohibitory measures of a despotic government could not annihilate this intellectual trade.'[1]

Such, then, was the country and such the people from whence came the ancestors of the English Houblons. But meanwhile they bore their share in the stress of industrial life, and the time had not yet arrived when religious persecution, having reduced their smiling and prosperous home to ruin and endangered their own lives, forced them to abandon it for their faith's sake, and join in the great exodus from the Low Countries to England in the early years of Queen Elizabeth.

When Jehan des Houbelon left his old home to settle in Flanders he was accompanied by his wife and son, and the latter appears to have been apprenticed by his father to a burgher of Lille very early in the sixteenth century. He would have been, according to the custom, about fifteen years old on thus beginning his industrial life, the bond between master and apprentice being unbreakable. During this time the elder Jehan became possessed of land in or near the village of Fives, and lived there till the close of his life.

Fives, the home of the elder Jehan, was situated so close to the city under the ramparts, as to be separated from them only by the massive stone bridge across the *fosse*, or moat, which encircled the town. About a hundred years later Fives, together with bridge, moat, and defended gate, was absorbed into the city itself, and, the *enceinte* having been thus enlarged, fresh fortifications were raised on the new boundary.[2] The free citizens of Lille were justly proud of their ancient city,

---

[1] J. L. Motley, *Rise of the Dutch Republic*, i. 225.
[2] On six several occasions the city of Lille was thus enlarged.

which, as the capital of Flanders, had held a distinguished place in the history of the country. Now,
French boulevards and cafés have taken the place of
the ancient *Halles* and stately squares of the old
mediæval town, for French Flanders, and Lille in particular, have become undistinguishably French.

The ancient vassalage to the French King as suzerain
was interrupted by the Spanish interregnum during one
hundred and forty-six years, for the Emperor Charles v.
repudiated fealty to France on behalf of the provinces,
and incorporated them with his Spanish dominions;
but the taking of the stronghold of Lille by Louis xiv.
1667 in 1667 once more restored the ancient allegiance to
France, and the city finally ranked as fifth among her
commercial towns, and is now one of the most active of
French industrial centres.[1]

From old engravings of the city we are able to form
some conception of her appearance as a mediæval town.
Enclosing within her strong walls groups of tall towers,
spires, and high-roofed buildings, Lille was built on
the originally insignificant river Deûle. Surrounded by
water—partly by the river itself greatly deepened and
enlarged—the city was intersected by numerous canals,
while outside the ramparts it was entirely encircled by
a deep and wide *fosse* or 'town-ditch,' spanned by massive
stone bridges. The only approach possible was thus
by means of the bridges, each of which was closed at
its inner extremity by a city gate. The great walls,
1296 constructed by the Lillois in 1296, were flanked by
fourteen towers, each gate being further protected from
assault from without, by an outer portal or wicket-
gate opening sideways upon the rampart, so as to enable
the defenders within to take an enemy in the flank when
endeavouring to force an entry. At the close of the fifteenth century these gates were eight in number. Built

[1] *Gazetteer of the World,* p. 734.

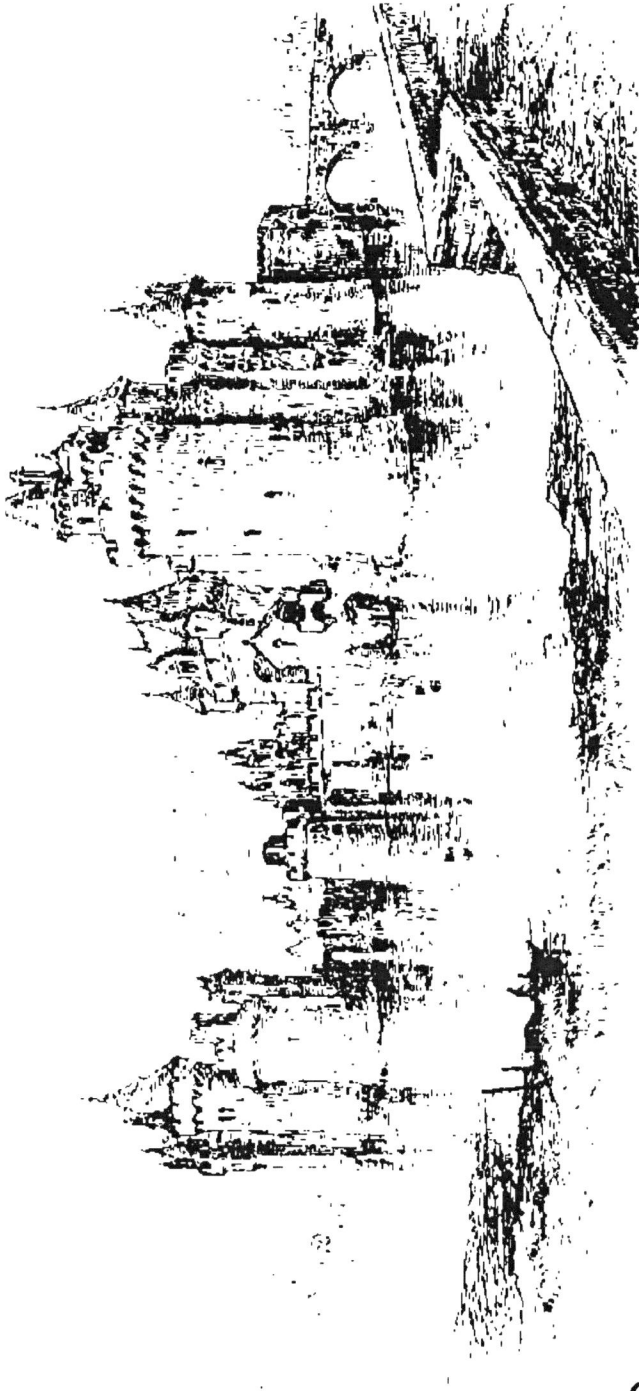

FORTIFIED LILLE, 1582.

of huge blocks of dressed stone, these grim portals of
fortified towns were usually protected on each side by
towers, from which depended the chains which served
to lower or raise the drawbridge. Here, day and night,
watch and ward was kept by the municipal guard, composed exclusively of members of the bourgeoisie. The
gates were closed every night, and each burgess was
called upon to take his turn in the safeguard of his
native city.[1]

Jehan Houbelon the younger, on entering his apprenticeship in the early dawn of the sixteenth century, did
not go far, for in the parish of St. Sauveur, that most
contiguous to Fives, the youth found his home. There
he remained during the rest of his life, and there also
his children married and settled down, as may be seen
in the early registers and archives in which Lille is
rich.

'Jehan Houbelon, natif de Fives,' as he is designated,
became probably what was called a *forain* or *bourgeois-
forain*, that is to say, a foreigner or outside burgess.[2]
This title of *forain* was applied to those country proprietors or yeomen throughout the Chatellenie who,
though not possessing the full privileges attendant on
the freedom of a city, yet enjoyed rights of bourgeoisie,
which distinguished them from the rest of the country
population. Indeed, had he not been 'free born,' Jehan's
son would have been ineligible for apprenticeship within

[1] A Florentine gentleman, in a work published in 1567, says that 'Pour
le trafic des marchandises et les mestiers exercés en Lille on la tient pour
la principale, apres Anvers et Amsterdam, entre toutes les Villes des Pays-
Bas sujet au roy Catholique' (Traduction contemporaine de Louis Guic-
cardin. Anvers, 1567).

[2] All who lived within the walls of a Flemish city were collectively
entitled *intranes* (? interned). They were divided into two distinct groups:
that of the bourgeois or freeman, and that of the *manant*, a name which
comprised every individual who paid taxes without possessing the freedom
of the city. The term *extranes* included the population extraneous to
the city (see Van Hende, *Lille et ses Institutions Communales*, p. 8). In
England these groups were termed respectively *forenseci* and *intrinseci*,
while strangers were called *extranei* (Gross, *Gild Merchant*, i. 67). In
the sixteenth century Stow speaks of 'forains' in his *Survey of London*.

the city.[1]   It is probable that after his settlement in the
country he became a cultivator of those plants which
were largely grown throughout the Chatellenie for the
purpose of dyeing the wools and silks of which the
splendid tapestries and woven cloths were made.   The
skill of the dyers of Lille contributed greatly to the
fame of these stuffs,[2] and immense pains were bestowed
on the cultivation of the *wedde* and *garance* (woad and
madder) and other plants then most used as dyes.[3]   So
important was it to maintain the high reputation of the
Lille dyes, that strict regulations were enforced as to
their production and use, while heavy penalties were
attached to any infringement of these rules.

It would appear that in Lille itself Jehan Houbelon
of Fives was well known.   Indeed, if our conjecture is
correct as to his occupation, he would have been in
constant communication with those craft-gilds which
he supplied with the plants from which they produced
their dyes.[4]   Although it is possible that Houbelon
apprenticed his son to some master-craftsman in the
gild of the *teinturiers* or dyers, it is more probable
that young Jehan's master belonged to one of the gilds
specially concerned in the making of the stuffs.   These
fine cloths were largely exported, and it was by this
trade that the family at a later date waxed rich.

Young Jehan Houbelon then, with all the world before

[1] On the Continent only the sons of freeborn forains were admitted to
apprenticeships in the towns, while in England, so stringent were the laws
against emigration off the land into the towns, that no one was allowed to
become an apprentice in a town unless he had property qualifications
equivalent to £200, modern value (see Denton, *England in the Fifteenth
Century*, p. 223).

[2] Van Hende, *Lille et ses Institutions Communales*, p. 158.

[3] Cochineal was also much used, but indigo was not yet known in the
Netherlands (*Ibid.*, p. 150).

[4] Mr. Gross says that burgesses possessed of country property who were
not merchants, found it advisable to join the gild of a town in order that
they might dispose of the produce of their lands and the manufactures of
their *villeins*, viz. labourers. 'The same would be true,' he adds, 'though
to a less degree, of the humble agricultural Burgher' (see Gross, *Gild
Merchant*, v. 74).

him, entered on his new life as apprentice to some prosperous bourgeois of Lille about the year 1502, when he must have been fifteen or sixteen years old. He would serve his indentures under his master's roof, and the length of service varied according to the rules of the gild. At the end of his apprenticeship he would probably continue in his master's workshop as journeyman or handicraftsman, until such time as he had acquired sufficient experience to admit of his establishing an *atelier* or a *comptoir*, as was the privilege of a master-craftsman. Once a master, employing journeymen of his own,[1] he would possess the right of exposing the *draperies* woven on his looms, for sale in the open market or on the quays of the river Deûle, in that place which was allotted for the merchandise of his particular gild. But whether he sold his goods there or at home, all that was produced under his auspices was subject to the inspection of the *égards*, or examiners of merchandise, and it could not be sold until the plummet or leaden seal (called the *Plomb de Commerce*) bearing the arms of Lille had been attached to each bale.

The tradition was held by their descendants that early in the sixteenth century the Houbelons of Lille were flourishing merchants in that city; and Jehan₂ Houbelon, before his death in 1555, appears to have reached a position of prosperity in the town, having carried on during the latter part of his life an extended commerce in conjunction with his sons. From the character for rectitude combined with business capacity borne by many of his descendants, we may perhaps

[1] It was a rule among the gilds that any craftsman desirous of setting up as a master, and as such employing others, should first submit to an examination, and produce evidence of his skill in his craft, so as to satisfy the *Échevins* and *Conseil* of his town—that is to say the governing body—as to his fitness to employ others.

infer that their progenitor possessed the same qualities, and that they contributed to his success both in business transactions and in obtaining the regard and respect of his fellow-citizens. Be that as it may, Jehan, Houbelon, whatever future success was in store for him, had by the year 1523 attained to such a position in the town as to be accepted by the daughter of a wealthy citizen, and to claim admission to that rank of bourgeois which was so highly coveted.

1523

The registers of the bourgeoisie of Lille, preserved among the *archives communales* of the city, form an unbroken series for a period of very nearly five hundred years, dating from 1292. In these *Registres aux Bourgeois* are to be found the names of all Lillois belonging to the bourgeoisie of the town, the dates of their admission to the privileges, the names of their children, and much incidental information throwing light upon their family history.[1] The following entry relating to Jehan, Houbelon occurs in folio 67 of the registers :

'Jehan Houbelon fitz de feu Jehan natif de Fives, ayant de sa premiere femme quatre enfans nommez Jennin, Pierchon, Hubert et Pasquette, fut reçu Bourgeois de Lille par achat le vi° jour de Mai 1523. Payé, xv Livres.'

At the time that Jehan, Houbelon was admitted to the rights of bourgeoisie and the above entry was made, they were not difficult to obtain by wealthy townsmen who were possessed of a house and a sufficient competence to admit of their contributing not less than thirty

---

[1] The modern French word *bourgeois* hardly conveys to our English ears the impression of dignity and importance which was attached to it in the days of which we write; nor does the modern bourgeois class on the Continent much resemble the old. The great Revolution of 1789 over-threw the 'old order,' and with it the ancient bourgeoisie of the towns; for the privileges it conveyed were incompatible with the new doctrines of liberty, equality, and fraternity. French Flanders was now part of France proper. The title of bourgeois was therefore abolished, the Échevinage or magistracy was likewise done away with, and the name citizen henceforth embraced the whole body of inhabitants.

livres per annum towards the municipal burdens of the city.[1] But as the freedom of the city could only be obtained, even by substantial citizens, when they bore a good name and reputation, and had obtained the consent of the Échevinage, the bourgeoisie of the Chatellenie of Lille was practically limited to the most honourable and wealthy among its citizens.[2]

The freedom of the city was conferred on certain fixed days of the year, and the ceremony, which took place in the Halle d'Échevinage, or Gildhall, was followed by a feast. At the sound of the *bancloche*, itself the type and evidence of a free city,[3] the eight treasurers (*huit-hommes*; later, *prud-hommes*), who formed part of the government of the town, assembled together in the Halle, where they were met by the other municipal officers, and by the candidates for admission. The choice of the new bourgeois and their reception in the Halle d'Échevinage lay in the hands of the huit-hommes, and here, dressed in their robes of office, they performed the ceremony of admitting them and of administering the oaths. The oath accompanying the admission was regarded as of great solemnity. The bourgeois elect promised to 'rester un bon, honnête et loyal maitre,'[4] but bound himself above all to maintain the privileges of his order; at all times was his personal interest and that of his family to be subordinated to that of the burghal community; its secrets were to be respected and its injuries avenged; while he strictly

---

[1] In England the burgess was required to be the owner of a burgage tenement within the town (see Gross, *Gild Merchant*, i. 71).

[2] Van Hende, *Lille et ses Institutions Communales*, p. 48.

[3] In some cities a special bell was used for this purpose. In England sometimes a horn was blown.

> 'If the citie horn twice sound
> Every burgher will be found
> Eager in the warlike labour
> Striving to out-do his neighbour.'

From the Norman French (see Gross, *Gild Merchant*, i. 74). For *bancloche*, see Houdoy's *Halle d'Échevinage de Lille*, i. 4.

[4] Félix de Vigne, *Mœurs et Usages des Corporations de Métiers de la Belgique et du Nord de la France*. Gand, 1857.

engaged himself never at any time to take part against a fellow-bourgeois in any dispute with a stranger; for the support and assistance of their fellows in a quarrel could be claimed by every bourgeois, whether he were in the right or whether he were in the wrong. If he were admitted by purchase to the freedom of his city, the bourgeois was called upon to pay into the city exchequer a duty of six livres, a further sum being required of him of fifteen *livres parisis* as a *hanse* or commercial tribute, while he had also to place in the hands of the *Rewart*, or sheriff of the city, five marks of 'fine silver,' or its equivalent in bonds, as caution-money.

The ceremony over, as we have seen, it was followed by a feast, and it would appear that on these occasions it was the custom for the burgesses' wives to take part in the banquet. Catherine Bave, Jehan, Houbelon's second wife, was a freewoman by birth, and she, doubtless, as well as her husband, dined in the Halle d'Échevinage after the ceremony of his admission as a bourgeois of Lille. That his first wife had been drawn from a French family of the same class as the elder Jehan is probable, for marriages were then arranged by the parents of the parties concerned, and he would have been too short a time in his democratic Flemish surroundings to admit of his choosing a bourgeois bride for his son.[1] But in his second matrimonial venture, Jehan, it would seem, greatly advanced his fortunes.

By the wording of the 'acte' of his bourgeoisie we find that by his first wife Jehan had four young children. It will be observed that in the case of two of them, their *prénoms* (*petits noms* or 'pet' names) are made use of in the act. Jennin and Pierchon were, amongst other forms, then in use as *prénoms* of Jean, or Jehan (as the name

---

[1] There were many other French families of noble extraction in the country.

was then written), and of Pierre; such variations are frequently to be met with in the archives of Lille and other towns.[1] We shall later come across both boys, as also their younger brother Hubert, the latter in connection with a story of conspiracy and exile. The eldest child Jennin, or Jehan, afterwards became the ancestor of the English Houblons. No trace remains to us of the little sister Pasquette; the lost registers of the parish of St. Sauveur probably alone could have told us something of her life-history.

The marriage of a bourgeois or of the son of a bourgeois—who by virtue of his birth enjoyed the privileges of bourgeoisie — obliged him to *relever* or renew his bourgeoisie on the celebration of the ceremony.[2] That is to say, he was expected to seek readmission to the rank he forfeited by marrying, and to take afresh the oath to maintain the rights of his city and of his order. Failing this claim, and his name being registered anew in the book of acts of registration, he ceased to enjoy the freedom of the city. Marriage was also the occasion for the admission of new bourgeois *par achat*, and Jehan, Houbelon's marriage with Catherine Bave was the signal for the event which now took place. No children of this marriage had yet been born; the law was distinct and emphatic; within a year and a day of the date of the marriage must the claim of renewal of bourgeoisie be made; and it probably was in most instances made immediately afterwards.

Catherine Bave came of a good bourgeois stock, of a family then prosperous at Lille.[3] The old story of the successful craftsman marrying the daughter of the wealthy master in whose atelier he had served his indentures is

---

[1] 'Des prénoms autrefois très-usités, aujourd'hui tombés en oubli' (Derode, *Histoire de Lille*, i. 144).   [2] *Ibid.*, p. 80.

[3] At a later date Antoine Bave served as an Échevin of Lille during several years. The family, however, became extinct in the eighteenth century. They then bore for arms, 'D'or à la rose de gueules feuillée de cinq pointes de sinople' (see Allard).

familiar to all fellow-countrymen of the famous Dick
Whittington, and it may well be that Catherine's ample
portion helped to found the fortunes of the Lille Houbelons. Such marriages were very frequent, and doubtless
were often expedient for the avoidance of the breaking
up of ateliers. In any case the marriage and bourgeoisie
of Jehan, Houbelon was probably followed by an
increase of fortune and business connection, while,
owing to the narrow exclusiveness of the bourgeois
coterie, his entry into it materially altered the social
and domestic aspects of his life.

The bourgeois of Lille were proud of their city and
its traditions; and in especial did they prize the
municipal government and craft organisations, regarded
in those days as types and emblems of liberties,
but which, in their principle of exclusiveness from
outsiders, we now should condemn as narrow and
tyrannical; but the busy hive within the ancient
walls gloried in their very restraints, and called them
freedom. The bourgeoisie of Lille had obtained no
voice in municipal affairs till near the close of the twelfth
century, when their Count purchased from his suzerain,
the King of France, the hereditary offices of the city.
These were then abolished, giving place to a municipal
government with an elected Mayor, and Échevins or
Magistrates,[1] holding office by virtue of the authority
delegated to them year by year by the Counts of
Flanders or their representatives.[2] The special functions
of the new officers were administrative and judicial,
and they chose their mayor from among themselves.
About a hundred years later, the demands of the

---

[1] In England the equivalent for the name of Échevin was Skevin or
Warden, frequently Scabini on the Continent (see Gross, *Gild Merchant*,
i. 27, and Stubbs, *Constitutional History*, i. 121, 135, 237, and 684).

[2] Amongst the towns affiliated to the city of Lille whose Échevins con-
sulted thers as their natural superior, were La Bassée Raimbeaucourt,
Comines, Point-à-Vendin, Seclin St. Amand, Bovines, Camphin, and others
(Derode, *Histoire de Lille*, i. 302).

citizens of the free towns of Flanders had become so urgent, and their power so vast, that it became necessary to grant them great concessions. The city of Ghent, for instance, was so powerful and turbulent as successfully to defy all authority, and, having wrested her liberty from the hands of her princes, she remained practically independent, until the Emperor Charles v., in wrath at her arrogance, humbled her to the dust, at the same time ruining her trade and reducing her rich citizens to poverty.

We are accustomed to think of the commercial and political energy of the present day as unprecedented, but the activity in the past was fully as great, and at the same time demanded more effort, from the limited facilities then possessed for accomplishing the designs on hand. The trend of commercial enterprise in Flanders had of late tended greatly to stimulate the trade of the provinces. The fatal advent of the tyrant Alva in 1567 checked that prosperity when at its height; but the sixty years comprised between 1505 and the date of his coming were years of an astonishing increase in the trade and commerce of the country, and in its ethical and intellectual development. With regard to Lille herself, many of her most prominent bourgeois families traced the rise of their wealth and importance to this period. Attracted by the prospect of an opening for their energy and enterprise within the city walls, many country families came from the surrounding neighbourhood and settled there, and in course of time enjoyed those rights of bourgeoisie which their success placed them in a position to claim.[1] Many amassed great fortunes and founded flourishing families, the descendants of some of whom are to be found to this day in French Flanders.

_1505-1567_

[1] Van Hende, _Lille et ses Institutions Communales_, p. 170.

CHAPTER II

JEHAN HOUBELON; PÈRE ET FILS

'If not equal all, yet free,
Equally free; for orders and degrees
Jar not with liberty, but well consist.'
Paradise Lost, book V. 791.

AT the time of his second marriage, Jehan, Houbelon
was still living in the parish of St. Sauveur, not far from
the Porte de Fives, which many years before he had
entered as a youth. His father was dead, and he
appears to have been the sole member of his family
at that time in Lille. An old timbered house, the
massive beams of which were elaborately carved and
ornamented, till lately stood in the Rue de Fives, and
was doubtless inhabited by just such another burgess
as Jehan Houbelon, at the time he first took home
his young wife. The interiors of these houses we may
see pictured by the Flemish artists of the time, and
many choice specimens of their household furniture and
effects have been preserved. The chief living rooms or
parlours were usually panelled with carved and moulded
oak, sometimes elaborately inlaid with *intarsia* work;
but all who could afford it adorned the walls of these
apartments with the tapestry hangings of *haute-lisse*—
at this period of prosperity produced in vast quantities
in both French and Teutonic Flanders—for which
there was an immense demand both at home and abroad.
So prized and admired were these splendid fabrics, that
on gala occasions it was the pride of the citizens to

expose them on the outer walls of the houses, whole streets being hung with them from end to end.[1] The apartments thus furnished were sometimes lighted by oriel windows, but more frequently by shallow square bays which, being supported externally on corbels, overhung the street below. Within, the angles afforded space for cosy seats, often on a raised platform above the floor of the room, enabling the occupants to overlook the street; or, if they so desired, to converse with their opposite neighbours, so narrow was the roadway. The casements, delicately latticed in diamond panes, were occasionally filled with the stained glass for which the Lillois were at that time noted. Behind the dwelling-house, or perhaps underneath it on the ground floor, were the workshop or atelier of the bourgeois, and, if he happened also to be a master-craftsman, the looms at which his apprentices and journeymen laboured, these being in close proximity to each other; for space was precious. Indeed the extreme narrowness of the streets of mediæval cities was probably in great measure owing to the value of space. With a teeming population hemmed in by the narrow limits of the city walls, a population always growing in spite of the efforts of the privileged classes to discourage its increase, all alike at times must have suffered from the difficulty of expansion.[2] Doubtless the terrible outbreaks of the plague and other epidemics served, by their periodical recurrence, to check this growth; but it was only at long intervals that the pressure was relieved by the absorption of suburbs into the *enceinte* of the city. The rigid

[1] The tapestries of *haute-lisse* which were made in the towns of the Low Countries were sent in great numbers to Antwerp, where they were exposed for sale in vast galleries. And here the merchants of all Europe came to purchase them, (M. Alexandre Pinchart, *Histoire Générale de la Tapisserie dans les Flandres*, viii. Introd. 1). At an earlier date they were exhibited at Bruges.

[2] See Zechariah ii. 4 : 'Run, speak to this young man, saying : "Jerusalem shall be inhabited as towns without walls, for the multitude of men and cattle therein."'

exclusiveness of the gilds also tended to reduce the surplus population, of which large numbers were frequently obliged to emigrate. This obligation doubtless contributed, indirectly, further to increase the wealth and prosperity of those who remained behind, for not only was the pressure on the privileged class from the artisans and journeymen relieved, but their skill and the produce of their industry became better known and in greater demand abroad through means of the emigrants. Of that produce—especially that of the fabrics, in the exportation of which we believe the Houbelon family to have been engaged—it may be permitted to give a short account, for not only were they prized and admired all over Europe during the period in which they were manufactured, but in some particulars they have never since been surpassed, in either beauty or excellence of workmanship.[1]

By the commencement of the sixteenth century rules limiting the amount of the output by the gilds were no longer so strictly enforced, and it had become possible for a master to employ more workmen, and undertake a larger business, than had before been allowed by the jealousy of the gilds. It was probably owing to this greater freedom from restraint that enterprising burgesses like Jehan Houbelon were enabled to extend an already developed business, till as foreign merchants they traded on a large scale to other countries. It was always open to the more enterprising among the burgesses of Lille and other towns, to send their merchandise to Antwerp, Cologne, Worms, or Frankfort, where the merchants from all parts of the world came to purchase, and where many of the Flemish merchants possessed *comptoirs* or dépôts for their goods. Others,

---

[1] The exquisite productions from the looms of the late Mr. Helbronner owe their beauty to his exhaustive study of old specimens of the Flemish, Italian, and German industries, both textile and of the needle.

meanwhile, among the richer merchants exported them direct by means of the water communication which connected the interior of the country with the seaports, whence their own ships conveyed them to foreign countries.[1] The greater part of the exports of Walloon Flanders to the north was shipped at Nieuport, and we find the Houbelons trading from there to London. Nieuport, then a thriving seaport, is now a desolate town between Jurnes and Ostend.

The sumptuary laws, by which the middle classes were for long restrained from wearing rich clothes of silk and velvet, materials reserved for the use of the nobles only, had come to be disregarded, although the Emperor Charles v. by frequent enactments strove to re-enforce them. But, in spite of his efforts, the rich and powerful bourgeoisie displayed almost as great a luxury in their dress as did the nobles. The great care and taste which were expended upon the making of woollen stuffs was doubtless partly due to the existence of these laws, a care which under other conditions might have been exclusively reserved for silken materials; but it is certain that many of the woollen fabrics of the period preceding the sixteenth century were both of exquisite texture and of endless variety, and so long as any attempt was made to enforce the sumptuary laws the same care continued to be expended upon woollen fabrics. But Charles's frequent residence at Lille, and the lavish luxury of his court, not only incited the Lillois to emulation in their dress, but stimulated the manufacture of everything which could contribute to the luxurious tastes of the day. Thus the bourgeoisie, Jehan Houbelon included, clad themselves in velvets, fine cloth, rich furs and gold chains, while their wives were not behind the noble

[1] In the Chatellenie of Lille there were four rivers made navigable by canalisation.

ladies of the court in the richness and elegance of their attire.[1] By the close of the sixteenth century much of the luxury of the past reign had, however, passed away; for the poverty resulting from the wars and persecutions which had prevailed throughout the reign of Philip II. brought about that simplicity in dress which the Emperor had in vain endeavoured to impose upon the once proud and opulent citizens of the free towns.[2]

To one or other of the two great gilds or corporations concerned in the manufacture of stuffs, whether of wool or silk, Jehan₂ Houbelon doubtless belonged. These two powerful gilds had for a long period maintained an attitude of antagonism towards each other.[3] One of them—the *bourgetteurs*—whose fabrics were at this time highly prized both at home and abroad for their great beauty and richness, came originally to Lille from Bourges, and were at first received into the gild of the *tisserands en toile* of Lille, who gave the strangers hospitality. But, as many of the stuffs they produced partook of the character of those made by the great rival gild of *sayetteurs*, much friction resulted, each corporation deeming its exclusive privileges of manufacture infringed by the other; nor were these difficulties finally adjusted till the Emperor Charles V. bestowed on the bourgetteurs a separate corporation. The new regulations with respect to the rival gilds of Lille which were at the same time inaugurated by the Emperor, also added to the number of fabrics to which they had the exclusive right of manufacture, and henceforth the making of velvets, satins, and *bourettes*,[4]—(woollen materials into which silk or gold

---

[1] A sumptuous robe called the *plichon*, lined and edged with fur, invariably formed part of the dress of a wealthy bourgeois.

[2] Derode, *Histoire de Lille*, p. 27.

[3] M. Alex. Pinchart, *Histoire Générale de la Tapisserie dans les Flandres*, iii. 47.

[4] Bourette: 'Laine et soie mélangées' (Van Hende, *Lille et ses Institutions Communales*, p. 216).

and silver threads were introduced), was reserved to
the bourgetteurs.

The varied materials in pure wool of the sayetteurs—
the most powerful gild in the Chatellenie, and the most
ancient—had long been greatly prized, and many years
later were popular in England, where their manufacture
was introduced by the Flemish refugees. The famous
blue dyes used largely in the making of *Sayetteries* were
chiefly derived from the *wedde* or woad plants so extensively grown in the Chatellenie of Lille, to which we
have already alluded as having probably been cultivated by the elder Jehan Houbelon. To the sayetteurs
were accorded the privilege of making the fabrics called
saies, œstades, demi-œstades, pièces de purenne (pure)
sayette; changeants (shot), *des couleurs blanches et bleues,
à part soye,* etc. etc.[1] That many of these materials
were of great magnificence may be seen by an examination of tapestries depicting scenes, in which the individuals represented are clothed in garments made of the
most sumptuous stuffs, the cut velvets, figured satins and
damasks, or brocades in bold and beautiful designs,
being minutely reproduced by the looms. Among the
many fine examples in the South Kensington Museum,
may be seen a series of beautiful hangings made at
Brussels shortly before this period—viz. the reign of
Charles v.—which give a brilliant picture of the fashion
in dress of the time.

In the panel pictures of Crivelli, Carpaccio, the
Vivarini, and other artists of the north of Italy—whose

[1] The subject has been exhaustively treated by M. Francisque Michel,
in his work on *Les Étoffes.* See also *Mémoires de* Jules Houdoy, *Tapisserie de Haute Lisse,* p. 21 : ' Les Bourgetteurs et nuls autres, feront toutes
sortes de manières d'ouvrage à la tire, haute et basse lisse,—marcheterie
ou au pied'. In reference to 'les ouvrages de haute et basse lisse ou au
pied' M. Houdoy thinks he finds the solution of a much vexed question as to
the meaning of the term *marcheteur, marcheterie* or *basse lisse,* so named
owing to the horizontal position of the chain on the loom (see Houdoy, p.
38, and Van Hende, p. 49). And it was doubtless this particular distinction
with regard to the position of the chain on the loom, that regulated the
apportionment of the various fabrics to the rival gilds.

art, like that of the early German and Flemish schools
was often influenced by that of the east—the gorgeous
stuffs of the bourgetteurs are as vividly depicted as in
these tapestries, and bear the same stamp of oriental
influence, an influence probably due to the imports from
the east by the Venetian merchants.   Not only were the
silken damasks and brocades of bourgetterie represented with fidelity by those artists, who loved their
beauty of colour and design, but the more humble
woollen materials of sayetterie, in which the schools of
painting of Tuscany, Lombardy, and Rome clothed
their saints and votaries and draped their Madonnas,—
were as faithfully portrayed.   These stuffs would appear
to have been for the most part closely woven and of
smooth texture, at the same time soft and clinging.
Painters such as Mantegna and the Lippis in Italy, and
Albert Dürer, Van Eyck, or Memling of the Flemish
schools, painted a somewhat different textile, which,
when draped, fell in angular stiff folds.   The wonderful
triptych of Andrea Mantegna in the Uffizi Palace at
Florence, and the no less superb *Calomnia* of Filippino
Lippi, would alone illustrate this treatment of woollen
fabrics in art.   Later again, materials of a less close
texture found favour with artists such as Andrea del
Sarto, who was himself one of those who loved to portray
the blending of colours produced by the Flemish weavers
in their *changeants* or shot materials.   In his pictures,
oil as well as frescoes, we find draperies of the palest
violet shaded into crimson, lemon-yellow into apple-
green ; or purple, with ' high lights ' of faintest pink or
gold.   Andrea's sartorial instincts revelled in these
' creations ' of the Flemish weavers, no other artist
equalling him in representing them, unless it be the
sumptuous Paul Veronese.

As they grew up, most of Jehan₂ Houbelon's sons were
associated with him in the commerce in which he was

now engaged; but each one of them would first have
served his time as apprentice either under his father
or some one of his fellow-citizens. Much of their
commerce appears to have been with England, and as
we shall see later, when, owing to persecution, their
expatriation took place, their relations with this country
facilitated their emigration. The merchants, *marchands en gros*, of the Netherlands to foreign countries,
in those days were called *Spéculateurs*,[1] a name somewhat analogous to that of the Merchant Adventurers
of England, with whom in fact they now shared the
commerce in Europe formerly monopolised by the
ancient Hanses. The Spéculateurs, like the English
Adventurers, ranked high in the social scale of commercial life, being distinct from and altogether superior
to the *marchands en demi gros* and the *boutiquiers
en détail* or retail traders of a humbler sphere. So
eager was Queen Elizabeth to encourage the traffic
between the countries, and so constant was already the
passing to and fro of the merchants of both, that special
exemption from assessment for subsidies was ordered by
the Queen in respect of both her own Adventurers and
the factors of Flemish merchants residing in London,
with the object of still further increasing trade.

The extreme luxury and love of display, the gorgeous
pageants and lavish expenditure which during this
period were almost universal in Europe, created an
immense demand for the *étoffes de luxe* produced by the
famous looms of Flanders, and exported from thence by
the Spéculateurs. Everywhere there was prosperity
and plenty, and both the will and the power to possess
and enjoy the coveted products of the Flemish crafts.

If it was during the period comprised between the
dawn of the sixteenth century and the commencement
of the Alva persecutions, that this extended commerce

---

[1] *i.e.* one who speculates upon the success of an adventure in trade.

of the Lillois was at its height, it was also during this period that Jehan, Houbelon and his sons laid the foundation of their fortunes. Though their chief trade was with England, they also traded with Spain, and not only had comptoirs in London and at Antwerp, but very possibly at Cologne, Worms, or Frankfort; all of which places they must occasionally have visited.

Though ranking among the more important and wealthy citizens of Lille, it does not appear that either Jehan, or his sons attained to any office of dignity in the government of their native city. Civic dignities in early times were frequently looked upon as a burden rather than a coveted honour,[1] the duties they entailed being of such an onerous nature as substantially to interfere with the business of those burgesses upon whom they were bestowed; and if the Houbelons of the sixteenth century were indeed the flourishing foreign merchants we have been led to believe, doubtless they were not unwilling to forgo the dignity of office-holding for the sake of the greater liberty they enjoyed.

Thus surrounded by his family and engaged in the business which his industry and intelligence had developed, Jehan, Houbelon for many years lived in peace and plenty. It has been possible approximately to fix the date of the good merchant's death through the evidence of the investment of a small sum of money, the record of which is found in the Municipal Archives of Lille. This, in conjunction with other evidence, shows it to have taken place during the course of the year 1555 or at the commencement of 1556, when he was about sixty-seven years of age. In consequence of the 'grans et urgens affaires que le roi Philippe ii. avait à supporter, pour l'entretenement des gens de guerre, estant en son service pour la defence des Pays de Pardeça,' (des Pays bas) against the French King Henri

---

[1] 'Office-holding was held to be a burden' (see Gross, *Gild Merchant*, v. 75).

II., a loan of 200,000 livres was raised for his use by the commonalty of the city of Lille. Among the names of the bourgeois who came forward to buy *lettres de rente* on the loan appears that of Jehan, Houbelon. 'De Jehan Houbelon fitz de feu Jehan, pour achat fait le 2

A MERCHANT (SIXTEENTH CENTURY).[1]

aôut 1554, de VI livres v sol de rente heritière par an, écheant (en deux termes) le 11ᵉ jour de Febvrier et d'âout, au denier XVI, au rachat de cent livres.'[2] For this sum, then, of a hundred livres, Houbelon received six per cent. payable twice a year; and the payment of

[1] From an engraving in the *Wappen und Stammbuch* of Jost Amman. Published at Frankfort in 1589.
[2] Résolutions des Bourgeois de Lille.

the interest comes into the accounts of the city and is shown for many years to have been regularly paid. Georges Houbelon, one of the sons of Jehan₂, married and renewed his bourgeoisie early in 1556 ; and in the *Registre aux bourgeois*, in which the fact is recorded, Georges is designated as the son of 'le feu Jehan Houbelon' of Lille.[1]   The death of Jehan must there-

1554 fore have occurred after the 2nd of August 1554, when the security on the royal loan was purchased, and before the renewal of the bourgeoisie of his son Georges,

1556 on the 12th of March 1556.   Henceforth the interest of this loan was paid to his widow, Catherine Bave, and the accounts of the town of Lille show it to have been

1578 paid to her every year till 1578, when Catherine herself died.   The next recipients of the interest of the loan were the heirs of Franchois Desquyre, her son-in-law. Both François and his wife being already dead, their children inherited the security under their grandmother's will.

[1] 3ᵉ Registre aux Bourgeois, Lille, fol. 67.

CHAPTER III

PERSECUTION

'No more shall Commerce be all in all, and Peace
Pipe on her pastoral hillock a languid note.'
TENNYSON'S *Maud.*

THE overmastering passion in the life of Philip II. of
Spain was his devotion to the idea of the universal
supremacy of the Church; and on his succession to
the throne he determined at all costs to stamp out
the reformed opinions in his vast dominions. In this
resolution he but continued the policy of the Emperor
Charles V., by whom the tendency of the Reformation
was fully apprehended. Charles directed his energies
towards stifling heresy for the same reasons that he
attacked the privileges and franchises of the great
communes, both alike being in his eyes 'un obstacle
qui le génait dans son chemin';[1] but the policy of
his son was prompted wholly by religious zeal irrespective of all other considerations, and the end to
Philip's mind justified the means. As later he brought
disaster upon himself by the infatuation which led him
to embark upon the invasion of England, so the ardour
with which he pursued the persecutions in the Netherlands resulted in the loss of their richest provinces.

Although in the Dutch Netherlands a vast number
had early adopted the reformed opinions, with respect to
Walloon Flanders it appears that until the year 1544, **1544**
the movement in this direction—unlike that in the

[1] Derode, *Histoire de Lille,* ii. 18.

northern provinces—was in part restrained by the great
influence possessed by the Church. Moreover, after
the persecutions inaugurated by the Inquisition and
later by the Duke of Alva had subsided,—the country
having meanwhile been *purged* of heretics, most of whom
had been either killed or had fled into exile,—this influence reasserted itself in strength.

1544-50   It was at an early stage in the religious movement
at Lille, that Pierre and Nicolas, two of the sons of
Jehan, Houbelon the merchant, fled from their home.
Edward VI. was on the throne when they found
refuge in England, where many Flemish artisans had
already arrived and received a hospitable welcome.
Anxious to profit by their skill and encourage their
industry, the King granted a charter to those of the
refugees who desired to settle in London, and they
accordingly set to work to gain their living under
his protection. The Walloon church in Threadneedle
Street, afterwards called the French protestant church,
1550   was founded in 1550, and Nicolas Houbelon was one
of the earliest members of its congregation. But the
1553   refugees had only a few years of peace; at the death
of Edward they were again forced to wander into
exile, for on the accession of Mary and during the persecutions which followed, the Queen caused the 'poor
Protestants' from the Low Countries and elsewhere
to whom her brother had given refuge, to leave the
kingdom, and from this order the denizens, or naturalised
foreigners only, were excepted. So great a stringency
was certainly not exercised in respect of those 'Merchant
Strangers' who had already begun in London to develop
an extensive business with the Netherlands and elsewhere; for Nicolas Houbelon and the other foreign
merchants lived on in London undisturbed throughout
the five years of Mary's stormy reign. Pierre, however,
had already left London for Cornwall.

Before their departure from Lille, the brothers had become so much identified with the new teachings as to entirely alter their relations with other men of their class; but active persecution had not yet begun in respect of those of the bourgeoisie who had adopted the new religion; their privileges protected them. What, then, caused their flight? Writers who have followed the story of the refugees, the times at which periodical emigrations took place, the character and social status of the people, etc., all agree that at this stage of the reform movement —at any rate in the Netherlands—the overwhelming majority of the Protestants were drawn from the common people. The poor, that is to say those who had nothing to lose socially or politically in all the busy centres of industry, followed and drank in the new teaching with avidity. For years the translated Scriptures, long withheld from the people, had been secretly disseminated with other literature, for many books and pamphlets were brought over from England and elsewhere (chiefly packed with merchandise), and scattered broadcast by means of the pedlars or *colporteurs*; but with respect of the bourgeoisie, at the date of the expatriation of Pierre and Nicolas, very few had as yet thrown in their lot with reform. Unlike their catholic brothers they had never claimed the privilege of bourgeoisie. Though the son of a freeman was privileged to do this as of right, his being freeborn did not of necessity make him a burgess; he had to present himself for election to the magistracy of the city; and as Protestants, the brothers would scarcely have been considered eligible by their exclusive fellow-citizens. Their flight would thus appear to have been voluntary, and because they were unable to meet the contempt of their class. On the other hand, Jehan, their eldest brother, who shared their religious opinions, remained for many years in his native country, though his personal mortifications apparently interfered in no way with his business as a merchant *spéculateur*; for he was a rich man with a great business, when he finally transferred both his person and his trade to London.

Jehan Houbelon₁ of Fives.

1st wife. =	Jehan₂	= Catherine Bave,	
	of Lille.	2nd wife.	

Jean₃. Pierre₁. Hubert. Nicolas₁. Regnault. Georges. A daughter.
Pasquette.

Meanwhile the people of the Netherlands in the strength of their numbers waxed bolder, and they began openly to worship God in their own way. At all the great towns in the provinces it became the custom on the afternoons of Sunday for the protestant population to attend in thousands the 'field-preaching' outside the city walls, where their fiery ministers or *diacres* inflamed their religious zeal. For more secret communication, the various towns were given names; for example, Armentières was called amongst the followers of 'the Religion,' *Le Bouton*; Valenciennes, *l'Aigle*; while Lille herself was known as *La Rose*.[1] At Lille the preachings were attended by large bodies of the Lillois—among the number of whom, without doubt, Jean₂ Houbelon was to be found—and the attendance was further swelled by the Protestants belonging to the surrounding country and villages of the Chatellenie. From five leagues around Lille, we learn, all those who followed the 'Religion' flocked to these gatherings, to listen to the preaching, and to sing the hymns of Marot; whose *quatrains*,—especially the following,— became veritable war-songs to the now excited and fanatical people.

[1] Huguenot Society Publications, vol. I. part ii. p. 6.

'Tailler ne te feras image
De quelque chose que ce soit ;
Ni l'honneur lui fais ou homage
Ton Dieu jalousie en reçoit.'[1]

The zeal of the Échevinage of Lille, feverishly anxious
to meet the requirements of the Holy Office, now led
them to make fresh efforts to check the spread of heresy.
In order to punish those citizens who thus continually
defied their authority and that of the Church, the magistrates devised a way of identifying them ; they caused
the city gates to be closed on Sunday afternoon after all
had gone forth to the preaching,[2] and on their return the
reformers found themselves obliged to re-enter the city
by the small posterns or wicket-gates, which, admitting
them one by one, thus allowed of a close scrutiny by
such of the Échevins as were on duty for the purpose
of this inspection.   The town was guarded night and
day as if undergoing a siege, and in order to prevent
any of the Lillois from joining the *Gueux* or other bands
now assembling all over the country, the inhabitants
were forbidden to come and go through the gates of the
city without a passport.   This passport consisted of the
impression of a seal on wax, affixed to the thumb-nail of
the right hand.   The seal bore a letter of the alphabet,
which was changed according to the day of the week or
month on which it was issued.[3]

The time had now arrived when concealment or class
privilege would no longer avail.   The bold front with
which the citizens had attended the field-preachings had

[1] Derode, *Histoire de Lille*, ii. 33.   The *quatrain* may be translated
thus :

'Thou shalt shape thee no image
Of any sort or kind ;
But if honour thou pay it or homage
A jealous God thou'lt find.'

[2] Strada says in his *De Bello Belgico*, that near Lille the people attended
the preachings 'in great shoals . . . armed with pikes and muskets   See
translation by Sir Robert Stapleton, Kt., 1650.

[3] Derode, *Histoire de Lille*, ii. 37.

enabled the Échevinage to identify individuals, and in respect of Lille every Lillois who had joined the ranks of the reformers was now known and proscribed. It would seem from the immense increase in the numbers of individuals of the educated classes who fled from the Netherlands or suffered martyrdom after the coming of the Duke of Alva, that one of the King's chief objects in sending him as governor was that of attacking the more wealthy and influential among the people. Alva, fresh from Spain, armed with full powers from the King, cared nothing for the circumstances of his intended victims,[1] nor yet for the injury inflicted upon the country by the loss of her most valuable inhabitants; he therefore struck indiscriminately at every individual among the heretics, regardless of all but the main object of his mission. Wealth and importance were now in themselves a reason for persecution and confiscation, and the exchequer of Philip was daily enriched by the spoil.[2] Nobles and citizens alike fell victims to the sentences of the Council of Troubles—or Blood Council, as it was popularly called—the arbitrary court superseding all others which the Duke established for the trial of the heretics. And so for the first time the free citizens of the provinces found

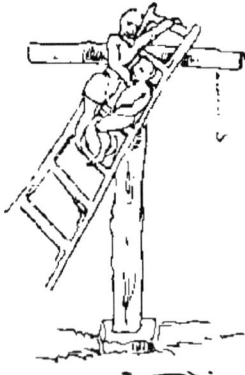

---

[1] The *Greffier Criminel* of Lille made memoranda of his executions by means of sketches on the margin of the *Registre aux sentences criminelles*. Facsimiles of many of these are given in a *brochure* by M. Frossart, Pasteur of the Reformed Church of Lille. See *L'Église sous la Croix*. Paris, 1857.

[2] Alva had promised the King a revenue of 500,000 ducats from the confiscations which were to accompany the executions (Motley, *Rise of the Dutch Republic*, ii. 123).

that neither riches, rank, nor civic privileges would avail to protect them, and that choice must promptly be made between submission or flight.

The question of emigration must often have presented itself to the minds of the reformers before the time actually arrived when it could be postponed no longer, and from the fact of the appearance so soon afterwards in London of a rich and important body of 'Merchant Strangers' (among whom we recognise Jean Houbelon), we may conclude that some of them had made use of the facilities afforded by their commercial relations with England, to transfer to that country at least part of their wealth, even though they may have been forced to forsake much of it in their flight.

Not till he had been seventeen years or more in the reformed faith, did the 'confessor' ancestor of the English Houblons fly for the saving of his life before the storm and tempest of persecution inaugurated by Alva. In hiding, going with his life in his hand, his flight at last must have been one of hairbreadth escapes and cruel privations; for although thousands fled at first, the authorities, seeing the country depopulated, later sought to check an emigration which threatened its ruin, and took such measures as to render flight almost impossible.

The bitterness experienced by the fugitive Protestants was the greater, that most of them had already been estranged from relations and friends who had remained faithful to the old forms; and as a rule, the closer the ties of the past, the wider the gulf that is caused by divergence of opinion and sentiment with regard to religion. Jean Houbelon probably drank to the dregs this bitterness. Gauging the immensity of the sacrifice, the future verdict as to the character and principles of the exiles was none too high as held by men of their own convictions in this country; but it is to be questioned if their friends and kinsmen at home who had not shared their religious views regarded their so-called fanaticism in any other light than as foolish and unnecessary; while they cherished no little ill-will against them as having been the direct cause of the acts of tyranny from which all alike, whether catholic or protestant, were suffering.

After the final departure of Jean, Houbelon to England in 1567, the family commercial house at Lille was carried on by his two brothers, Regnault and Georges. They had long been prosperous merchants, and probably were still more so after the presence of Jean in London; they certainly increased in riches in spite of troubles in church and state. Strangely enough, except for a comparatively short period, trade was not interrupted by the internal ferment going on in the country; but the final readjustment of law and order was not accomplished without a long and patient struggle. The story of Hubert Houbelon and of a conspiracy the failure of which resulted in his punishment and exile is illustrative of the complicated political situation then existing in the southern provinces of the Netherlands. We know nothing of the earlier years of this son of old Jean Houbelon, merchant of Lille; he neither followed the calling of his father, nor was he in character like him.

When Hubert was still young, the restlessness of the age had already more or less affected all men; but while in the large majority of the law-abiding Walloons their rebellion against authority was chiefly bounded by the claim to freedom of thought and religious observance, it found its vent in him—as in others of his type—in political plots and agitations. Impatient of any yoke, whether municipal or ecclesiastic, Hubert cared not to be bound by what seemed to him ponderous duties and privileges of bourgeoisie; nor yet does he appear to have sympathised with religious reform. Although the great body of the people was slow to break through the

peaceful traditions of generations, the more independent
and restless spirits had already begun to band themselves together into what would now be called secret
societies; but only when war and bloodshed—the consequence of persecution—began to devastate the provinces, did the real strength of these societies become
apparent. In the most famous of them, the Band of
Gueux—the lusty so-called Beggars—Philip II. later
found his most powerful opponent; but others scarcely
less formidable, though more lawless, began to infest
the country as the revolt became more general; and of
these, the '*Malcontents*' of Montigny were raised within
the forests and vales and busy cities of Walloon
Flanders, by one of their own nobles. With the Sieur
de Montigny and his Malcontents, in fact, Hubert
Houbelon finally threw in his lot, and with them, many
years later, met his fate.

The restless activity of the Malcontents in the Chatellenie of Lille added greatly to the general confusion
and distress in the country following upon the war.
They were concerned in frequent conspiracies and plots
within Lille itself, in which they were frequently aided
and abetted by the people of the town of Tournai,
between whom and those of Lille a hereditary feud had
long existed. Almost daily skirmishes took place at this
time, 'les gens de Tournai' (in concert with their friends
inside the city) making many unavailing efforts to over-
throw the increasing power of the Roman Catholic or
King's party in Lille. A conspiracy, in which Hubert
Houbelon was concerned, appears to have been a culmin-
ating effort on the part of the Malcontents, but the plot
was discovered on the eve of its development, and a
number of Lillois, including some prominent members
of the bourgeoisie, were found to be implicated in it.
The conspirators were thrown into prison on the 17th of   1581
June 1581; and though some of them were subsequently

pardoned, while the civic privileges of others served to mitigate their punishment, a few less fortunate were summarily banished from the city. Among these were Hubert and five or six others, who had, it is to be presumed, taken too active a part in the plot to escape a heavy penalty. The indictment, together with an account of the affair, is to be found in the Résolutions of the Magistracy of the 28th of June.[1]

Hubert was now a homeless exile; but it is certain he did not find his way to England. The Flemings had close commercial relations with other countries besides this, and doubtless he, though now no longer young, was at no loss whither to turn his footsteps; but he probably preferred to remain in hiding with others of the more reckless members of Montigny's Malcontents, till after the final break-up of that body, which took place towards the close of the same year.[2]

Though it was not long before the town of Lille once more returned to her old allegiance to the King, we find the protestant element still existing in the country, and books and papers of the reformed cult still industriously circulated, in spite of the heavy penalties attached to their discovery. The commerce with England, which had languished during the stress of persecution, had now resumed much of its former activity, and afforded opportunities for this traffic, of which the protestant Lillois were not slow to avail themselves. It is at this point that the name of Nicolas Houbelon again appears upon the scene in connection with his old home. The 1544-84 first to quit his native country, he had been thirty years an exile, when we find him actively pursuing the traffic in books above alluded to. In the present instance it

[1] Résolutions du Magistrat de Lille, 28 Juin 1581.
[2] A family of Hubert's name exists in Austrian Galicia. The arms of this family (described in Rietstap as 'Herb, edle (noble) von Houblon') would appear to indicate, somewhat fantastically, an origin in a fortified city.

would appear that the Échevinage of Lille had some
reason to suspect that heretical books were being introduced into the city, and the ultimate discovery was
probably due to intercepted correspondence. We gather
from the archives of the year 1584,[1] that other towns
besides Lille were co-operating with her in her endeavour to trace out and check this traffic. In consequence of the watch thus set, on the 7th of June 1584
the *mayor et conseil* of St. Omer notified to 'ces
Messieurs de Lille,' that they had traced and discovered
the books. They were found *mesly*,—mixed or con-
cealed,—in bales of merchandise, despatched by 'ung
(one) Nicolas Houbelon, habitant de Londres,' by
whom they were consigned to Denis Lecat, a prominent
bourgeois of Lille. The bales were found packed 'sur
un chariot' at Ligny. Ligny—now called Ligny Saint
Flochel—was a small village near Saint Pol in the Pas-
de-Calais, situated a short distance off the direct water-
route between Lille and St. Omer; and here the goods
were probably awaiting an opportunity, through the
agency of the consignee Lecat, for their dispersal
throughout the towns and villages, by means of the
travelling pedlars. The *greffier criminel* or common
hangman of Lille was now despatched by the Échevinage
to St. Omer, and from thence this grim functionary proceeded to the little village, to receive the fateful books
into his custody, and to collect evidence for the information of the magistrates for the trial of the prisoner
Lecat. For the chief offender in the matter being safe
in England and out of reach, the person to whom the
books were consigned had meanwhile been arrested and
imprisoned. In so serious an offence his privileges as a
bourgeois could not avail further than to lighten his
punishment. Lecat was tried and banished, with the
caution not to venture to return under peril of 'more

[1] Registre de Résolutions, 1584.

grievous punishment.' The fact that among the books Foxe's *Book of Martyrs* was included would seem to have greatly aggravated the crime committed. Had Lecat been other than a privileged burgess, his punishment would have been far more severe ; the *Manants*, for such offences, were usually hanged and quartered. As a matter of fact Lecat came to England and settled in London, where amongst the registers of the Walloon congregation we find frequent mention of his name, and those of subsequent members of his family.

As to the catholic Houbelons of the now chastened and orthodox Lille, we can imagine with what disgust they found their protestant brother in London dragging their respected name into disrepute in the matter of the books ! All alike now desired to bury the past in oblivion, and they doubtless hastened to repudiate any complicity in Nicolas's misdemeanour.

There are many entries relating to the brothers Georges and Regnault Houbelon and their children in the archives of Lille, both as to their bourgeoisie, and in the parish registers. These show them to have flourished till the third generation, in Lille. Though Georges had no son, his brother Regnault left two, named Jehan and Pierre. The latter's son, Antoine, was born in the year 1585, and when young became a Protestant, and soon after went to London, where he was subsequently followed by his brother François. With their departure from Lille, went the last males of the name of Houbelon ; for their father's only brother, Pierre, and his wife Françoise Delespierre, had but one child, named Catherine. In the descendants of Catherine, who was a rich heiress, now lies the representation of the catholic branch of the Houbelons. She married Antoine, a member of the family of Van Ackère, well known in Lille, but formerly of burgher stock in Ghent. Their son Denis is said to have been 'tres riche Bourgeois de

Lille,' a fact which tends to support the hypothesis that he had inherited a great part of the riches of the Houbelon family through his mother. From Denis Van Ackère, his son, descend the present Comtes Van de Cruisse de Waziers, of the Château de Lignières near Senarpont, in the department of la Somme.

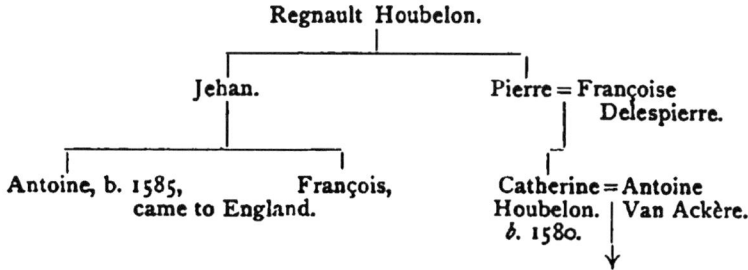

```
                    Regnault Houbelon.
          ┌──────────────────────────┴──────────────┐
       Jehan.                              Pierre = Françoise
          │                                   │      Delespierre.
   ┌──────┴──────────┐                        │
Antoine, b. 1585,       François,        Catherine = Antoine
   came to England.              Houbelon. │ Van Ackère.
                                  b. 1580.  │
                                            ↓
```

The name of Houbelon ceases to appear among the entries in the registers after the close of the seventeenth century, nor do the parish registers contain any further evidence of their existence subsequent to that date.[1]

[1] All these particulars and many others as to the Houbelon family in Lille are derived from various documents preserved in the city, and were copied and certified as correct by M. Frémaux of Lille, to whom the author owes many obligations both for his courtesy in this respect, and for much interesting information relating to his native town.

CHAPTER IV

CHRISTI ASYLUM

'Ici, au milieu d'un grand Peuple,
Nos Pères ont trouvé la douce hospitalité—le repos :
Nous, avec le Toit paternel,—
Nous y avons trouvé la Patrie !'[1]

OWING to the commercial relations which had existed
from the earliest times between the Low Countries and
England, and to the fact that many of their countrymen
were already settled in this country, it was hardly strange
that the persecuted inhabitants of the United Provinces
in their time of need should have turned to England as
a place of refuge.

The first Flemings and Walloons who had settled in
England did so in the reign and by the invitation of
Edward III., whose frequent warlike excursions on the
Continent had no doubt enlightened him as to their
superior skill in their several trades to that of his own
subjects; while, keenly alive to the advantages to be
gained by their introduction into the country, he sought
to tempt them over with promises of protection and encouragement. A large number of artisans and journeymen accepted the King's invitation, not only on account
of the religious persecutions which already assailed them,
but owing to the trade jealousies which existed within
their own gilds at home. As we have seen, Edward VI.
followed the same policy, and Queen Elizabeth, recognising the value and anxious to profit by the skill of the

[1] Part of inscription in the Walloon Temple, Threadneedle Street,
London.

refugees, welcomed all who reached these shores. From the first, the coming of these 'gentle strangers' was a boon to this country, and exerted a lasting influence both upon the trade and the character of the English people; for, as Mr. Smiles tells us, 'wherever the refugees settled they acted as so many missionaries of skilled work, exhibiting the best practical examples of diligence, industry and thrift, and teaching the English people in the most effective manner, the beginnings of those various industrial arts in which they have since acquired so much distinction and wealth.'[1] As a return for the hospitality extended to them, a single condition was made by order of the Queen, viz. that of their admitting a proportion of English apprentices into their workshops. It was thus that the English industrial class profited, for the artisans became possessed of the trade secrets of the foreign crafts.

But large as had been the number of artisans who thus settled in England during the early years of Elizabeth's reign, the influx from the Netherlands both of Flemish and Dutch after Alva's persecutions was far greater. Strype in his *Annals* tells us, that the hospitality afforded by England to the 'Strangers' gave great offence on the Continent, and that the country was ironically called 'Christi Asylum' or the 'Sanctuary of Christ.'[2] A haven of peace and safety she must indeed have been to the homeless wanderers, whose exhaustion in both strength and means is pathetically shown by the fact, that on arriving in troops on the seacoast (sometimes in open boats) many never went beyond the place of their first disembarkation, but settled down on the spot, setting to work patiently at their several trades and occupations, and quickly establishing branches of industry by which to gain their living. The Queen meanwhile

[1] Smiles, *Huguenots*, p. 125.
[2] *Apud* Burn, *Protestant Refugees*, p. 6.

was supported in her enlightened hospitality by the strong feeling which existed in the country against the arrogant pretensions of the Spaniards, inseparably connected as they were with the horrors of the Inquisition.

Although the strangers were on the whole well received by the English working-classes, many of whom were content to profit by their skill and friendly willingness to impart it to others, it was but natural that the advent of so many strangers to this country should have been the cause of some ill-will. But although a prejudice remains to this day against the foreigner who freely takes advantage of the wide hospitality which permits him to come and go at his will, the spirit of fair play to all has ever been a tradition with the English people. Our countrymen have always given a free hand to those who have sought either shelter or a livelihood here; though, owing to the narrow bounds of our sea-girt country, the English welcome to aliens would appear to have been a potent factor in the history of her own colonisation.

If the poorest emigrants were well received by those who foresaw what useful and industrious citizens they would make, the rich and intelligent men, whose religious convictions had induced them to forsake their native country for London, would be doubly welcome. Writers on this period testify to the fact that the Merchant Strangers, from the time of their arrival and settlement here, constituted a powerful and prosperous group. 'Several of the foreigners,' writes Mr. Smiles, 'now became known as leading men in commercial affairs, who had already been distinguished as merchants in their own country, and they brought with them a spirit and enterprise which infused quite a new life into London business.' Jean's name heads the list given by Mr. Smiles of the leading foreign merchants of Elizabeth's time, among whom he recognises 'the names of Houblon, Palavicino, De Malines, Corsellis, Van Peine, Tryon, Buskell (De Bosquelles), Cursini (Corsini), De Best, and Cotett.'[1] And be it remarked that these men did not apparently seek denization, *i.e.* naturalisation—as yet not hard to obtain—but were content, under the special protection of the Queen, to carry on their business as 'Merchant Strangers' or 'Merchants of the Intercourse,' as they were called, in the Christi Asylum which had given them refuge.[2]

Some hundred and twenty years after the expatriation of Jean Houbelon, a sermon was preached by the famous Dr. Gilbert Burnet, afterwards Bishop of Salisbury, on the occasion of the funeral of his descendant. The bishop was a friend of the family, and the details of the short memoir embodied in his sermon were, as he states in the preface to the published edition, supplied him by the sons of the deceased. With respect of Jean and the reasons for his settlement in England, the words of the English bishop would seem to imply that even at that date—1682—the fear of persecution in their own country had not wholly disappeared from men's minds, while the sufferings of their ancestors were still fresh in the memories of the anglicised foreign families. Of the ancestor of the English Houblons the bishop spoke as :

1682

[1] Smiles, *Huguenots*, p. 108.

[2] Burn is under a misapprehension when he assumes in his *History of the Protestant Refugees*, p. 94, that the ancestor of the English Houblons came to Rye from France in 1572. Quoting Stow as his authority he says : 'He [Stow] mentions having seen an authentic catalogue of such French as fled to Rye in Sussex, anno 1572,' and 'that there were the names of Le Tellier and Tellier, one a Merchant the other a Minister, who with John Houblowe' (already mentioned in the text) 'were very probably the ancestors of those eminent merchants and citizens, bearing the name of Houblon and Le Thieullier, which at this present flourish here in wealth and reputation, and some of them such as have and do partake of the government of the city as well as places of honour and trust.' If so be that a Jean Houblon from Normandy landed at Rye in 1572, he would probably have been a member of the old French house of Des Houbelon, if indeed any still remained. Gabriel Ogilvy in his *Pedigree of the Houblon Family* (1873) assumes this. But he was not identical with the Merchant Stranger in any case, whom we know to have come to England some years before, and from Flanders.'

'That worthy Mr. Houblon, a gentleman of Flanders, who above a hundred years ago fled to England from the persecution that was raised there against all that embraced the purity of the Christian religion . . . by the Duke of Alva. Then all that received the reformation were reduced to those hard straits (which how far they are from *us* the only wise God knows), either to act against their consciences, to seal their faith with their blood, or, as the least dreadful, to suffer loss of all that they had and fly for their lives to other countries. This was the choice of that noble person who did by this act ennoble himself and all that descended from him.'[1]

Although Jean arrived as a fugitive in this country, his great prosperity and that of his brother merchants soon after their arrival in London may be explained by their not being strange to the city. A transference of their property, or a portion of it—for part of a merchant's wealth is in the country with which he trades—would have been natural. Only when it became evident that Alva's orders were so stringent as to include the sacrifice of the vast trade of the Netherlands, did the merchants leave. Having gathered at Antwerp from their native cities they were doubtless employed to the last in hastily making arrangements for the transfer of their business to London. That all the best of them were Protestants is probable, for after the holocaust was over, the trade of Antwerp had disappeared; it had gone to London.

Since the abolition of the monopoly of trade with northern ports enjoyed by the famous Hansa merchants (or merchants of the Steel Yard) in London, English trade had received a great stimulus; for so long as the Germans held their own, except in so far as the exchange

---

[1] Sermon preached 28 June 1682, by Dr. Gilbert Burnet, D.D., Bishop of Salisbury, at the funeral of Mr. James Houblon, senior, grandson of the 'gentleman of Flanders' here alluded to. Printed for Rich. Chiswel at the Rose and Crown in St. Paul's Churchyard. London, 1682.

with Flanders was concerned, the trade of the English was confined to distant ports.[1] The Queen's factor, Sir Thomas Gresham, was a far-seeing politician as well as a commercial pioneer. Far from being jealous of the newly-arrived Merchant Strangers from the Netherlands, he facilitated their business and cordially encouraged the Queen in her gracious acts towards them ; and the event proved the wisdom of Elizabeth and her advisers, for not only did the strangers enrich the country by their trade, but they in time became some of the most loyal and most intelligent of her inhabitants.

Jean Houbelon joined his brother Nicolas in London, **1567** and soon after his arrival we hear of them living together in the same house. That Jean quitted the home of his birth most unwillingly we may infer from the yearning with which he continued to regard it, and it is possible that the hope that Walloon Flanders might in time be open for his return induced him to postpone sending for his family, for several years elapsed before they joined him in London. Jean was about forty-four when he came to England ; his descendants possessed his picture, which was carefully handed down through the generations amongst the 'ffamily portraits.' Together with the rest of these, neglected and dusty, thrust out of sight since the early years of the nineteenth century, the old Elizabethan panel picture has again come to light. The Merchant Stranger wears a black dress, over which is the fur-lined *plichon*, then the characteristic dress of his order ; his right hand rests upon the skull often portrayed in the portraits of 'confessors' who preferred death to parting with their faith. He came of a dark-haired race, and Jean Houbelon's short black hair and pointed beard streaked with grey testify to his Gallican or Frankish descent.

[1] But little is known of the powerful league called the *Hanse de Londres*, under the auspices of which, trade was carried on in early times between this country and Flanders.

The picture shows him to have had a scar over one eye.

That the vicissitudes of their persecuted countrymen were followed with anxious solicitude by those now in prosperous security, there is ample evidence to show, and also that help in money was repeatedly sent to aid the Prince of Orange and his party in their efforts to emancipate the Provinces from the tyranny of Spain.[1] When, in 1572, the first success was attained in the taking of Brill on the coast of Zeeland,[2] the victory was partly owing to the assistance afforded to the *Gueux de Mer* by the English and French ships in the Channel, but partly also to the fact that some of the more prosperous of the refugees in London, among whom was Jean Houbelon, had become (to quote a student of Belgian history) 'sufficiently rich to enable the Consistory of the refugees in England to raise a company of two hundred soldiers, whom they despatched to Launcelot de Broderode, the brave Captain of the Gueux de Mer.' He adds: 'This fact, which I mention at random, is the more worthy of note, that it enabled the English refugees to claim a large share in the taking of Brill, which operation proved to be the commencement of the eventual discomfiture of the Spaniards. Jean Houblon, Roger van Peene, Pierre Tryon, and Jean Longhuet were of the number of those who contributed to the cost of this levy of troops.'[3]

From this time Queen Elizabeth was gradually drawn

[1] Seeley, *Growth of British Policy*, i. 182; and Motley's *Rise of the Dutch Republic*, ii. 359.

[2] Strada, in his *De Bello Belgico*, states that after the taking of Brill, the people pictured the Duke of Alva with spectacles on his nose; for the Low Dutch call spectacles 'brills': Strada, trans. by Sir Robert Stapleton, Kt., book vii. p. 72.

[3] See *Quelques Notes sur les réformés Flamands et Wallons du 16⁰ Siècle réfugiés en Angleterre*, par Charles A. Rahlenbeck, Secrétaire de la Société d'Histoire de Belgique. (See *Proceedings of the Huguenot Society*, vol. iv. No. 1.) For an account of the war and the fall of Brill, see Van Grusinger, *Geschiedenes Werke*, vol. viii.: Watergusen, and Groen von Prinsterer, *Archives de la maison d'Orange Nassau*, vol. i., l'an 1572.

JEHAN₃ HOUBELON, "MERCHANT STRANGER."

into the vortex of continental politics, in spite of her efforts to retain her isolation, for the success at Brill, followed by that of Flushing in 1578, changed the aspect of affairs, and the struggle in the Netherlands now for the first time assumed a European importance.[1] It is true that the Provinces were now wellnigh subdued by Alva's heavy hand, while the protestant cause in France had received a crushing blow in the massacre of 1572 St. Bartholomew. But apart from the question of the Church, the power and success of Spain—especially in regard to her recent great victory over the Turks[2]—had at last excited the jealousy and apprehension of Europe. France and England were thus seeking, though in secret, to embarrass Philip by aiding and encouraging his unfortunate subjects in the Netherlands in their struggle for liberty; while not only did the English people watch with sympathy the sufferings of the Protestants, but the question of their own commercial interests began to be an important factor in their foreign relations.

Hitherto the Spaniards had been practically masters of the New World, basing their claim on a Papal Bull of the early part of the sixteenth century; but the union 1580 of Portugal with Spain had completed the monopoly of Spanish dominion in the East, making her indisputably the single state in Europe of unlimited maritime supremacy;[3] and this supremacy was of the greater grievance to the English from their growing spirit of adventure in trade and commerce. During the long peace of the earlier years of Elizabeth's reign, the prosperity of this country had steadily advanced. In those countries where trade had hitherto chiefly flourished, it was now languishing under the influence of internal troubles, and England was not slow to avail herself of

[1] Seeley, *Growth of British Policy*, i. 133, 142, and 147.
[2] The battle of Lepanto, 1571.
[3] Seeley, *Growth of British Policy*, i. 163.

the openings thus afforded her.[1]   The English company
of Merchant Adventurers were diligently pushing their
way all over Europe and the East, and had likewise
found their opportunity in the wars in the Netherlands for the absorption of a great part of the trade of
Flanders in Europe.[2]   That of London was also being
still further enlarged and developed by the transference
there of the experience and business connections of the
Merchant Strangers, who at this time appear to have
traded almost exclusively with European ports.   But
British commerce was now undergoing a change; the
old and dignified traditions as represented by the
Thornes of Bristol, the Greshams and other merchant
princes of London, etc., were passing away.   The
Merchant Adventurer had won for himself, by his
individual energy and enterprise, a trade untrammelled
by the restrictions of the past; while a still newer school
had lately arisen with the daring exploits of the ‘sea-
dogs’ of Elizabeth.

While the Queen was still resolute not to break the
peace which she had successfully maintained while all
around her were at war, she had not been unwilling to
allow her great enemy in Spain to be harassed and
annoyed by her sea-captains.   A guerilla warfare was
long carried on in this manner unchecked by the Queen.
Hawkins and Drake were primarily animated by a bitter
hatred against Spain, and of her claim to a monopoly of
the New World, while the cruelties there practised by
the Spanish Inquisition they also regarded as specially
calling for their interference;[3] the annoyance of Spain

---

[1] ‘Queen Elizabeth, by the vigorous application of her Ministry, found
methods of removing the woollen manufacture from Flanders, and establishing it here, which has made a mighty progress and spread itself all
over the Kingdom.’—Joshua Gee, *Trade and Navigation of Great Britain*,
p. 147. London, 1738.

[2] W. Cunningham, *The Growth of English Industry and Commerce in
Modern Times*. 1892. See Introduction to vol. ii. p. 24.

[3] Seeley, *Growth of British Policy*, i. 205.

was thus the first object with the sea-captains, but all opportunity for trade was eagerly seized upon, and the riches they brought home with them in abundance added materially to the warmth of the welcome they received on returning from their adventurous expeditions. Not only did the 'silver ships' bound for Spain occasionally fall into their hands, but 'prizes' laden with rich merchandise destined for the grandees of the Peninsula found through their means a different destination. Thus the Spanish trade in the East was everywhere made to suffer at the hands of the sea-rovers, whose nimble vessels and bold crews were more than a match for their great unwieldy carracks laden with the riches of India and China, and bound for Spain.[1] The efficiency of the English navy owed its birth to this irregular warfare; it was being trained through a course of daring privateering for the great work to which it was destined at a later date. When in 1585 the Queen 'let loose Drake,'[2] and the long delayed moment arrived when open war took the place of the past irregular strife, Elizabeth found that she had a good navy able to cope with Spain. The quarrel widened with the execution of the Queen of Scots, and finally, after a prolonged period of preparation, of false starts and of much vain-glorious boasting, the Spanish Armada set sail for England in the year 1588, to take possession in the King's name, and to restore to the Roman Church her lost supremacy in England.

1585

1588

Jean Houbelon had been twenty years in this country when we find him again coming forward with the other Merchant Strangers, in concert with the City of London, to aid the Queen in the strait she was now in. For

---

[1] The capture of a Spanish carrack laden with Eastern merchandise is said to have first opened up to the English the knowledge of the treasures of the East, and inspired them with the ambition to trade themselves. See R. Fox-Bourne, *English Merchants*, vol. i. pp. 209-10. Bentley, 1866.
[2] Seeley, *Growth of British Policy*, i. 206.

Elizabeth was unprepared for war ; she had postponed too long the needful preparations, in the expectation and hope that by means of the dexterous negotiations she had hitherto found so successful, direct hostilities might still be avoided.   Under this procrastination her people had fretted in vain, nor would she listen to their expostulations.   But now that the Great Armada had sailed, and that all Europe was watching in awe for the anticipated disaster to the English arms, the country rose as one man in response to the spirited appeal of the Queen. Having failed in her efforts to preserve the peace which had blessed the earlier years of her reign, no sooner was war unavoidable than she met the necessity with a bold front.   A voluntary loan was immediately raised in the City to meet her necessities, and a large sum was placed at her disposition; while the twelve great companies of the City of London alone subscribed upwards of £50,000, the little group of Merchant Strangers fulfilled their part by contributing £5000, and of the thirty-eight names given as subscribing this sum, all, with the exception of four Italians, were Walloons, Flemings, or Dutch. The name of ' John Houblon ' occurs among those who subscribed £100 to the fund.   The worldly affairs of the Strangers had certainly prospered in the country of their adoption, or they would hardly have been able to advance so considerable a sum towards the loan raised to meet the necessities of the Queen ; the more so that the amount of their contribution, if multiplied by about twelve—some even say fifteen—would be of nearer approximate value to our modern standard of money. But few knew better than did the refugees—and that from dire experience—the consequences which would have followed a successful Spanish invasion.   Indeed, it would be difficult to overestimate the importance of the issue of the struggle then impending between the two countries—a struggle involving not only the fate of the reformed religion, but of the balance of power in Europe.[1]

But the event showed that the Vatican had miscalculated its power to pervert the patriotic instincts of Englishmen ; for at the approach of the Armada none were found to hang back—Protestants and Catholics, alike irrespective of creed, rallied round the banner of their Queen, resolute to resist invasion by the foreigner.[2] Far from the danger having been averted in great part by the accidents of natural causes of ' wind and wave,' it is evident from the story of the sea-fight off Gravelines on Monday the 25th of July, that the English navy was now well able to cope with the enemy, and was fully confident of its power to do so; while it is also plain that the Spaniards were themselves aware of the fact.[3] According to a contemporary Report among the State Papers, there was 'great fear throughout the Spanish fleet that England was strong enough and well prepared to encounter them ; . . . though they make account of their beastly great ships, any good English ship is able to combat with them.'[4] It is enough to say that the English ships were equipped and victualled in time—

1588

[1] Strype in his *Annals* records the preparations for encountering the Spanish Armada. 'The Queen,' he says, 'took up great sums of money of her City of London, which they lent her readily, each merchant and citizen according to his ability. And so did the Strangers also, both Merchants and Tradesmen that came to inhabit here for their business and liberty of the Protestant Religion ; in all to a sum of £4900. Whereof among the strangers John Houblon was one, of whose pedigree—no question—is the present worshipful spreading family of that name.' Strype's *Annals*, vol. iii. book ii. p. 517. See also Smiles, *Huguenots*, pp. 111, 112, and Agnew, *French Protestant Exiles*, Index vol., p. 16.

[2] This spirit of independence and loyalty is illustrated in the quaint pamphlet *Transactions of Count Gondomar* (Spanish ambassador) in 1624, where Sir Walter Raleigh's ghost is made to say to the Count, with whom —together with a ' Fryer ' and a Jesuit—he is conversing : ' There is never a Catholic Gentleman in our country will give you leave to tread upon the ground by way of invasion.' *Phœnix Britannicus* (Collection of Tracts), i. 321.

[3] See *Publications of the Navy Records Society*, vol. i., 1894. Edited by Professor Laughton. See also Seeley, *Growth of British Policy*, I. chaps. vi. and vii.

[4] State Papers, Domestic, Elizabeth, vol. 211, No. 97.

though scantily—and that as usual the pluck and energy of Englishmen rose to the occasion. The great storm indeed scattered and destroyed the Armada, but only after the English admirals—Drake, Sir John Hawkins, and the catholic Lord Howard—had defeated it, and this by virtue of their skill and the gallantry of their men, as well as by the essential superiority which they possessed in naval tactics over the commanders of the formidable galleons of the Spanish fleet.

CHAPTER V

MERCHANT STRANGERS OF ELIZABETH

'Blessed is that land that hath all commodities to increase the Commonwealth ; happy is that island that hath wise councillors to maintain it, virtuous courtiers to beautify it, noble gentlemen to advance it, and ... such a Prince to govern it as is their Sovereign Queen !'—JOHN LYLY, *Euphues and his England,* 1580.

BETWEEN the years 1560 and 1569, all wards of the City of London were required to send in returns of the strangers within their gates, giving their names and occupations, how long they had been living in England, and to what churches they resorted.[1] Nicolas Houbelon had already been twenty years in England, and had long been a denizen and naturalised citizen, before his name occurs in one of these searches. The returns were very incomplete, and many of the documents which have escaped destruction are much damaged and faded. In 1571 a more exhaustive inquiry 1571 was attempted, and apparently undertaken by the Lord Mayor at the instance of the Privy Council.[2] The distinctions drawn were broad ; all were classified according to the language they spoke. Nicolas and his wife, who are described as residing in the parish of St. Martin le Grand, were classed as 'Frenche,' and as 'borne in Fraunce,' although they were formerly 'subjects to the King of Spain.' But their speech was French,

[1] See Burn, *Protestant Refugees,* p. 6.
[2] Huguenot Society Publications, x. part i. p. 402. The result of the search disclosed the fact that upwards of 4000 strangers were then living in London. Of these by far the larger number were Dutch, principally artisans.

and that was enough.[1]   The Walloons, many of whom, like the Houblons, were of French origin, were in fact usually counted as 'French' in these returns of strangers, while occasionally they were included under the classification of Burgundians.   At this time Nicolas's brother Jean, had been four or five years in England, but as his name does not appear in the list, it is probable that he evaded the search.   The father of his wife—Nicolas de la Fontaine—appears to have accompanied Jean to England, and their names are frequently found mentioned together.   The family (originally French) came from Ypres in Hainault, and De Fontaine, like his son-in-law, was a merchant.

1571   Nicolas Houbelon left his home in the precincts of St. Martin le Grand soon after the return of strangers above-mentioned was made, and it would appear that Jean's wife and children arrived this same year.   The brothers, however, did not separate though they moved into another house.   This house belonged to a Merchant Stranger, by name Pierre de Bosquelles, who had likewise come over to England in 1567.[2]   His wife's name first appears in the returns at this time, and as they were natives of Lille, it is possible that she and Marie Houbelon came to England together.   The latter's eldest son, Pierre (who was born in 1559), Nicolas, his younger brother, and a daughter named Edeth, accompanied their mother.   Pierre de Bosquelles was then living in the parish of Saint Andrew Undershaft, and, according to the foreign custom, the house

---

[1] The entry is as follows: November 1571. Sainte Martyns le Graund Aldrichegate Warde. Nicholas Heblen Dennizein and his wife borne in Fraunce. Have byn here XXtie yeares, and are of the frenche Churche.
> —French Churche ii.
> —Dennizein   i.
> Frenche pson   ii.

State Papers, Domestic, Elizabeth, vol. 82, p. 38.

[2] Together with Pierre de Bosquelles, Nicolas de la Fontaine contributed £1000 to one of the war loans of Elizabeth. See Stow, *Survey of London*, I. i. 283. Ed. 1720.

was occupied by different families in separate apartments, the occupants of which were said in the returns to be 'sojourning within him,' viz. the owner of the house.[1]

When, at a later date, Jean Houbelon and his family removed to another part of the city, Nicolas₁ remained in the same apartment in De Bosquelles' house. The names of both brothers occur frequently from this time in connection with the subsidies assessed upon the inhabitants of London for the use of the 'Queene's Majestie.'[2] Jean's new abode was in Aldgate Ward;[3] according to Stow and other evidence, his house was near the corner of Lime Street in one of the best and most convenient parts of the city, and it remained the home of the family till well on in the next century. At the age of twenty-four, Pierre, his eldest son, was (as we find by an assessment of 1582) already launched on his career as a Merchant Stranger,[4] and from this time forward his name is frequently mentioned in connection with commercial matters. Although he was only fifteen at the time of his expatriation, it would appear that it was by his own initiative that he joined his father in England, and for this reason he was afterwards called a Confessor.   1582

During the long years following upon their hurried flight from Flanders, Jean Houbelon and his fellow-countrymen passed through many trials and varied experiences. Although their interests, both commercially and politically, were now bound up in the country of their adoption, there are many evidences of the love

---

[1] Indenture made the 25th October, 19 Elizabeth. Lay Subsidy, London 145/252.
[2] At an earlier date we find De Bosquelles to have been living in Tower Ward with two servants also aliens (State Papers, Domestic, Elizabeth, vol. 84. Certificate of Lord Mayor).
[3] Lay Subsidy. Additional. London, 257/16. 1st August, 24 Elizabeth (1582).
[4] *Ibid.*

of 'home' felt by the refugees, and of their concern for the sufferings being there endured by many dear ones, of whose fate they frequently were in complete ignorance. This solicitude is pathetically illustrated by the records in the registers of some of their churches, which tell of fasts held by their members on the various occasions on which they conceived God's help to be specially needed. Thus we find that every success or reverse experienced by the Prince of Orange's party caused corresponding joy or sorrow. Smiles quotes the following, from the records of the refugees at Southampton : ' L'an 1586 le 3ᵉ jour de Septembre fut célébré le jeusne publique; l'occasion estoit que Monsigneur le Prince d'orange descendoit dalemaigne aux paiis bas pour assaié (essayer) avec l'aide de Dieu de délivrer les poures (pauvres) églises dafliction ; et pour prier plus ardament le Seigneur à la délivrance de son peuple—le jeusne fut célébré.'[1] The refugees in England, Jean Houbelon included, had contributed a large sum of money towards the equipment of this expedition, which, however, to their grief was doomed to failure. This and many other extracts given by Mr. Smiles from the registers of the Huguenot Church at Southampton—'God's house,' as it was called—form a curious commentary upon the history of the struggle being enacted in the Netherlands, reflecting as they do each event, and illustrating the hopes and fears of the exiles. Thus, a public fast was ordered in the year 1583, when the wild doings of the *Malcontents* had introduced fresh complications to those already existing in Walloon Flanders. It will be remembered that a conspiracy in Lille, in which the Malcontents bore a part, was the cause of the exile of Hubert, one of the Houbelon brothers from that city. The exiles complain that their churches in 'les paiis bas sont affligées par les Espagnols et les Malcontents,' and

1586

---

[1] Smiles, *Huguenots*, Ap. p. 476.

again 'que les horribles guerres des Espagnols et des Malcontents gattent (gâtent) la Flandres, et remettent la Papauté et l'idolatrie por toutes les villes quy prennent.'[1] A wail of woe was raised on the terrible news of the massacre of St. Bartholomew reaching this country; while the ravages of the plague at their own doors demanded the constant prayers of the foreign congregations. We may well believe that the blow given to the cause by the murder of the patriot William the Silent must have seemed the end to all hope of emancipation for the Provinces; but it once more revived, and their own position was secured to the refugees, by the triumph of 1588. After the destruction of the Spanish Armada, fervent thanksgivings to God were offered in all the refugee churches for the successful issue to the peril.

(margin: 1572) *(margin: 1585)* *(margin: 1588)*

The next Lay Subsidy, in the records of which we recognise the name of Jean Houbelon, was granted to the Queen in this same year, viz. 30-31 of Elizabeth. That is to say, it covered the period dating from the beginning of the thirtieth year of the Queen's reign (the 17th November 1587) to the end of the thirty-first year (the 16th November 1589), thus including within it the memorable event of the invasion by the Armada, which took place in August 1588. The Queen showed her gratitude towards the Merchant Strangers who had helped her with money, by making a special exemption in their favour with regard to all payments of subsequent subsidies. A document in the Record Office sets forth that, by the Queen's letter, dated Greenwich January 23rd, in the thirty-second year of her reign, she signified her pleasure that all merchants born in Antwerp, or in any other place in the Low Countries, 'resorting to London for traffic of merchandise only,

---

[1] Smiles, *Huguenots*, Ap. pp. 476-7. See also Huguenot Society Publications for transcript of these registers.

should, with their servants, etc., be discharged of the several payments of the said subsidies,[1] power and authority for the same being granted to the Lord High Treasurer of England' (Lord Burleigh), 'the Barons of the Exchequer,' etc. etc.[2]   In consequence of this command, certificates were drawn up by the successive Lord Mayors of London, within their respective years of office, through means of which their lordships approached the Ministers of State 'sending greetings,' and submitting the names of the 'Aliens borne,' who, living in the various wards of the city, by virtue of the Queen's favour, 'claimed exemption from being taxed and assessed towards the Subsydies graunted to the Quene's Majesty that nowe is, by the Laitie.'   Five such certificates are preserved in the Record Office, and on each one of them the name of ' John Hublone' occurs third on the list of ' Merchants of Antwerp and others.'   The first of them contains sixty-three names,[3]—the last of the series is dated the 11th of January 1592-3,—and a few months later the old merchant passed away.   Jean's death occurred shortly before the 18th of May 1593, on which date his will was proved.   The original will was in French, written throughout 'in his own hand,' the certified translation in Somerset House being 'done into English' by Paul Typook, Public Notary, on its being proved some nine months after its execution.   In effect it is as follows : 'Being in perfect health and strength, he desyres that his body may be layde into the earthe and be buried without any pompe;' . . . that 'besyde the articles and conditions conteyned in his Marriage Contract,' he leaves all his property to Marie Fontayne,[4] his wife;

1593

---

[1] Each 'Entire Subsidy' was usually assessed in three separate payments.

[2] Lay Subsidy, London, No. 146/301, 30-31 Elizabeth, Membrane 4.

[3] The certificates are included in the Subsidy, 146/301.

[4] The document is torn, and the word Fontayne obliterated in the translated copy P.C.C. 'Nevell' No. 45 ; but occurs in the registered transcript.   Room No. 9 in Somerset House.

absolutely, the legacies to be left to her discretion and will, trusting that 'even as she hath been unto me a faithful spouse, that she shall be a careful and faithful mother for the goodes of her children and myne. Our uncle Erasme de la Fontayne and my brother Nicolas Houbelon are required and prayed to act as executors and administrators with my wife and spouse above mencioned.' It was commonly the habit of the refugees to bequeath the bulk of their property to their wives, while by the 'Custom of London' one equal part of the whole estate was the wife's due. Leaving the bestowal of legacies to the discretion of the widow was also a frequent arrangement in those days ; for example, by the will of Sir William Craven, who died in 1617, he left certain legacies 'with the consent and good liking of my wife.'[1]

The affectionate tone in which Jean alludes to his wife, the companion of his chequered career, would lead us to think of him as of a kindly nature, and of her as a woman both capable in mind, and worthy of trust and confidence. But long e'er their father's death, 'her children and myne' had been launched on the great world of commercial enterprise—the sons as merchants, while their daughter was married.[2] Marie's family continued for three generations to be closely united

De la Fontaine—Arms.

with the Houbelons in affection as well as in business. 'Notre oncle,' the executor of Jean Houbelon's will, was much younger than his wife's father, Nicolas de la Fontaine ; so much so that Erasme's son and hers were of the same age. Erasme, afterwards Sir Erasmus,

---

[1] Stow, *Survey of London*, I. ii. 68.
[2] Edeth Houbelon was married to George Careterith (Cartwright ?) the 30th May 1588. See *Registers of St. Andrew Undershaft*.

was one of the earliest examples of the descendant of a refugee settling in the country and founding a county family.[1]

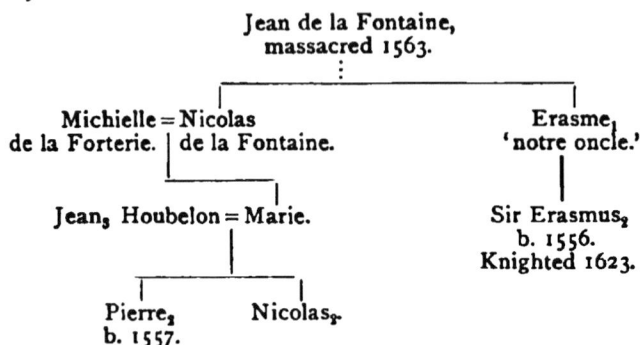

Jean de la Fontaine,
massacred 1563.

Michielle = Nicolas
de la Forterie. | de la Fontaine.

Erasme,
'notre oncle.'

Jean, Houbelon = Marie.

Sir Erasmus,
b. 1556.
Knighted 1623.

Pierre,
b. 1557.

Nicolas,.

Jean Houbelon, the Merchant Stranger, was advanced in years at the time of his death; over forty when he came over from Flanders, he had been twenty-six years in this country.

As the years passed by, doubtless the refugees became more reconciled to the country of their adoption; but those of the exiles who were men of middle age when expatriated, never wholly forgot their situation as of sufferance in a foreign country. Eagerly as the far-seeing wisdom of Elizabeth and Lord Burleigh might welcome the strangers, they were yet subject to many grudging and inquisitorial mortifications. The 'Searches for Strangers' were in themselves evidence of ill-will, and the impertinent questioning of officials as to every

[1] Sir Erasmus de la Fontaine purchased the Manor of Kirkby Beter, otherwise Kirby Betters or Bellhouse, in Leicestershire in 1603, and was High Sheriff of Leicestershire in 1628. He married Mary, daughter of Edward Noel, Viscount Campden, by whom he had a son John, and another named Erasmus. A Jean Fontagne living in Amsterdam sent 'his cousin,' Sir Erasmus, some old family plate in 1640, who bequeathed it in his will to his son John. John married Frances, daughter of Sir George Palmer, and died in 1672. The family were staunch Protestants and Roundheads. The arms of the family are 'Per bend sable and gules, a bend or in chief a cinque foil pierced of the third.'—(See Morant, *History and Antiquities of Essex*.) In earlier times the De la Fontaines were frequently spoken of as *alias* Wicart, to distinguish them from others of the same name, who were called 'Maçon' in the same way.

detail of domestic family arrangement, and of age and place of birth, cannot but have been annoying and distasteful to men whose early surroundings had been republican in character. Not the least inquisitorial was the diligent search among the strangers as to their attendance at a place of worship. The good people of England prided themselves on having discarded the jurisdiction of the ' Pope of Rome,' but they only found other feet planted on their necks in the way of sacerdotal authority. Most men submitted themselves without question to the discipline of their own denomination, also requiring the strangers to do the same ; for mankind had been accustomed to be state-directed in their worship from the time of Constantine ; while in England men had not yet tasted to the full the persecution which burns the dross and refines the gold, as had done their gentle guests. Attendance at the roll-call of ' divine service' satisfied the authorities, and was to them the evidence of a proper and decorous piety ; and so, very few, either English or foreign, had the temerity to absent themselves from public worship.

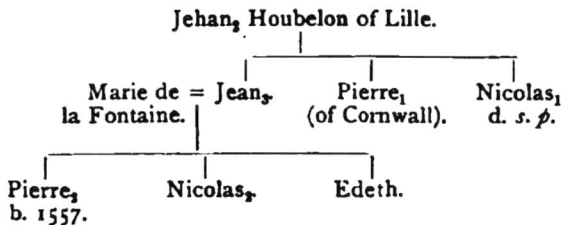

Jehan, Houbelon of Lille.

Marie de = Jean,   Pierre$_1$ Nicolas$_1$
la Fontaine.   (of Cornwall).   d. s. p.

Pierre,   Nicolas,   Edeth.
b. 1557.

The elder Nicolas, did not long survive his brother. He left no children and outlived his wife many years ; but owing to his being a denizen, his name is missing from the lists of Merchant Strangers claiming exemption from assessment for the Queen's subsidies.[1] When next we come across a Nicolas Houbelon, it will be

[1] Only Merchant Strangers were exempt.

has a Letter of Denization. Witness the Queen at Westminster, 3 February [1589-90].'[1] The early records of the Dyers' Company having perished in the Great Fire, we have been unable further to trace Pierre's connection with it; the Company is an ancient one, and ranks first in order after the twelve greater London Companies. It.does not of course follow from a person's admittance to the freedom of a Company that he himself practised the particular branch of industry it represented, but it is nevertheless possible that Pierre exported to the Netherlands, in his capacity of a merchant, white woollen goods to be dyed there. Indeed, until the year 1608 all English woollen stuffs were sent to Holland for this purpose, after which they were brought back to this country to be placed on the market.[2]

Subsequent to the date of his naturalisation, Pierre traded as an English merchant, or Merchant Adventurer, and as such were his descendants in future years to trade. Although it has not been possible with any certainty to discover in what manner he gained his high reputation as 'an eminent merchant of Elizabeth's reign,' it is probable that he was one of those *pioneers* who, at this time of change and development, prepared the way by their vigour and initiative for that great increase in the commerce of this country which was soon to follow. We should doubtless have known more of Pierre's history, but for the loss of that portion of a MS. work preserved in the British Museum which relates to him. Joseph Gulston, in his *Biographical Dictionary of Foreigners who have resided in or visited England from the earliest times down to the year* 1777, refers to his Appendix, page 159, for an account of Pierre Houbelon, merchant. The appendix to the manuscript is unfortunately not now in the Museum.[3]

[1] Patent Roll, 32 Elizabeth, Part iv. Membrane 35 [1589/90].
[2] Burn, *Protestant Refugees*, 1846, p. 259.
[3] Additional Manuscripts, 34. 282.

Pierre left a large fortune, so large that his youngest son began his career twenty years after the death of his father with the aid of the 'ample fortune' he had inherited from him. But Pierre was nevertheless cut off prematurely at the early age of thirty-six; while in full health and strength he was struck down by the plague, which at that time was bringing desolation to so many homes. His will, nuncupative—that is to say, unsigned and witnessed only—is dated the 10th of August 1593, but three months after the proving of that of his father; the following day he was carried to his grave. The hurried burial is briefly recorded in the parish register of St. Olave's, Southwark.

1593

Burials	1593. August 11.
Peter Hoblyn.[1]	Dyer

The nuncupative testament of Pierre Houbelon by its brevity witnesses to the haste and terror of the surroundings of his death-bed, the testator being already past the power of appending his signature to the document. 'In the name of God, Amen. Mr. Peter Hoblowne dothe leave unto Marye his wyfe to be full Execatrix of all that he hathe. The debts being paide. His brother Nicolas to be Overseer for the children.' Witnessed by John Goodwyne, Philipe Dupuis, Thomas Howse, and Katherine Goodwyne.[2] The will, being irregular, was not proved.

Pierre had been married some seven or eight years at this time, and five children had been born. Though the family was living in the parish of St. Olave's, Southwark, they had continued to attend the French Walloon church in Threadneedle Street, in the registers of which the baptisms of the children were recorded. Pierre's first thought would doubtless have been to secure the safety

---

[1] The name was frequently spelt thus by English scribes.
[2] John Goodwyne, citizen and grocer of London, died 8 Sept. 1608. See his will P.C.C. 'Dorset,' No. 80. He appointed his wife Katherine his sole executrix and residuary legatee.

of his wife and young children; we find, accordingly, that he sent them away, and in his extremity his French servant tended him, who was himself later to fall a victim. The man's name was Philipe Dupuis, and it occurs as one of the witnesses to his master's nuncupative will. Alone then, but for the kindly ministrations of his man, and the brief and terrified visit of the notary and witnesses to his will, Pierre Houbelon fought his grim fight with the plague. The bitter fate was a common one, for the recovery of the victim was generally regarded as hopeless, while so great was the terror of infection, that the attendants frequently succumbed to their fears. A few days later this fate overtook Pierre's servant, and the registers of the parish church record the burial of Philipe Dupuis.

Of the three sons and two daughters left by Pierre, James, the youngest, was born on the 2nd of July 1592,[1] and was thus at the time of his father's death less than a year old. Of Pierre's other children we know but little, but in this child we recognise the first truly English Houblon, and the ancestor from whom the present family descends.

At the time of his brother's death of the plague, Nicolas, was living alone with his mother in his late father's house in Lime Street; and here he continued to reside till his death. Strype, in his edition of Stow's *Survey of London* (1633), mentions this house in Lime Street when describing the bounds and limits of 'Ealdgate' Ward. 'Then they turn back,' he says, 'into Lime Street South, on both sides of the way, so far as the house of Nicolas Houbelon, Merchant Stranger, which is situated in Lime Street near where it turns into Leadenhall Street South on the one side, and Cornhill

1592

---

[1] Registers of St. Olave's, Southwark. Chester MSS., College of Arms, Surrey, iii. 307-400, IV. i. 185. Pierre's other children were baptized in the French church, Threadneedle Street, but the registers prior to 1599 have been lost.

on the other.'[1]   It appears that Pierre's young widow
and her children found a home with her mother-
in-law under the same roof; but she did not long
survive her husband.   Within a month of his death
and five of that of his father we find, in the parish
registers of St. Andrew Undershaft, the certificate of
her burial.   Whether she fell a victim to the ravages
of the plague still devastating London we have no
means of knowing, but the subsequent silence respecting her, the fact that her children were brought up by
their uncle Nicolas, and that she died in the house in
Lime Street where the children continued to live, leads
us to believe that the Marie Houbelon buried on the
7th of September 1593 was Pierre's wife rather than   1593
his mother, who also bore the name of Marie.[2]   And
so it was that with the death of both parents the past
was closed to the orphans; doubtless the charge of her
son's young children, thus thrown upon her protecting
care, gave comfort and consolation to the elder Marie
in the sorrow of her recent losses of husband, son, and
son's wife.

In the year 1600 the foreign merchants found them-   1600
selves called upon for a heavy loan to the Queen.   She
had helped the people of the Netherlands with men and
money; but when she wanted repayment and failed to
receive it, she turned to the Strangers to whom she had
given asylum.   She ordered Privy Seals to be issued
to the 'Aliens of Abilitie resident in London,' informing
them that 'having borrowed of our own subjects, we
have now recourse to your help, and especially to those

---

[1] Stow, *Survey of London*, II. ii. 73.   See also Map of the Ward, p. 55.
[2] See Pedigree, p. 70.   It is a curious fact that ten days after his death
Pierre Houbelon's name occurs in the list of inhabitants of the Borough of
Southwark for the first payment of the Lay Subsidy granted the 19th of
February, 35 of Elizabeth (Lay Subsidy, Surrey, 186/349); while the second
subsidy the following August was assessed upon his 'Wydowe.'   Doubtless
both payments would have been regarded as due, and were paid accordingly
by his executors.

of the Low Countries who have enjoyed the benefit of
Intercourse and freedom of Conscience, and trust you
will comply.' The threat follows that if the Strangers
hesitate, her Majesty might be necessitated to take
'severe courses.' Meanwhile we find by a letter to the
Hague that they were to look to the States for repayment, in the money due to the Queen.[1] Amongst the
lists of aliens in London thus taxed, whether free
denizens or 'Merchant Strangers of the Intercourse,'
we find many familiar names, and Nicolas Houbelon's
occurs amongst the latter category for £200. The
appellation of Strangers of the *Intercourse*, as given
to unnaturalised foreigners, may perhaps be explained
by the Queen's plea as to the privileges they enjoyed
in this country. From twenty-three Strangers nearly
£22,000 was raised by this loan, most of them contributing two or three hundred pounds or more, large
sums for those days; each £200 representing approximately two or three thousand in modern money.

At this time the refugees still maintained a separate
coterie of their own, their families mingling almost
exclusively with others of their own faith and nationality,
while their strict religious principles, allowing of no
relaxation of pleasure or excitement, doubtless were the
cause of their keeping aloof from the mirth and jollity
which was a characteristic of the Elizabethan age.
The surroundings of the refugees, however, were fast
being attuned to their own taste; the levity of the
past was passing away with the closing years of the
Queen's reign, while Puritanism waxed steadily stronger.
It was said that Elizabeth cared nothing for theology,
and this is probable; but that a sense of duty inspired
her policy of resistance to change in respect of ritual,

---

[1] 'Privy Seals for £29,000 are come among the Strangers; which money
the States are to repay.'—John Chamberlain to Dudley Carleton at the
Hague, 3 Feb. 1600. London State Papers, Domestic, Elizabeth, vol. 278,
No. 27. See also Stow.

is evident, for it cost her that popularity which was indeed as the 'breath of her nostrils.' 'Far above all earthly treasure,' she says in her pathetic last speech to her 'Good Commons,' 'I esteem my people's love.'[1] The struggle between the Church and the Puritan party[2] was to continue till near the close of the Queen's reign, embittering her last days. And so it was that the brilliant personality which had at once dazzled and bewildered Europe by its contradictions, its greatnesses and its apparent frivolities, set in gloom and discontent.

The plague was raging the year the Queen died, a bitter year of sickness and unrest. Of its ravages it was said: 'It would make your cheek grow pale and your hearts to shake with telling of it';[3] while Pym related in his diary that two thousand a week were its victims. At her death the people's pride in their Queen broke out afresh, and their grief at her loss was shown in that 'never did the English nation behold so much black worne as there was at her funeral.'[4] With the year 1603, and with the death of Elizabeth, the old order ended and a new began. None knew what the future might bring forth; the Queen had indeed named the Queen of Scots' son as her successor, but only when on her deathbed; and so great was the uncertainty that 'Upon Thursday it was treason to cry God save James, King of England, and upon Friday high treason not to cry so, for S. George and S. Andrew, that many hundred yeares had defied one another, were now sworne brothers.'[5]

It is very probable that the funeral obsequies of the

1603

---

[1] Queen Elizabeth's speech to her last Parliament, made 30th November 1601. Printed 10th March 1647.

[2] The virulency of the famous Marprelate Pamphlets created a reaction in favour of the Church.

[3] See old tract 'The wonderful yeare, 1603,' reprinted in *Phœnix Britannicus* collection, by J. Morgan, gent, London, 1732. i. 31.

[4] *Ibid.*, i. 31.

[5] *Ibid.*, i. 35.

last and greatest of the Tudors were witnessed by Pierre, Houbelon's children. The Queen died at Richmond, and her body was brought by water to Whitehall in a state barge, accompanied by her court and the great officers of state.[1] It was there disembarked and carried in procession to the Abbey, where the members of the great and important City, as well as the families of those Merchant Strangers whom Elizabeth had delighted to honour, would doubtless have witnessed the funeral pageant. Pierre's youngest son James was now eleven years old; as he lived to the age of ninety, he was to become a link with a past which before his death had so completely passed away, that his childhood's memories must have been to him like a strange dream.

The character of the new King was not one to inspire either loyalty at home or respect abroad. No sooner was Salisbury—the son and successor of Elizabeth's veteran Minister, Lord Burleigh—removed by death, than the traditional policy with regard to Spain was reversed for one of timid conciliation of the national enemy; a change which first stirred the proud English nation to ridicule, and then to anger. What was thought on the Continent of his policy and character, is scornfully expressed by the following French epigram, given in Rapin's *Life of King James I.*

'Tandis qu' Elizabeth fût Roy
L'Anglois fut d'Espagne l'Effroy,
Maintenant devise et caquette
Régi par le Reine Jacquette.'[2]

---

[1] The popular rhyme
'The Queen was brought by water to Whitehall,
At ev'ry stroke the Oars Tears let fall.'
is quoted in Stow, *Survey of London*, II. vi. 27.

[2] *Phœnix Britannicus*, i. 324. The lines may be roughly translated thus :—
'Whilst Elizabeth was King,
With England's greatness Spain did ring,
But now with silly plots and chatter,
Queen Janey loves to make a clatter.'

James I. inherited the tradition of hospitality towards the strangers bequeathed to him by his predecessors, and for some years the merchants from the Low Countries, including Nicolas₂ Houbelon, were exempted from payment of the Lay Subsidies as before.[1]

In addition to his private commercial adventures, Nicolas₂ acted as agent or factor to Flemish merchants abroad, and we have evidence of his having acted in this capacity for French merchants also. Elizabeth had the faculty of choosing her men with peculiar shrewdness; seldom has a sovereign been so served, whether by her statesmen or by the gallant soldiers and seamen who made her name and their own famous. But the daring born of the recklessness of the age was doomed to pass away with changing circumstances, more especially as the stress and danger of her service had somewhat blunted the moral sense of some of her servants. With the death of the Queen the prosperity of many of them came to an end, for while some had embroiled themselves in the plots relating to the succession to the throne, others had grown old in her service. It is in connection with the fall of Lord Cobham, Lord Warden of the Cinque Ports and Constable of Dover Castle, that we obtain a glimpse of some of the life-work of Nicolas₂ Houbelon. The complicity of Lord Cobham was conclusively proved with regard to the so-called 'Main Plot' for placing Lady Arabella Stuart upon the throne. In his fall, Cobham tried to drag down his friend Sir Walter Raleigh, who with himself, Lord Grey, and some others, were all tried and condemned to death. The prosecution and imprisonment of the noble Raleigh is a dark blot on the character of James, whose desire to propitiate Spain led him to sacrifice the hero to the foes whom he had made to tremble

[1] See Alien Subsidies, 146/460, membranes 2, 3, 4, 6, 7, 8, in each of which the name of Nicolas Houbelon occurs. The date of the last certificate being 18 May 1610.

in the days of the great Elizabeth. Though at first reprieved from sentence of death, Raleigh was stripped of his property, left to languish in prison, and finally laid his head upon the block to satisfy the revenge of Spain.

Meanwhile Cobham and Grey were brought to the scaffold, and, at the last moment only, were pardoned by the King. Their vast estates were forfeited to the Crown, and they, like Raleigh, spent a great part of the remainder of their lives in the Tower. Lord Cobham was a man of great ambition and a lover of literature and art [1]; but in the hour of his adversity he proved himself a coward, while subsequent disclosures showed him to have been none too honest. Arbitrary practices in his capacity of Lord Warden were disclosed in his trial, in which practices Raleigh's enemies endeavoured to implicate him also. The King, while appropriating the estates of the attainted noblemen, undertook their liabilities, and we find among the State Papers a list of Lord Cobham's debts. An item endorsed as follows is included in this list. [2]

1605   Nicholas Houbelon, Merchant Straunger, for Barrs of Sylver taken out of a French Shipp. } 530 li.

The Lord Warden had so far abused his power as to commit an act of piracy upon a French subject, and probably upon his fall vehement complaints were made to the new King of this and similar acts. [3] James subsequently ordered restitution to be made, and we find a warrant in the British Museum for the payment of the first instalment of this sum of £530 to Nicolas Houbelon (as acting for the aggrieved subject of the

[1] He had a library of 1000 volumes. Stebbing's *Life of Sir W. Raleigh*, p. 384, and Alien Subsidies, 228.

[2] State Papers, Domestic, James I., vol. xii. No. 79. Feb. 1605.

[3] That such acts of piracy were reciprocated by the French may be seen by a draft of an appeal to the French King preserved in the British Museum on behalf of the owners of an English ship taken by a French man-of-war this same year. See Add. MSS., vol. vi., 1604, Jan.-Mar. (Docquet).

French King), and ordering that his acquittance should be taken for the receipt thereof.[1]

This same year, 1605, Nicolas₁ married Marie, daughter of Jacques and Jeanne Godescal. This family had been refugees from Flanders, and the names of both Jacques and his brother Jean are to be found among the Merchant Strangers who subscribed to the Loan of 1588.[2] Two years after the birth of his youngest child, Nicolas₁ Houbelon died. His will was proved by his wife, 18th April 1618. He left five children named respectively, Nicolas₂, Jeanne, Jean, Anne, and Judith, of whom the eldest was but eleven years old at the time of his father's decease; their baptisms were registered in the French Church of Threadneedle Street. At the time of their uncle's death the children of Pierre were already grown up and his sons launched on the world; this fact may possibly account for the relative prosperity of the two families at a later date; for although Nicolas left a not inconsiderable fortune at his death, his children were deprived of his guardianship at an age when they needed it most, while—unlike those of his brother Pierre₂, who were English subjects by right of their father's naturalisation —Nicolas₂'s sons laboured under the disabilities of their foreign extraction; for their father remained an alien to the end of his life.

1605

1618

[1] See Brit. Mus. Add. MSS. 5755. The document is signed by Lords Nottingham, Shrewsbury, Buckhurst, Worcester, Howard, the Duke of Suffolk, Rob. Cecyl, and others.

[2] Jean subscribed £200, and Jacques £100. At the death of the latter he left legacies to several members of the Houbelon family. See Will in the Muniment Room, Abbey, Westminster. Their descendants were wealthy and influential citizens of London.

CHAPTER VI

REFUGEE FAMILIES : THEIR ORIGIN AND ARMS

'Astra Castra Numen Lumen Munimen.'[1]

THE 'Gentle Art' of Heraldry—called *Le beau Science* by the French—but few now either reverence or understand. And yet there was a time when not only Armigeri—viz. persons entitled to bear arms— but every one else, considered it as part of their education to be more or less familiar with the language of heraldry, and even to be able to 'emblazon a coat.' In days when few were able to write, each man had his mark or insignia, usually engraved upon a seal. Not only did the rich and noble make use of seals, but all alike did the same ; gilds of crafts, corporations, ecclesiastical establishments, commercial companies and towns, even individuals of industrial trades, — all possessed some sort of insignia, and these were generally engraved upon seals, or sculptured in stone and affixed to the façades of their owners' houses or over gateways.[2] Thus, while some claimed the privilege of bearing arms on a heraldic shield, others of humbler position used insignia of the nature of a modern trade-mark, in England often consisting of a monogram only.[3] In the case of the commercial towns, leaden plummets bearing the

[1] Lindsay motto.
[2] F. de Vigne, *Mœurs et usages des corporations des Métiers de Belgique, etc.*, p. 118. Gand, 1857.
[3] See Monogram on Tapestry hanging, at Hallingbury Place.

impression of the seal of the city were attached to every bale of goods before it could be sold. Thus the *plomb de commerce*, as it was called, of the town of Lille, consisted of a fleur-de-lis, the lion rampant of Flanders, and the label ' Lille.'

In the earliest days of chivalry, the practical use of heraldry was to be found in the facility it afforded for recognising an individual in armour; it was indeed (as is now believed), the outcome of the custom of using insignia rather than its origin.[1] After a time the heraldic art became altered and enlarged in scope. Deeds of daring and adventure, the desire for fame, or a chivalrous devotion to a 'liege lady,' found expression in our knightly ancestors through the emblematic language and imagery of heraldry, which was regarded as the exponent or trustee of these sentiments; and in an age when letters were in great part the possession of the cloister or higher branches of the clergy, the civilising influences of the art had their value. A still later development supervened, when men began to multiply the quarterings to which they had a right by marriage or descent, upon their shields, which no longer were characterised by that simplicity which formerly enabled the individual who bore them, easily to be recognised. Armorial bearings thus in time became solely the outward sign of gentle birth and the evidence of lineage.

The laws of chivalry and the rules and language of heraldry were practically international, while the same may be said with regard to many of the laws and customs of municipal life, and of the privileges and restrictions of its members. In Flanders, for example, as elsewhere, though no ordinary bourgeois could bear arms, the Échevins or magistrates of the great free cities (though themselves bourgeois) were privileged to do so;

---

[1] *Encyclo. Brit.*, HERALDRY.

and hence the origin of *canting arms*.   On the Continent
insignia were usually of a nature suggestive of the name
or occupation of the individual, or bearing on the origin
of the name ; and while some, like the Houbelons,
resorted to the productions of nature, whether of animal
or vegetable life, others had recourse to something
emblematic of their craft, or of the name of the place
of their birth, or even of some personal characteristic.[1]
The more elaborate of these insignia, such for instance
as were used by the important citizens, were termed
'canting' or *armes parlantes*.[2]   With the lapse of time,
these canting arms in many instances ceased to be
distinguishable from the armorial bearings of chivalry,
more especially as it was frequently the custom on the
Continent for the nobles to introduce quarterings of this
description into their coats; for the privileges of citizenship were eagerly coveted by the noble classes, and as
no one was eligible unless he was a member of some one
of the gilds, many sought admission, frequently adopting
at the same time the insignia or arms of the craft of
which he was made free.

A familiar example of a canting coat is to be found
in the armorial bearings of the great Tuscan family of
Medici, who had no patrician origin.   Whether they
derived their famous *palle* from the insignia of the
Lombardy merchants of the Middle Ages, as did the
pawnbrokers;[3] or from the *pills* of a mythical Medico
ancestor, as some have thought;[4] the arms would alike
be canting.   Their coat may be seen emblazoned in the
palaces and sculptured on the walls of the municipal
buildings of Florence, side by side with the armorial

---

[1] Derode, *Histoire de Lille*, i. 287, 8.

[2] For example, the family of Frémaux 'avait des gueules à trois fermails
d'or. (Fermaux—Frémaux.) Morier trois têtes de nègre.   De Mailly portait
trois maillets d'or,' etc.   *Ibid.*, i. 392.

[3] *Encyclo. Brit.*, PAWNBROKING.   The name 'Lombardy Merchant'
comprised Central Italy.

[4] Verini, *apud* Roscoe's *Life of Lorenzo de Medici*, note p. 5, 7th ed.

bearings of the great patrician families. Besides many English, other instances of canting coats of much interest are to be found among the German and Flemish bourgeois families, such as that of Albert Dürer. The father of the great painter was a goldsmith of Nuremberg, and on the back of his portrait, painted in 1491, are his canting arms : *Thüre*—an open door.

So far as the Flemish Houbelons are concerned, they would soon have given up the use of their former armorial bearings in their new surroundings, as they (and some others) ceased to employ the prefix *de* or *des* to their name. The canting arms (used to this day) of the *houblon* or hop plant on three poles, probably served them as their insignia in Flanders. The name, doubtless, was originally associated in some way with the plant ; and not only the Des Houblons, but the Poitou families of Des Cerisiers and Des Rosiers, owed their patronymics to the fact that in the fiefs of which they were the Seigneurs,

ARMS OF
DES HOUBELON.

these respective plants were largely grown. To this day Les Cerisiers is a small fief in the Commune de Loudun ;[1] while in a protestant register of that place (1580), the name of Jehan des Rosiers occurs, styled *Ecuyer et Seigneur du dit lieu.*[2]

HOUBELON 'CANTING
ARMS.'

Among the French refugees of 1685 there were some who could trace a common origin with the French-speaking Flemings already settled in England.

Every student of French history is familiar with the intimate connection between France

1685

---

[1] *Registres de Loudun.* Huguenot Society Publications.
[2] *Ibid.*

and Flanders in early times—the Counts of the latter
country paying homage as vassals of the French Kings.
The 'Picardian Jurisdiction' in the thirteenth century
comprised Picardy, Artois, Flanders, Hainault, Bas-
Maine, Meranche and Rothelois;[1] so that it will be
conceived how easily a transition of individuals would have
taken place.   Many Walloon families were descended
from Frenchmen who, like Jehan₁ des Houbelons,
found their way into the towns and villages of Flanders:
families of the same name flourishing in Normandy and
Picardy on the one part, and in the Flemish provinces
formerly subject to the King of France on the other;
all alike speaking the same tongue.   Many of these
families were originally noble, as may be seen by such
names as De Ligne,[2] De Francqueville; De la Haye;
De Béhault; De Lillers; De la Motte; Du Quesne; De
la Fontaine; De la Forterie, and Des Bouveries; not to
mention the Des Houbelons; these particular names
being mentioned here, only because of their connection
with the Houbelons or with those families with whom
the Houbelons were related by marriage.   Thus we find
in Monstrelet's *Chronicle* that amongst the knights who
in 1408 fought under the banner of the Duke of Burgundy in the battle of Eichtfeld (near Tongres) against
the Liégeois, Roland de la Motte was slain; while on
the same occasion the Lord of Ligne served in the
Duke's army.[3]

Of the families above-mentioned, many can be traced
in the various French works dealing with the noble
families of France.   We are told by Aubert de la Chenage
du Bois (in his *Recueil des Généalogies*), that the French
family of Du Quesne belonged to Picardy, and he adds

---

[1] Fallot, in *Recherches sur les Formes Grammaticales*, quoted by Diez.   See *Some Account of the Family of Du Quesne*, by Sir Edmund du Cane, K.C.B.
[2] Some of the De Lignes settled in Essex.   See Morant, *Essex*, vol. ii. p. 333.
[3] Monstrelet, *Chronicle*, vol. i. pp. 120-122.

'on peut présumer que cette famille noble est ancienne';[1] and the English Du Quesnes—now spelt Du Cane—claim to be descended from the ancient French house. A Vicomte de Quesne died on the field of Agincourt,[2] and Monstrelet mentions more than one member of the family in his *Chronicle*. From the Norman branch it is probable that the great Admiral was descended, as he was a native of Dieppe. It is curious to note, in a *Généalogie de la Maison du Quesne* (*Seigneurs de Broton, et de la Marabroc, et en Normandie*), the record of an alliance (in 1538) between a Jean du Quesne and a daughter of the family of de la Haye, members of whom also found their way into French Flanders. Coming to England during the persecutions,[3] they again became connected by marriage with the English Du Quesnes and other families, notably with that of De la Forterie.[4]

The family of De Francqueville was similarly allied. Marie,[3] wife of James Houblon, was the daughter of Jean du Quesne and Sara de Francqueville, whose marriage took place in 1599. The De Francquevilles may be traced to Normandy, where we find them in close alliance with the Norman Du Quesnes, both in marriage (in 1532) and in connection with an act of homage to the King in the year 1538. The following is from the Dépôt des Fiefs, Chambres des Comptes, Paris[5] :—

'7 Fevrier 1538. Verification d'aveu par noble

---

[1] Messieurs Feret and de Magny write at length on the family of Du Quesne; the latter in his *Nobiliaire de Normandie* and the former in his *Esquisse de la vie de Du Quesne*, the Admiral. From the hard pronunciation of Quesne—*chêne*, oak—which prevailed in Picardy, it appears probable that that province was the original home of the family.

[2] See Monstrelet, *Chronicle*, ed. Buchon, vol. 3. Paris.

[3] In the sixteenth century there were Protestants of this family in Loudun, *i.e.* L'honorable homme Jehan de la Haie, Seigneur de Malaguet, 1566, also—de la Haye, Sieur de Sanzeau and his daughter Marguerite, 1576. See *Loudun Registers*, Huguenot Society Publications.

[4] The mother of Marie de la Fontaine (wife of Jean, Houbelon) was Michielle de la Forterie. See *Canterbury Registers*, Huguenot Society Publications. The de la Forterie family was originally French, as also the Des Bouveries.

[5] Vol. 279, No. 38.

homme, Jehan de Francqueville, fait au Roi, 23 Septembre 1532, de hommage, a cause de son dit fief.
Entre les témoins sont Robert du Quesne, Seigneur de
la Marbroc, agé de 35 ans ou environ, et Jehan de
Quesne le jeune de la paroisse de Bournevillle, agé de
35 ans ou environ.'   In a *Nobiliaire* in the library of
Rouen, of the time of Louis XIV., the records of the
family of De Francqueville are given as far back as 1402.
The Du Quesnes were also connected with the noble
Flemish family of De Lillers, which traced its descent
from Raoul de Lillers living in 1348.   Jean de Lillers
was buried in Lille in 1430, and his epitaph is in the
church of St. Stephen there.   François de Lillers married Jeanne le Maire in 1500, whose sister (or niece),
Anne le Maire, was the mother of Sara de Francqueville, grandmother of Marie₈ Houbelon, née Du Quesne.[1]
The ancestor of the Flemish du Quesnes probably
found his way to Walloon Flanders at an early date.

Admiral du Quesne (who, as we have seen, was born
at Dieppe) shared with the Lille offshoots of the race
the same protestant proclivities that caused their exile
from the dominions of Philip of Spain; but the bigotry
of his master Louis XIV. was not so great as to prevent
the King's reaping to the full the advantages to be
gained by the services of his great subject; and so it
came to pass that the 'Marquis du Quesne, Admiral
of the French Fleet,' was unmolested in his religious
opinions.

While claiming for some of the protestant refugees
to this country a descent from well-born ancestors, it
must be remembered that not only in the great cities of
the Continent was citizenship deemed a privilege, while

---

[1] The pedigree of the de Lillers, who settled at Canterbury, is in the Heralds'
College down to 1663, extracted by Monsieur Le Blon, Pursuivant of Arms
at Valenciennes, and attested before the officers of the Court of Haynault
and Mons. See du Quesne Pedigree, p. 19. There is a Fief named Lillers
'près de Thérouane en Picardie.' See *Mémoires de la Société des Antiquaires de Picardie*, ii. p. 434.

many youths of good birth were enrolled as apprentices to their master-craftsmen ; but in England the same conditions prevailed. It is a mistake to think that but few of the citizens of London were of good birth. Those who were apprenticed to the greater citizens, and destined in the future to belong to that section of the community from which were drawn the foremost members of the Companies,—the great 'Merchant Princes,' the Court of Aldermen, Sheriffs and other functionaries of the municipal body,—were gentlemen ; while in earlier times this condition extended to every one who aspired to be admitted to the freedom of the City. Stow tells us that by the ancient laws and customs (many of them still in force till long after his time) 'none was admitted to the freedom of this City unless he were *Liberae Conditionis*, that is of the quality of a gentleman born,'[1] and this condition would have to be proved by those refugees in the sixteenth century who were admitted to a City Company, as was Pierre₂ Houbelon in 1590. Numbers of names connected with the City of London down to the period of the Revolution of 1688 can be traced to the English county families or minor nobility,[2] whose younger sons, seeking their fortunes, came to London to enter on a career of commerce and trade, not then thought otherwise than honourable and advantageous for all. An examination of the monuments and epitaphs in the London churches reveals the fact that large numbers of great citizens, of whom it has been said that 'they rose from being simple apprentices,' were armigeri ; the names of their relatives also occurring in the Heralds' Visitations in their several counties.

The 'Radnor group' (so classed by Mr. Agnew in

[1] Stow, *Survey of London*, II. v. 328.
[2] Lords of Manors in England, whether noblemen or commoners, correspond to the Seigneurs in France.

his *History of the Protestant Exiles*) comprised the most prominent among the foreign families in England in the sixteenth century, and with regard to the Houbelons, they took this place as of right, not only amongst their own countrymen, but among those of France and Italy, and their high character and position were recognised by such writers as the historian Stow.

CHAPTER VII

JAMES HOUBLON, MERCHANT ADVENTURER
AND ROUNDHEAD

'When gospel Trumpeter, surrounded
With long-eared rout, to battle sounded ;
And Pulpit, drum ecclesiastic,
Was beat with fist, instead of a stick ;
Then did Sir Knight abandon dwelling,
And out he rode a colonelling.'

Hudibras.

JAMES HOUBLON was probably apprenticed between the
ages of sixteen and twenty, according to the custom
among the citizens of London. Sir John Gresham apprenticed his son to his brother at the age of seventeen,
and the youth remained for eight years an apprentice
before he was admitted to the freedom of the Company
of Mercers, and became his own master; and this
although, as he himself expressed it in later years, 'I
was born free by my father's copy.'[1] On the admission
of a free-born apprentice to his full rights, he was sworn
and 'made free by patrimony, and paide as of custome';
while according to the old laws concerning freedom (still
in force in the seventeenth century), a man 'made free
by his father's copy, payeth eighteen pence.'[2] But as the
greater merchants were in great demand as masters,
and the citizens were allowed a limited number of

[1] See Ward's *Lives of the Professors of Gresham College*, pp. 1, 6.
[2] Stow, *Survey of London*, II. v. 308. See also for laws on freedom
(ancient and modern) *A Practical Treatise on the Laws, Customs, Usages
and Regulations of the City and Port of London*, by Alex. Pulling, p. 66.
(Henry Butterworth.)

apprentices, it followed that the former sometimes asked and received large sums from the parents of would-be apprentices.[1]

Many circumstances point to his uncle, Jean de la Motte, as having been the master of James Houblon in the days of his apprenticeship, on the completion of which he was admitted to the freedom of the Drapers' Company. James and his brothers were strictly trained according to the tenets of the French Reformed Church, of which the elder, Pierre,, ultimately became a *diacre* or minister. The influence of Mr. de la Motte may also be traced in their political tendencies, as he was himself an ardent Parliamentarian. Throughout the period of unrest and controversy which distracted the religious world of England during the childhood and early manhood of James, the French and Dutch protestant Churches remained practically untouched, and while each form of worship had its day of persecution or triumph, the strangers by common consent were permitted to carry on their own meek devotions undisturbed. It would appear that the pride and self-righteousness which was characteristic of the sects was absent in the Walloons. Indeed their humility, and quiet unassuming care for their own poor, inspired respect in both rigid Anglican and unbending Presbyterian; and to this attitude they in great measure owed the privilege of being allowed to live in peace. But apart from these considerations, the strangers had now become identified with the commercial and industrial world of London, and their removal in any large numbers would have been prejudicial to its prosperity. Already some had emigrated, and it was felt that their religious zeal would have braced them to

---

[1] £500 was not considered as too great a sum. See *Temple Bar, or some account of 'ye Marygold,'* No. 1 *Fleet Street,* p. 13, by F. G. H. Price. 1875.

further sacrifices were it put to the test by persecution; for, in the first year of his Archbishopric, the zealous and uncompromising Laud had ventured for a time to interfere with them, and the privileges they had enjoyed since the charter of Edward VI. were withdrawn. They were ordered to translate the English liturgy into French or Dutch, and enjoined to send their children to attend divine service, and be catechised in their parish churches.[1] This some of the strangers declined to do, preferring once again to wander forth in search of unrestricted freedom in their religious worship. Of those who emigrated at this time, some went over to Holland, but more to North America, to ‘ swell the numbers of the little colony already formed in Massachusetts Bay.’[2]

1633

A member of the Houblon family is found in or near New York in the earlier half of the seventeenth century, and it is possible that it was now that he emigrated to America. His name is spelt Houplein, but there can be but little doubt as to its identity.[3] In Baird's *History of the Huguenot Emigration to America* he mentions him as one of four settlers[4] of Flemish origin among many French. But that his christian name, Juste or Justin, is not elsewhere to be recognised in the family, we might perhaps hazard the suggestion that he was a brother of James Houblon. Pierre, had three sons, but we are without any trace of the third, and it may well be that he and Houplein of New York were one and the same. In another place we have the name of Houpleine given in a list of families established in New York City or its neighbourhood, before 1788.[5]

---

[1] Prynne's *Trial of Laud.* See also Burn, *History of the Refugees,* p. 15.
[2] *The Walloons and their Church at Norwich,* vol. I. part ii. p. 94.
[3] See *ante,* chap. i. p. 8.
[4] Two of these, named Tournay and Luten, or Luton, are to be found in the Registers of the Walloon Church in London.
[5] *Collections of the Huguenot Society of America,* vol. i. Introduction, note, p. x.

Pierre, = Marie de
Houbelon | la Motte.

Pierre,   ? Justin   James.
Diacre.   Houplein
    of New York.

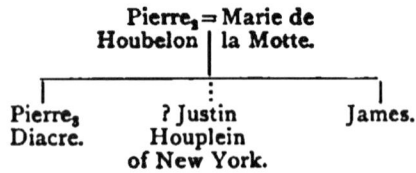

While the majority of the descendants of the refugees remained outside the stir of religious strife going on around them, it was not so with regard to the world of politics, and still less with that of trade and commerce, in both of which they exercised an influence in business circles which was steadily increasing. In spite of the ancient prejudice against them, it is patent that among the number of those men whose names figure prominently in the history of London during the seventeenth century and onwards, a considerable proportion were the descendants (by now completely anglicised) of the refugees of the previous century. After the opening of the recently erected Burse, or Royal Exchange (as it had been named by Elizabeth), with the accompanying opportunities it afforded for discussion and co-operation, the power of the great monied class began to take shape and silently grow in strength, although it was long before that strength was fully recognised by the State. But henceforth the possession of wealth, the fruit of industry, apart from that derived from territorial possessions, was to constitute a power which entitled its possessor to political influence.

James Houblon's father and grandfather were successful merchants of their day in London, but their business there had been carried on without the facilities the strangers had possessed while still living in their native country. The Flemish merchants had long enjoyed the use of a Burse at Antwerp, at a time when their correspondents in London—together with their English brother-merchants—were still meeting together for business in the open air. As Stow tells us in his *Survey of London* : 'Lombard Street, before the building of the Exchange, was the central haunt of the merchants. There, especially in the open space near Grace Church, they were accustomed to meet at all hours and in all weathers, to manage their affairs.'[1] It is not surprising that the change in the conditions under which business was transacted should quickly have borne fruit, in the manner we have indicated.[2]

A great gap of silence yawns between the death in 1593 of Peter Houbelon, the Merchant Stranger—a denizen only three years before his death—and the time when his son appears as a successful and prominent London citizen. During this interval many changes had taken place; James was an Englishman pure and simple in all but origin and name, and it would seem that to him the memories of the past were already shadowy. The refugees had now lost many of their foreign characteristics, while many had changed the spelling of their names to suit the English tongue ; in ceasing to pronounce their name in the French way the Houblons dropped the *e* mute, and henceforth we propose to do the same in these memoirs.

Possessing in an eminent degree the talents and business qualifications which had distinguished his ancestors, James identified himself with the new Royal Exchange of London from his earliest youth, and as we shall see, in his extreme old age, this bond was understood and acknowledged by his fellow-merchants, who conferred on him the title of *Pater Bursae Londinensis*, or 'Father of the London Burse.' By this title he is still honoured in the City through the epitaph composed for him by Mr. Samuel Pepys, the diarist, a copy of which is

[1] Stow's *Survey of London*, 1. ii. 152.
[2] The Royal Exchange, once so thronged with busy citizens, is now but little used, specialisation having broken up business 'into many groups, meeting at their several centres.

inscribed under his portrait which hangs in an ante-room in the Bank of England.[1]

On his marriage, James Houblon settled in the precincts of St. Mary Abchurch in Walbroke Ward, where he lived for some years. During the reign of Elizabeth, London had been much enlarged and beautified, and many fine buildings erected both by the nobles and the greater citizens; but until the Great Fire swept them away, the timbered houses in which the greater part of the population dwelt were rather picturesque than sanitary and convenient. Most of the merchants dwelt near the Royal Exchange, the seat of their business, and it was in one of these houses built of timber, and possessing, probably, a 'fair garden with trees,' that James and his wife passed their early married life. On the 16th of November 1620, at the age of twenty-eight, James Houblon was—as he himself expressed it in the evening of his long life—'in a happie day married' to Marie, daughter of Jean du Quesne

1620

DU QUESNE ARMS.[2]

le jeune (merchant of London), and of Sara, née de Francqueville, his wife. Marie was born on the 17th of October 1602, and was therefore eighteen years old at the date of her marriage. The earliest book extant of marriage registers belonging to the Walloon Church in Threadneedle Street, opens with the close of the sixteenth century, and the first marriage recorded in it was that of Marie₈'s

1599

---

[1]
Jacobus Houblon,
Londinas Petri Filius,
Ob fidem Flandria exulantis:
Ex C. nepotibus habuit LXX. superstites:
Filios V. videns Mercatores florentissimos;
Ipse Londinensis Bursae Pater;
Piissime obiit Nonagenarius,
Aº D. CIƆIƆCLXXXII. (1682.)

[2] The *canton* in the Du Quesne coat was added at a later date to their expatriation.

parents. Her grandfather and his family took refuge in England during the Alva persecutions, and settled at Canterbury, but subsequently removed to London. Here the friendship began which resulted in the marriage of James's elder brother Pierre, with Marie the daughter of the elder du Quesne, and some seven years later, in that of James himself with the niece of his brother's wife.[1]

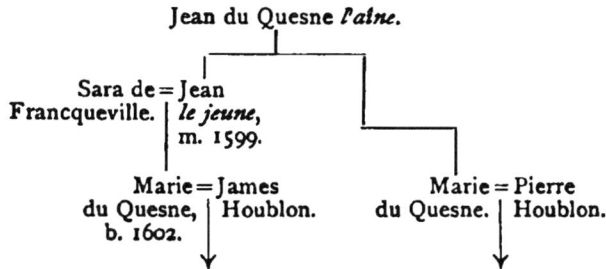

```
                    Jean du Quesne l'aîné.
                            |
          _____|_____
          |                                        |
   Sara de = Jean                                   |
Francqueville. | le jeune,                          |
               | m. 1599.                           |
          |                                         |
    Marie = James                          Marie = Pierre
 du Quesne, | Houblon.                   du Quesne. | Houblon.
   b. 1602.  |                                      |
             ↓                                      ↓
```

We find James at an early age engaged in commercial 'adventures' carried on in his own ships and in his own name. The commodities in which he dealt, and other evidence, show him to have been a Merchant Adventurer, trading exclusively (at that date) with European ports.[2] He appears to have been at one time, early in his career, a member of the French Company of Merchants trading into France and Spain, a company which was dissolved towards the middle of the seventeenth century; no evidence exists of his having engaged in trade with the East or in the New World. With the opening of

---

[1] The Registers kept by the foreign churches are of great interest, and, from the manner in which they were kept, facilitate a study, and recognition, of kinship between the various families, especially as the married women were almost always designated by their family name, as is the case in Scotland to this day. We are further helped by the fact that usually the eldest child of either sex was named after one or other of its grandparents. In the case of the Houblons, both James and his brother Pierre having married members of the Du Quesne family, common relationships are to be traced in the registers for both, whether of De Fontaine, De la Motte, or Du Quesne. The sponsors of infants were invariably nearly related to them.

[2] Bourne's *English Merchants*, i. 246. For lists of the commodities dealt in by the several companies of merchants, see Stow, *Survey of London*.

the seventeenth century many trading companies had
been established, all of which more or less developed a
great business.   These were not, like the East India
Company, worked on the joint-stock principle; but the
merchants who belonged to them, while enjoying the
mutual advantages of co-operation and support derived
from their charters, were yet independent Adventurers
either engaging singly in trade or in partnership with
others.   All possessed their own ships in whole or in
part, which sailed either in combined fleets at stated
times in the year, or in twos and threes upon private
adventures, according to the individual initiative of the
merchants who owned them.

After a time James Houblon and his wife removed
to a larger house in Walbroke Ward.   Of their numerous
family of sons and daughters, almost all of whom sooner
or later struck out careers for themselves in the great
commercial world of London, the writer of a MS.
memoir compiled in the following century says, that
'they laid the foundation of a most flourishing family
bred to marchandise, that made as considerable a figure
as any during the last Century.'[1]

James early identified himself with the fortunes of the
little French church in Threadneedle Street, in the
congregation of which he held the post of *ancien* or
elder.   In a community where religion and its free
exercise had been now for three generations the very
foundation and spring of existence, the habit of piety
and discipline had become a second nature.   To the
anciens was accorded the title of *Sire*, while their wives
(with those of the diacres) were alone distinguished
as *Madame* in the books of registration in their
church.   The names of Le Sire Jacques Houblon
and his wife Marie du Quesne are often to be found in
these books, whether as acting as sponsors to their

[1] MS. *ante* 1740.

friends' children, or as registering the births of their own.

The common practice in times of puritan zeal of giving biblical names to children was a far-reaching one among the refugee families, especially as it was also the invariable habit to give the baptized child the name of one of its sponsors. Thus the continuity of biblical names was perpetuated throughout several generations. James and Mary Houblon strictly conformed to this custom; and being blessed with a goodly quiverful of many sons, began with the names of Peter, James, and John, reverted to the patriarchs Jacob, Isaac, and Abraham, and finally resorted to more than one name chosen from among the prophets; and all these children were named after their godparents! Of the mother of this large family her husband speaks long years after her death with the tenderest affection. James's married life seems to have been for many years altogether happy and prosperous; his mercantile 'adventures' were successful, and to the 'good estate that his father left him,' he added large commercial gains, so that he was possessed—as Bishop Burnet records of him at the time of his death—'of as visible and large a share of the good things of this life as, all things being put together, any man in this age has had.'[1]

In the year 1635 James Houblon was severely injured at a 'Training near Morefields.' The Moor Fields and Artillery ground adjoining them then comprised a large tract of open ground outside the city walls, and planted round with trees. It was here customary for the City Train Bands and Artillery Company to exercise. James Houblon was a member of the Honourable Artillery Company, and was wounded, on the occasion of an explosion taking place in the Artillery garden, where there was a small arsenal or

[1] Funeral sermon by Dr. Gilbert Burnet, Bishop of Salisbury. 1683.

armoury in which their arms and ammunition were kept.
While his comrades belonging to the corps were killed
outright by the explosion, James, we are told, escaped
with serious injuries, from which he eventually recovered
after a long illness.   His biographer attributes this recovery 'to the strength of his constitution.' His military
career appears to have come to an end after this
event.

The Artillery Company of London had a later origin
than that of the Train Bands.   A company of between
two and three hundred merchants and other citizens 'of
1585   like position,' during the time of stress and danger which
preceded the coming of the Great Armada, banded
themselves together with the object of teaching and
training a strong corps of rank and file, as well as
each other, in military exercises.   They drilled in
the Artillery garden, where they erected the 'strong
and well furnished armory,' which was the scene of
James Houblon's accident.   Stow tells us that these
military exercises took precedent from those of the
merchants of Antwerp,[1] and they probably owed their
origin in London to the initiation of the refugee merchants.   The corps was accustomed to meet every
Thursday throughout the year, and these musters were
for many years very popular, attracting numerous
spectators, amongst whom 'Prince Charles' was sometimes to be found.[2]   The military ardour displayed by
the citizens cooled after a time, and the weekly training
ceased about 1610, but it was again revived with re-
1614   newed vigour in 1614, in which year King James I.
appointed a general muster over all England.   James
Houblon was at this time a young man of two-and-
twenty, and it is probable that he joined the corps on
this occasion; only the most active and able citizens
were selected as officers, and these for the most part

[1] Stow, *Survey of London*, II. v. 457.   [2] *Ibid.*

PETER₍ᵢᵥ₎ HOUBLON.
(CAPTAIN OF THE BLUE REGIMENT (TRAIN BANDS).

were householders.[1] Train Bands had existed in London from an early period; unlike the *Gardes bourgeoises* of foreign towns, which were solely composed of freemen, and were designed primarily to protect and uphold the rights and privileges of the cities, those of London formed a portion of the only military force of this country. The united Train Bands of the whole country constituted the militia, and were recruited from among able-bodied men throughout the kingdom.

Some years after James Houblon's accident the death of his elder brother Peter occurred, who left several sons all considerably older than those of James. The eldest (also named Peter$_{iv}$) belonged to the Dyers Company, and was likewise a merchant. Peter$_{iv}$ was an officer for many years in the London Train Bands, and his name occurs as Captain of the Blue regiment in Stow's list of the bands and of their officers in 1659.[2] The Blue regiment was one of the six belonging to London, the other five being respectively the Green, Red, White, Orange, and Yellow. At the time of the publication of the *Little Directory* of 1677 he was still an officer, and is there mentioned as Major Peter Houblon, Merchant; at that time his residence was in Budge Row.[3] There is a portrait of him at Hallingbury Place, in armour, by T. Jouay, bearing the date of 1651; with pale stern face and long nose, he appears a typical specimen of the rigid Puritan.

The strained relations subsisting between Charles I. and his people were now such that the King saw no way but in struggling on as best he could without calling a Parliament. This desperate endeavour to carry on the government of the country without resorting to the only legitimate way of obtaining supplies of money

---

[1] Stow, *Survey of London*, II. v. 450. [2] *Ibid.*, I. ii. 302.
[3] See reprint (1863) of *The Little Directory* of 1677; the oldest printed list of the merchants and bankers of London.

by the granting of subsidies, involved him deeply in the displeasure of his subjects, for it was only by the straining of the royal prerogative to breaking-point, and by divers illegal measures, that he was able to raise any revenue at all. The enforced economy of the King, however, resulted in a peace marked during the so-called 'personal government' by a general prosperity; and both James Houblon and his cousin Anthony became during this time increasingly prosperous in their business as merchants. Trade and commerce flourished, fresh manufactures were started, land was brought into culti-vation, and wealth and culture increased everywhere.[1] But in their prosperity the people, though apparently forgetful of their wrongs, were, in the words of the royalist Clarendon, 'full of pride and mutiny and dis-content.'

Amongst other devices for the raising of money, the Earl of Strafford is reported to have 'laid before the Council a memorial about the French method of raising forced loans from the wealthy,' and to have 'advised imitation of that practice.'[2] Although it is said that at this juncture the Lord Mayor and Aldermen actually refused the loan to the King which he requested[3] (and it is certain that at this time the City was filled with discontent and anxiety), a close inquiry was nevertheless instituted by the Aldermen of the several wards on the lines suggested by Strafford, and in consequence of an order of Privy Council of the 10th of May 1640, but a few days after the dissolving of the Short Parliament. The original returns made by the Aldermen of the names of the 'men of wealth' in their several wards, whom they conceived to be of 'ability' to contribute to the proposed loan, are in the British Museum; the sum proposed to be raised in this manner was £200,000 upon security.

1640

[1] Green, *Short History*, p. 518.
[2] Von Ranke, *History of England*, ii. 196-7.   [3] *Ibid.*, ii. 209.

James Houblon's house was in Walbroke Ward, and in the return given in on the 13th of May by Sir Edward Bromfield, knight and alderman of his ward, James's name as a 'person of abillitie' had its place amongst others on the list.[1] That of Anthony Houblon also appears as an 'able person of worth in esteme' among the inhabitants of Cheape Ward.[2]

One of the first acts of the Long Parliament, when the King departed for Scotland after the execution of Strafford, was to levy a poll-tax upon the inhabitants of London. The return given of the occupants of James Houblon's house includes his own name, that of his wife, two children, and five servants, two of whom were French; the tax was assessed on adults only.[3] Although James and his family were at this time still living in Walbroke Ward, they had again changed their residence; the house they now occupied was in Bearbinder or Burbinder Lane, within the precincts of St. Mary Woolchurch. In this house (probably more suitable for so many inmates than his old one) James remained until the street was destroyed by the Great Fire of 1666. It will be found, however, that after that event he rebuilt it on the old site, overlooking the Stocks Market and the belt of lime-trees which grew on the east side of the square. James continued to inhabit Bearbinder Lane, whenever he was not living in the country, till his death; and his eldest son resided there after him for many years. 1632

As we have seen, the foreign protestant Churches were left in peace during the years of trouble and strife which raged round the Church of England during this period. Intolerance characterised both parties, and while

---

[1] List of the principal inhabitants of the City, 1640, p. 18.

[2] *Ibid.*, p. 12. Many references are to be found to Anthony Houblon, who was a Merchant Stranger. He was born at Lille in 1585, and died in London in 1648 without children, leaving his property to his wife Ruth Hama, remarking in his will that 'it lyeth somewhat confusedly abroade.'

[3] Lay Subsidies, Additional. London, 252/13.

'Parliament men' displayed a temper full of arrogance and self-righteousness, 'King's men' no less hated and despised their adversaries, seeing nothing but *cant* in their religious professions. The religious sentiment was doubtless largely political, but it was none the less present among both Cavaliers and Roundheads; reform was in the air, and a bold and inquiring spirit, in which the ancient submission to persons and things was fast making way for an uncompromising criticism of Church and State, and of the encroachments of the King upon constitutional usage. And this attitude was in time,—though its development was temporarily suspended by the Restoration,—to crystallise in England into the great Whig party which brought about the Revolution and placed its stamp upon both religion and politics in the eighteenth century. With regard to James Houblon, the line of conduct on which he embarked in his early manhood was one of uncompromising hostility to all invasion of personal or religious freedom; this was the keynote of his political creed throughout his long life, as it was also that of his many sons after him. That his naturally gentle and well-balanced mind in time brought about a change in his political attitude there is no doubt, for he was unprepared to go the lengths of puritan dogmatism and military government. We shall see that before the establishment of the Protectorate, he withdrew entirely from any active co-operation with parliamentary affairs.

Though the City of London was at this time presbyterian in its sympathies and predilections, its traditions of loyalty led to the display of much irresolution and apparent changeableness during the succeeding years of Charles's stormy reign; while the good sense of the citizens made them both deprecate the violence of the parliamentary party, and keenly alive to the dangers attendant upon the proposed oversetting of the old order for one wholly untried, which promised to be equally despotic. Less cautious than the wealthy City, the Commons were hastening, by virtue of their new powers wrung from the King, to make sweeping changes; republican sentiments were now heard openly expressed, and the House began the difficult and critical task of attempting to amend the Constitution to its special taste. It is easy to read the trend of opinion and prejudice in Parliament with regard to the Church, in the destructive zeal it now displayed. The City had been eager to curb the power of the Church, and had rightly resented the arbitrary measures of Archbishop Laud, now lying in prison; but it is inconceivable that the vandalism enacted by order of Parliament could have been witnessed without indignation and disgust by the citizens. No sooner had the edict of destruction gone forth, than the speedy consequence followed, in 'a bleak and hideous defacement of beautiful and comely things in most of the cathedrals and great churches all over England.' When we hear that all the crosses about London were pulled down to the ground, and the churches and altars desecrated, we do not wonder that a great reaction, if temporary, did in fact supervene.[1]

It was the King himself who finally precipitated the struggle which had so long been impending. The 'Five Members' impeached at Westminster were brought back by the citizens in triumph; while the Train Bands who formed their escort (amongst whom marched Captain Peter$_{iv}$ Houblon) took a solemn oath 'to guard and defend the Parliament, the Kingdom and the King.'[2] The return of the five members was the signal for Charles's retirement from Whitehall, and the City's long

---

[1] Writing in September this year (1641) to the King, Sir Edward Nicholas says, 'The late crosse orders and unusuall passages in Parliament a little before the recess, are so distasteful to the wiser sort as it hath taken off the edge of their confidence in parliamentary proceedings.' Von Ranke, ii. p. 293.

[2] Green, *Short History*, p. 546.

hesitation was for the time at an end. War being now inevitable, Parliament delayed no longer in assuming control over the militia of the country by means of an ordinance of the two Houses.[1] With enthusiasm the citizens threw themselves into the work; a loan was raised in the City, and in a very short time a regiment of horse was enlisted by the citizens for service in the war. The 'listing' for men and horses was opened on the 21st of June 1642.[2]

But for his retirement from service in the Artillery Company of London after his accident some years previously, James Houblon's zeal would probably have led to his taking an active part in the rebellion, as did his cousin Peter$_{iv}$, who fought with his regiment in the first Civil War. Unable himself to bear arms, James, in common with other rich and zealous citizens, provided a horse and man for the service. Two days after the 'listing' was opened, we find by the contemporary army accounts that he 'entred one able bay gelding, his rider James Dandoe, armed with a Carabine, a case of pistolls, buffe coate and sword, all valued by the Commissaryes at 22.00.00 (£22).'[3] James Houblon of Southwark shortly afterwards 'listed one sorell horse with a blase, his rider Cuthbert Ridley,' armed also with the requisite pistols, carbine, buff coat and sword; the horse and arms being valued by the commissaries at £18. This other 'James' was a son of Peter the diacre, and younger brother of Captain Peter Houblon now in arms. The ardour of both James Houblon and his cousin and namesake induced them in November following again to come forward, when the former 'listed one daple gray gelding' to the City regiment, and

[1] 17 May 1642, see *Commons' Journals*, ii. p. 577; see also *Lords' Journals*, v. p. 70.

[2] See Army Accounts. Account of horses listed for the Parliament, June 1642.

[3] *Ibid.* Four Commissaries had been appointed on the 16th of June to enrol, and value the horses and arms.

the latter 'one gray nagg and one browne-bay nagg with sadles and bridles';[1] as the battle of Edgehill was fought the previous month (23rd October 1642) it is possible that both Captain Peter Houblon of the Blue regiment, and the troopers James Dandoe and Cuthbert Ridley, may thus have been furnished with remounts. Later the name of James Houblon of Southwark again appears in the 'listing,' when he contributed 'one browne-bay gelding with a starr, and a brown Mosell, furnished with a case of pistolls and a sadle and furniture valued att 20.00.00.'[2]

It would appear that in their zeal for the cause of the Parliament, and their anxiety at the supposed danger to the protestant religion, the citizens subscribed largely to the cost of the war, and that without expectation of a return for their sacrifices. But the following year Parliament, now exercising uncontrolled authority over the finances of the kingdom, was able to accept the offerings of the people with the promise of eventual repayment, 'engaging the publique faith' for the same,[3]—though it is noticeable that the declaration was now issued in the name of the Commons only. We again find the name of James Houblon[4] in connection with a fresh 'listing' of dragoons in 1645, for the New Model Army of Cromwell; the horse and man he provided being accepted as a loan only. 'Whereas by virtue of an Ordinance of Parliament of 8 September 1645 the Committee of the Militia of London was authorised to send forth 500 horses and 500 dragoones into the publique service of the Kingdom,' the commissaries 'do in pursuance of the said Ordinance certifie as followeth.' Here follow the names of those

1642

1643

1645

---

[1] See Army Accounts. [2] *Ibid.*
[3] 17th July 1643. See *Commons' Journals*, iii. p. 171. The Commons here appeal 'for aid to the Committee of the Militia in London and others' for 'men, moneys, horse or ammunition to my Lord General.'
[4] Of Bearbinder Lane.

citizens (under the heading of the wards they lived in) who had either come forward with a loan in money amounting to £12, or had furnished a man and horse with arms. To those who sent horses, etc., we find they were returned at the end of the war, while the balance of the value of the worn-out animal when returned, was refunded to his owner. To those who gave money, the horse and arms purchased therewith for service were likewise returned.

Of James Houblon's contribution to this levy, the horse 'was lost in the service,' and its value being set at £12, this sum was paid him by the commissaries. Among the Exchequer army accounts is a volume of ' Acquittances,' and under date the 17th of March 1646-7 we find that of James Houblon for the sum of ' 12.00.00,' the value of his horse lost in the war.[1]

[1] Army Accounts, London Militia, 1645.

CHAPTER VIII

CIVIL WAR

'The men before us are so rigid and love so much their own notions . . . that let a man be never so godly, yet if he jumps not with them in all things, they thrust him out of their company.'— *Pilgrim's Progress.*

IF in England there was general disapproval of King Charles's unconstitutional proceedings, it was far greater in Scotland, where the King had made determined efforts to reduce his northern subjects to obedience to his will. On the renewal, in 1640, of the war he had waged against them, the Scots responded by boldly marching beyond the Tweed, where in an engagement on the Tyne they routed a portion of the English army. The quarrel, however, being with the King only, negotiations were ultimately opened by which they were for the time left in possession of Durham and Northumberland till a treaty could be arranged;[1] meanwhile their army was to be maintained at the cost of the State.

It is curious to find the descendants of the two branches of the Picardy Houblons coming into touch at this juncture, inasmuch as both were engaged in the same work.

Commanding the bodyguard of Leslie, the Scottish general, which had been raised by the College of Justice of Scotland, was Sir Thomas Hope of Kerse, a son of the King's Advocate. Sir Thomas was a lawyer; though such was his covenanting zeal as to incite him to martial

[1] Gardiner, *Student's History*, ii. 529.

deeds and daring; but he was soon to lay aside the
sword, for at the breaking out of the rebellion in Ireland, the King (who was in Scotland when he heard
the news) in his perplexity appealed to the Parliament
at Edinburgh for assistance and counsel.[1] This request
was responded to by the appointment of a committee.
Hope, the colonel of dragoons in Leslie's army, being also
a man of the law, was nominated one of the 'Commissioners now appointed to treat with the Parliament of
England[2] with respect of Ireland, as to the best method
of reducing her to obedience,' and he was at the same
time created a Lord of Session and Lord Justice
General of Scotland.   This was the way the Scots
proposed to help the King, and in truth he had better
have declined their aid.

It has cost those who have striven to unravel the
tangled skein of events at this time much trouble to
distinguish one committee from another; for in quick
succession they followed one after the other.   Now that
so many busybodies were helping the King to govern,
possibly they were a useful safety-valve for superfluous
political energy; but the fact remains that they absorbed
the business of the State into their hands.   The Scottish
1642   commissioners came to London in January 1641-2, and
there delivered themselves of their good advice to the
English Committee, which had just been appointed to
deal with the 'Affairs of Ireland'; and in February they
were still at work, striving with certain of the English
commissioners to devise a way for reducing Ireland.[3]
The English Committee—sometimes called of Lords and
Commons—soon found it necessary to engage help in
the practical details of their work, and this resulted in
the formation of a supplementary Committee of Citizens
and Adventurers of London.   Of this committee James

---

[1] See Preface to Calendar of State Papers, 1625-1649, p. xxxvii.
[2] See *Peerage of Scotland*, Sir Robert Douglas, 1704; revised, 1813.
[3] Preface to Calendar of State Papers, 1625-1649, p. xxxvii.

Houblon was made a member. He had already, in his private capacity as a merchant, been providing the Scottish army with stores according to the agreement with the Scots above mentioned, and we now find, through the evidence of State Papers, that he continued this and other work in the service of his committee in respect of Irish affairs. In view of Sir Thomas Hope, now Lord Kerse, being engaged in London as one of the Scottish commissioners in constant communication with the Committee for the Affairs of Ireland, there can be but little doubt that the kinsmen met, whether on business or private grounds. Hope, however, was not long in England, for he died the following year, to the great grief of his father, who lamented bitterly his 'grevous wound of sorrow in the loss of his son.'[1]

James Houblon's committee sat in Grocers' Hall, and is often referred to by that name. It was appointed in July 1643, and many of the Citizen Adventurers who   1643 sat on it were also members of the House of Commons; as all were associated with the City of London and its interests, it was likewise frequently spoken of as the City Committee.[2]

It would appear that after a time the Citizen Adventurers had waxed suspicious that they were being called upon to make too many sacrifices, and instituted an inquiry as to whether the merchants of Dublin were indeed bearing their fair share in the supply and maintenance of the English army in Ireland; saying, 'they would be content to beare the greatest burthen, but for them to bear all, they weare not able.'[3] This was on the 12th of February 1642-3. Many of the Adven-

[1] See Diary. In 1644 another of Sir Thomas Hope's kin was chosen a Commissioner to the English Parliament by the Scots, viz. Sir Charles Erskine, son of the 7th Earl of Mar, who was married to Sir Thomas Hope's daughter Marie.

[2] Preface to Calendar of State Papers, 1625-1649, Addenda, p. xxxvii, *re* Irish Loan.

[3] *History of the Confederate War in Ireland*, 1641-1643. Ed. J. T. Gilbert, from R. Bellings. Tucker's *Journal*, ii. 192.

turers had advanced their money before proper security had been given, or their subscriptions confirmed by Act of Parliament; the English officers in the Irish army were in the same plight, and were doubtful as to 'that the Parliament should deal fayrely with them'—a state of things suggestive of the difficulties that surrounded parliamentary government pure and simple. It was apparently in consequence of this uncertainty, that the new committee of July 1643 was appointed on which James Houblon had a seat, for that the Citizen Adventurers having lent their money considered themselves entitled to a vote in the management of the affairs of Ireland.[1]

After a time the original Committee for the Affairs of Ireland was reconstituted. At first composed of twenty-six members of each House, it presently became apparent that the Lords who sat on it were no longer in sympathy with either the opinions or the proceedings of those among them who were Commoners; so they were replaced by other members of the House of Commons, all of whom were likewise Adventurers.[2] John Goodwyn, member of Parliament, was its chairman, and it sat in the Exchequer Chamber at Westminster. Through the hands of the 'City committee for the Affairs of Ireland' (of which James Houblon was a member) passed most of the practical details of the business of both, such as the levying of assessments, the furnishing of arms, ammunition, and provisions for the army, the organisation of supply and transport, etc. etc.,[3] and this continued to be its work, notwithstanding the changes which took place in the composition of other committees appointed from time to time, during the years which succeeded.

[1] See Preface to Calendar of State Papers, Domestic, Addenda, 1625-1649, p. xxxvii. A few original orders for the year 1643, issued by this committee, besides some books containing copies of orders, have been preserved among the State Papers Interregnum, to some of which the signature of James Houblon is attached.

[2] Ibid.   [3] Ibid.

The two committees for the Affairs of Ireland working, as they did, together, John Goodwyn, the chairman of the one, had a seat likewise on the other. He was a prominent parliamentarian and 'committee-man,' and was active for the Parliament upon all that appertained to Ireland, and he served also upon the Committee for 'choosing officers for service in Ireland.'[1]

We find by the State Papers of Ireland, that James Houblon was among the merchant Citizen Adventurers who subscribed to the parliamentary loan for the reduction of Ireland. Captain Peter Houblon also subscribed £200, and James's young brother-in-law and ward, Peter du Quesne, was likewise a subscriber.[2] James's first investment amounted to £650 in two sums, the interest guaranteed being 8 per cent. He thus became entitled to upwards of a thousand acres of Irish land at the close of the war. The same documents show that on a later appeal (in 1643) for funds by the Parliament, he was of the number of Adventurers who 'doubled their original money'; the first sum subscribed in the City was £56,556, while that contributed on the subsequent occasion was upwards of £60,000, the total money being £117,487, 16s. 0½d. Thus '142,000 Acres, sett at 1s. 6d. p. Acre (being a very moderate rate by worth per annum),'[3] were disposed of by Parliament in this manner.

What became of the two thousand Irish acres allotted to James Houblon, 'bogs and barren mountains cast in in addition,'[4] we have not been able to discover, though we are told that the receipts constituted a claim upon the forfeited lands in Ireland, and were afterwards made the basis of the allotment in July 1653.[5] It seems 1653

---

[1] See à Declaration from both Houses, 17 May 1642, for a list of the Irish committee for choosing of officers.

[2] State Papers, Ireland, 294; 114 and 115.

[3] State Papers, Ireland, Charles I., vol. 260.

[4] *History of the Confederate War in Ireland*, 1641-1643, Ed. J. T. Gilbert, from R. Bellings, i. xxxi.

[5] State Papers, Ireland, Charles I., vol. 260.

that Parliament went so far as to institute lotteries in respect of the more advantageous estates, and in a list of those who drew lots for lands in the Barony of Connello, in Limerick, we find James Houblon's name.[1] Regarded purely as an investment, it were perhaps invidious to look too closely into the motive which prompted the acceptance of such a cruel bargain on the part of the citizens of London; while it is a strange fact, that not only 'Parliament-men' availed themselves of the offer of Irish acres, but 'Kings-men' were also eager in large numbers to invest their money in this manner.[2] Doubtless the horrible cruelties perpetrated upon their countrymen by the Irish insurgents justified in the minds of Englishmen the confiscations involved in the plan of the parliamentary committee for raising money.

Various orders and warrants which have escaped destruction show James to have been still taking an active part in the employment of Parliament, after the establishment of the famous Committee for both Kingdoms. This committee was, from the time of its creation (in 1644) on the conclusion of the compact of the Parliament with the Scottish presbyterian party—the work of Pym,—the paramount agent of authority in the conduct of the civil war; while keeping at the same time 'good intelligence between the forces in the three kingdoms, and whatsoever may concern the peace of his Majesty's dominions.'[3] Among the proceedings of this great Committee we find a warrant dated 6th of June of this year, directing 'that James Houbelon, merchant, who hath the custody of arms, ammunition, and other provisions made for the armies in Ireland now lying in the stores in Bucklersbury and Smart's Quay in London, shall presently deliver them to the committee of Citizen

1644

[1] State Papers, Ireland, Charles I., vol. 300, p. 351.
[2] See Preface to Calendar of State Papers, Domestic, Addenda, 1625-1649, p. xxxvii., *re* Irish Loan.
[3] See *Commons' Journals*, iii. 504.

Adventurers for lands in *Ireland*, or to such others as they shall employ.'[1] It would appear from the document that the stores of which James Houblon was in charge, and which he was directed by the Committee for Both Kingdoms to deliver into the hands of his own committee, were destined not for Ireland, but for the use of the parliamentary troops under Fairfax.[2] Meanwhile lay subsidies were regularly assessed for the war expenses *in the King's name* by the authority of Parliament; while during the campaign in Scotland under the Earl of Leven, monthly subsidies were charged upon the various wards for the 'maintenance of the Scottish Armie'; and in these the names of several of the Houblons appear.[3]

Soon after this, James was required by a letter from John Goodwyn, chairman of the Parliament committee, addressing him as his 'very loving friend Mr. Houblond one of the committee for the affairs of Ireland,' —by the presentation of a 'note in writing' (said to be in his keeping), to claim the return of a number of muskets which had been lent to the City by the said committee for the use of the militia of London; Alderman Bunce, on behalf of the City, having undertaken to return them on the presentation of the said note. Having obtained the arms, which consisted of 'one hundred and twenty-eight musquetts of snaphanceworke,'[4] Mr. Houblon was requested to deliver them to Sir John Clotworthy, knight, whose orders were to convey them to Ireland.[5] Sir John was a violent Presbyterian, a member of the Commons, and greatly distrusted and dreaded in Ireland.[6] It is noteworthy that this order was twice

---

[1] State Papers, Domestic, Interregnum, E. 7, p. 80.
[2] Ordinance of the Lords and Commons, 15 February 1644-5. Pamphlet, B.M. Also *Lords' Journals*, vii. pp. 204-9.
[3] For instance, Lay Subsidy, London, 147-594. 1645.
[4] The snaphance, or flint-lock.
[5] State Papers, Domestic, Charles I., vol. 539, No. 181.
[6] See *History of the Confederation and War in Ireland*, edited by J. T. Gilbert.

repeated ere it was obeyed by James Houblon, expostulations having apparently been exchanged between
the presentation of the two warrants. (Peace was now
subsisting between the countries ; both being exhausted
by the terrible struggle they had maintained with
each other ; 'articles of cessation of hostilities between
the English and Irish for the space of one year' having
meanwhile been signed at Dublin on the 15th of Sep-
1643   tember 1643.[1]) It is also significant that the style of
the second warrant, unlike that of the first, is peremp-
tory in tone, and merely signed.[2]   It was, as is shown
by the endorsement, obeyed ; but it is also the last of
the documents relating to Ireland in which the name of
James Houblon appears.

Though he apparently ceased to serve on the Committee for the Affairs of Ireland, the parliamentary
authorities continued to avail themselves of Houblon's
experience in the matter of supply, and barely had the
1644   campaign of 1644 opened than he, together with a Mr.
Johnstone, was called upon for advice and assistance in
the organisation of 'supply to the Scottish armyes in
the field.' Besides that of Both Kingdoms (which, as we
have seen, was the chief authority at this time in the
regulation of hostilities against the King), we find two
committees working in the matter of supply ; viz. one
sitting at Goldsmiths' Hall—commonly called the committee for Compounding,—and a small sub-committee
under Sir James Watkins, which directly supplied 'the
necessaryes for the Scottish armies.'[3]   In the Order
book of the former is the warrant addressed to the sub-
committee, whereby 'Mr. Houbelon and Mr. Johnstone
were intreated to be keeping and assisting unto them
(if they shall have occasion to desire their company and

---

[1] See *History of the Confederation and War in Ireland*, edited by
J. T. Gilbert.
[2] State Papers, Domestic, Charles I., vol. 539, No. 182.
[3] This committee was also concerned in the supply to the Irish army.

advice) for the despatch of this businesse.' The committee then proceeded to order that they should 'take care speedily to provide one thowsand Backe Breste and Potte,'[1] besides 'a thowsand payre of Pistolls and Holsters: and soe much cloth of the goodnesse of that formerly sent as may answeare the quantity of Eleaven thousand yarde of broadcloth to be forthwith sent to Newcastle for the use of the army.'[2] The sub-committee is likewise authorised to make a contract for the said provisions to be paid in quarterly instalments. Eight days after the date of this order, an ordinance of the Lords and Commons for raising and maintaining a 'force for the defence of the Kingdom' was issued, consisting of eleven regiments of horse, and 14,000 foot.[3]

In the campaign now commencing, Waller and Essex were in the field in command of the parliamentary forces against the King, while in the north the Earl of Leven with the Scottish army was advancing to co-operate with that under Fairfax. The movements of the parliamentary generals were at first controlled by the Committee for Both Kingdoms; but, as might be expected, the result of this control was scarcely as successful as were the generals when left to their own discretion. In spite of the fact that the committee was named in the first instance with the express object of controlling the armies of both countries—the result of the arrangement made with the Scottish presbyterian party in return for their aid and support in the war[4]—the good sense of the City of London finally forced it to leave to the generals the conduct of the campaign, and henceforth

---

[1] 'Back, Breste,' probably the back- and breast-plates worn by the parliamentary troops over their buff jerkins; while Potte could only mean the steel headpiece—in vulgar phrase 'steel pot' or helmet.

[2] Committee for Compounding, vol. G. 2, p. 49, 7 February 1644-5.

[3] Pamphlet, B.M. Ordinance of the Lords and Commons, 15 February 1644-5.

[4] Gardiner, *Student's History*, ii. 542.

the chief work of the committee was in the supply and maintenance of the troops.

It would appear that in common with many others who had at first vehemently taken up the quarrel of Parliament with the King, James Houblon had been scarcely prepared to carry the quarrel to the length to which it had been brought by passion and fanaticism. The compromise long hoped for by many of those who took up arms at the outset was no nearer than at the beginning; for the demands of Parliament were now such as made compromise impossible,[1] and for those who were not prepared to take part in the over-throw of the constitution and in driving the King to extremity, the time had come to pause. Charles's attitude was one from which it was practically impos-sible to recede, for he had been driven into it by the Parliament's hostility towards the national Church, from which, as he himself said, 'he who took one stone, did take two from his crown.'[2]   In 1645, in the

1645   words of the historian Gardiner, 'when compelled to retreat to Oxford with all his followers ardently plead-ing for peace, he still maintained that his conscience would not allow him to accept any terms with rebels, or to surrender the Church of England into their hands.'[3] So again did he refuse the Scots when they promised to fight for him to a man, if only he would accept pres-byterianism; and the result of his refusal was, that they abandoned him and his cause into the hands of the English Parliament.   Cromwell did his best to come to an understanding with the King, while the English people had no such quarrel with him as had the House of Commons and the army; but Cromwell's advances

---

[1] 'Every day they were asking the King for the impossible!' See J. Morley, *Oliver Cromwell*, p. 210.

[2] Repeated to S. Pepys by Pierce the surgeon.   See *Diary*, 29 March 1669.

[3] See Gardiner, *Student's History*, ii. 549, and Von Ranke.

were also unacceptable, as they threatened episcopacy, the integrity of which must be untouched.

In the deadlock which followed, the increasing power of the army became more and more manifest, and the attitude of the stern Independents of Cromwell more and more menacing to the crown and constitution. As we are told that at this time London was full of people loyal to the King and discontented with the violence of the soldiers, it is evident that the great City was now again 'torn with doubt' and uncertainty as how to act for the best. But while powerless to stem the tide of revolution for which they had so largely helped to open the sluices, the many citizens who, like James Houblon, had arrayed themselves against the King from conscientious motives, now found themselves and their counsels thrust aside and disregarded. In the end, ' Pride's Purge' reduced a mutilated House to the desired obedience to the will of the victorious soldiers, and the King was condemned to death by a handful of his enemies. In that he suffered death rather than abandon the Church and her property and privileges (which, had he done so, could never again have been recovered), he has been accorded the title of ' Martyr, if indeed the man who values his own life less than the cause for which he is fighting, and in perishing himself saves it for the future, may be regarded as such.'[1] If the King laid his head on the block rather than abandon the English Church to the destructive zeal of her enemies,—after having vainly endeavoured to force them to conform to her authority and usage,—on the other hand, the Presbyterian and Independent conscience was equally sensitive in its objections to the ritual of that Church; while it was also more violent. And so it came to pass that the King succumbed in the struggle, and his enemies reigned in his stead.

[1] Von Ranke, *History of England*, ii. 553.

CHAPTER IX

TRADE

'The Sea's our own : and now all nations greet,
 With bending sails, each vessel of our Fleet.
 Our pow'r extends as far as winds can blow,
 Or swelling sails upon the globe may go.'
 EDMUND WALLER : *A Panegyric to my Lord Protector.*

JAMES HOUBLON seems to have spared no pains with
regard to the early training of his children, which his
own good education rendered him well competent to
supervise. It was open to the citizens and merchants of
London to obtain for their sons a first-rate education at
such schools as that of St. Paul, founded by Dean
Colet, the 'Blue Coat' school which had been built
upon the site of the old Grey-Friars Monastery, or else
at one of the numerous excellent schools which had
been founded by the city companies. It was doubtless
at one of these that James's young sons received
their education. Handwriting is an interesting study in
respect of a man's general education and culture as
well as of his character and idiosyncrasies; and perhaps
it was as much an indication then, as it is now. Though
in the case of some individuals their accomplishments
and learning were of a very high order, handwriting as
well as grammar and spelling was in those days—even
in the case of men of high social standing—often extremely bad. That the uneducated and ignorant were
numerous we may perhaps infer from the half-playful,
half-scornful remark of the polished Lord Falkland, as

JAMES HOUBLON, MERCHANT.

he stood one day in the window of his library at Tew: 'I pity unlearned gentlemen in a wet day.'[1] Some manuscripts of James Houblon's are in existence, written in a clear and beautiful hand, and exhibiting every characteristic of a refined and cultivated mind; and in this particular of good handwriting we find that his sons afterwards resembled him. While he was careful to teach them the simple faith and high standard of morality of his 'confessor' ancestors, James also set his children a practical example in his own conduct. Strict business habits and an uncompromising integrity characterised the generations both before and after that of James; but the Walloon families appear to have had the happy faculty of inculcating the manifold virtues of their race, without wearying the rising generations with tedious repetitions of 'precept upon precept, line upon line.' Upon their general education a greater insistence was brought to bear, and some of James's sons became accomplished men. All spoke French with native fluency, and all were at different times sent abroad by their father to acquire languages, and to acquaint themselves with the conditions of those countries with which the family carried on a great trade. 'Having been all abroad,' wrote Mr. Pepys, 'their discourse very fine.'[2]

In the year 1646 the domestic happiness which had blessed James's early life was broken by a great trouble. Ever since the death of his parents late in the previous century, the plague had continued to break out from time to time, and was still to do so until it reached the full climax of its virulence in the epidemic of 1665. During one of these intermediate visitations, one of James and Mary Houblon's children contracted the disease, and was nursed by his mother. The child

1646

---

[1] See *Lloyd's Memoirs*: Life and Death of Lucius Carey, Viscount Faulkland, p. 333.
[2] Pepys's *Diary*.

died; no other *dénouement* would then have been expected, as also the sequel to the event, in the death
of Mary herself.   The heroism of people in giving
their ministrations to the sick under so strong a fear
must have been great; but it was to be found everywhere among families similarly situated.   James's wife
and child were buried in their parish church of St. Mary
1646 Woolchurch, in August 1646, within the short interval
of a few days.

Mary's death cut her off in the full career of a useful
and happy life, and at the age of little more than forty.
Her two daughters, who might partly have filled
their mother's place, had both lately married; and
James was left alone with a troop of lads of all
ages![1]   His spirit might well have quailed before such
a task as that before him; but his unselfish character
and good sense nerved him to the work, and he seems
to have henceforth filled the place of both father and
mother to his many children.   That he succeeded in the
task he set himself is certain, for many evidences of his
success have come down to us.   James's sons loved
their father, and obeyed his lightest wish, and when he
died in extreme old age, they mourned and regretted
him as a friend as well as parent.   Throughout their
lives the brothers (five of whom were also merchants)
remained the closest friends, so that their unity became
almost a proverb in the London world of the day; this
mutual affection we shall find Samuel Pepys alluding to
more than once in his *Diary*.

Meanwhile the civil wars had brought in their train
the inevitable consequences of disorder, and stagnation
in trade.   The citizens of London soon came to entertain
grave doubts as to the dangers attendant upon a reversal

---

[1] Besides the child who died of the plague in 1646, two sons and a
daughter had died young.   Peter, the eldest, was about two-and-twenty at
this time; James was seventeen, John fifteen, Jacob twelve; while the three
younger ones who survived were but eight, seven, and three years old.

of authority so great as had taken place; hence their
'changeableness,' and the City's 'terrors,' which brought
contempt upon it from both parties in turn. It had
already been made to pay for its doubts and vacillation
by the masterful Lord General on his victorious entrance
into London on the 16th of December 1648. Clarendon   1648
tells us of its embarrassment on this occasion,[1] its doubt
how to act, and of its final attempt to conciliate Cromwell;
and how the Corporation went out to meet him in Hyde
Park, but was treated with contempt, and its offers of
gifts roughly rejected. Oliver and his soldiers marched
through the City which, as sole answer to its overtures,
was ordered to contribute one hundred thousand pounds
towards the payment of the army.[2] And so it came to
pass that, having learned this rough lesson, on the assumption of the Protectorate by Oliver in 1653, the City   1653
received him with all submission, while he, having thus
humbled the proud citizens, allowed himself to be entertained by them at a magnificent banquet, where, as
Clarendon sarcastically remarks, he 'as like a King'
graciously conferred the honour of knighthood on the
Lord Mayor.[3]

But Cromwell, though he could treat the powerful
City with rudeness, was yet desirous of doing all in his
power to restore her flagging trade; and while he
sought to revive English commerce, his vigorous measures brought new life to that navy in the building
up of which the unfortunate King had sacrificed his
popularity.[4] The Navigation Act of Cromwell was the
central fact dominating commerce and trade during this
period. No doubt the Act greatly stimulated ship-
building in England; but pending the creation or vast

---

[1] Lord Clarendon, *History of the Rebellion*, III. x. 103.
[2] S. R. Gardiner, *History of the Commonwealth and Protectorate*, iii. 308;
and Clarendon, III. x. 107.
[3] *Ibid.*, III. x. 107.
[4] 'Ship-Money' was for this purpose.

increase in the mercantile fleets, (for during the civil wars, 'Dutch bottoms' were generally used by the English merchants) great embarrassment resulted. A large number of documents, addressed to the Commissioners of Customs and containing petitions relating to trade, are to be found among the State Papers of this time; and amongst these some presented by the merchant members of the Houblon family are in themselves illustrative of the immense difficulties brought about by these new regulations, and of how trade itself was hampered by the restrictions which were designed to foster it. That Cromwell's measures succeeded in the end was the more remarkable, because the Dutch war was the direct outcome of the Navigation Act.

The struggle for commercial supremacy between England and Holland following upon the Act was long and severe, for the Dutch saw clearly the injury its enforcement would inflict upon their trade, which during the civil wars had prospered so greatly. On the whole, the advantage in this war remained on the side of England. Holland's immense success in trade and commerce had been due, partly to the lack of enterprise among her neighbours, and partly to their internal troubles, of both of which weaknesses she was quick to take advantage, seizing upon every opportunity that presented itself for the advancement of her home industries and commerce. Through the apathy of the English, for instance, the Dutch had for ages enjoyed undisturbed the privilege of fishing in English waters, an industry which brought them enormous profit.[1] The arbitrary removal of this privilege had consequently caused the greatest embarrassment, and was the more irritating to the Dutch, that the English made but little effort to develop the fishing industry themselves; a

[1] Yeats, *Growth and Vicissitudes of Commerce*, p. 211.

neglect partly due to the fact that since the Reformation
the habit of eating fish had for the time nearly ceased.

Although the English had neglected the herring
fisheries in their own waters, those of Newfoundland
were a source of much profit, and employed large
numbers of Englishmen from the towns on the west
coast, the fishing fleets mostly carrying their cargoes to
Portugal and Spain. The Houblons, and other London
merchants associated with them, engaged in this trade,
which, like most other enterprises, suffered seriously
through the quarrels with the Dutch. A story illustrative of these troubles is to be found in connection
with an exchange of prisoners between the two countries. In 1657 Joseph Haddock,[1] master of the ship   1657
Diligence of London, complains in a petition backed
by the Houblons, and presented to the Protector and
Council, that while sailing, laden with fish, from
Newfoundland to Portugal, he and his ship's company
were captured by two Ostend men-of-war and carried
to Vigo in Galicia, where, after being hardly used,
they were released on parole, on the understanding
that they were to obtain the liberty of nine Ostend
seamen who had been made prisoners out of the ' *St.
Peter* of Ostend,' and were now lying in Chelsea
College. Joseph Haddock and his ship's company
therefore make humble petition for the release of the
said nine seamen, praying that they may be delivered
up in exchange for their own freedom. With the petition two certificates were handed in by the petitioners,
one from the Deputy-Marshal, stating that he had
the Dutch seamen in his custody, and the other from
James Houblon and ten other London merchants,
their owners, verifying the petition. At the head of
the signatures on this document appears that of the
elder James, followed by the signatures of his sons

[1] For many years a master in the employment of James Houblon.

James and John, his sons-in-law James Lordell and John Jurin, and his nephew Peter Ducane or Du Quesne.[1]

The Dutch were especially active at this time in all parts of the world where the two nations had been wont to trade, in their efforts to hamper and annoy British commerce. During this same year an interesting letter from Genoa to his brother, from Thomas Hill, a well-known merchant and friend of the Houblon family, describes the misadventures of their ship *Olive Branch* in the East Indies, which, shadowed by the Dutch Admiral off Bantam, and delayed by storms, finally 'lost her monsoon,' and was forced to winter in the Mauritius. 'I hope you will take care to lay it before his highness,' wrote Hill, 'who I am sure will not suffer his subjects to be trampled on by any power on earth, especially by the Hollanders.'[2]

1655   But the embarrassment to trade was now still further increased by the war with Spain, which was consequent upon the alliance with France, recently concluded by the Protector. The history of the long negotiations with both countries which preceded this step[3] shows with what hesitation it was taken by Oliver. In the end, however, the result was, that of the two great nations who had long and eagerly been soliciting his alliance, the offers and bribes of France were accepted. It is possible that the hesitation exhibited by Oliver may have been partly due to his desire to encourage the fruitful trade between this country and Spain by an alliance; but in his subsequent policy with regard to her, this passing consideration was entirely superseded by the hatred inspired by her bigotry and fanaticism. 1657 The exploits of Blake and the English navy in 1657

[1] State Papers, Domestic, Interregnum, vol. 189, pp. 1-3.
[2] MS. in the Hill family.
[3] For a detailed account of Oliver's intrigues with Spain and France, see Gardiner's *Commonwealth and Protectorate*, ii. 476.

were fruitful in glory, but scarcely advantageous to the commerce of this country, which suffered severely during the whole of the latter part of the Protectorate. The Spanish prizes captured by the English fleet might flood the City with gold and silver—thirty-eight wagon-loads of silver from Spain's treasure-ships were once drawn through the streets of London—but this was small amends for the loss of the lucrative trade between the countries, or for the English merchantmen taken as prizes by the Spaniards.[1] The discontent of the merchants trading with the Peninsula—among whom were James Houblon and his sons—found expression in a memorial on the trade with Spain printed in 1659, after the death of Oliver.[2] It was entitled 'The Merchants Humble Petition and Remonstrance to his late Highness; With an Account of the Losses of their Shipping and Estates since the War with Spain.'[3] This memorial or 'remonstrance' sets forth 'the great value of the Traffique with Spain as redounding more to the essential benefit of this Commonwealth than all others whatsoever.' Although it is easy to see how intolerable the loss to trade caused by the breach with Spain at the time appeared to the great commercial class, one cannot but recognise the enormous compensating advantage later to accrue to it, through the West Indian conquests of Oliver—the spoils of war wrested from the hand of Spain.[4]

Long before the death of the Protector, he found the government of the country increasingly difficult, nor could he maintain his authority without the aid of the military despotism which he had established. Meanwhile all alike were sick of the soldiers, while the mutilated Rump Parliament was both despised and detested. So

---

[1] Von Ranke, *History of England*, iii. 207-8.
[2] Drawn up before the Protector's death.
[3] London, 1659, 4to, 18 pages.
[4] Von Ranke, *History*, iii. 222.

when the great and powerful personality of Oliver was removed, the rule of his weak successor could only be regarded as temporary till the 'bringing in' of the King could be safely accomplished; for the return to the old order of King, Lords and Commons was now a foregone conclusion. Not only was the country determined never again to be subject to the rule of the army, but it was openly said of the late Protector that 'he hath had a far greater power than what cost so much blood and treasure to oppose in the last King.'[1] In the interim the City of London was as usual anxious and doubtful. 'The City looks mighty blank, and cannot tell what in the world to do,' writes Mr. Pepys in his *Diary* on the 10th of February. But General Monk's arrival from the north,[2] and his strong and vigorous measures (after he had satisfied himself as to the bent of public opinion), presently eased their mind, and by the 16th of the following month Pepys again writes of Westminster Hall, the resort of the citizens, 'the whole Hall talk loud for the King'; while a few weeks after this he remarks that the royal ensign could be seen flying from the masts of the merchant-ships in the river.[3]

To the persistent call of the City, supported by General Monk, for a free Parliament, its election was said to be chiefly due, and once assembled, the will of the country was immediately apparent.[4] It had had enough of both Presbyterian and Independent; the tyranny of the army was at an end, and with a sense of relief the country turned once more towards the ancient order of the English constitutional monarchy.

1659
1660
1660

[1] Tracts: *Phœnix Britannicus*, i. 125.
[2] 'The new Common Council of the City do speak very high, and had sent to Monk, their sword-bearer, to acquaint him with their desires for a free and full Parliament which is at present the desires and the hopes and expectations of all.'—Pepys's *Diary*, 1 January 1659-60.
[3] *Ibid.* 21 April 1660.
[4] 'Henceforth he (Monk) sided effectually with the City. I say the City, which if well or ill affected, was then able to make us a happy or unhappy nation.'—Thomas Fuller's *Worthies of England*, 1608-1661.

Before coming over to take possession of his crown, Charles II. offered a free pardon to all but those specially exempted by Parliament, excluding, of course, the regicides. Though the new Parliament was vehemently in favour of the execution of those concerned in the trial and condemnation of the King, in the end more moderate counsels prevailed, and thirteen only of the regicides were put to death in the barbarous manner of the time. Among the lists of persons originally excluded from pardon by the parliamentary vote, we find the name of an official intimately connected with the work of James Houblon in his employment under the Parliament during the civil wars, viz. John Goodwyn, member of Parliament, and chairman of the Committee for the Affairs of Ireland.[1] His name, however, was finally struck off the list, and included in that of those 'omitted from the exception, and incapacitated for public employment.'[2]

The policy of the Protector with regard to the navy was not reversed; Charles II. showed himself anxious to encourage trade and commerce, and soon after his arrival in England, he inaugurated a system for the protection of the merchant shipping in war time. The Act of Navigation was (for good or ill) still enforced, while the struggle with the Dutch, the outcome of the jealousy it had engendered, was continued with increased vigour; in his desire to encourage the herring fishery in English-built craft, Charles II. even promised a reward of £200 to any man who would 'set out a new English-made busse.'[3] English trade was at the beginning of Charles's reign comparatively unhampered so far as foreign commerce was concerned;

---

[1] Index to *Commons' Journals*, 1547-1714. Resolution excepting him (John Goodwyn) from the Bill of Pardon and Oblivion, viii. 68.
[2] *Ibid.*, 118.
[3] Viz. a small sea vessel as used by the Dutch. See Pepys's *Diary*, 28 November 1662.

but England had set an example in the Navigation Act which was bound sooner or later to be met in a similar spirit by other nations; and so the precedent set by Oliver was followed by Colbert, the great minister of Louis XIV., some years later. Colbert sought by imposing heavy customs upon foreign imports into France to stimulate French commerce, and by the correlative creation of native industries to supply the demand at home; raw material was therefore admitted free into the country, but all manufactured commodities were either heavily taxed or entirely prohibited.[1] This policy was naturally reciprocated by England, and the commerce of both countries suffered in consequence; though, in spite of all, it was said that trade between England and France was very active during the twenty years of Colbert's rule. The whole traffic, however, French as well as English, was carried on in either English or Dutch vessels. In linen alone, it was estimated that £700,000 worth was brought into this country during Colbert's time,[2] and Peter, Houblon, the eldest of the five merchant brothers, engaged in this trade; among the State Papers there is a record, dated July 1667, of the grant to him of a licence for a ship to bring linen from France to England, the cargo being composed of linen only.[3] It is evident that the commercial warfare between the countries caused both embarrassment and confusion, often resulting in serious loss. As illustrative of this state of things, we find a petition presented by James Houblon, senior, to the Privy Council, in which he pleads that he 'has ever been regular in the payment of his Majesty's customs and duties,' and that 'a year ago he laded in the *David Alexander* of Dieppe for the account of Nicholas

---

[1] Yeats, *Growth and Vicissitudes of Commerce*, p. 234.
[2] *Ibid.*, p. 237.
[3] State Papers, Domestic, Entry Book, Charles II., vol. 25, p. 25b.

Cognard of Rouen, certain merchandise, which was seized by his Majesty's commissioners as *French goods*, and were still stayed in their custody.' He therefore prays an order from the commissioners for French goods, for the redelivery to himself (the petitioner) of the *perpetuanos* and serge 'which had thus been stayed by the customs; his own goods (of far greater value) being now stayed at Rouen in Cognard's hands, in respect that the latter's goods are stayed here.'[1]

Not long after, we find one of Mr. Houblon's sons writing to Mr. Williamson (afterwards Sir Joseph), a Principal Officer of the navy, referring to the grievances of the English merchants against the French, in reference to which they had forwarded a formal complaint to the Navy Office; while again another of the brothers in applying to the Council of State (the 3rd of December 1653), for a pass for his ship between France and England—affirms she is carrying no prohibited goods.[2] The policy of the two governments was ultimately ruinous to their mutual trade, and it was probably in consequence of it that the French Company of English merchants was soon after broken up. It is a fact that henceforth we find but few traces of any commerce with France carried on by the Houblons; and this in spite of the fresh alliance concluded between the monarchs of both countries. Trade had flourished under conditions which must have stifled any enterprise less vigorous;[3] but commerce with France was deliberately sacrificed to these beginnings of a *haute politique* which found expression in the doctrine of the Mercantilists, who subordinated all advantage to trade proper, to the supposed necessity for thwarting and injuring that of France.

---

[1] State Papers, Domestic, Entry Book, Charles I., vol. 519, No. 29.
[2] State Papers, Domestic, Interregnum, i. 72, pp. 154, 162.
[3] *Ibid.*, i. 72, pp. 162-164. *Ibid.*, i. 39, p. 90, and *Ibid.*, i. 75, p. 322, No. 36. Besides these evidences, see other documents bearing on the trade of the Houblon family with France.

The Protectorate wars with Spain being at an end,
the trade with that country again revived, and henceforth it was mainly as Portuguese and Spanish merchants
that the Houblons traded in the old world; and this
commerce became increasingly important, as through
the weakness and decay of those countries its conduct passed gradually into the hands of the English
merchants.   So far as Portugal was concerned, England
possessed almost a monopoly of her trade both at home
and in her territories beyond the sea, the country having
become, as Captain Mahan expresses it, dependent upon
and a mere outpost of England.[1]   This position was
brought about by means of treaties and alliances ac-
quiesced in by the French King with a strange want of
foresight as to their results;[2] for while his heart and
ambition were set upon his own aggrandisement by land,
Louis XIV. failed to see the danger to himself in the
growing power of England upon the seas.[3]

The Houblons were all deeply concerned in the new
openings for enterprise and trade in Tangiers, which
had formed part of the dowry of Queen Catherine of
Braganza, and was soon to be strongly fortified by the
English.   In the course of a few years their commerce in the Mediterranean, especially on the coasts
of Africa, greatly developed.   Charles II. endeavoured
to maintain friendly relations with his new and turbulent neighbours on the African coast by means
of treaties and engagements, while many European
states even paid them tribute in order to secure immunity from piracy;[4] but their attacks on merchant
ships of all nations made the risks of commerce very
great at this time, the pirates of the Barbary States and

[1] Mahan, *Influence of Sea Power upon History*, p. 105.
[2] For the treaty of 1654, see Gardiner's *Commonwealth and Protectorate*,
ii. 387
[3] Mahan, *Influence of Sea Power upon History*, p. 105.
[4] Longman's *Gazetteer of the World*—ALGERIA.

the Sallee Ports of Morocco being specially held in terror by peaceful traders. The Algerian government, it is true, made some efforts to 'comply with its promises not to suffer any attempt upon the English, . . . nor offer any affront to *their* imbarcations,'[1] but it was quite unable to control the piratical instincts which had long been characteristic of the races.

A letter from the English consul at Algiers to a Principal Officer of the navy, dated September 1668, is illustrative of these difficulties. It informs him of the capture by a 'Man-of-war of this place . . . which had revolted to Sally,' of certain merchant vessels both English and French, and how that he had made 'complaint of y[e] action,' they excusing it by the plea that the port of 'Sallee is not onder their correction,' though they had desired their men-of-war 'to endeavour to meete with the shipe in revolt, and bring her to this Porte.'[2] Probably the revolted frigate hoped by joining these bold marauders to reap great gains. We find, however, in another document among the State Papers, endorsed 'Advices from Salley,' and written some eight or nine months after that from the consul at Algiers, some further information relating to one of the merchant ships taken by the Algerians. This letter was from the Sallee port itself, and announces the arrival there of the pirate ship with two of her prizes, one of which was the *Ruby*, ketch of London, which with all 'hir ladeinge, belongueinged (*sic*) to Mr. Hublond.' The loss to the owner would have been great; she had on board '80 Chests of Bahia shugger' (sugar from Brazil, then greatly prized), and '50 pipes of oyle.' The vessel and goods, the writer says, were bought up by 'a jew of Amsterdam.'[3] Starting from the New World with her cargo of sugar, the

[1] State Papers, Foreign : Barbary States, Algiers, vol. i. p. 623.
[2] *Ibid.*
[3] *Ibid.*, Morocco, vol. ii. 8 July 1669.

merchant vessel *Ruby* doubtless shipped her oil in Portugal, and was on her way to some port in the Mediterranean, when captured by the little pirate frigate, bristling with her formidable equipment of '12 guns and 14 pedreros.'[1]

We know that the Houblon brothers frequently travelled abroad, and it is not unlikely that one or more of them may have been among the many English merchants to be found in Spain and Portugal at this time; in the contemporary memoirs of Lady Fanshawe, wife of the English minister of Charles II. at Lisbon, there are some interesting details relating to the now waning splendour of both Spain and Portugal, as well as many references to the active part that English merchants were taking in the conduct of their trade in the Peninsula. Sir Richard Fanshawe was sent to Lisbon a few months after the King's marriage; and the recent acquisition of Tangiers by this country as part of the Queen's dowry had, as we have seen, already drawn the attention of English merchants to this and other fresh openings for their trade on the African coast. Lady Fanshawe speaks not only of the large number of English merchants then at Lisbon, but also of those at Madrid and other Spanish towns visited by the English minister and his party, when on a diplomatic excursion into Spain; of the relics of former luxury and splendour exhibited to the eyes of the English lady, she gives a vivid picture in her memoirs.[2]

1666

[1] State Papers, Foreign: Morocco, vol. ii. 8 July 1669. 'Pedro,' an early gun of large calibre. See Admiral W. H. Smyth, *Sailor's Word Book*, p. 522.

[2] Of a piece of the true Tyrian dye seen at Granada she says, 'It hath the glory of scarlet, the beauty of purple, and is so bright that when the eye is removed upon any other object it seems as white as snow.'—*Memoirs of Lady Fanshawe*, p. 96.

CHAPTER X

FIRE AND PESTILENCE

'La crainte gouverne le monde.'
Maximes de M. le Duc le Lévis.

FOR some ten years before the terrible outbreak of plague in London in 1665—the year before the Great Fire—we hear of its existence at Rotterdam and other places on the Continent, and of anxious fears lest it should appear in this country.   In the early part of 1665, however, all went on as usual in the busy, throbbing life of the great City.   Unmindful of the scourge which was to scatter them for so many months, the Houblon brothers were intent upon the organisation of the new adventure in Tangiers which they had undertaken.

The earliest entry containing an allusion to the Houblon family to be found in Mr. Pepys's *Diary* was in February 1664-5, scarcely more than a year before this 1664-5 terrible epidemic.   He here mentions having supped at the Sun Tavern behind the Exchange in company with 'Mr. Hubland[1] a pretty serious man, together with Mr. Hill and Andrews,'[2]—both London merchants. This interview, and another the following day, related to a matter of business with regard to a ship bound for Tangiers, before the dispatch of which Pepys had to read over and approve the charter-party or agreement, for its carrying goods to that place.   As commissioner and

[1] James Houblon, Junior.
[2] *Diary*, 1 February 1664-5.   Mr. Wheatley's edition.

treasurer for the affairs of Tangiers, the dispatch of
ships to and from Morocco for purposes of commerce
was under his control, and for his goodwill in the matter
—according to the invariable custom of the time—he considered that he had a legitimate right to a consideration
as part of the prerogatives of his office ; adding in respect
of the affair in question, that 'herein he hoped to get
some money.'[1]   Pepys, whose industry and integrity at
the Naval Office had made his services valued in high
places and given him many friends, now held, as Clerk
of the Acts of the Navy, a position in which the London
merchants frequently required to be in communication
with him,[2] the more so that their ships were liable to be
requisitioned at any time for the King's service.   On such
a subject we find James Houblon, junior, writing in March
1665, 'to my honoured Friend Saml. Pepys, Esq.—
Principal Officer of the Navy—these,' with reference to
a merchant ship, the *St. Lucar*, belonging to himself
and his brothers.   Having heard from her master, Joseph
Haddock, 'that she is prict for your Service,' he begs
that she may be discharged, 'both Ship and Master
being unfit for the Norward, she being sharpe and he
never used that way,' while he adds that the ship
'wholely concerns my brothers and myself and wee have
a voyadge for her ;'[3] we have already come across the
ship's master, Haddock, who was in the service of the
Houblons in 1657.[4]   This paper is endorsed in Mr.
Pepys's handwriting : 'Mr. Houbland about the unfitt-
ness of the Lucar Merchant hyred for his Mats. Service.'
The requisition of the ship in question was made during
the progress of the Dutch war ; a sudden alarm of the

1665

[1] *Diary*, 2 February. Ed. Wheatley.
[2] Samuel Pepys was at this time Clerk of the Acts of the Navy, Clerk of the
Privy Seal, and Commissioner and Treasurer for Tangiers. The following
year he was made a Younger Brother of Trinity House, and was elected
Burgess for Portsmouth.
[3] State Papers, Domestic, Charles II., vol. 120, No. 3.
[4] *Ibid.*, Interregnum, vol. 189, 1-3.

enemy's fleet having been seen off the coast of Scotland
—'on the back of Scotland' as Pepys expressed it,—
caused the King to issue an order to the Duke of York
to appoint a fleet to sail northward to meet them.[1]

If the merchants were subject to the King's com-
pulsory hiring of their ships according to his need
of them, 'pricking for the navy' as it was called,[2]—
they in their turn benefited by an interchange of ships
belonging to the Admiralty, which when not required
for other purposes appear to have been frequently
placed by the commissioners of the navy at their disposal for hire.[3]   Hence we find in February the following
year, among the State Papers, articles of agreement
between the navy commissioners and the Houblons for
hire of one of the King's ships for one journey to Jersey.[4]
It was in such services as this that Mr. Pepys was able
to oblige his friends among the merchants: favours for
which frequent expressions of thanks were tendered him
by the Houblon brothers and others, to the former of
whom he repeatedly protests his desire to oblige ; while
they in their turn were often able to be of service to the
Clerk of the Acts of the Navy in both public and private
matters.

In view of the great strain put upon the resources of
the country by the Dutch war, it had been found neces-   1665
sary to interfere with trade by forbidding the sailing of
the merchant fleets this year.   For example, in January
the Turkey merchants had not been allowed to send out
the fleet they usually dispatched at that time, as it was
argued that it would be ' neither safe for the Merchants

[1] Pepys's *Diary*, 17 April 1665.

[2] If a merchant ship hired for the service of the State was meant to go
into action, the State took the risk of loss, paid and provisioned the men,
and supplied powder and any guns necessary beyond the normal number.
See M. Oppenheim, *Administration of the Royal Navy*, 1509-1660, p. 343.

[3] For example: '23 March 1663. This evening come Captain Grove
about hiring ships for Tangier. I did hint to him my desire that I could
make some lawfull profit thereof which he promises.'—Pepys's *Diary*.

[4] State Papers, Domestic, Charles II., vol. 147, No. 76.

nor honourable for the King to expose these rich ships
. . . when we can neither spare them ships to go nor
men, nor King's ships to convoy them. . . . For it was
not possible to support the war and trade together.'[1]
The Dutch had likewise determined to meet the war
with England with their whole resources, and temporarily suspended all trade for eighteen months.[2]   From
this state of things a considerable check to enterprise had
resulted, all the greater to the English that the Navigation
Act precluded the goods of the merchants from being carried in other than English shipping.[3]   The regulations
were often evaded, and the more adventurous of the English merchants continued to trade in spite of the embargo
which had been laid upon their ships in the vain effort
to keep them at home.   The officers of the Navy Office
indeed,—as in the instance above quoted, of the hire by
the Houblon brothers of a King's ship for a journey to
Jersey,—still occasionally gave leave to merchants to
send out their own ships or to hire those of the King,
though this was done only at the cost of considerable
trouble and manœuvring on their own part.

All trade was now suspended by the alarming
rapidity with which the plague was spreading in
London.   In the midst of the cares of his office,
doubly heavy on account of the naval war with the
Dutch at its height, Samuel Pepys, the Clerk of Acts,
records the slow but sure advance of the terrible
disease.   On the 30th of April 1665 he writes : 'great
fears of the sicknesse here in the City, it being said that
two or three houses are already shut up.   God preserve
us all.'   On the 7th of June it had further increased, and
he remarks on its being 'the hottest day that ever I felt
in my life.   This day much against my will I did in
Drury Lane see two or three houses marked with a red

1665

[1] Pepys's *Diary*, 15 January 1664-5.
[2] *Ibid.*, 24 January 1664-5.
[3] It was proposed to suspend the Act for a time, but it was not done.

cross upon the doors, and "Lord have mercy on us" writ there.'[1]   By the 21st he finds 'all the Town almost going out of town, the coaches and waggons of all who were in a position to leave the City being all full of people going into the country.'[2]   By the beginning of August the weekly bill of deaths from the plague had nearly reached the figure of 2000, while he presently adds 'the few people I see look like people who have taken leave of the world.'   And again : 'The town is like a place distressed and forsaken.'[3]   By the end of August, 6000 was the weekly sum of deaths, and in September more than 7000.   'Lord,' cried Mr. Pepys, 'a sad time it is to see no boat upon the river and grass growing up and down Whitehall Court; and nobody but poor wretches in the streets.'[4]   And again : 'There is never a physician and but one apothecary left—all being dead.'[5]   After this the numbers began gradually to decrease, and at the end of November a few people were to be seen going about, cautiously returning to their usual avocations.

By the end of December all was again going on as usual, though it was only then that the terrible havoc which had been made by the plague was completely realised.

1665

Before the close of the year, the Houblons were all once more in London.   There is little doubt that their father spent those months during which the plague was at its height, in the country, while some, at least, of his sons went abroad with the object of furthering their mercantile connections.   The terror and isolation in which people had lived when forced to remain in town during these weary months, is shown by the fact that after they were over, friends and neighbours met as if freshly come

---

[1] *Diary*, 7 June 1665.
[2] *Ibid.*, 21 June 1665.
[3] *Ibid.*, 30 August 1665.
[4] *Ibid.*, 20 September 1665.
[5] *Ibid.*, 16 October 1665.

back from a long journey.   Though they had lived next
door to each other all the time, they yet knew not if
each were dead or alive till they met again.

Hardly had the plague begun to subside, when the
negotiations between the Houblons and the Principal
Officer of the navy, with regard to their business in
Tangiers, were once more resumed.   The first of these
interviews after the return of the merchants to London,
took place on the 22nd of December 1665, on which occasion Pepys mentions in his *Diary* meeting Mr. Hill and
Mr. Houblon and going with them 'to the Beare and
dining with them and their brothers, of which Hill had
his, and the other, two of his, and mighty merry and
very fine company they are, and I glad to see them.'[1]
James, Houblon was on this occasion accompanied
by his brothers John, and Isaac, who were associated
with him in this matter.   Shortly after this, Pepys
records, 'I did also give a good step in a business of
Mr. Hubland's about getting a ship of his to go to
Tangier, which during this strict embargo is a great
matter, and I shall have a good reward for it I hope.'[2]

Later it would appear that Pepys himself had a mind to
make an 'adventure' on one of the Houblons' ships, on
which he advised with them, and by the 5th of February
he speaks of the affair as settled, and of the brothers
preparing for the going out of their ships (they were
now sending several) to Tangiers, and of Mr. Hill's
going in charge of them [3]   On this occasion they agreed
that 'I must sup with them to-night, . . . so I did some
little business and visited my Lord Sandwich,[4] and so,
it raining, went directly to the Sun behind the Exchange
about seven o'clock, where I find all the five brothers

[1] *Diary*, 22 December 1665.   Mr. Wheatley's edition.
[2] *Ibid.*, 22 January 1665-6.   Mr. Wheatley's edition.
[3] *Ibid.*, 5 February 1665-6.   Hill spent most of his life abroad.   He was a
great connoisseur in music.
[4] His patron and kinsman.

Houblons, and mighty fine gentlemen they are all, and used me mighty respectfully. We were mighty civilly merry, and their discourses, having been all abroad, very fine. Here late, and at last accompanied home with Mr. J. Houblon and Hill whom I invited to sup with me on Friday, and so parted and I home to bed.'[1]

A few days after this he records another meeting with the brothers at Westminster Hall, 'where the first day of Terme and the Hall very full of people, and much more than was expected considering the Plague that hath been.' He afterwards entertained them and Mr. Hill at his own house. 'Anon the five brothers Houblons come and Mr. Hill, and a very good supper we had and good company, and discourse with great pleasure. My new plate sets off my cupboard very nobly. A fine sight it is to see these five brothers thus loving one to another, and all industrious Merchants. Mr. Hill going for them to Portugall was the occasion of this entertainment.'[2]

Doubtless Pepys's regard for the Houblons was somewhat quickened by the solid advantages to be gained by their requirements in their commerce, and their willingness to pay liberally for his good-will in the matter of the breaking of the embargo. But these business relations later ripened into a warm friendship between the diarist and James, Houblon and his two young sons. With all his faults, Pepys was always quick to respond to kindness, and with regard to the Houblon family he ever showed himself as affectionately grateful for the many substantial services which he owed to their friendship throughout his life,[3] while he was at the same time keenly appreciative of the manly and upright character common to the brothers; 'gentlemen

---

[1] *Diary*, 9 February 1665-6.   [2] *Ibid.*, 10 February 1665-6.
[3] See J. E. Cussans, *History of Hertfordshire*. 1870-73. Chatto and Windus.

I honour mightily,' he says, after another meeting with
the fraternal group at the Exchange.[1]

What the Houblons promised him for his help in the
present instance we hear in the following entry, dated
March the 2nd, being the evening on which the supper
took place to which Pepys had invited James, Houblon
and Mr. Hill a few days before. 'By appointment find Mr.
Hill come to sup and take his last leave of me, and by and
by in comes Mr. James Houbland to bear us company,
a man I love mightily and will not lose his acquaintance.
He told me in my eare this night what he and his
brothers have resolved to give me, which is £200 for
helping them out with two or three ships. A good sum
and that which I did believe they would give me and I
did expect little less. Here we talked and very good
company till late, and then took leave of one another,
and indeed I am heartily sorry for Mr. Hills leaving
us, for he is a very worthy gentleman as most I know.'[2]

Whatever we may think of a practice now so
strongly condemned as the acceptance of fees or commissions, we must not condemn the diarist in respect of a
custom which was so universally practised at the time,
and in view of the low scale of salaries paid. Pepys
himself explains his receipts to be legitimate fees rightly
and justly his own to accept; 'the King receiving no
hurt or injury thereby,' while, unlike some others in a
like official position, he earned his fee by substantial
services often involving much trouble and labour.[3] But
'there's many a slip betwixt the cup and the lip,' and
we find by sundry other entries in the diaries that
matters did not run altogether smoothly with regard to
the dispatch of the ships to Tangiers ; neither did ' Mr.
James and brother Houblons' pay over their £200 till

---

[1] *Diary*, January 1668-9.
[2] *Ibid.*, 2 March 1665-6. He frequently calls Hill 'the little Merchant.'
[3] At the time of his death the State still owed Pepys a large sum of
money.

all had been satisfactorily arranged. In the meantime, Pepys describes his friend James's countenance as changed towards him; 'he looked coldly,' he complains.[1] From his account of his labours and many runnings to and fro in his efforts to settle the matter, Pepys certainly fully earned his money.[2] We are quite glad to hear that the chief obstacles were finally removed, and to see him complacently remarking of the brothers that 'they and I are likely to understand one another to very good purpose.'[3] The ships, however, did not sail before June, and of many formalities still to be gone through before they could finally be dispatched: 'share-parties' had to be agreed upon, 'charter-parties evened'; various advances on the value of the freight paid (of which Pepys himself paid a part); and then the freight itself had to be 'evened.'[4]

But though the adventure to Tangiers had lately occupied so large a share of the attention of the Houblons, they did not cease to engage in commercial adventures in other directions. For instance, in the Record Office there is a notice of articles of agreement between James, and John, and the navy commissioners, dated the 10th of February, for the hire of a King's ship, the *White Horse*, for a voyage; for which the merchants paid the King £120.[5]

Business was now once more suspended in the City, by the second calamity which befell her in the Great 1666 Fire. Until about two months had passed after that event, no further record of commercial activity on the part of the Houblons is to be found, either in Pepys's *Diary* or anywhere else. The Great Fire broke out early on Sunday morning, the 2nd of September 1666. From

[1] *Diary*, 8 February 1665-6.
[2] See entries dated Feb. 5, 9, 15, and 16. The chief obstacles were raised by Colonel Norwood, the Deputy-Governor of Tangiers.
[3] *Ibid.*, 16 February 1665-6.
[4] See entries dated 13 April, 15 May, 15 June, 1666.
[5] State Papers, Domestic, Charles II., vol. 147, No. 76.

a small beginning in an obscure house in Pudding Lane, in a dense part of the City, this mighty fire spread till the flames had devoured nearly all the ancient and splendid City which had been the pride and delight of her citizens for so many centuries. Old London was not only one of the most beautiful cities in the world, but it was the freest, and with the fire, the monuments with which this freedom and greatness were associated, municipal buildings, palaces, churches, all were swept away. The sense of desolation and waste must have made every citizen who witnessed the conflagration—as did Samuel Pepys—'weep to see it.'[1] Apart from the pathos of the scene, it must have been magnificent in the extreme, the fire being so fierce and so great. Pepys describes it thus: 'As the day grew darker we saw the fire grow . . . and in corners and upon steeples and between Churches and houses as far as we could see up the hill of the City, in a most horrid malicious bloody flame, not like the fine flame of an ordinary fire. . . . We staid till it being darkish we saw the fire as one only entire arch of fire from this to the other side the Bridge,[2] and in a bow up the hill for an arch of above a mile long.'[3] This was after many hours of fruitless effort to bring some order into what was being done to check the conflagration. But it was too great to cope with, and the organisation too weak to deal with so great a matter. Pepys describes meeting my Lord Mayor on the day of the breaking out of the fire in Cannon Street: 'Like a man spent: with a hankercher about his neck,' and how to the King's message to pull down houses, 'he cried, like a fainting woman, " Lord, what can I do? I am spent! people will not obey me." '[4]

And so, men bent their minds solely to the saving each man his own goods before the steady advance of

[1] *Diary*, 2 September 1666. [2] London Bridge.
[3] *Diary*, 3 September 1666. [4] *Ibid.*

the flames should overwhelm their houses. Thus, while much was saved and carried away, most of the citizens of London were made homeless by this great destruction of their city.   This fate befell most of the Houblons. With the exception of that of the younger James, the houses of all the brothers, as well as of their father, were situated in those parts of the City which were destroyed. Bearbinder Lane, in which was the house of old Mr. Houblon, was burnt from end to end; while his parish church of St. Mary Woolchurch, where his wife and young children were buried, and which stood in the centre of the Stocks Market close at hand, was also burnt to the ground.   Mr. Houblon's friend and relation, John de la Motte, lived in Billiter Lane but a short distance off, and at this point the fire was checked on that side, from further advance.[1]

The fire lasted four days, and left London a heap of ruins.   At first all men seemed stunned by the magnitude of the disaster, but then the Duke of Albemarle— Monk—who had before saved and comforted the City in its doubt and trouble before the 'coming in' of the King, arrived from the fleet at the summons of Charles II.; and in his quiet sober way brought back confidence and order.   For all men were acquainted with his interest in the City, and turned to him from the weak and foolish Lord Mayor of the year, who had failed so miserably in his duty in the crisis.   The Duke 'lays by all business,' says Pepys, 'and minds the City.'[2]

The Exchange had been burnt, and the merchants by proclamation first met at Gresham College the following day, and there the Duke of Albemarle hastened to discourse with the Aldermen.   Shortly after this, confidence was again partly restored, and Pepys cheerfully writes that certainly never so great a loss as this was borne by citizens in the world '. . . and that not one

---

[1] Stow, *Survey of London*, I. ii. 64, 163.   [2] *Diary*, 8 September 1666.

Merchant upon the 'Change will break upon it' . . .
nor 'any disturbances in State, for that all men are busy
in looking after their own business to save themselves.'[1]
And this, although it was computed at the time that the
loss in the rents of houses alone would amount to
£600,000 per annum.[2]

A fortnight after the fire, Pepys tells of the daily
return of the Londoners, and of the high prices paid for
lodgings to those who had the good fortune not to be
burnt out.[3] But as for the state and magnificence of
the City and of its functions, they were all at an end for
the time. On the 29th of October Pepys exclaims of
the Aldermen almost in derision : 'How meanly they
now look, who upon this day used to be all little lords
—is a sad sight, and worthy consideration : and how
everybody did reflect with pity upon the poor City
to whom they are now coming to choose and swear
their Lord Mayor, compared with what it heretofore
was.'[4] Early in November the City was still lying
silent in its ruins, men taking walks through the midst
of it to see its desolation ; while the shock from which
the citizens had suffered made them nervous and superstitious, seeing ill omens and portents of misfortune
in everything that happened. And until this load of
anxiety which oppressed all men was removed, no
attempt was made to cope with the ruins. At the end
of December Pepys writes, 'The City less and less
likely to be built again, everybody settling elsewhere,
and nobody encouraged to trade';[5] while on the vexed
question of the proposed plans for rebuilding, he

1666

---

[1] *Diary*, 15 September 1666.
[2] The fire destroyed St. Paul's, the great Gild Hall (nine Courts were held in it), the Royal Exchange of Queen Elizabeth, eighty-nine parish churches, the King's Custom House, the Justice Hall, four prisons, four of the city gates, and fifty Halls of Companies. See Stow, *Survey of London*, I. i. 226.
[3] *Diary*, 26 September 1666.   [4] *Ibid.*, 29 October 1666.
[5] *Ibid.*, 31 December 1666.

remarks, 'The City will never be built again while any restraint is laid on them.'[1]

It was indeed a time of anxiety. The long and costly Dutch war had strained the resources of the nation, while a strong suspicion had grown up in men's minds that on the waste and profligacy of the court much of the money voted for the war had been expended. The Cavalier Parliament, once so strong in the maxim that the King could do no wrong, was now face to face with the problem how to check the King in his extravagance, and yet not discredit the crown. The anger of the people was deep against the court, and they showed it by their rejection of court candidates at by-elections. Thus the people of Winchelsea this year would have none but a private gentleman, saying openly that 'they would have no Court Pimp to be their Burgesse,'[2] nor could Mr. Williamson, the Commissioner of the navy, fare any better; they said of him 'that they would have no courtier.'

There were many schemes for the rebuilding of London. That of Sir Christopher Wren would have made it very beautiful had it been carried out;[3] but in the end it was left pretty much to the citizens to build as they would; and so the City rose up like a phœnix from amidst ashes, while those great and in authority had scarcely finished debating upon what lines to design the new town. Once left to himself, the indomitable spirit of his race set each homeless citizen to clear the ruins and rebuild his house, while public spirit was not lacking to replace the old public buildings and churches with others larger and finer than those which had been destroyed; though nothing could replace their many

[1] *Diary*, 1 January 1666-7.
[2] *Ibid.*, 21 October 1666.
[3] On 25th November Pepys writes: 'Mr. May...tells me that the design of building the City do go on apace, and by his description it will be mighty handsome; but I pray God it come not out too late.'—*Diary*, 25 November 1666.

valuable records and documents destroyed in the fire.[1] Clean and wholesome, purified by the flames from the dirt of centuries and from ancient 'nests of fever and pestilence,' the new city must have been. Perhaps in those days when the world was younger, the loss, æsthetic and archæological, of so much that would have been priceless to us in this age had it still existed, was but little felt; as little, perhaps, as the destruction of an early-Victorian town with all its contents, the product of contemporary taste and industry, would be by ourselves.

James Houblon, the elder, rebuilt his house on the same site as before, but on a larger scale. Of this we have circumstantial evidence in the surveys of Stow's *London*; in the earlier edition to that of Strype, the number of houses in Bearbinder Lane on the one side having then been seven or eight, while after the rebuilding of London, they were but three or four.[2] The chimney tax of 1662 likewise shows the old house to have been smaller than the new, for its owner was assessed for fewer firehearths then than in 1674, when the new hearth tax of that year was charged upon the City of London.

The neighbourhood of James's house was much improved by the changes consequent upon the fire. His house closely abutted on the old Stocks Market, which took its name from the presence there of the parish stocks.[3] After the fire the stocks were not replaced, and the market was henceforward used for the sale of fruit, herbs, and flowers only,[4] the booths on

---

[1] The Royal Insurance Company was among the many who thus lost all their early records. From the evidence of business papers in the Du Quesne (Du Cane) family, we find that members both of that family and of the Houblons were among the first founders of the company.

[2] Strype's Stow's *Survey of London*, I. ii. 196.

[3] 'You are to take Order that there be provided and set up a pair of Stocks and a whipping Post in some convenient place in every parish within your Ward for the punishment of Vagrants and other offenders.' See the Maior's Precept to the Aldermen as to their duties. Old City Customes. *Ibid.*, II. v. 314.   [4] *Ibid.*, I. ii. 195.

which they were displayed occupying the centre on which the church had formerly stood. On the side of the square where Bearbinder Lane opened upon it, a broad space was planted with rows of trees forming a green alley, and extending as far as Lombard Street.[1] In this alley the citizens were wont to walk on summer evenings.[2]

After the burning of the Church of St. Mary Woolchurch, it was not rebuilt, but, as in the case of many others in the City, that parish and the neighbouring one of St. Mary Woolnoth were thrown into one. The latter then became the parish church of Mr. Houblon, in which, in fact, he was, many years later, buried. Upon the site of the old Stocks Market, and of the Church of St. Mary Woolchurch burnt in the fire, the Mansion-house now stands.

On November the 13th and 14th, after the Great Fire, 1666 we find entries in Pepys's *Diary* which show us that the Houblons were by that time busy again with commercial matters, though anxious and disturbed at the serious political outlook, and at the carelessness of the King with regard to all matters appertaining to business. All their houses except that of James, having been burnt, it is probable that the brothers were lodging with him at his house in Winchester Street; or, at any rate, that for the time it served them all as their place of business. 'This evening,' writes Pepys, 'come all the Houblons to me, to invite me to sup with them to-morrow night. I did take them home, and there we sat and talked a good while—and a glass of wine, and then we parted till to-morrow night.'[3]

The supper to which the brothers had invited him

---

[1] Strype's Stow's *Survey of London*, I. ii. 199. See also map.
[2] There is an interesting picture by Van Ackere of that part of the old Stocks Market occupied by the booths, in the Bank of England, lately presented to the bank by one of its directors.
[3] Pepys's *Diary*, 13 November 1666.

took place the following day at the Pope's Head tavern, 'where all the Houblons were, and Dr. Croone.'[1] During supper the Doctor,—who was a learned physician and Rhetoric Professor at Gresham College,—discoursed to the company on some surgical experiments in which he had just taken part; but after supper, at least one other object of the entertainment appeared, for 'James Houblon and another brother took me aside, and to talk of some businesses of their owne where I am to serve them, and will.' The talk then became general 'of publique matters, and I do find that they and all the merchants else do give over trade and the nation for lost, nothing being done with care or foresight, no convoys granted nor anything done to satisfaction; but do think that the Dutch and French will master us the next yeare, do what we can : and so do I unless necessity makes the King to mind his business, which might yet save all. Here we sat talking till past one in the morning, and then home, where my people sat up for me, my wife and all, and so to bed.'[2]

English merchants were still fretting under the difficulties and embarrassments to trade consequent upon the Dutch war, of which both nations were heartily weary. 'Our Merchants do much pray for peace,' writes Mr. Pepys, after one of his many meetings with the Houblon brothers.[3] There was also a vague fear of invasion in many men's minds at this time, the French King's ambition, and the hostile mercantile regulations of his minister Colbert, adding to the discontent and uneasiness. With regard to the fear of invasion by the French, Mr. Pepys quotes the opinion of the Houblons, whom he met on the 2nd 1666-7 of January in Westminster Hall. They, at any rate,

---

[1] William Croune, M.D., of Emmanuel College, Cambridge, and Fellow of the Royal Society. Ob. 1684.
[2] *Diary*, 14 November 1666.
[3] *Ibid.*, 10 April 1667.

were always outwardly optimistic as to such proba-
bilities, laughing at what James Houblon on another
occasion calls 'a clutter of arming in Dutchland.' In
the present instance: 'They,' says Pepys, 'do laugh at
it,' and suggest that 'we at Court do blow up a design
of invading us only to make the Parliament make more
haste in the money matters. . . . Nevertheless, they
lament our ill condition in not being able to set out
a Fleet (we doubt) this year, and the certain ill effect
that must bring, which is lamentable.'[1]

The event was to show how just was this prophecy;
not six months afterwards this country suffered an affront
(though it did not come from the French), to which there
is no parallel in her history.   Charles II., confident in the
successful termination of the negotiations then going on
with the Dutch at Breda, and deeply harassed for money,
far from 'setting out a fleet' for service, dismantled and
disarmed those ships he possessed, and dismissed the
sailors.   His expectation that the embarrassments to the
Dutch, consequent upon the French King's designs
upon the Spanish Netherlands, would ensure the speedy
ratification of the treaty, was not realised; for Admiral
de Ruyter, who had become aware of Charles's hasty
action, adroitly took advantage of the defenceless
situation in which the King had placed himself, and
hoping to extract better conditions of peace, suddenly
appeared off Chatham, reduced it, sailed up the Medway, burning the empty English ships lying in the
river as he went, and carrying off others.   He took
Sheerness, and for some days entirely blockaded the
Thames itself.   The helpless rage and terror of the
Londoners is ably described in Pepys's record of this
disgraceful episode in his *Diary*.

When these events took place, Charles II. had but
lately concluded the secret treaty with Louis XIV.

[1] *Diary*, 2 January 1666-7.

which discredited the rest of his reign. In return
for a yearly subsidy in money (by means of which
he was rendered independent of Parliament), he con-
sented to leave Louis a free hand with regard to the
absorption of Flanders, and to shut his eyes to other
ambitious designs of the French King, of whom he
now became the tool and laughing-stock. 'It seems,'
writes Mr. Pepys, 'as if the King of France did
think other Princes fit for nothing but to make sport
for him : but the simple Princes they are that are forced
to suffer this from him.'[1]   As illustrative of the small
account in which the country and the English King were
then held by the French, is the following—one of many
affronts of the same kind. 'At noon,' writes Mr. Pepys,
'to the 'Change, and there hear by Mr. Hublon of the
loss of a little East Indiaman, valued at about £20,000,
coming home alone, and safe to within ten leagues of
Scilly, and there snapt by a French Caper.'[2]   The ambition of Colbert was to substitute French for English
trade in both the East and West Indies, and every
encouragement possible was given to the trading companies he had inaugurated for that purpose, as well as
to the new French Plantations, which he hoped would
rival those of the English. The minister of the 'grand
Monarque' was not above taking advantage of his ally's
present weakness, and of furthering his end of embarrassing her trade, by the encouragement of privateering
while the countries were at peace ; and thus the English
merchants suffered insult and loss, as no convoys were
now to be had from home to protect their fleets. For
this reason, perhaps, the East India Company at this
time deemed solitary vessels more likely to escape notice

[1] *Diary*, 11 March 1667.
[2] This was a light-armed vessel used in the seventeenth century for
privateering. The word used was that employed by the Dutch. Smyth's
Sailor's Word Book. The Houblons had large interests in East India
stock.

from both enemies and friends, than ships that sailed together in a fleet.

Yet luck often attended the English merchants; and great were the rejoicings in London when fleets of merchantmen came safely in.   On December the 3rd 1666 Mr. Pepys was jubilant over the arrival of four New England ships at Falmouth 'with masts for the King'; then we hear of his anxiety about the safety of 'our Hamburgh and Gottenburg fleets,' and his saying, 'we shall be safe for this winter' if they come in.[1] Pepys's interest in these particular fleets was on account of their bringing stores for the navy, which alas! was not to be fitted out this year.   Again he mentions the arrival in the Downs of four ships from Smyrna without convoy—a long and dangerous voyage for unprotected ships in these troublous times.[2]   But a month or two after the coming in of these vessels, the fatal determination having been arrived at that it was unnecessary to equip a fleet to carry on the Dutch war that year, liberty was granted to the East India merchants for the setting out of ships for their trade, and this was done by the Company on so great a scale that ten to fifteen thousand seamen found employment and left the country, being thus unavailable at the time of emergency. And this was the more unfortunate as that many valuable ships of the fleets sent out were lost or captured. This want of foresight in allowing so many seamen to leave the country before the conclusion of peace was afterwards acknowledged by Sir William Penn and the other Commissioners of the navy when called upon by Parliament to make their defence to the accusations brought against the Navy Office, with respect to the disasters at the hand of the Dutch.

Some six months after de Ruyter's exploit in the

[1] *Diary*, 15 December 1666.
[2] *Ibid.*, 12 December 1666.   The dangers run by merchant ships were so great that nobody would insure them.

Medway, a general apathy and depression seems to have succeeded the excitement and indignation it caused. Every one was anxious about the badness of the times, while the merchants are described as angry and sad at the discreditable peace and at the breaking up of Parliament. The heavy losses through the capture of valuable ships by the enemy meanwhile obliged them for the time to abstain altogether from mercantile adventures. In their enforced idleness we find the heretofore busy merchant passing the heavy time in amusing himself as best he could. Mr. Andrews, the friend of the Houblons and of Pepys, is described by the latter—'as all other Merchants do all—give over any hopes of things doing well, and so he spends his

1667   time here (at Bow) most, playing at bowles.'[1] We likewise see the Houblons forsaking the Exchange and Westminster Hall for the fashionable resort of the Wells at Epsom, where in recreation as in business they still clung to each other's society. There Pepys, going down in a coach and four with his wife and friends 'to take the ayre,' found them 'and much company.' Having left 'his women' at the King's Head, he walked to church, 'where few people to what I expected, but all the Houblon brothers, and them after Sermon I did salute and walk with towards my Inne.' The general indignation excited by the late events, and the fear of what punishment Parliament was likely to inflict upon the officials of the Navy Office, had been hanging like a sword of Damocles over the head of Pepys, notwithstanding that of all his colleagues he was the only one who had made any earnest attempt to bring order into the confusion which reigned in the administration of the navy. Indeed, Pepys's well-known assiduity at his work caused him to be very generally excepted from the chorus of indignation which assailed his brother-officials. He

[1] *Diary*, 8 August 1667.

was, however, at this time very anxious as to how matters would turn out, and so rejoices over the assurances of James, Houblon, as to how men speak of him. During the walk from church to his 'Inne,' 'James did tell me I was the only happy man of the Navy, of whom he says, during all the freedom the people have taken to speaking treason,[1] he hath not heard one bad word of me, which is a great joy to me ; for I hear the same of others, but do know that I have deserved as well as most. We parted to meet anon.'[2]   1667

The year 1668 opened with gloom and many heart-burnings. All who had had anything to do with the conduct of the late war were full of apprehension as to what might befall them when Parliament met, while the searching inquiries being now made into the internal administration of the navy filled not only Mr. Pepys but all others with dismay, whether they were conscious of corruption or not. So narrow was the margin between the legitimate and the corrupt absorption of money, that it was at this time scarcely possible to discriminate between the bribe and the lawful fee.[3]   1668

After the Commons had met, full of 'madness' at the mismanagement and neglect which had borne the bitter fruit of the peace of Breda, the King brought before the Houses his necessities ; 'his debts, his want of a fleet, and therefore want of money,' and then—with lamentable want of tact at such a time—sprung upon the House his proposal for a bill of comprehension, as it was called ; the measure which he had bound himself by his treaty with Louis xiv. to bring before the Commons. The Cavalier Parliament had throughout its career maintained so loyal a devotion to the English Church, and to her supremacy as against Roman Catholics and

---

[1] Viz. abuse of the Court and of the Navy Office.
[2] *Diary*, 14 July 1667.
[3] Mr. Coventry in June 1663 sent in a demand to have 'his Fees set.' See *Diary* of Mr. Pepys.

Dissenters alike, that the side blow which they saw in the King's proposal stung them to indignation, rightly regarding it as designed to stultify the Act of Uniformity, by means of which they prided themselves on having, after her long dethronement, re-established the supremacy of the old English Church in this country. 'So furious are they,' writes Mr. Pepys; though 'tis 'a thing much desired by much the greater part of the nation.'[1] In the meantime the Navy Office found itself confronted by determined committees of inquiry as to accounts and miscarriages; who, as Pepys remarks, 'sit all day; and only eat a bit of bread at noon and a glass of wine; and are resolved to go through their business with great severity and method.'[2] 'Mighty hot they are, which makes me mad to see them bite at the stone and not at the hand that flings it.'[3] For it was well known that the Commons desired indirectly to drive home to the King their disapproval of his wanton waste of the money they had voted for the war. Pepys himself, though at one time in danger of being involved in the general condemnation of his office, seems early to have impressed the commissioners with the clearness of his mind and with his businesslike suggestions for amending the management for which he was not himself responsible. Keenly alive to the necessity for reform, he drew up reports, and composed narratives of past events, vindicating the office of which he was a member, while consulting with the friends most able to advise on the various questions at issue. Of the burning questions involved, some of them were of a nature to affect the merchants with whom the interests of the navy were closely bound up; and we find Pepys at this time more than once in consultation with the merchant, James, Houblon. On the 13th of February he tells us in his

---

[1] *Diary*, 10 February 1667-8.   [2] *Ibid.*, 7 February 1667-8.
[3] *Ibid.*, 11 February 1667-8.

Diary of James coming to him 'late at night,' and after a long conversation, of their going together to the gate, where to Pepys's amazement he discovers Mr. Houblon's 'Lady and another fine Lady, sitting in their coach for an hour together,' waiting; 'which,' adds the diarist, 'is so like my wife'—in her devotion and patience, it is to be presumed—'that I was mightily taken with it, though troubled for it.'[1]   The next day he appears, hurrying to the Old Exchange 'with his head busy but his heart at pretty good ease,' for his narrative on the vexed question of prize goods had been 'respectfully' received by the Committee of Accounts.   There he met Mr. Houblon, and anxious to hear what impression had been produced by his paper, 'I prayed him,' he tells us, 'to discourse with some of the merchants that are on the Committee of Accounts,' 'to see how they do resent my Paper, and in general my particular in relation to the business of the Navy; and this he hath promised to do carefully for me.'[2]

The climax of all this trouble and stir was reached a few weeks later, when the Navy Office commissioners   1668 and Principal Officers were summoned to the bar of the House of Commons, there to answer the charges made against them of mismanagement and waste in the affairs of the navy.   It fell to Mr. Pepys to be spokesman on this occasion, when he delivered himself of the famous speech prepared in fear and trembling, but which in its eloquence, close pleading, and ingenuity of argument for the time weathered the storm, and, amidst a chorus of congratulations and approval, called forth the cheery greeting from Sir William Coventry, the man he most honoured and reverenced: 'Good morrow, Mr. Pepys, that must be Speaker of the Parliament House!'[3]

---

[1] *Diary*, 13 February 1667-8.   [2] *Ibid.*, 14 February 1667-8.
[3] 6 March 1668.   Pepys after this date possessed the entire confidence of his 'chief,' the Duke of York.   H. B. Wheatley, *Pepysiana*, 1899.

CHAPTER XI

PATER BURSAE LONDINENSIS

'I cannot call Riches better, than the Baggage of Virtue.'
BACON: *Essays.*

'THENCE I away . . . to the Old Exchange. . . . Here it
1667-8 was a mighty pretty sight to see old Mr. Houblon whom
I never saw before, and all his sons about him ; all good
Merchants.'[1]

Old Mr. Houblon was now seventy-six years old;
and although he did not retire entirely from business
till some years after this date, it is probable that he had
already for some time ceased to take an active part in
commercial life, acting rather as the referee or sleeping
partner in the little company of merchant brothers
whose interests were bound up in one.   Doubtless his
sons were well content to profit by his large experience,
and by the prestige attached to his name, as one of the
last of those Merchant Adventurers who had been the
pioneers of the great trade to which they had succeeded.
The position of their father with regard to their business was probably in some measure the reason of the
habit of the brothers of moving about in each other's
society.   In Westminster Hall or at the Exchange,
where much business was done during the 'walking' to
and fro according to the invariable custom, their common interests would in any case have necessitated
frequent meetings.   'A very eminent merchant of
London,' Strype calls Mr. Houblon in his edition of

---

[1] *Diary,* 14 February 1667-8.

Stow's *Survey*, 'and as eminent for his plainness and piety; his family descended from confessors on both sides.'[1] The 'plainness' for which he was remarkable was one of those characteristics which had distinguished the Flemish refugee merchants; characteristics which had been partly instrumental in placing them in the position to which they ultimately attained. The word, now suggestive (in this connection) of ugliness or dullness, at that time was used to express the idea of the plain uprightness or straightforward dealing which belonged to the character of one whose word could be trusted and his promise relied on.[2] Indeed the very memory of the sacrifices formerly made by their ancestors, together with the traditions of piety they left behind them, appears to have very sensibly influenced the lives and conduct of the descendants of the refugees, in a time when corruption was eating into the very heart of society. 'Descended from confessors on both sides' was then no mere form of words, but a fact constituting a right to consideration and respect, and carrying with it a tradition of integrity especially valuable to business men. As persecution has had invariably the effect of strengthening and deepening a religious faith, even through long distances of time, so may we trace, we think, that same inherited influence upon many generations of Houblons, many of whom were remarkable for the same piety and 'plain' dealing as were their confessor ancestors.

The last years of Mr. Houblon's life were spent uninterruptedly in the country. In the year 1672 he took a final leave of London, and of the work on which he had been engaged from his youth. It has not been

1672

---

[1] Stow, *Survey of London*, I. ii. 162.
[2] In Pennant's *London* he used the same word in his note about Mr. Houblon, while Mr. Pepys uses it of Mr. Spong, a distinguished and accomplished man of his acquaintance, calling him 'a man I mightily love for his plainness and engenuity.'—*Diary*, 21 January 1668-9.

possible to identify the situation of his country house with any certainty, except that it was in Essex, and probably not far from Wanstead, which was then a favourite resort of the London citizens, and in the neighbourhood of which more than one of his sons had their country residences.   But except for the occasional visits of his sons—especially of Jacob, the fifth, who was a 'Clerk in Orders'—he seems to have lived alone.   While still in the midst of business, James had always found time for religious exercises, and for the active work of ministration to the poor and needy.   His purse was always open, and his kind hand ready to help those in trouble or poverty.   Dr. Burnet says of his charities that ' he took care to manage them so secretly that often the persons knew not from whence their relief came.' Indeed, so generous to their poor had the early Flemish refugees of wealth and position always been, that it was never said of them at any time that their sick and needy were a charge on the general community.   And now, before the close of his long life, James sought and obtained the opportunity he had coveted, in quiet and retirement wholly ' to fear God and do good.   Having so entire a health, so plentiful a fortune, and the freedom of that leisure which he gave himself, he added to his crown of gray hairs and the crown of his children, that of good works.'[1]

Thus, withdrawn from the stir of life and the cares which had been his portion, James Houblon employed his time in prayer and meditation, but chiefly in intercession for the children he loved so well ; his ' sweet ones,' as he called them, though all now grown men and women of advanced years, with families and busy lives full of cares and joys of their own ; but ' children ' still to their venerable father, who must have united with a patriarchal authority a

[1] A Sermon preached at the funeral of Mr. James Houblon, June 28, 1682, by Gilbert Burnet, D.D., p. 35.   Printed at the Rose and Crown in St. Paul's Churchyard, MDCLXXXII.

judicious tact in his rule, which ensured their love and reverence and the fulfilment of his most ardent prayers for the unity and love among themselves which we know to have been theirs.

It was during these last years that Mr. Houblon employed himself in writing his Pious Memoirs, or 'Various notes and exhortations written with mine own hand for direction and government of all my children in their pilgrimage on earth.' These writings are singularly broad-minded for those days in the matter of religion. They are entirely free from dogmatism, while a sound practical common-sense pervades every word of them. Religion to James meant right-thinking; but if any injunction more than another is to be found in the memoirs, it is the earnest beseeching of his children to love God and their fellowmen. In his early manhood their author was in the very hot-bed of puritanical zeal and prejudice; and the English Puritans bore but a slender resemblance to his own gentle and persecuted ancestors! The tide had turned in so far as persecution went—though the dread of Rome survived to the last. But on the other hand, the old 'Roundhead' had been early sickened with the intolerance and self-righteousness of his party in the years gone by, when he worked for and with the Parliamentarians during the civil wars. He then learnt the lessons of peace and tolerance—we may believe—which lasted him his life.

The MSS. of these Memoirs have been preserved, and some of them printed in 1886 by the late John Archer Houblon 'in memory of his good Ancestor.' While some of the sheets were written in the strong and beautiful handwriting of his earlier years, others are inscribed in extreme old age, the writing feeble, and the frequent erasures and corrections pathetically suggestive of the earnest care and labour bestowed on their

composition. Of the wife lost in the prime of his manhood, the gentle mother of his children, the memory
remained green to the last, though she had been dead
for thirty-six years. Exhorting his sons as to their
home life he writes: 'Children, comport yourselves
towards your wives with mildness and gentleness.
Pray often together; . . . I and your mother (who
nursed you all), a woman of a meek and humble spirit,
did daily so in our family, and jointly together in
private.'[1]

Thus, in the quiet and retirement he had chosen,
James₁ Houblon lived on for ten years. He never re-
visited the City that he had loved and served. Its hum
of busy life—the tramp of feet—the street cries so
familiar and musical in those days—the clang of Bow
Bell at curfew—the swish of the river racing under
'Bridge'—sights and sounds familiar to his youth—
must often have floated across his mind as he sat alone
at his window gazing across the green landscape towards
the faint haze on the horizon, where the great City lay.
For though he lived alone and at a distance, after communion with his God, his chief and constant thought
was of the loved ones who dwelt there. And so he
passed his long and quiet days, writing, reading, and
praying, and dreaming of the past and of the 'woman of
a meek and humble spirit' he hoped soon to meet again.
A miniature painted of Mr. Houblon about this time
shows his countenance to have been a faithful mirror of
the serenity of his mind. A broad smooth forehead,
the face pale as ivory; a thin-cut, sensitive mouth, the
sweet expression of which is not hidden by the spare
moustache and imperial surrounding it; while in the
large blue, heavily lidded eyes we find a characteristic
still to be traced in many of his descendants. Soft grey

---

[1] See Appendix A. for extracts from the Pious Memoirs of Mr. James
Houblon.

MR. JAMES HOUBLON.
" PATER BURSÆ LONDINENSIS."

distinctly. . . . He lived to see his children's children,
and some of their children, to so great an increase, that
in his time a full hundred came into the world descended
from him, all born in full time and all baptized save one.
Of these, sixty-seven are yet alive, to which if eleven
that are come into his family by marriage be joined,
there wanted but two to fourscore that had a right to
his daily blessing.'   Looking down on the upturned
faces of the many sons whose duty and affection to their
father had been well known, the following words of the
Bishop could have been no empty compliment, for all
knew them to be true : 'I shall not add anything of the
comfort he had in his children, though that is a
necessary ingredient to make such things blessings
indeed ; but that belongs too much to the living to be
insisted on by me.' [1]

The old jealousy of the strangers and of their prosperity had not died out yet.   After so many years they
were by a section of the population still regarded as
aliens, while men wilfully shut their eyes to the benefits
obtained through their coming in what Bishop Burnet
calls 'the last age.'   Knowing well the common prejudice, and perhaps in the signs of the times foreseeing
what would soon happen in France,[2] the accomplished
divine seized the opportunity presented by the foreign
origin of the man whose past life he was eulogising,
to appeal to his congregation to continue their charities
and readiness to relieve those that are forced to come
and take sanctuary among them.   'You see,' he added,
'what the nation and this City has gained by the
reception of the strangers that fled hither for refuge in
the last age ; you see how great a citizen you had in
him that is now dead, and into how many he is now
divided who by their interest could almost make a city

[1] Sermon preached on the occasion of the funeral of Mr. James Houblon
by Dr. Burnet, June 1682.
[2] The Revocation of the Edict of Nantes in 1683.

alone; and you do not know how many such others there may be if those that now come among you, who may produce many to be as great blessings to the next age, as this family is to the present.'[1]

Mr. Houblon was nearly ninety when he died on the 20th of June 1682. He was buried eight days later under the chancel of St. Mary Woolnoth in Lombard Street, 'on the north side of the altar.'[2] His will, dated the 12th of January 1681, was witnessed by his son Jacob, by James Lordell, his son-in-law, and his old friend Isaac Jurin. After enumerating various sums left for charitable purposes, including one to the parish of Moreton in Essex,—'where my son Jacob is rector,'—and to 'Bovinger[3] where my grandson Butler is rector, —for the schooling of poor children,' he gave special legacies to his sons and daughters. To his eldest son Peter he left his 'sapphire ring,' and we afterwards find this ring mentioned in the will of another Peter, his grandson. To his 'loving son' James, he bequeathed 'one of my silver fflaggons,' and to his son John the other. His large fortune he divided equally amongst all his six sons then living, 'share and share alike.' Legacies were also left to two ladies of the name of Durand, said to have been his sisters; but they were probably his nieces, daughters of one of his sisters, both of whom had married early in the century brothers named Jean and Benjamin Durand, members probably of a Flemish branch of the distinguished French family of Dauphiny of that name, some of whom afterwards settled in the island of Guernsey.

1682

---

[1] Bishop Burnet practised what he preached. Dr. King eulogises him as 'a good pastor,' and tells us that unlike many prelates of his day who amassed large sums of money from the revenue of their Sees, Dr. Burnet at his death had nothing to bequeath to his children but their mother's fortune. See King's *Anecdotes*. See also for an interesting portrait of this great churchman: Lecky, *England in the Eighteenth Century*, i. 80-83.

[2] Registers of St. Mary Woolnoth. Edited by Mr. Philips.

[3] Pronounced Bovinger; but spelt to this day: Bubbingworth (Essex).

The parish registers of St. Mary Woolnoth up to the date of 1760 have been printed, and contain a vast number of entries relating to the Houblon family, which was now extremely numerous. The editor of the work states that 'At St. Mary Woolnoth is an inscription to the memory of Mr. James Houblon,' whose 'epitaph was composed for him by Samuel Pepys, Esq., Secretary to the Admiralty in the reigns of Charles II. and James II.' He adds that the tablet has now disappeared.[1] Pennant, writing in 1793, also affirms that this epitaph was written for Mr. Houblon by Samuel Pepys, and that it was placed on the tablet in this church.[2] It was probably displaced early in the nineteenth century when many alterations were made in the church and crypt, and the coffins moved. The epitaph, of which several contemporary copies exist, is as follows :—

Jacobus Houblon
Londinas Petri Filius
Ob fidem Flandria exuiantis
Ex c nepotibus habuit LXX superstites:
Filios v videns Mercatores florentissimos
Ipse Londinensis Bursae Pater,
Piissime obiit Nonagenarius
A° D. MDCLXXXII.[3]

Mr. Houblon requested that after his death each of his children should possess his picture, and owing to this wish copies were made of the miniature we have

---

[1] Registers of St. Mary Woolnoth. Edited by Mr. Philips.

[2] See Pennant, *Some Account of London*, p. 455, 3rd Edition. 1793. Pennant was descended through his mother from Arabella, daughter of Sir John Houblon ; she married Richard Mytton of Halston, Esq., M.P. for Shrewsbury.

[3] (Translation):   James Houblon of London,
    Son of Peter, who for faith's sake fled out of Flanders.
    Of one hundred grandchildren he had seventy survivors.
    Seeing five sons most flourishing merchants :
    He himself, the Father of the London Exchange,
    Died ; full of piety ; aged ninety. .
        A° D. 1682.

already described. The original of these copies is unfinished, but it is by a master hand, and almost certainly the work of Samuel Cooper, 'the great limner in little,' as Pepys calls him. One of the copies made after the death of Mr. Houblon is a good specimen of miniature painting on vellum like the original, ivory not having yet been used at that date for miniatures. It belonged, in the eighteenth century, to a grandson of Mr. James Houblon, and was left by him to his nephew, the great-great-grandfather of the present head of the family and direct descendant of Mr. James Houblon. The portrait itself occupies the centre of the picture, the upper portion of which consists of arabesque ornamentation chiefly composed of the hop or *houblon* plant, and a shield bearing the arms of the family. Below is the blue sea in which two dolphins disport themselves, while on either side of an illuminated inscription a merchant galley is depicted, her sails furled and laid up in harbour. The inscription consists of the epitaph written by Samuel Pepys and quoted above. Another of these pictures, and exactly similar, hangs in one of the anterooms in the Bank of England. In addition to his portrait, each of his children and grandchildren received a MS. copy of James Houblon's Pious Memoirs. One of these at Hallingbury is in a beautiful contemporary binding.

And so the Father of the Exchange—that great Burse of Elizabeth, of which he was the oldest living member—slept in peace, full of years and honour; leaving behind him a memory and example to his children and children's children, and their children after them. The mild eyes in the tender old face still look wistfully out of his picture and carry on the appeal they made in his parting words to his own 'sweet ones'; preaching the patience, the duty, the justice and integrity of his own life to the young ones of this day and their elders, of whom he was the ancestor more than two hundred years

ago.   Perhaps the saintly Jeremy Taylor may have had
such another good man as James in his mind, when
he wrote the following in the epistle dedicatory to his
Holy Living and Dying: 'No man is a better merchant
than he that laies out his time upon God and his money
upon the Poor.'[1]

[1] Chap. i. p. 3, edition of 1703.

CHAPTER XII

'BROTHERS HOUBLON'

'For the King's ships went to Tarshish; . . . every three years once came the ships of Tarshish bringing gold, and silver, ivory, and apes, and peacocks.'—2 CHRON. ix. 21.

THE banking accounts of the brothers throw some light upon their mercantile undertakings, especially with regard to Portugal. It appears from the earliest books belonging to Messrs. Child and Co., that the Houblons were among the first customers of their predecessors in their business, at a time when banking in this country was still in a very early stage of development. In days yet earlier, the care of wealth was often most embarrassing to its possessors; and ancient cabinets and escritoires with ingenious secret drawers, as well as iron strong-boxes with intricate locks, bear witness to this fact. For people were forced to keep their money *en cassette*, hidden away as best they could; while in time of danger they generally buried it, as did Mr. Pepys his hoarded wealth at the time of the Great Fire.

The City Company of Goldsmiths were the first bankers in this country; and in London they kept the money and bullion deposited in their hands for safe custody, in the Exchequer, or at the Mint. Alderman Edward Backwell was a great merchant and goldsmith on his own account, and he also kept the cash accounts of a number of the wealthy London citizens, while on his books many of the most distinguished names of the day are likewise to be found. It was with him that the

Houblon brothers kept their accounts. Some interesting old ledgers have been preserved by his successors— Messrs. Child—in a series beginning in the year 1663, and extending to 1672, at which date Backwell was ruined and his business destroyed, by the 'closing of the Exchequer.' The ledgers show large sums to have been continually passing through his hands in connection with his banking business, and his customers doubtless all suffered severely by this act of Charles II.

1672

From the entries under the Houblon name, it is clear that the larger number of deposits made by them were in *pieces of eight*, the Portuguese coin. Silver bars were also frequently accounted for on the credit side, and on more than one occasion blocks of tin. The Houblons traded extensively with Spain and Portugal, and the pieces of eight being sent so freely to this country is illustrative of the small productiveness of these countries as to commodities. In an old pamphlet of 1659, on the importance to this country of the trade with the Peninsula, the writer speaks of the 'great store of monies' brought to this country from there,[1] an aspect of commercial exchange dear to the exponents of the 'mercantile theory,' to whom the import of the precious metals was ever welcome.

In the early ledgers now in the possession of Messrs. Child, the names of no less than eight Houblons appear, all of whom engaged in commerce at that period. Messrs. Child assert that old Mr. Houblon was of the number of Alderman Backwell's earliest customers ; but we are inclined to think that he kept no current cash account, and though the name of James occurs frequently, it was really that of his second son. James Houblon senior's name is indeed shown on the books, but only in the banking account kept by the East India Company at

---

[1] It was an offence punishable with death to export the precious metals from Spain, but the law failed to stop the outflow.

Backwell's, and here, while the christian names of all his sons are mentioned, he only is designated as Mr. Houblon.

Alderman Backwell's first ledger extant opens the 28th of March 1663. Between this date and December the sum of £1372, 1s. 4d. passed through his hands in the name of James, Houblon. John's account, carried forward from an earlier ledger not now in existence, opens at the same time, and at the end of the year it stood at £2431, 12s. 11d. These brothers were then about thirty years old ; Abraham and Isaac but twenty-three and twenty-five. A joint account at Backwell's in their name was opened this year ; and at the end of it it stood at £961, 12s. 8d. The younger brothers quickly improved their position, for the following year the amount to their credit, during the course of five months, reached £3286, 1s. 7d. Major Peter Houblon in 1664 paid in, in pieces of eight and 'Spanish Barrs,' £1097 worth ; and on the 30th of August we find on the debtor side the sum of £80, 1s. 9d. 'paid to my Sonn.' Between October this year and the following March, John Houblon paid in Portuguese money £3308, 1s. 9d. Such entries occur throughout the series of ledgers still in existence.[1]

As a portion of their commerce with Spain and Portugal would have been paid by the exchange of commodities, these deposits of the merchants represent that part only which was paid in 'monies' by those countries, showing that, with regard to the Peninsula, their exports greatly exceeded their imports. Beyond the carrying forward of the balance in their favour, no entries are made in the ledgers of other money than the pieces of eight ; and it would thus appear with regard to their trade with other ports, that it was balanced by mutual exchange of commodities. An entry dated

1663

[1] Examined by kind permission of Messrs. Child and Co.

November 1666, shows the value of nineteen 'blocks of Tynne' to have been placed to the credit of the brothers James and John Houblon at Backwell's, and the same amount occurs the following year. In each case the value allowed was £315.

1665 From early in the year 1665 till June 1666, a long pause occurs in the banking accounts of the brothers, broken only by a single entry in the name of Peter. During this interval the two calamities of the Plague and the Great Fire occurred; but no sooner had the citizens begun to recover from the effect of the latter misfortune, than John Houblon began again to pay in pieces of eight and Spanish bars, and the entries 1666 continue as before.

James and John's 'bills for Amsterdam,' in September, on the credit side of the account, were for the sums of £400, £600, and £1000; and again in October for £1000 'per their man.'[1] Bills for Spain and Seville likewise occur from time to time in the accounts of the brothers. Throughout, the entries in the name of Mr. Houblon's eldest son Peter are insignificant compared to those of his brothers. From the be-1670 ginning of the year 1670, the deposits are less in amount in the banking books, perhaps because the Houblons began in April that year to invest largely in East India stock. These sums appear in the banking account of that company who kept it at Alderman Backwell's. About £5000 was invested by the brothers and their father in this manner, between April and November 1670. Their name is likewise to be found in the accounts of other merchants banking with Backwell, notably with Michael Dunkin, a principal of the East India Company.

The sums of money entrusted to the keeping of the

[1] These appear to have been bills of exchange drawn upon Amsterdam firms, and paid into Backwell's so that the merchants might send them to their correspondents in Amsterdam for encashment.

bankers, and by them deposited in the Exchequer, fluctuated considerably, as the merchants withdrew what cash they required once a week to meet their engagements.[1] Charles I. had forced a loan upon the City of London in 1640, by helping himself to £200,000 which was lodged in the Mint; but the act of Charles II. was more disastrous. When in 1672 he seized £1,500,000 which was in the Exchequer, many merchants of the City were unable to meet their current engagements,[2] and great embarrassment ensued. Alderman Backwell had advanced large sums to the King before this time, the crown already owing him nearly £300,000. Although the King henceforth paid interest upon the debt, the principal is owing to this day, and Backwell was of course ruined,—as were many other goldsmiths—by the King's dishonest act. After a few years the broken fortunes of Backwell's business were transferred to Messrs. Child at Temple Bar, together with some of the ancient ledgers, which are still their cherished possessions.

The greater number of Backwell's customers opened accounts with Child after the ruin of Backwell's bank, but the Houblon name did not reappear upon the books till the year 1735.[3] The high reputation of Child was a byword in the corrupt days of the Restoration, and Mr. Pepys records in the year 1669 a speech of Sir T. Littleton, who declared 'that he never heard any honest man speak ill of Child.'[4] Nevertheless the diarist was not slow to cry out with his neighbours 'against the King for dealing so much with the Goldsmiths, and suffering himself to have his purse kept and commanded by them,'

1640
1672

---

[1] B. B. Turner Sonnenschein, *Chronicles of the Bank of England*, p. 3. 1897.

[2] *Ibid.*, pp. 3, 4.

[3] After the establishment of the Bank of England in 1694, the Houblons kept their banking accounts there.

[4] The banking house of Child dates back to 1559, while those of Gosling and Hoare in Fleet Street existed respectively in 1620 and 1677.

a mortification (if he felt it) grimly avenged by the wily
monarch in 1672!

Although during the lifetime of old Mr. Houblon, his
sons had continued to act in concert in most of their
commercial undertakings, we find that after his death
two among them came much more prominently forward
than the others, both in the management of their
common adventures and in municipal life. For instance,
while no less than seven of the name appear on the
lists of Spanish and Portuguese merchants, James, and
John, Houblon were foremost among these as Chairmen
of their respective Companies; while their names also
figure prominently upon a variety of other documents of
all kinds. Before proceeding to relate what there is to
tell of the life and work of these two, a slight sketch of
what concerns the other members may perhaps not be
considered uninteresting.

The two sisters of this large family married in extreme
youth before the death of their mother; and both their
husbands were descended from Flemish refugees. Anne's
first husband was Jacques Jurin or Jorion. This marriage, as was customary at the time, appears to have been
arranged by the respective parents. Isaac Jurin was
a close friend of Mr. James Houblon throughout his life,
and acted as one of his executors at his death; the husband of Anne was probably his brother. He died after
but few years' married life, and left his wife with one
daughter named Esther; and Anne married again in 1653
an English merchant named Milner Tempest, a member
of the Drapers' Company, and afterwards Alderman of
London. This was a happy and prosperous marriage,
and the couple had numerous children.

Sara Houblon married in 1645. Her husband, James
Lordell, was a London merchant of large fortune. He
and his brother John were constantly associated with his
brothers-in-law in all their commercial transactions, and

later in the directorate of the Bank of England ; they were also, like the Houblons, Spanish and Portuguese merchants. The Lordells were armigeri, of good Flemish stock, their grandfather having fled from Flanders during the Alva persecutions.[1] We have been unable to trace descendants of either of these Flemish families beyond the second generation from their alliance with the Houblons.

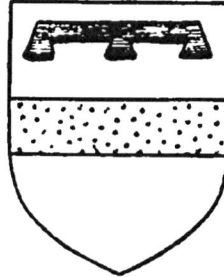

ARMS OF LORDELL.

The eldest of the Houblon brothers, Peter, a member of the Cordwainers Company, was at one time foreman of the inquest of the ward; the company's mace still bears his name. It was purchased in the year 1669 by the inquest, and is engraved with an inscription to that effect, followed by the names of 'Peeter Houblon, fforeman,' and others. The new mace was doubtless made in order to be used on the occasion of the formal opening of the Royal Exchange, which took place with every circumstance of pomp and ceremony in September 1669, when the mace was probably carried in the procession of the companies by 'Peeter Houblon, fforeman,' himself.[2]

1669

Of the newly built Royal Exchange, reopened to the merchants on this occasion, an interesting picture by Marlowe is in the Bank of England. After the three years which had passed since the Fire, during which time they had received hospitality at Gresham College as a temporary Exchange, the merchants must have hailed with joy the inauguration of the noble building of Wren which now replaced the old Burse of Elizabeth, destroyed in 1666. Peter, Houblon was some years

---

[1] Their arms were registered at Heralds' College at the visitation of London, 1687. College of Arms, K.G. A certificate from De Launay, Brabant King of Arms, of 22 September 1694, gives the arms of Lordell. The label in the English coat is said to distinguish it from the foreign.
[2] Exhibited in 1860 before the Society of Antiquaries.

older than his brothers. He married, at an early age, Elizabeth, daughter of Courtois Dingley, a merchant of London, and until his father's retirement to the country, —when he removed to the family home in Bearbinder Lane,—Peter lived in the parish of St. Antholin, in the registers of whose church numerous entries relating to himself and his family are to be found. After the fire he was still residing in the same place, which was called Dodson's Court, so it is to be supposed that he rebuilt his house. His son, also named Peter₅, served for many years in the City militia and eventually commanded his regiment; his name being submitted by the City

1690 Lieutenancy for the post of colonel in 1690, which appointment was approved by Queen Mary in July that year.[1] We come across the name of the elder

1683 Peter₄ incidentally in 1683, the year of the Rye House Plot and its attendant troubles. Among the papers in the British Museum relating to the mysterious death of the Earl of Essex, which caused so great a stir at the time, is a pamphlet by Laurence Braddon in which an account is given of the evidence of various witnesses who were examined under oath in reference to the supposed murder. We find that ' Mr. Peter Houblond (merchant)[2] and his wife both sweare that about ten of the clock that very morning my Lord dy'd, they heard it reported nigh Tunbridge Welles that the Earl of Essex had cut his throat in the Tower; which report was imediately contradicted and hushed up untill nigh twelve of the clock. But as soon as chappell was ended the same was received again and so continued.'[3] This evidence clearly shows that the effort to hush up the affair was wholly unsuccessful.

Peter₄ died in 1691 at the age of sixty-four, and was

---

[1] See letter from the Earl of Nottingham to the Lieutenancy of London, 21 July 1690. Whitehall, H. O. Letter Book (Secretary's), 11, 143.
[2] This word occurs in another copy of the pamphlet.
[3] Harl. MSS. 1221 f. 299.

buried at Wimbledon in Surrey, where he had his country house; his death was probably sudden, as he left no will. As old Mr. Houblon's eldest son, he inherited his father's personal effects, which we find his own son 'Colonel' Peter, bequeathing, in 1712, to his uncles Abraham and John. To the former he left the 'ffamily pictures,' including the portrait of his Flemish ancestor, and to the latter 'my blew ring which belonged to Mr. James Houblon, my grandfather. Peter, who never married, appointed his cousin Esther Jurin, spinster (the daughter of his aunt Anne by her first marriage), his residuary legatee. As he had two sisters to whom he bequeathed but £10 apiece, he was either very indifferent to them or very much attached to his earliest friend and playmate, now upwards of sixty years old.

We find that on several occasions his relations advanced money to Peter, and that when he died he was still in their debt. His debts to his family were probably cancelled, but it appears that others were only in part satisfied at the time of his death. Nearly forty years after it occurred, an advertisement appeared in the *London Gazette* to the effect that any creditors and legatees of the late Mr. Peter Houblon, merchant, whose claims on his estate were still partly unsatisfied, would be paid in full by the advertiser on application.[1]

Isaac was another of the five brothers who were merchants. Pepys called him 'the handsome man,' and implied that by his 'pretty dress' he was aware of the fact. Although Isaac had his place of business at his brother's house in Winchester Street, he lived elsewhere; in Samuel Pepys's relation of his experiences during the raging of the Great Fire when all was confusion and dismay, he mentions how, walking through the City after his interview with the King,

---

[1] *London Gazette*, 11 August 1747. The advertisement was inserted by the solicitors of Jacob Houblon, Esq., of Hallingbury.

'Here I saw Mr. Isaac Houblon, the handsome man, prettily drest and dirty at his door at Dowgate, receiving some of his brothers' things whose houses were on fire, and as he says have been removed twice already, and he doubts, as it soon proved, that they must be in a little time removed from his house also, which was a sad consideration.'[1]

Isaac's good looks or good humour later procured him a happy and prosperous alliance. His wife Elizabeth was the grand-daughter of Henry King, Bishop of Chichester, who was himself the son of John King, Bishop of London. Her father, Henry King, was one of the gentlemen of the Privy Chamber to Charles II. The inscription on his monument in Chichester Cathedral describes the King family as very ancient, dating from Saxon times.[2]

All the sons of Mr. James Houblon were closely united in their mutual interests and affection, but while James and John were more especially so as regards each other, the same was the case in respect of their younger brothers Isaac and Abraham. And now we find that the family connection formed by Isaac brought about another marriage, for within little more than a year of the wedding of Isaac, Abraham was married to Dorothy[2] Hubert, the cousin of his wife; the one being the grand-daughter of the Bishop of Chichester, and the other his niece.

The Bishop's sister, Dorothy[1] King, had been married to Sir Richard Hubert, knight, of Langley in Bucks, early in the seventeenth century, and it was at the house of his brother-in-law, and his sister Dorothy, 1642 that Dr. King found a refuge, when he was driven from his Bishopric in 1642 after the siege of Chichester

[1] Pepys's *Diary*, 2 September 1666.
[2] The arms of the King family are sable, a lion rampant crowned between three cross crosslets or. See Dallaway's *West Sussex*, vol. i. See also monuments in Langley Church and Chichester Cathedral.

by Sir William Waller and the parliamentary forces. The siege was carried on with the greater animus that the Bishop was supposed to have at one time sympathised with the views of the puritan party. Owing to this circumstance he was made the object of a violent personal attack by the soldiers, who, not content with the desecration of the cathedral, directed their energies towards wrecking the episcopal palace, destroying the Bishop's private property, and even to the 'barbarous illtreatment of his person.' He was,

ARMS OF KING.

however, subsequently allowed his liberty, and as a special act of clemency permitted to retire to Langley, where he remained till the Restoration enabled him to return to his See.[1] Sir Richard Hubert had held the post of Groom-porter to King Charles I., and, after the Restoration, filled the same position in the service of Charles II. His wife, Dorothy King, died the 17th of November 1658, leaving a daughter Dorothy[2] and two sons; and these children were brought up at Langley, which place the King family made their home during the years of parliamentary government and the Commonwealth.

Elizabeth King, the grand-daughter of the Bishop of Chichester, and afterwards his heir, was married to Isaac Houblon in the year 1670, and the marriage of Dorothy Hubert with Abraham took place early in 1672; both weddings were celebrated in Westminster Abbey.[3] The Langley property devolved upon Dorothy, Abraham Houblon's wife, after the death of her father, Sir Richard in 1679 (his sons having predeceased him);[3] and she

---

[1] See Dallaway, *West Sussex*. (Chichester Cathedral.)
[2] Harleian Society's Publications, vol. x., *Westminster Abbey Registers*.
[3] One of them, Richard Hubert, was a Gentleman of the Privy Chamber to Charles II. He left one child Dorothy. The arms of Hubert are: Arg. quarterly, Arg. and Sab. Over all a bend Gu., 3 Lionals Or. See many monuments in Langley church, etc.

1703   and her husband lived there till 1703, when she died and,—the registers inform us,—was buried 'in a velvett coffin.' Mr. Houblon lived on at Langley till
1722   his death in 1722. A son and a daughter were the issue of this marriage, viz. Richard, afterwards Sir Richard Houblon, knight; and Anne, married to Henry Temple, first Viscount Palmerston.

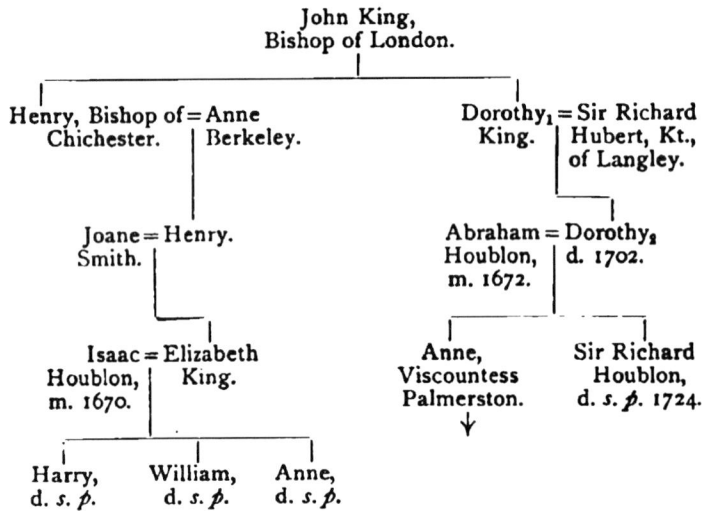

John King,
Bishop of London.

Henry, Bishop of = Anne   Dorothy₁ = Sir Richard
Chichester.   Berkeley.   King.   Hubert, Kt.,
                                           of Langley.

Joane = Henry.   Abraham = Dorothy₂
Smith.   Houblon, d. 1702.
                                  m. 1672.

Isaac = Elizabeth   Anne,   Sir Richard
Houblon, King.   Viscountess   Houblon,
m. 1670.   Palmerston.   d. s. p. 1724.
                                     ↓

Harry,   William,   Anne,
d. s. p.   d. s. p.   d. s. p.

Isaac Houblon's wife survived him many years. They had two sons: Henry (usually called Harry) and William, the latter of whom married and died *s. p.*, and a daughter Anne. Harry Houblon[1] made his sister Anne his heir, with the proviso that after her decease, his cousin Sir Richard, the son of his uncle Abraham and Dorothy₂ Hubert, should succeed to certain property left him by his father. This was Hormead Hall in Hertfordshire, in which estate Abraham had also

ARMS OF HUBERT.

possessed a share. It appears from Isaac's will that Hormead and the manor of Broughing, also in Herts,

[1] He was High Sheriff of Herts in 1707.

were bequeathed to the two brothers jointly by a
very dear friend, Mr. William Delawood.[1] On bestow-
ing Hormead on his son Harry, his father requested
that it might for ever remain in the possession of the
Houblons and their descendants, 'for the sake of the
great love the donor had borne to himself and his
brother.' Broughing subsequently found its way into
the hands of Sir James Houblon, who bestowed it on
his daughter Elizabeth on her marriage with John
Harvey of Norfolk, Esq., in the possession of whose
descendants it long remained.[2] Hormead was for many
years the residence of Sir Richard Houblon ; the old
manor-house is in good preservation still, the brick
chimney-stacks alone being worthy of attention. In the
parlour, wainscoted with oak, the arms of Delawood
appear over the mantelpiece ; those of Houblon, carved
on a shield of oak, are in the church ; the property
still remains in the possession of the head of the Houblon
family.[3]

After their father's death Isaac Houblon, alone of all
the brothers, traded in the East, while still carrying on
the Portuguese and Mediterranean commerce in which
all were engaged. In 1694-5 we find his name included
among the twenty-four members of the new board of
direction of the East India Company. By its first charter,
dating from the dawn of the seventeenth century, this
company enjoyed the exclusive privilege of trade with
the East Indies. By the magnitude of its scope and
the brilliancy of its achievements it eclipsed all other
companies, while its great privileges excited the envy of
the free lances among the English merchants, who found
themselves shut out from the most lucrative portion of

1695

---

[1] A London merchant. See J. E. Cussan, *History of Herts.*
[2] *Ibid.*
[3] There was an ancient privilege attached to the lordship of Hormead,
by virtue of which its Lord claimed the post of Chamberlain to the Queen.
(College of Arms.)

the world's trade and commerce; so jealously did the company, by privilege of their charter, exclude all adventurers of private enterprise from the field of their operations in the East. The old East India Company was originally inaugurated by a few vigorous business men; the ostensible object of its formation being the solving of the vexed question of a route to the East not already monopolised by the then chief trading nations, Spain, Portugal, and the Netherlands; and the company was founded upon the strictest business principles. When the dream of the north-west passage faded away in failure and disappointment, on the return of the first expedition a fresh one was immediately organised and despatched by way of the Cape, on the more fruitful errand of trade and commerce; a beginning which inaugurated a career of splendid success for the company. So exclusive was the court of directors, that not only was no Flemish or Dutch name to be found on the list of the first members of the company, but we are told that 'they refused to imploy anie *gent*,' and requested 'leave to sort ther business wth men of ther owne quality.'[1] This refusal was in response to an urgent appeal by one high in authority on behalf of a young gentleman of family, who was desirous of being allowed to accompany the first expedition as factor on board one of the vessels of the fleet.[2] The management of the company, being on joint stock principles, admitted of no private trading of any kind; bills of adventure being allotted to the merchants and factors for the mutual benefit of all. In course of time a rival East India Company was started by Merchant Adventurers of London, which obtained a charter and privileges from King Charles II. But so great were the power and influence of Sir Josiah Child (the chairman of the old company) in the East itself, that

---

[1] *Dawn of British Trade to the East Indies*, Introduction, xiii.
[2] *Ibid.*

it was able for long to defy all interference from the new; a bitter war was, however, waged between the rivals, much to the detriment of both. At length, after the strongest pressure had been brought to bear upon the original directors, a compromise was effected, the new company being in part absorbed by the old, after which a fresh charter of William and Mary confirmed its ancient privileges. For the obtaining of this charter, it was said that an immense bribe was offered and accepted by those through whose influence the charter was finally granted; by this means, the privileges of 'John Company' were prolonged till the middle of the nineteenth century. Upon the board of directors newly appointed on the granting of the charter of William and Mary, Isaac Houblon had a seat, and there is evidence of the sympathies of the Houblon family having been strongly in favour of the amalgamation of the two companies. Among the names on the board are Sir Thomas Cooke, Governor, Francis Tyssen, Deputy-governor, George, Earl of Berkeley, Sir John Fleet (Lord Mayor), Sir Josiah Child, Sir John Moore, and fifteen others, including Mr. Isaac Houblon.[1]

Isaac Houblon left considerable property at his death 1700 in 1700 (a few months before that of his brother Sir James), his wife's own ample fortune enabling him to bestow it directly upon his sons, subject however to a long list of charitable bequests, among which the hospitals of Bethlehem,[2] St. Bartholomew, Christ Church, and St. Thomas each received £100, while the French Church and its poor were left £300.[3] Isaac was buried under the chancel of Great Hormead church, where there is a monument to his memory; his wife, Elizabeth King, subsequently made her home in London, where she

[1] For the terms of the charter see Lord Somers's *Tracts*. Second Edition by Sir W. Scott, x. 629, 31.
[2] *New View of London*, ii. 732.
[3] See Will.

lived in great comfort and even luxury.   In her will
she bestowed handsome legacies on numerous members
of her husband's family, while old and faithful servants,
both male and female, were substantially rewarded for
their services.

Abraham Houblon was his father's eighth son and was
a Portuguese merchant, but he was also a member of
the Rotterdam Company.   Board of Trade papers show
him at one time to have taken an active part, together
with 'divers merchants and owners of ships trading to
Rotterdam,' in the presentation of a petition to the Lords
Justices of England in council, against the English
consul of that place.[1]   This is not the only occasion on
which we have found a British consul the object of
bitter complaint from the merchants, the position of
this official, rendering it extremely important that he
should be both efficient and zealous in forwarding the
commercial interests of his fellow-countrymen ; for, then
as now, a lack of these qualities in a consul seriously
handicapped the merchants in their business.   On the
founding of the Bank of England in 1694 Abraham was
one of the four Houblon brothers who were elected by
ballot on the board of its direction.   He was destined
at a later date to take an active part in its management.

[1] Board of Trade.   Trade Papers, vol. 20, part ii. pp. 21-33, 1696-98.

CHAPTER XIII

THE FELLOW OF PETERHOUSE, CAMBRIDGE

'You are now become a Searcher after Truth. . . . Let your Example confirm your doctrine; and let no man ever have it in his Power to reproach you with practising contrary to what you preach.'—Lord Lansdowne to his Nephew, *Works*, 1732.

IT will now be necessary to go back some distance of time in the history of James Houblon's sons in order to give an account of that one of them, the lines of whose life lay in different places from those of his brothers. Of all James and Mary's many sons, Jacob alone is, so far as we know, represented by male descendants at the present time; none of the other branches of the family survived the third generation in the male line. It is said that the issue of an unusually numerous offspring are seldom equally prolific in succeeding generations. In spite of the fact mentioned by Bishop Burnet in his sermon preached on the occasion of Mr. James Houblon's funeral, that 'a full hundred came into the world descended from him, and that at the time of his death sixty-seven were yet alive,' many of his grandsons died unmarried, and others without any male offspring; so that it came to pass in course of time, that in the grandson of his fifth son, Jacob, 'the sole heir male of his race' remained.[1]

Jacob$_1$ was born in London on the 22nd of December 1634, and was baptized in the French church in Threadneedle Street on the 1st of January following. We find

---

[1] Jacob, only son of Charles Houblon, born in 1710.

that his parents chose for his sponsors 'Madame Ester Honiewood, femme de Sir Thomas Honiewood, Chevalier,' and Jacob de la Forterie ; from the latter of whom he took his Christian name.[1]   Lady Honywood was the daughter of Mr. Jean de Lamotte, Mr. Houblon's uncle.

While all his sons were trained to their father's profession almost as a matter of course, Jacob alone turned his mind in another direction.   The injunctions of Laud respecting the catechising of the children of the refugees ultimately resulted in the merging into the English Church of many of those so taught.   During those years of King Charles's reign when the injunctions were enforced, James Houblon's young sons were of an age when impressions made upon the mind are deepest; and in spite of his father's roundhead and puritan predilections, it is probable that the character and opinions of young Jacob had already taken their *pli* before the commencement of the civil wars.   It was no doubt owing to the revival of ecclesiastical discipline and observance under Archbishop Laud, and to the training then given to the young, that the re-establishment of the Church and episcopate at the Restoration was possible in England.

From his early youth it would appear that Jacob₁ was destined for the Church.   The prospects of English churchmen received a rude blow with the death of the King and the establishment of the Commonwealth, but nevertheless no change was made by Mr. Houblon in his plans for his son's education.   One year only after the execution of King Charles, Jacob was sent to Oxford University.   He matriculated at Pembroke College on 1650   the 27th of November 1650 at the age of sixteen, and took his B.A. degree in March 1652/3.[2]   It was not uncommon in those days for students of one University to be subsequently 'incorporated' into the other, and

[1] See Threadneedle Street Church registers, also the Table of family alliances.
[2] Joseph Foster, M.A., *Alumni Oxonienses*, vol. ii.   Early Series, p. 751.

this seems to have been the case with Jacob Houblon. After being five years at Oxford he was transferred to Peterhouse, Cambridge, and at the same time took his degree as M.A., and was elected to a Fellowship at that College. He was, however, re-'incorporated' at Oxford the same year.[1] Only after the Restoration did he take Orders, nor would it have been possible for him to do this before, while holding the views in which he had been trained; for although the sects were allowed to worship in what way they pleased during the Commonwealth and Protectorate, the use of the book of Common Prayer of the Church of England was forbidden even in private.[2]

1657

Lord Clarendon gives an interesting account of the visitation by order of Parliament of the University of Cambridge in 1647, and the almost unanimous refusal of the Governors and Masters of Colleges and Fellows to conform to the Covenant, the then 'standard of all men's learning and ability to govern,' as he sarcastically calls it. In consequence of this refusal they were expelled from their places, and Presbyterians placed in their 'rooms in the government of the several halls and colleges.'[3] In spite of the origin and training of the new Masters of colleges, etc., it is recorded that the 'splendid tradition of learning and allegiance' for which the University was distinguished, instead of being 'extirpated of all that learning, religion, and loyalty which had so eminently flourished there, after several tyrannical governments mutually succeeding each other, . . . finally yielded a harvest of extraordinary good and sound knowledge in all parts of learning,' and acquired that 'inclination to duty and obedience they had *never been taught.*' So that at the Restoration the University

[1] Joseph Foster, M.A., *Alumni Oxonienses*, vol. ii. Early Series, p. 751. A mistake in identity occurs in the biographical notice following these particulars between Jacob and his brother James.
[2] Wakeman, *History of the Church of England*, p. 378.
[3] Lord Clarendon, *History of the Rebellion*, III. x. 115-116.

Jacob Houblon, one of the lads who came under the notice of the learned Doctor, was of studious habits, presenting a strong contrast to his brothers; for while the ecclesiastical influences exercised upon their child-hood left but slight impression upon them, Jacob's more susceptible temperament was deeply and indelibly permeated by them. His University career and trans-ference from one University to the other, as well as the interest which resulted in his presentation to a Fellow-ship, were thus probably due to the intervention of this friend, of whose only surviving child he was many years later to become the husband.

Dr. Whincop appears to have spent the interim of parliamentary government and Protectorate at Elsworth, his house near Cambridge, and during this time his pulpits would have been 'occupied' by presbyterian divines; nor would he have been permitted to retain his livings by the Commission of Ejectors appointed by Oliver, who summarily turned out of their cures those of the episcopalian clergy whom they considered as unfit to fill them. At the Restoration, the doctor would have been restored to his rectorates had he not died before that event; both his churches were after-wards destroyed in the Great Fire. By his will, made 1654 in the year 1654, his daughter Elizabeth eventually became sole heir to property of some importance.[1] Amongst other legacies Dr. Whincop bequeathed £30 to Trinity College, Cambridge, besides a sum of money for the purpose of purchasing it a piece of plate.

[1] A contemporary pedigree on vellum is at Hallingbury, showing the descent of Elizabeth's mother. She was the daughter of John Pellet, Esq. (son of Sir Benjamin, Kt.), and Anne, daughter of Thomas West, Lord de la Warr, who, through the Knowles and Carys, was descended from Mary, daughter of Sir Thomas Bullen, Earl of Ormond, the sister of Anne Boleyn. A small book, enclosed in a pocket or satchel of beautiful workmanship, was cherished by several generations of Whincops. The interior (containing many memoranda of family interest) was apparently renewed early in the seventeenth century, for both book and satchel are older.

SATCHEL AND BOOK BELONGING TO WHINCOP FAMILY.

Jacob₁ Houblon from his early youth had thus withdrawn himself from the City, and the excitement and anxiety from which the exercise of commerce has always been inseparable. Where a whole race had followed a particular calling, as the Houblons had now done for five generations, a member of it who chose to retire from all the associations of his family, in order to devote himself to so opposite a career, must have had widely different tastes from those of his ancestors. Those of Jacob were in fact mainly contemplative and scholastic, not unmixed probably with that narrowness and illogical reasoning which the great John Locke observed as often characteristic of the theological mind.[1] But that he became a man of some literary attainment, the result of hard work during his college career, is certain from the evidence of manuscript notes and references which he left behind him, which betray a wide range of reading and study, both of the works of the Fathers of the Church, and of classic authors, Latin, Greek, and Hebrew. He also was acquainted with Italian, and was a lover of Petrarch.

The loyalty of the Masters and Fellows of Peterhouse had led them, during the civil wars, to sacrifice the valuable collection of plate belonging to the College to the royal cause; but a few years after the sacrifice, much plate was presented to the College by the Fellows and others in order to replace this loss. The following entry, in an old MS. volume at the College, enumerates, ' Item a tankerd Poculum ex dono Jacobi Houbelon. Soc. D. Perne[2] oz 26½ - 04ᵈ - 00ᵍ.' Jacob's gift is again frequently referred to in the volume above mentioned, and on one occasion, when the periodical checking of the inventory was taking place, it was not forthcoming, as it was 'sayd to be now lockt up in Sʳ.

---

[1] See *The Human Understanding.*
[2] The name of his Fellowship.

steward's study, who is at prisent in the country.' But the old 'piece' was destined to make way for changing taste and requirements.   In the year 1709 it is stated that a large quantity of plate was 'taken out of ye Treasury in order to be changed'; 'Twelve pottingers' now replacing the old 'Plates.'   Of these 'number one' was engraved on the one side with the College arms, and on the other with those (together with the name) of 'Jacob Houbelon.'   The pottingers in their turn disappeared.

Peterhouse was beautifully restored some years ago by Mr. Bodley, and so much remains of what is old and venerable, that we can imagine pretty vividly the surroundings in which Jacob Houblon spent his early manhood.   In those days college life was both simpler and more monastic, the relations between the 'scholars' and the Master and Fellows having been gradually altered during the lapse of years; for the Master—once regarded as the father living in the midst of his community—was ultimately succeeded by the pretentious and pompous Don of the eighteenth century, who by effectually destroying all traces of the earlier social conditions, raised a gulf between himself and the collegiate life which has never since been bridged over.

The turret staircase still exists by which the Master of Peterhouse, in Jacob's day still resident in the College buildings, reached his chamber from the 'stone parlour' below on the one side, and the great dining-hall on the other.   The hall, the oldest portion of the College, is now hung with numerous portraits of its benefactors, which in former days adorned the stone parlour since wainscoted with oak.   This range of buildings faces the south, upon which side lies the sunny Fellows' garden, where, together with the rest of the college Fellows, Jacob Houblon went in and out, or paced, book in hand, under the shady trees.   The 'worthiest library in England,'[1] whose picturesque oriel still faces the street, supplied him with the means of study; and here, as was then the custom in all such libraries, those books which were regarded as valuable or rare were chained to the fixed desks below the shelves upon which they were ranged, and could be perused only in the library itself; other volumes less precious might be taken away by the Fellows to be studied at their leisure in their chambers.[2]

Thus Jacob Houblon's life did in truth present a strong contrast in its quiet and monotony of study to that of his father and brothers in the distant City throbbing with the stir and stress of work, and of the coming and going of men.   May we not imagine Mr. Houblon, senior, now advanced in years, visiting the one son who had chosen this retreat, and while gazing wistfully on the calm and peace around him, forming the resolution, many years later carried into effect, of himself retiring to pass the evening of his days at a distance from the busy scenes in which his life had been passed?

After he had been some years at Cambridge, Jacob drew up what he called 'the true copy of the time of my father his marriage, with yᵉ ages of all his children.' The document is dated the 21st of February 1658, and included memoranda of such events as had occurred in the family history to that time.   These entries were made in Jacob's own handwriting, but long afterwards another hand than his, added the single word 'dead' against the names of no less than nine of the children of James, including that of Jacob himself.   Besides these notes, which consisted merely of names and dates, he collected and wrote a memoir of his family, a docu-

1658

---

[1] The library at Peterhouse was erected in 1431.   Fuller's *History of Cambridge*, p. 217.
[2] *Ibid.*   The former books came under the category of the 'inner library,' as it was called, while the latter belonged to the 'outer' or working portion of the collection.

ment for which we have searched in vain.   Not only
is this manuscript mentioned by a certain William
Holman, who was employed by a son of its author to
draw up a pedigree of the Houblon family, but we find,
by a letter preserved among the Sloane correspondence
in the British Museum, that the 'Narrative of Mr.
Houblon' had excited the curiosity of the well-known
Dr. Sloane, who expressed to Dr. Woodward of Gresham
College his desire to read it.   Having borrowed the
MS., Woodward, on sending it to Sloane on the 20th of
February 1713, apologised for not having sent it before,
and wrote: 'Here is Mr. Houblon's Narrative.   You
had had it according to my promise sooner, but 'twas
mislaid, and not found till now.'   After remarking that
'a thing of this sort' was not of public interest, he adds:
'When you have read it, be pleased to send it me back.'
The MS. was neither returned into the hands of its owner,
nor did it remain amongst the Sloane papers.   It was
probably sent back by Sloane to Dr. Woodward, and
subsequently again mislaid or lost.   It cannot but
be a matter of regret that a document which probably
contained much of supreme interest to the Houblon
family should have been lost.   Family history in those
days was in truth considered of no general interest,
nor worthy of 'public discourse';[1] but the fact remains
that the narrative was considered interesting by such
men as Sloane and Woodward.[2]

The Restoration brought about great changes in the
University of Cambridge, and the old traditions and
ritual of Peterhouse were once more restored.   Jacob
Houblon was now ordained; but he kept his Fellowship
at Peterhouse till his marriage in 1662.   It was doubtless

1662

[1] See letter.   British Museum.

[2] Another pedigree exists bearing the date 1674, and purporting to be a
complete scheme of the descendants of Mr. James Houblon at the time it
was made.   It is, however, incomplete, and in some instances incorrect.
It is drawn out on a large skin of parchment, and above the family tree, are
shields of arms.

ELIZABETH WHINCOP.
m. JACOB HOUBLON (CLERK).

by such young churchmen as he, trained and nurtured according to the traditions which had flourished at the Universities in spite of presbyterian influences, that many of the vacant incumbencies were filled at the Restoration. Of these a large number were vacated by presbyterian ministers, who, refusing to submit to the Act of Uniformity and receive ordination as priests of the Church of England, were ejected from the livings they had occupied during the Commonwealth and Protectorate.[1]

Three months after his marriage, Jacob was instituted to the rectory of Moreton in Essex. His wedding took place in London by special licence,[2] the bride and her mother having apparently come from Cambridge for the ceremony. A miniature of Elizabeth Whincop represents her as dark, with large brown eyes, and a serious oval countenance; her hair (under a little black velvet cap) arranged in tendrils or curls on the neck, a fashion which possibly may have been considered

ARMS OF WHINCOP.

antiquated in the early days of the Restoration, but which suited well the gentle face and slender throat. Elizabeth was twenty at the time of her marriage, and Jacob—who is described as of St. Mary Woolchurch, London, clerk, showing him to have been living at the time under his father's roof—was twenty-eight. It was some two years after his marriage, that Jacob's miniature was painted by Samuel Cooper, who was now at the height of his fame.[3] While the portrait which he painted of Mr. Houblon in his old age was,

---

[1] 'It is thought,' wrote Mr. Pepys, 'it will make wild work amongst the presbyterian ministers.' *Diary*, 31 May 1662.

[2] London Marriage Licences, 1521-1869.

[3] Pepys says that these 'pictures in little' cost £30. *Diary*, 2 January 1661.

like much of Cooper's work, left unfinished, and has somewhat faded, the miniature of his son is a beautiful and highly finished specimen of the artist's work, and is signed, and dated 1664. He is represented in his academical gown and lace bands, and with his own brown hair, long and curled according to the fashion of the time, the disfiguring periwig of some years later not having yet been adopted. Keen dark eyes, a long nose, and full lips, were the characteristic features of an interesting face, but with some traces, in the expression, of restlessness and discontent. `

1664

Jacob's life henceforth was passed in the quiet country village in which his lot was cast, where he devoted himself assiduously to his duties as its pastor. Meanwhile the young ones of his own family grew up around him, claiming the care and attention formerly lavished upon books and study, and though (as is shown by notes and MSS.) he continued to bestow time upon both, and collected a considerable library, he was content henceforward to live with and for his people.

Throughout his career Jacob Houblon appears as an orthodox 'high churchman,' according to the teaching of Laud, and the writings of Andrewes, Hooker, and Jeremy Taylor; but by the latitudinarian doctrines held by a section of English thinking men,—the successors of Lord Falkland and his friends at Great Tew,[1]—he seems to have been but little influenced, though it is apparent by his notes and references, that his reading and study extended into the sphere of their thought and speculations. The Church revival of the days of Queen Anne he did not see, for he died four years before her accession to the throne; but his beginnings of work as a parish priest must have demanded of him much energy, unselfishness, and tact, for he came to his parish bringing again the old forbidden

[1] Green, *Short History*, p. 591 ; ed. 1875.

ritual and sacraments, and with the discarded book of Common Prayer in his hand. Fifteen years had passed since, in the struggle with Charles I. and Archbishop Laud, the presbyterian party had imposed their authority upon the English Church and laid the hand of destruction upon all that was deemed superstitious in the churches. The new rector doubtless found at Moreton a neglected, ruinous edifice; in place of the old altar a bare table placed lengthwise in the nave, the ancient font broken or turned out of the church —a rude basin being used in its place;—unhung or injured bells, broken windows rudely patched, carved work mutilated, and probably the structure itself in a dangerous condition through want of repair![1]

In Thorne's *Environs of London*, he describes the 'pretty old church of Moreton embowered in trees.'[2] Its walls, he tells us, were formerly decorated with paintings, some traces of which could still be discerned through the white plaster with which it was the custom of the Puritans to blot out 'remnants of Popery.' If the church itself wanted all the care and expenditure its rector could bestow on it in its ruin and decay, the people presented no less perplexing a problem. With broken habits of worship, together with the unfamiliarity bred of long disuse, the difficulties presented by the book of Common Prayer (formerly familiar, but now strange and intricate to the illiterate, unaccustomed peasant of the little Essex village) must during the first years of Jacob's rectorate have taxed to the utmost his energy, his temper, and his strength. But our young parson would have been indeed unlike the race from which he had sprung, if he had been content to meet

[1] In April 1643 the Commons at Westminster had appointed a Committee to destroy painted glass and carved stone-work in London churches and streets as monuments of superstition. (Wakeman, *History of the Church*, p. 374).
[2] Thorne, *Environs of London*, i. 438-9. Murray, 1876.

these difficulties with apathy or discouragement. As the energy and *savoir faire* of his ancestors had overcome obstacles in the past, so now would tact and patience accomplish the work of reconstruction in the little realm of his parish.

Moreton, surrounded by the fat green pastures of the 'garden of England,' is scarcely changed since the lean, cassocked parish priest went in and out of its humble dwellings, and patiently taught the little children round his knee. The keen sensitive face of his earlier years betrayed a character which might have degenerated under the circumstances of monotony in which he passed the greater part of his life; but the sweet amenities of his good old father's influence and love doubtless kept tender the temper and character of the son. There is evidence to show that the young rector's chief energies were devoted to the teaching of the little ones of his flock; a duty in which old Mr. Houblon shared his enthusiasm, and to which he contributed liberally with his purse. For now began the first stirrings of the great movement in this direction, a movement born of an immense want, which was ultimately to find its culmination in the establishment of schools for the poor all over the country.

The reconstruction going on in the national Church throughout the country was not interrupted by the changes consequent upon the Revolution, though it affected the Church through the loss she sustained by the refusal of the Non-jurors to take the oath of allegiance demanded of them by the new sovereigns. To Jacob Houblon the test of the oath of allegiance to 1689 William and Mary, in 1689, hardly presented the conscientious difficulties that it did to some of the clergy. He had been trained in his youth in what would in later times have been called Whig principles; and although as a churchman he was now a Tory, in common with practically the whole body of the parochial clergy of the Restoration, we cannot conceive of a son of the 'Pater Bursae,' that in common with them he held the doctrines of 'indefeasible right,' nor yet that of the 'sinfulness of resistance.'[1] In his quiet rectory, far away from the busy scenes where his brothers and their Whig friends were now for the first time stepping to the forefront of the councils of their fellow-citizens, and assuming a political importance commensurate to the part the City had taken in bringing about the Revolution,—the rector of Moreton was doubtless deeply stirred in his mind. We can imagine his visit to London, and his conferences with the brothers who had hailed the Revolution with so much joy and hope. The long years apart would have made no difference in the mutual affection which was characteristic of James Houblon's sons; and we may conclude that their representations, together with the influence of his own early training and surroundings, resulted in the quieting of his conscience, and his acceptance of the oath of allegiance which proved so sore a stumbling-block to those of his brother-clergy who were henceforth known as the famous Non-jurors.

And so Jacob Houblon returned to his work and his home, and for another nine years laboured amongst his people; when, having given them the thirty-six best years of his life and of his health and strength as their friend and pastor, he died at Moreton on the 12th of December 1698, at the age of sixty-four, and was buried there, below the chancel of his church. 1698

[1] Mr. Lecky says that 'the immense majority (of the clergy) held the doctrine of the indefeasible title of hereditary royalty and of the sinfulness of all resistance to oppression, and they only took the oaths of the Revolutionary Government with much equivocation, and after long and painful misgiving' (*History of England*, i. 62).

[2] The parish registers of Moreton have been printed.

CHAPTER XIV

THE FRIEND OF PEPYS

‘A man that I love mightily.’—SAMUEL PEPYS : *Diary*.

OF the sons of Mr. Houblon, senior, James was the one possessed of the most qualifications for social success ; while we find that with regard to their profession, he was generally spokesman and actor in times of stress. Generous and hospitable, he welcomed his friends and acquaintance at his house in Winchester Street, where he lived in a comfort and luxury to which we find various references. When describing Broad Street Ward, Strype speaks of James's house in Winchester Street, as a ‘great messuage, formerly called the Spanish Ambassador's, and of late inhabited by Sir James Houblon, Knight and Alderman of London.’ The ground floor served as his place of business, his two younger brothers' business address being likewise given in the *Little Directory* of 1677 as at their brother's house. Of the ‘great messuage’ in Winchester Street there is a water-colour drawing in the Soane collection,[1] and from this it would seem to have been a fine and dignified mansion.

‘A pretty serious man,’ Pepys called James ; meaning that to his other qualities he added those of piety and good manners. This was in the early days of the Royal Society,[2] and James, though he was not himself a member, counted many of its most distinguished

---

[1] By J. H. Shepherd.   [2] It was incorporated in 1660.

SAMUEL PEPYS.
(GIVEN TO SIR JAMES HOUBLON, 1681.)

Fellows among his *habitués*; indeed, Mr. Pepys (afterwards President of the society) speaks of the number of 'ingenious men' he was accustomed to meet at the house in Winchester Street. During the earlier years of Mr. Pepys's acquaintance with him, its master was still young, full of life and *bonhomie*; and while possessing a large circle of acquaintance, was above all devoted to his brothers, forming one of the somewhat boyish troop of five, so frequently to be seen in each other's society.

Shortly before the outbreak of the plague had scattered all the guests, Pepys mentions in his *Diary* having dined in Winchester Street, 'at Mr. Houblon's, the merchant [till then a stranger to him], in company with Sir William Petty,[1] and abundance of most ingenious men, and with most excellent discourse.'

'After dinner,' he continues, 'Mr. Hill took me with Mrs. Houblon into another room, and there made her sing, which she do very well to my great content.'[2] Of James Houblon's wife Pepys speaks elsewhere as 'a fine gentlewoman,' while his musical soul appreciated her singing. Mr. Hill was likewise a great amateur of music, and the Houblons were his lifelong friends.[3]

James Houblon, while he could enjoy the society of his friends, and surround himself with all that the advancing science and requirements of the day permitted, was nevertheless a most painstaking and hard-working man of business. Genius has been said to consist in the infinite capacity for taking pains; if so, James Houblon deserved the appellation. He was laborious in making

---

[1] The eminent political economist and Fellow of the Royal Society.

[2] Pepys's *Diary*, 22 March 1665.

[3] Sarah Houblon was the daughter of Charles Wynne, and was married in 1658. Her portrait by Mrs. Beale represents her as a dark young woman with a profusion of wavy hair, and attired in the négligé style affected by the 'beauties' of Charles II.'s day, a mode of dress really more pictorial than real. The couple had two sons named Wynne and James. The arms of Wynne are Vert, three eagles displayed in fess or. See Le Neve's *Knights* for the arms of Sir James Houblon's wife, p. 440.

himself minutely acquainted with all details connected with his calling, especially with regard to shipping and navigation—on which matters the Government frequently sought the advice of the Royal Society. At a later date he was often requested, through the medium of the Secretary to the Admiralty, to draw up reports on various subjects on which it required information and data; and the drafts of some of these papers have been preserved among the Pepysian and other MSS. The connection between the merchant marine and the royal navy was a close one, while through the medium of the merchants, much 'foreign office' work was still carried on. We owe to Mr. Pepys's acquaintance with James$_2$ Houblon the younger the preservation of these documents, of considerable interest, partly on account of their intrinsic merit, and partly as bearing upon the character of the famous diarist, and the ingenuity with which he collected information, and absorbed the time and energies of his friends to the purposes he had in view.

ARMS OF WYNNE.

Besides the great mass of papers bequeathed by Mr. Pepys, together with his library, to Magdalene College, Cambridge, a large collection of Pepysiana has been preserved among the Rawlinson MSS. in the Bodleian Library at Oxford;[1] and these include, besides letters from his friends, many copies and drafts of letters penned by himself, mostly at a later date than the close of the *Diary*, the last page of which was written on 1669 the 31st of May 1669. The papers relating to James Houblon in this collection comprise letters to and from him to Mr. Pepys, and reports, bearing upon naval and mercantile matters, drawn up at different times at the

---

[1] Viz. fifty volumes of MSS.

SARA WYNNE.
m. SIR JAMES HOUBLON.

request of the Secretary of the Admiralty, during the tenure of his office and before it. Such documents of his as have been preserved, reveal the fact that James, Houblon was in the habit of rendering assistance to Mr. Pepys in his work at Trinity House and at the Admiralty; his indefatigable energy and experience in his own profession being frequently placed at the disposal of his friend, who appears to have assimilated his ideas, adopted his suggestions, and made use of his data and statistics, even to the laborious copying of them in his own hand before submitting them—in the words of James Houblon himself—for the consideration of 'those for whom you intend them.'[1] In connection with these papers, it must be borne in mind that the scope of Trinity House embraced not only much of that which related to the royal navy, but everything appertaining to the regulation of the merchant service, and trade and commerce in general.[2]

Pepys was made Clerk of the Acts of the Navy in 1659,   1659 through the influence of his patron and kinsman Lord Sandwich; and from this time forward, his zeal and ability were unceasingly devoted to the work which devolved upon him: at first, as is betrayed by his diaries, chiefly with the object of making money by his position; but as time went on, through the intense interest excited in his keen and intelligent mind in the whole scope of his work, together with an absorbing desire to improve and reform the organisation which he found. He appears to have inspired some of the other 'Principal Officers' with his enthusiasm, though his zeal was both annoying and inconvenient to others whose interests and gains were interfered with by his assiduity. As early as 1666 his services had been sufficiently recognised[3] as to bring about his election as a 'Younger

---

[1] See *Letter*.   [2] Stow, *Survey of London*, II. v. 288.
[3] Admiral the Duke of York called him the 'right hand of the Navy.'

Brother' of Trinity House, after which his work and interests were extended into the domain of commerce and trade, as well as of the royal navy. The ancient corporation of Trinity House had been established in the reign of Henry VIII., by whom it was given control over the dockyards and arsenals, and his newly-made building-yard at Deptford. To the corporation was also deputed the management of the arms, ammunition, and provisions required for the maintenance of the navy, as well as the control and superintendence of the merchant fleets, and the supply of materials necessary for their equipment. Their duties also included the granting of certificates to pilots, and the recommendation of ships' masters. Buoys, beacons, and lighthouses also came under the control of the Elder Brethren of the Guild, while the charitable side of their many functions included the care and succour of widows and orphans, the important duties of the suppression of piracy, and the redemption of captives from slavery.[1]

During the rule of Parliament and the Commonwealth, the work of Trinity House had been suppressed, and its functions discharged by the employés of the various committees of that period. It will be remembered that James$_1$ Houblon, senior, was in charge of warlike stores for the army during the Civil Wars, a trust which, but for its suppression, would otherwise have devolved upon the officials of Trinity House.

1672 'Late at night,' on the 14th of December 1672, Mr. Samuel Pepys wrote to James$_2$ Houblon, requesting him to be at Whitehall at one o'clock the following day to wait on the King. 'I am every houre lesse and lesse at ease about the safety of our ships for Spayne, and therefore doe wish you and some of our friends about you had been with the King to discourse it, who [the King] has appointed mee to attend them and you to

[1] See *Trinity House of Deptford Strond*, by C. R. B. Barrett, 1893

(Sir) James Houblon.

him at his riseing from table tomorrow, which wilbe about one aclocke or a little sooner.'[1]

After the passing of the Test Act and the resignation by the Duke of York of his offices,[2] Pepys came into close communication with the King in matters relating to the navy and commerce. As we have seen, Charles II. was very solicitous to encourage and support the trade of the country, and he was now anxious as to the effect which the late breaking of the Triple Alliance and his new war with the Dutch might have on commerce. For the City merchants were touched in their most vulnerable part when the rich trade with Spain and Portugal was endangered, as it now was, by de Ruyter and his hostile fleet ; the more so as the King was also finding to his chagrin, that he could look for neither help nor protection upon his coasts from his selfish ally, Louis XIV. of France. In the late naval engagement with the Dutch, while the English fleet bore the whole brunt of the battle, that of Louis, by his express order, stood aloof from the contest.

The wish of Charles to oblige the merchants is clearly demonstrated in the following letter, in which it appears that, at the request of the Secretary of the Admiralty, he went so far as to order one of his yachts to be at the disposal of James, Houblon for the conveyance of a sum of money to Dieppe. The Mr. Barr mentioned in the letter, or one of his name, had been agent there to the Houblon family for three or more generations. 'This serves only to notifye to you,' writes Mr. Pepys, 'that his Majesty (upon my motion since my seeing you in the morning), is pleased to appoint Captain Lovell in the Katherine yacht to your service,' whom 'I have directed to wait upon you and gett his yacht in readiness for you, against Tuesday. Whereof I leave to you the advertiseing Mr. Barr.'

[1] Pepysian Library MSS., ii. 399.   [2] The Duke was Lord High Admiral.

1674   In 1674 we find the Secretary of the Admiralty well embarked upon a work he set himself, viz., of hunting down and punishing the irregularities of certain captains of vessels — especially those commanding H. M. SS. *Reserve* and *Adventurer*—in foreign ports.   Letters to Mr. James₂ Houblon (or rather their copies) show Pepys to have requested him by desire of the Lords of the Admiralty to undertake the procuring of testimony by oath from St. Malo, Cadiz, and elsewhere, as to these reported misdemeanours.[1]   Indeed the anxiety and embarrassment caused to the Admiralty by the lack of information and absence of any organisation for receiving it, with reference to naval and commercial matters abroad, were frequently the subject of consultation between the secretary and the merchants, among whom James₂ Houblon was the former's friend and assistant.

    Some three months after his receipt of the letter relating to the men-of-war *Reserve* and *Adventurer*, Mr. Houblon wrote a paper on the subject of marine
1674 intelligence at the request of Mr. Pepys.   The MS., which is in the Rawlinson collection, is endorsed in the secretary's handwriting as follows: 'Mr. James Houblon to S. P. upon his proposal of having a course of universall marine Intelligence kept by the Secretary of the Admiralty.'   The paper presents a vivid picture of marine Europe at the time, from the point of view of an English merchant, and appears to us as the more interesting, from the fact that the suggestions made, obvious to any one in these days,—as to the advantage of the State, the development of commerce, and increasing dangers from piracy,—were then new.   For, until this period in our history, but little effort had as yet been made in the directions aimed at by Mr. Houblon's paper.   Students of the history of our navy and commercial marine have indeed traced to Mr. Pepys's term

[1] Pepysian Library, Rawlinson MSS., vol. v. p. 329, etc. etc.

of office at the Admiralty and Trinity House many measures which afterwards formed the foundations of important developments in naval matters, though it is to be doubted if many of the reforms suggested by Mr. James Houblon were carried out in his day. In the covering letter which accompanied the document, James apologises for 'its rough composition,' which he fears 'is without method or order, according to my usual way of writing.'[1]

The much-vexed question of the Newfoundland Fisheries was greatly exercising the minds of English merchants in 1675, when James Houblon was summoned before the Lords Committee of Trade and Plantations in order to advise with it as to the reasons for the decay of the industry, etc.[2] This board had been erected by Charles II. for the better encouragement of colonial enterprise and management,[3] but it does not appear to have shown much initiative on this occasion. A long letter addressed to Sir R. Southwell was the outcome of the order to James Houblon to attend the board, for he was unable to do so in person. It gives an interesting account of existing circumstances, and suggests remedies. Although this letter was read a second time at an adjourned meeting, and there was 'a great debate thereon,' the Lords finally 'did much incline to adhere to the old way'; so nothing was done.[4] Meanwhile the Dutch profited; and during these years were quietly capturing the larger part of the fishery trade from both French and English.[5] That they had already an organisation of intelligence on naval matters may be seen by another paper of Mr. James Houblon's, dated

1675

---

[1] Rawlinson MS. A. 185, fol. 93. The text of this document will be found in a note at the end of the chapter.
[2] Colonial Papers, vol. 34, no. 27.
[3] F. S. Thomas, *History of the Public Offices*, pp. 77-82.
[4] Colonial Papers, vol. 34, p. 197. 30 March 1675. Whitehall.
[5] Tract : Considerations upon the East India Trade. Anon. London, 1701.

1679 the 18th of October 1679. It contains a digest of a Dutch book which had been sent to him by Mr. Pepys to read, and upon which he desires the information which James's knowledge of the language would enable him to give. This book exhibits a close acquaintance with the vessels of the English fleet.[1]   Pepys arranged a meeting at Mr. Houblon's house the next day in order to discuss the Dutch 'Shipwright's Art,' but found him absent, though 'noe further' as James explains 'than with my brother at our usuall meeting which kept us longer than ordinary. He adds his 'Sonne Wynne had had a good chiding' for suffering Mr. Pepys to depart.[2]   The meeting mentioned here, took place daily between James and his brother John at the latter's house in Threadneedle Street.

In the same letter explaining his absence on this occasion, James Houblon speaks of the efforts now being made to discredit Mr. Secretary Pepys,—soon to be successful. 'I see the malice of the enemy increases,' he says, 'God forgive them for that vilanous paper published yesterday.   If they call the master Beelseebub they will not spare them of the household.' The prophecy was not long in its fulfilment; and Mr. Pepys shared the fate of his master, the Duke of York, and was deprived of his offices.   His imprisonment in the Tower, however, was not of long duration, the accusations brought against him being so trivial that they could not be substantiated.   James Houblon continued to render assistance to the officials of the Navy office during the period of Mr. Pepys's disgrace, an interregnum characterised by an inefficiency which roused the commercial world to indignation, so great was the neglect of the interests of commerce and trade.

1681   About this time Mr. Pepys, whose time was now at

[1] Rawlinson MS. A. 173, fol. 12. The Dutch caused an engraving—now in the Museum of Amsterdam—to be made of the stern of the *Royal Charles* captured in the Medway.
[2] *Ibid.*, 185, fol. 93.

his own disposal, made an excursion into the country, leaving his faithful friend and secretary, William Hewer, in charge of his goods and interests. A letter from Mr. Hewer (with whom Pepys now made his home), informing him how that during his absence he had minutely carried out certain instructions given him by Mr. Pepys, has been preserved. 'First,' he writes, 'as regards the severall things wrapped up in paper, I left them with your owne picture carefully done upp in a course cloath early this morning at Mr. Houblon's as from you; and two howers after, I sent him your letter, and afterwards acquainted him myselfe upon the 'Change[1] with your determination touching your retourne to town.'[2]   The enforced leisure of the heretofore busy Pepys had enabled him to contrive a minutiæ of proceeding for the accommodating Hewer, which shows with what importance the good man regarded the gift which he had prepared for his friend. For it was the fashion at this time for men to present each other with their portraits. An enormous number exist, painted during this period, many of them being very indifferent as works of art. In the portrait of Samuel Pepys, presented by him on this occasion, the diarist wears the usual huge periwig, and a brown velvet coat. In his will Pepys bequeathed to Sir James Houblon's two sons (Sir James having predeceased him) the pictures of their father, mother, and grandfather in his possession,[3] all of which, including Pepys's own portrait, are now at Hallingbury Place.

Soon after the exchange of portraits, Mr. Pepys's life was in considerable danger. In 1682 the Duke of   1682

[1] The Royal Exchange.
[2] See letter, Rawlinson MS., A. 29, 33.
[3] See Appendix to diary. Together with a large number of family portraits, this picture was found some years ago stacked in one of the turrets which flank the angles of the house at Hallingbury, witnessing by their neglect to the contempt felt by their descendants for the love of portraiture of their ancestors and their friends.

York found it expedient to retire to the north, and was accompanied in his travels by the late secretary. During a cruise off the east coast of Scotland the *Gloucester* (the vessel in which the Duke was embarked) was wrecked, though without loss of life. There was a great flutter of anxiety in the breasts of Pepys's many friends on hearing the news, though it was quickly allayed by a letter written from Edinburgh to Mr. Hewer wherein he bids him relieve the minds of his friends in Winchester Street and Portugal Row, as soon as he conveniently can 'concerning me.' Hewer, replying a few days later, assures him, 'You cannot imagine in what consternation all your friends in general were upon the report of your being cast away; but more especially at Crutched Fryars, Winchester St., and Portugal Row.'[1] Writing again from Newcastle, Pepys, touched by such evidence of kindness, sends them many messages of friendship, begging his friends meanwhile to 'stay their kind stomachs till that he may thank them, love them, long to see them, and having thus escaped will not despair of living to serve them.'

Some two years after his shipwreck, King Charles reappointed Mr. Pepys to his old place of secretary to the Admiralty, and he retained it till the Revolution. 1684 The year 1684 also witnessed his election to the post of President of the Royal Society, an appointment in itself suggestive of the high estimation in which Pepys was held by some of the best and most learned men of his time. Back at his old post of secretary, Pepys was once more active in all relating to the navy and commerce.

It happened that a great mortality among the seamen 1686 in the year 1686 impelled the Admiralty to institute inquiries into the treatment and condition of the sailors employed on the vast merchant fleets yearly sent out of

---

[1] 26 May 1682.

the country on long and dangerous voyages. During these investigations, a complaint was drawn up and lodged at Trinity House against the East India Company, with regard to the mortality amongst their men. This paper (which was the work of Sir M. Andrewes, a prominent Merchant Adventurer) exhibited considerable animus in its composition. We have seen how the great and powerful East India Company by its exclusive privileges excited the jealousy of the Adventurers, and it was perhaps for this reason that Mr. Pepys sent it to James Houblon for comment and counsel. In his reply Mr. Houblon suggests considerable alteration both in the matter and form of the document, and that all animadversions should be eliminated. With regard to the reasons for the 'said greate mortalities of seamen,' he believes them 'mostly to arise . . . for that the said E. I. C. have for some yeares past sent many of their ships from England to India at very unseasonable times, and so late that some of them have not arrived for ten months.'[1] From the annals of the Company itself, we find that the time of year in which the ships formerly sailed for India was in September.[2] Investigation into a still more serious allegation on which Mr. Houblon was asked to supply information, was as to the dispatch of unseaworthy ships to India. In response to this request, he laconically sends to Mr. Pepys the names of five merchantmen and their captains, who had lately 'all gone to the East Indies on condition that they never return.'[3]

An interesting fragment of a letter written by James Houblon about this time to Mr. Pepys comments on a 'Complaint' forwarded to Trinity House by his Majesty's consul at Lisbon touching on this same question of the welfare of English seamen. The consul

[1] Rawlinson MS. A. 171, fol. 228.
[2] *Dawn of British Trade to East Indies.*
[3] Rawlinson MS. A. 170, fol. 230, Nov. 1686.

begs for new powers that he may interpose between them and their commanders, thinking to remedy matters by his personal intervention. Mr. Houblon, however, shows conclusively that the consul's complaints are groundless, due to officiousness, and 'only noise,' while the remedies he proposes are merely 'to appeare to be an excellent officer and watchful in the King's service.' He then proceeds to give a clear and graphic account of 'the nature of the Ship Trade to Lisbon,' on which question nobody could speak with greater authority than himself, being, as he was, chairman of the Portugal merchants. It is unnecessary to enter into the particulars of his explanation, but suffice it to say that he shows the groundlessness of the consul's attack upon the merchants and their factors. In closing, he nevertheless laments the decay of discipline amongst the English seamen, and the many temptations to which they are subjected in port. To these he attributes the frequency of piracy and the 'running away' with merchant ships, 'of which more examples of this sorte wee have had within twenty years, than any old man can remember for forty years before that.'[1] With regard to the above, James and his brothers were ere long to become interested sufferers in a curious story about the carrying off of one of their vessels by her ship's company, and of her many subsequent adventures as a pirate.

The Houblon brothers certainly seem to have had the faculty of inspiring not only respect but affection in their private life, as also in their more public relations in connection with their profession; and we constantly find incidental proof of the high character they bore in the commercial world. A letter addressed to Mr. Pepys in 1687 by Sir Robert Robinson illustrates this fact. 'This comes to inquire about your health,' writes Mr. Pepys to James Houblon, 'and to tell you there is

[1] Rawlinson MS. A. 179, fol. 5.

this moment come to me an express from Sir Robert Robinson, Commander of his Maj^{ty}'s ships at Portsmouth, wherein . . . he advises me thus : Yesterday, viz. October 1, came in a small vessel from the Downes, loaden from Pharo, belonging to Mr. Jam: Houblon. The account the saylors give, is inclosed. I moored her last night at my stern with a hawser, and shall send her into ye harbour to secure her and stop her leaks, till care shall be taken about her, for no officer is aboard.' The sailors' account of the mishaps which had resulted in the disabling of the ship has not been preserved, but Sir Robert went on to assure Mr. Pepys that 'in respect of this vessel from Pharo with Faggs ' . . . 'he had had more than ordinary care of, in respect as, first belonging to his Majesty's subjects, and secondly as to *that family in particular*.' 'This misfortune, little as it is to you,' adds Mr. Pepys, 'I am heartily sorry for, and shall be glad any service of mine by aught that you would have me write to Sr Robt. Robinson, may conduce to ye rendering it less.'[1]

About this time the proceedings of the Dutch led to fears that peace might again be broken, a contingency which it appears would not have been displeasing to the Roman Catholics, whose intrigues were ever active in State matters at this time. James Houblon, in a postscript to a letter on business to Mr. Pepys, remarks : 'We hear from Dutchland such a Clutter of Arming both by sea and land that makes us poore merchants looke carefully at what may be the End of it. Glad wee are in the meane time to see heere a disposition for peace, and that wee shalbe happy in a profitable neutralitie, which wee traders think best for England! I wish the zelous R. Priesthood and Sword-men thought soe too.'[2]

---

[1] MS., Pepysian Library, vol. viii. 369.
[2] 12 March 1687. To Mr. Pepys. Rawlinson MS.

The friendship between the Houblon family and Mr. Secretary Pepys continued till the end of the life of the latter, and became closer as age and infirmity grew upon him.   The art of inspiring affection was also one of the many talents possessed by the famous Mr. Pepys. Most of the more remarkable men of his time felt it an honour to be called his friend; and many of them are to be found among his correspondents.   It is a matter of curious speculation as to what their feelings would have been had the inmost life of his earlier years been laid bare to them, as it was to students of his *Diary* in the nineteenth century; and the suggestion arises as to whose most secret mind would bear the test of so frank a dissection of motives and acts as are revealed by this man of himself, who was, nevertheless, as R. L. Stevenson observes, 'regarded as in a halo of almost historical pomp . . . and loved and respected by some of the best and wisest men in England.'[1] Jeremy Collier says of him that he was 'a philosopher of the severest morality.'[2]   What he had thought of himself in his younger days the *Diary* itself tells us : ' Let some contemporary light upon the journal, and Pepys were plunged for ever in social and political disgrace.'[3]

As shown in his *Diary*, Pepys's character was both impulsive and weak; while desirous of being virtuous and true, he yet was easily overcome by temptation. He was sincerely ashamed when he did wrong, and childishly glad when he resisted his evil impulses.   In November 1662 we see him congratulating himself upon his having kept his vow against intemperance, putting all his success in his official work down to this, and hoping 'yett to do God, the King, and myself good service.'[4]   Indeed, those who have studied his life apart

---

[1] R. L. Stevenson, *Familiar Studies of Men and Books*, p. 292.
[2] Wheatley's *Pepysiana*, p. 12.
[3] *Diary.*
[4] *Diary.*

from the wonderful journal which was kept during the short spell of only nine years, think that both Pepys's character and morals were mellowed and chastened as the years went by, and that the Pepys of the latter portion of his life was a different being from the writer of Pepys's *Diary*. Perhaps one of the most strongly marked characteristics of Mr. Samuel Pepys, especially in his later years, was his love of order and method. Half the charm of the exquisite little library of three thousand books bequeathed by him to Magdalene College, Cambridge, lies in its quaint and orderly arrangement. From the original bookcases carved and glazed and planned by himself, to the smallest volume in the collection, Pepys's library is cherished to this day in the silent, shaded room of the venerable college loved by the diarist.   Here the visitor seems to be transported into that atmosphere of culture and leisure and quiet study, in which Pepys, after his retirement from official work, passed his happiest days ; the happier perhaps from the somewhat tumultuous experiences of his early manhood.   The books bear upon them the impress of the care with which they have been treated, without a moment's intermission, since they came into the hands of their owner.   So determined was Mr. Pepys to secure the inviolability of his beloved library from dispersal or mutilation, that by a clause in his will he left it to Magdalene College on the condition that it was kept intact, and in order to insure this proviso, he directed that, in the event of the loss of a single volume, the entire collection was to be forfeited to Trinity College, which college had, in consequence, the right of periodical inspection.   All his life Pepys collected books, and the arrangement of his library cost him much time and labour.   He was fastidious and somewhat narrow in his choice, while the capacity of his bookshelves controlled the limits within which he confined the size of his library; nor was he tempted to overpass the number he had set himself. When new books crowded his space, others less precious were sacrificed, and made way for the newcomers. The acquisition of the best editions was his aim, and he was free from the modern craze for first editions.

In eleven large volumes Pepys caused to be transcribed, by his clerk William Hewer, a vast number of letters written by himself upon business and other matters. Under the heading of 'Admiralty Letters,' one of these volumes contains many addressed to James Houblon by Mr. Pepys, some of which we have already noticed. Another set of volumes cherished by their owner contained his 'Collection of Heads' in *Taille douce*, classified under the headings of 'Royal family, Noblemen, Gentlemen, Seamen, etc.' In the section 'Gentlemen' we find the portrait of Sir James Houblon. It is interesting to note the names of the friends with whom Pepys thus grouped him. On the one page are drawings of Sir John Hoskins, Dr. Lock (the great John Locke), Sir Isaac, then Mr., Newton, and Mr. Evelyn as a young man. On the opposite page we find the diarist himself, surrounded by Sir Anthony Deane, Mr. Evelyn (in more advanced years), Sir James Houblon, Dr. Gale, Dean of York, and his faithful friend, William Hewer.[1]

A mutual friend and acquaintance of Pepys and James Houblon, was the good Mr. Evelyn; a man of the highest character and endowed with every attribute to inspire affection and admiration. He speaks of Mr. Pepys as a 'genius,'[2] and in the secretary's trouble and fall at the 'King's withdrawing' in 1688, sends to 'know if in any sort I may serve you in this prodigious revolution. You have many friends, but no man living

1688

---

[1] See volume ii. of *Collection of Heads*, p. 127.
[2] Letter to S. P., 6 December 1691.

Sir James Houblon.
(From Pepys' Book of Portraits.)

who is more sincerely your servant or that has a greater value for you.'[1] Mr. Evelyn's acquaintance with James Houblon dated from 1679, when they were mutually made known to each other through the auspices of Mr. Pepys. Evelyn mentions this first interview in his *Diary*, recording that he accompanied Pepys to the house in Winchester Street, to a supper given by Mr. Houblon. 'I supped this night,' he says, 'with Mr. Secretary at one Mr. Houblon's, a French merchant who had his house furnished *en Prince*, and gave us a splendid entertainment.'[2] Elsewhere he speaks of a dinner at Mr. Pepys's house, where Mr. Houblon also was; and how that 'after dinner he had me and Mr. Houblon . . . into a private room' where a discussion took place on the vexed question as to whether or no Charles ii. had died a Papist.[3] In yet another place Evelyn speaks of James Houblon as a 'rich and gentile (genteel) French merchant,' and adds that 'he is building a house in the forest of Epping, near to Sir J. Child's; in a place where the late Earle of Norwich dwelt some time. . . . It will be a pretty villa about five miles from White Chapell.'[4] The neighbourhood of the famous Wanstead House, lately rebuilt by Sir Josiah Child, after its destruction by fire, was a favourite resort for the wealthy citizens of London in the seventeenth century. At a convenient distance from town, and situated in what was then a lovely country, the merchants delighted to build themselves 'fair houses' here, and surround them with well-watered gardens full of choice fruit and other trees, and adorned with the trim yew hedges and smooth lawns loved by Evelyn the great gardener of the age. Many of these old houses

[1] Letter dated Sayes Court, 2 December 1688.
[2] *Diary of John Evelyn*, ii. 135, edited by W. Bray, F.S.A.
[3] *Ibid.*, 5 October 1685.
[4] *Ibid.*, 16 March 1683. 'The Forest House' is in the parish of Leyton-stone, and close to Epping Forest.

remain; well-built, substantial mansions defying decay, but grey with age and mellow with time's beautifying touch. The Forest House mentioned by Evelyn, which was rebuilt or enlarged by Sir James Houblon, still stands; it also still goes by its old name and is in good preservation. The large and lofty hall and grand staircase are of the date of Sir James Houblon's additions to the house, and are fine examples of contemporary work. In the former there is an immense white marble chimney-piece with figures on either side. This fine old house now belongs to the West Ham Corporation and serves as an adjunct to the workhouse, for the accommodation of 'old and respectable paupers.' The Forest House and domain when it belonged to Sir James Houblon included some twenty acres of land and garden, the property being bounded on two sides by the open heath, and on another by woodlands, notably 'Sykes myles Grove.'[1]

The moral and political high pressure in which men were living both in London and in the country was now wellnigh intolerable. King James was on the throne, and by his reckless measures had quickly shown the inferiority of his political genius to that of his brother Charles. The latter, with all his faults and greed of power, had an instinctive knowledge as to how far he could safely go with his long-suffering subjects, and had the sense to give way when it became politic to do so. James had no such sense. It was a day when, first in English history, that cleavage of thought had begun to take shape which, while driving men holding antagonistic groups of opinions into opposite factions, was afterwards to crystallise into the party system of later times: factions which, in their first inception, were dubbed each

---

[1] Among the Chancery bills and answers we have found an account of the Forest House and Manor of 'Layton äls Lowleighton äls Leighton Grange'; as also of the curious history of its tenure. See Bridges, No. 629 (before 1714).

by the other with the then opprobrious nicknames of Whig and Tory. Although the struggle on the one hand of the Parliament for the predominant authority it claimed, and on the other of the King for irresponsibility to it in virtue of his divine right, marked the issues between King and people in both reigns, the situation was soon rendered acute on the accession of James by his action with regard to Roman Catholics. Whatever men may now think as to the injustice with which the prejudices of the day had surrounded them—prejudices probably justified by experience—the King's measures were highly calculated to arouse resentment and anxiety, and, failing his power to carry them through, to defeat their own object of restoring the supremacy of Rome to this country. Nor had he reckoned upon the spirit of independence and love of liberty which prevailed among his people ; his steady disregard of their feelings and prejudices, in fact, alienated the goodwill of all parties. Those who had at first turned to him hopefully in spite of his creed, regarding his person as the one guarantee against the strife and civil war with which they were threatened at the opening of his reign, now steeled themselves against him ; for this old dread of Rome had only grown in intensity with the march of the century. And so it came to pass that the theory of Divine Right of Kings was to melt away before the prospect now confronting the country of a popish dynasty, to be hereafter perpetuated in the person of the little unwished-for child of Mary of Modena.

The steady opposition of the City of London, which from the first had met the arbitrary government of Charles II. with quiet determination, was not even broken by the withdrawal by James of its charter. For with the growth of wealth throughout the country, and the consequent influence of those possessing it, the great City had become conscious of its own power ; and the need for a government under which that growth might be fostered and encouraged became more and more imperative. Thought and enlightenment, where-ever they were to be found, were ranging themselves on the side of progress; speculation, whether political, philosophical or scientific, was burning for legitimate expression, and ripening fast for the climax which was shortly to result in the Revolution, in which the old order was changed. Thus the outcome of the

1688   Revolution of 1688 (in the consummation of which the City had so large a share) was to establish in the country a government which represented a new era in English history. The revolution was bloodless, because all men felt its inevitability; the old loyalty was indeed to break out in fruitless struggles, mostly at a distance from the capital where the royal Stuarts had lived and failed and fallen; but the pathetic devotion of the Jacobite, and his many sacrifices to the lost cause, were doomed to failure and defeat, not because that cause was otherwise than righteous, but because James had now identified it with that of the Roman Church and the Pope's supremacy. William and Mary, the new heads of the State, were welcomed, because they were regarded as pledges of the continuity of protestantism in the country, and of a government in harmony with those ideas of liberty and progress in the light of which men desired to live.[1] Disappointment was to follow, discontent and much jealousy of the foreigner and his Dutch following. The situation was accepted as inevitable; but henceforth a sentiment which had belonged to the nation, and was indeed part of itself—the sentiment of personal loyalty—was gradually to die down in the breasts of the English people. William was tolerated, while both Stuart sisters were personally popular; but

---

[1] See Lecky, *Democracy and Liberty*, i. 3, and Cunningham, *Growth of Industry and Commerce*, i. Int. 5.

after the death of good Queen Anne, her successors, the
Hanoverian Georges, possessed no spark wherewith to
rekindle the fire quenched with the fall of the ancient
monarchy, which claimed to rule by divine right.

MAY 1677

CONSIDERATIONS TOUCHING THE IMPORTANCE OF SOME PROVISION TO BEE MADE FOR PUBLIQUE MARINE INTELLIGENCE [1]

'THE several Princes of Europe whose dominions border upon the
sea, having in imitation of England, for these twenty years last past
more than ever applyed themselves to increase their navall forces by
encouraging their people in their several trades, and in giveing them
countenance and protection, it may not be unnecessary for the
Secretary of the Lord Admiral to be enabled by a yearly allowance to
obtain intelligence from abroad as well in time of peace as of warr, soe
that being continually fully and faithfully instructed he may from time
to time give the King and the Lord Admiral in time of peace a true
accompt of the increase or decrease of the severale navall forces of
Europe, as also of that of their several trades and plantations and the
reasons of both ; as also in time of warr, of their several preparations,
the number of their shipps and men, the exact time of their putting to
sea, and which way their fleets are intended. Which being pre-
mised, it remaines to shew the several particulars wherein such an
Intelligence may be of great service to the King both in time of peace
and of warr ; and also that it is of absolute necessity.

' AND 1ST IN TIME OF PEACE.

' That he have full knowledge of the navall forces and trade of all
the European Princes.

' And first of FRANCE.

' By haveing constant and certaine knowledge from their chief ports,
of the number of shipps of warr, and their captains' names, guns,
burthen, and number of seamen and landmen in each shipp, and of
their sea stores and ammunition. Whether there be a want of seamen
in France to carry on trade and warr att the same time ; what course
there is taken to increase them ; what number of seamen there may be
in the French dominions ; what men of warr he hath abroad ; in what

---

[1] Paper by Mr. James Houblon. Rawlinson MS. A. 185, fol. 53.

parts of Europe, Africa, Asia, or America, and what designes they went upon. What number of fishing ships either upon our coasts, Greenland, or Newfoundland. What convoyes they have, and how their fishing shipps in Newfoundland are mann'd and gunned. What men of warr they have in their American plantations of St. Christopher, Guadaloupe, and Martinique, etc*., and other their Leeward Islands and East India.

'Of HOLLAND and the UNITED PROVINCES.

'That the Secretary informe himselfe strictly of all the necessary knowledge of their sea affairs in the several Provinces: their quotas of shipps constantly kept in repair, their stores, etc.; and alsoe when they build new ones; how many, and of what force in each Province; what sumes of moneys are directed to be raised for that purpose in each Province. The causes of their increase or decrease in trade, and the number of seamen; and where their sea forces are disposed abroad in the world. How their fishings on our coasts and Greenland goe forward. Their numbers of shipps and busses yearely employed: soe as to compare and compute their increasing or decaying in the said Trades. Their number of Men of warr and merchant men in the East India's. Their severall quarrels and warrs with those Princes; and whether their East India trade and forces decrease or diminish, and how they are either well or ill supplied with European seamen and navale stores.

'Of DENMARK and SWEDEN.

'The number, burthen, and gunns, etc., of their men of warr, and what are building or ordered to be built. Whether Sweden doth daylie increase in navigation since their laws about Trade, [they] have-ing encouraged their own subjects to build warlike shipps which are in a great measure freed from customes which other shipps pay. By which privilege they are oblidged to serve the King in his warrs. The probable numbers of seamen in both these Kingdoms, and what Men of warr they have abroad, and where.

'Of SPAINE, PORTUGALL, and VENICE.

'It may not be unnecessary—though they are but weake in shipping —to have an Intelligence of all sea affaires as above; but, from the severall African Ports of SALLEE, TUNIS, TRIPOLY, and ALGIERS, and of the designes and transactions of their men of warr, their disposi-tion to peace or warr—it is absolutely necessary that the Secretary keepe a constant correspondence. And that in those parts he may know the dispositions of those governments and peoples either to breake or keepe the peace: so that the English navigation may not suffer by their suddaine and unexpected breaking with us.

'It is needful alsoe that the Secretary keep a correspondence in all the most frequented PORTS of England, France, Portugall, Spaine, Italy, and Turkie, the better to gaine an accompt of the dilligence and behavior of the King's Comanders appointed for a guard and convoyes in those seas, viz. What time they arrive.   How much time they spend in each port, and for what occasion; whether by negligence opportunities of sailing out of any ports have been lost.   And chiefly this may serve to correct the debauched and scandalous lives of any Commanders, Officers, and seamen in those seas; to the dishonour of the King and the nation; and also by keeping them to their duty, prevent a mighty losse, which for many years the King has sustained.   For his Shipps of warr have misspent their time in Spaine and Italy for their own private gaines when they should have otherwise employed them for his honour, and the protection and careful convoy of his subjects.

'2ND IN TIME OF WARR.

'Nothing is of more indispensible necessitie than that the Secretary of the Lord Admirall should have true, frequent, and punctuale advices and intelligence from the enemy's PORTS; and this not from ignorant and slight hands, but from people of good understanding, and whose qualities and nearness to busynesse may capacitate them to give an accompt of the secret intentions and designs of the fleets or squadrons of Men-of-Warr, besides what else may be found out by his owne experience and observation.

'In time of Warr with FRANCE.

'For to defend ourselves or annoy the enemy, its needful the Secretary know the whole state of their NAVIES, where they are, and when they may bee ready to sail from their respective ports of Brest, Rochel, Rochford, Dunkirke, Haure de grace, and St. Malo in these seas; and from Toulon and Marseilles in the Mediterranean.   Where the *rendezvous* is to be; if they intend to keepe in a bodie or disperse, in squadrons or parties.

'It's alsoe reasonable to know if any shipps are sent from France to Norway, Sweden, or the Baltique, and to what ports for NAVALL STORES; the time of their departure and arrival at the said Ports, and when they may be dispatched from thence, and where: and what number, and what force: Soe as the better to be provided for to intercept them.

'It's reasonable alsoe that the Secretary be informed of the several times of departure and arrival of the FRENCH FISHERMEN of Newfound Land and Green Land, and other fleets and shipps to the American plantations and of what force they are; and whether with or without convoys—the better to disturb them in their trades and weaken them by takeing off their shipps. And because Privateers doe more harm to Merchantmen than the King's Men of Warr (the former having nothing else to mind), the better to preserve our coasts and seas from being infested by them, it's good to keepe a watchful eye over them, and to nipp them in the bud at first before they grow considerable; and for this purpose before a warr at any time breake out, it's needfull to know whence Privateers are sett out, their number and force; what kind of build they are, what markes they may be known by, and what stations they keepe; if they consort or separate, and the times of their setting to sea and returns, and whether they increase or decrease.

'In time of warr with HOLLAND.

'The same rules for Intelligence to be observed. But, as by how much their ports—and by consequence their navall forces—are nearer one another, and for that reason they can more readily joyne themselves, soe a most watchful eye must be kept upon them; and the Intelligences must from thence be as perfect to all intents and purposes as is possible to be had. And the better to annoy and weaken them is to know the times of the departures and returns of their GREEN LAND FLEETE and FISHING FLEET for HERRINGS; and to disturb and discourage all that may be the whole course of their trade. Alsoe to prevent the increase of their PRIVATEERS which are almost solely fitted out in Zealand. To have a true Intelligence from Middlebourgh and Flushing of all things relating to them as before; the better, by taking them or their prizes as they come out or goe in (and this upon the first beginning of the warr), to stop their increase.

'Which thing was neglected in our late warrs to the grievous destruction of the English merchants and dishonour to our nation. Which mischiefe might at first have been in great measure prevented, if by good Intelligence from those ports, the Lord Admirall had had an exact accompt of them, that he might have applyed some few Friggatts to have curbed them at their first starting. For being necessitous people that sett up those trades of stealing, the takeing of their shipps putts them quite out of capacitie to make new equipages: whereas on the contrary being covetous of gaines and people of great hopes and expectations, they generally employ all the produce of their prizes in fitting out more shipps. Insomuch that the Lamsines of Middleburgh and Vlushing had, the second warr with England, fourteen men of warr of their owne, to prey upon the English—of from ten to forty guns apiece.

'Alsoe, when we happen to be in warr with other nations as SPAINE, PORTUGALL, SWEDEN, or DENMARK, etc. As before; nothing can be of greater use to us—soe as to make the King's fleet of that effect it ought to bee, to us or our enemies—as that the Secretary to the Lord High Admirall be fully capacitated in a handsome and plentifull manner to *purchase Intelligence* in the courts of our neighbours concerning their navall affairs; and above all, to maintain by pensions (in the severall ports of Europe where the navall forces, communications, provisions and stores are), understanding prying men, to give him an accompt of all matters relating to them, as hath been said before. Soe that at any time when warrs breake out we may be soe farr from being ignorant of what is done among our neighbours, as to this point, that we may have a full knowlege of it, which will certainly with great satisfaction and profit, recompense the charge that shall be laid out to obtain it.'

CHAPTER XV

WHIGS AND THEIR WORK

'We made shift to gather out of one [of our guides] that this island was very much infested with a monstrous kind of animal in the shape of men, called Whigs. . . . These two creatures [Whigs and Tories] it seems are born with a secret antipathy for one another.'—ADDISON : *Spectator*, No. 50.

' THE City is loyal to their princes, but yet jealous of the invasion of their religion and liberty.   This was the cause the citizens so readily received the Prince of Orange, An° 1688, and that in their address they thanked him for his glorious design of rescuing England, Scotland, and Ireland from slavery and popery, and implored his highness' protection.'[1]   The long-awaited chance of the City had come, and, full of hope, it looked forward not only to freedom from that fear which had oppressed it, but to reaping the golden fruit that was to be the outcome of the new régime.

1688

We now find a new class of men advancing to the front.   The patient waiting of the great merchant princes was at length rewarded, and their weight and influence were henceforth felt in government councils. The Houblons were all Whigs, and now, for the first time, their name is mentioned in connection with municipal government and with parliamentary representation ; while they were also to be concerned in fresh financial developments of great importance.   John Houblon at

---

[1] Strype, Stow's *Survey*, I. ii. 302, 304.

once stepped into a place amongst the foremost of his fellow-citizens, and from this time till his death in 1712 he remained a prominent figure in all that appertained to the City, in which, of late years, royal influence had found a way to intervene.   During the troubles which followed the scare of the Popish Plot, John took a strong line in City affairs as one of the whig supporters of the Earl of Shaftesbury in his bold struggle with King Charles II. for parliamentary supremacy, and such a toleration as should exclude Roman Catholics while admitting Dissenters.   When the rashness of Shaftesbury had already brought about a reaction in the country, due to the fear lest a breach with the King should result in civil war, the City still clung to their 'daring pilot,' as he was called by Dryden,[1] and saved his life when he was impeached for high treason, through the refusal of   1681 the Grand Jury of Middlesex to find a true bill against him.   By a letter from Lord Fauconberg to Sir William Frankland,—written on the 22nd of November 1681, a few days before the trial was to take place—it is plain that this acquittal was regarded as a foregone conclusion, owing to the composition of the Grand Jury.   For, on the list of 'forty substantial men' offered for a jury to the court by the Sheriffs, were to be found the names of the most prominent and influential of the city Whigs, of whom John Houblon was one.   'Of these forty,' writes Lord Fauconberg, 'Sir Sam: Barnadiston, Dubois, Papillon, Rudge, Houblon, Boneale and the two Godfreys make a part; by which you may judge what we are to expect.'[2]

The City of London alone possessed the privilege, through their charter, of electing their sheriffs ; in all other cities these officers were nominated by the King. Hence this Grand Jury was composed of Whigs, and the

[1] In *Absalom and Achitophel.*
[2] Treasury Papers.   Report on the MSS. of Mrs. Frankland Russell-Astley, of Chequers Court, Bucks, p. 47.

sheriffs, in naming them to the court, were in a position to brave the displeasure of the King. The jury, as was expected, threw out the bill of indictment against Shaftesbury, and he was set at liberty. A silver medal was struck in London in commemoration of Lord Shaftesbury's release from the Tower, and of the part played ·by the bold Londoners in thus saving his life ; but although the City continued to protect him so long as the Whigs retained the majority, it was made to feel the resentment of Charles for its independence of his will. He procured the return of a Tory majority on the Common Council, and finally withdrew the City Charter, offering such terms for its renewal as should render independent action impossible in the future.[1]

From the time of the retirement of their father from active life, the brothers Houblon regarded John as his successor in the headship of their joint interests, and this in spite of two of them being older than he. James₂, as we have seen, went daily to John's house in Threadneedle Street for their 'usual Meeting,' and most likely the other brothers frequently went there also. James's good temper and vivacity made him a general favourite, but John was a quiet and serious man, caring little for pleasure or the society of his fellows ; and in him a keen, strong mind was united to a temper and intellect at once laborious and powerful. In the important events following upon the Revolution which he and his fellow-citizens had done so much to bring about, he was to bear no inconsiderable part ; for he was the chief and determined advocate of the financial support given by the Bank of England to the great game played with consummate statesmanship by William with regard to the ambition of Louis xiv. of France. Without the money provided by the Bank at

----

[1] Gardiner, *Student's History*, i. 624.

(Sir) John Houblon.

great cost and sacrifice, the King's success in the war would have been impossible. It may thus be claimed for John Houblon that he was prominently concerned in the first historical episode in which the power of wealth took that place in the politics of this country which it was ever after to retain; a power which was later fully apprehended by Louis himself, who truly remarked that the victor in the great European struggle in which England had crossed his path would be he who owned the last louis d'or.

The historian Von Ranke has drawn largely from foreign sources for his authorities on this period for his English history, and his remarks upon the influence of the refugees upon English politics are particularly interesting. The Huguenots had been the backbone of French commercial prosperity, and on their expatriation by the revocation of the Edict of Nantes, they 1685 brought with them large sums of money to this country. While they cherished a great hatred for the French king, whose religious bigotry had led to their banishment,[1] it is evident that the descendants of the Flemish and Dutch Protestants in England were no less interested in the success of King William's arms in the country of their ancestors. All had money to invest, and mindful of the immense stake they now possessed in the England of the Revolution, they boldly ventured it in State loans, and the more they added to their investments in these, the more bound up did their interests become in William's government. The contributions of the expatriated Huguenots may therefore be regarded as having been a substantial factor in the discomfiture of some of their persecutor's most cherished plans.[2]

The faithful chronicler of London life and politics at

[1] Von Ranke, *History of England*, v. 76.
[2] Before the landing of William of Orange, large sums of money were sent him to Holland by descendants of the refugees in England.—Macaulay, *History of England*, iii. 442.

this period was Narcissus Luttrell; and in his pages, City news—with which we are primarily concerned—hold an important place. Four months after the accession of the King and Queen he tells, in his *Brief Historical Relation of State Affairs*, how that on the 25th of June 1689, 'according to custom, yesterday there was a Common Hall at Guildhall, where they proceeded to chuse their officers for the year ensueing,' and that they had chosen Mr. John Houblon and Mr. Christopher Lethieullier, sheriffs.[1] Here, then, we see the City of London once more asserting its rights, and by its election of prominent whig sheriffs setting its seal upon the newly accomplished Revolution. The Lord Mayor, Sir Thomas Pilkington, was already in office during the crisis in 1688, having served the latter half of that year (the reigning Lord Mayor having died), no fresh election was necessary in his case for 1689.[2] John Houblon and his colleague were thus the first municipal officers elected in the City since the Revolution, and in September following Houblon was chosen Alderman of Cornhill ward. After the Lord Mayor's pageant in October, the City having invited the King and Queen and both Houses of Parliament to dine at the Guildhall, a great function took place, 'the splendor and good order of which outdid all that had been seen before upon the like occasion,'[3] that which was most 'particular to mention' being the 'royal Regiment of volunteer Horse made up of the chief citizens, and led by the Earl of Monmouth, which attended their Majesties from Whitehall.'[4] This cavalcade being passed by, the King and Queen were conducted by John Houblon and his brother sheriff to Guildhall, where a 'magnificent Feast' was served, and where 'his Majesty to express his satisfaction, conferred the honor

---

[1] Luttrell, *Brief Relation*, iii. 55.   [2] *New View of London*, 1708.
[3] Kennet, *History of England*, iii. 548.   [4] *Ibid.*

of knighthood on Christopher Lethieullier[1] and John Houblon, Esq⁏., the two sheriffs,' . . . as well as on two other prominent aldermen, viz. Edward Clerk and Francis Child, who afterwards in their turn were elected sheriffs.

The tory party was very strong in the country; the Revolution had indeed been made possible only by the temporary alliance, due to their mutual fear of Popery, between the two opposing factions.[2]   Their opposition was mostly based upon ecclesiastical lines; and while the traditions of the Tories above all bound them to uphold the exclusive supremacy of the English Church, the Whigs supported the broad principles of toleration, except with regard to Roman Catholics.   The English Revolution was indeed successful only because the exigencies of the time afforded the country no option but to secure the safety of much that it held dear by the sacrifice of part.   Only the inconceivable folly of James could have alienated the loyalty of his people from his person, as representing the royal family, for which they held an almost superstitious reverence.   As Mr. Lecky remarks in his *History of the Eighteenth Century*, the nation was unprepared for the great step which was forced upon it by the necessity of at once saving the country and themselves from Popery.[3]   Fear of Rome, affection for the English Church, and attachment to the throne were the three leading passions of the time.   The King had touched the people nearly in the first two, and so the 'doctrine of indefeasible right' of the legitimate sovereign, and the 'sinfulness of resistance,' as taught industriously by the English clergy since the Restoration,[4] were of necessity abandoned, and with this emancipation the English

---

[1] Lethieullier died before the close of his term of office.
[2] Lecky, *History of the Eighteenth Century*, i. 11.
[3] *Ibid.*, i. 10.   [4] *Ibid.*

people gained what they were as yet scarcely able to either appreciate or understand. Thus the few who shaped the policy of the Revolution stood far in advance of the sense of the country,[1] and were only able to accomplish their work because all were for the present united in the common object of supporting the government of William and Mary.

1690   In the new Parliament returned in February 1690, the Tories were in a majority throughout the kingdom, though in London the Whigs made a hard fight. Sir John Houblon was returned member for the Bodmin division of south-east Cornwall for this Parliament, and we are informed by his biographer in a MS. memoir, that he sat in three successive Parliaments as representing this seat. It

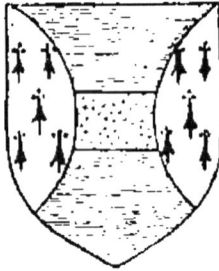

ARMS OF HOBLYN.

was probably due to the fact that he had family connections settled in that county that the City magnate sought the suffrages of Cornishmen, and that it was by their influence that he was returned. The Hoblyns of Nanswhyden in Cornwall were descended, it seems probable, from the brother of Sir John's own great-grandfather.[2]

Mr. James Houblon was put forward by the whig party in the City in 1690 for one of the City constituencies; and amongst Mr. Pepys's correspondence is a letter from his son James[3] requesting his support and interest in the matter of his father's candidature, the

---

[1] Lecky, *History of the Eighteenth Century*, i. 13, 15.

[2] Pierre₁ Houblon who fled to this country about 1550. The name occurs as Hoblyn. In the seventeenth century there were numerous members of the family in Cornwall. Originally wealthy and of good birth they quickly acquired landed property, and allied themselves with the best families of those parts. In local histories Sir John Houblon's name as representing the Cornish constituency is given as Hoblyn. See W. Prideaux Courtney, *Representation of Cornwall to 1832. London*, 1889. The arms of Hoblyn are: Az. a fess or between two flanches ermine.

[3] Born May 1665.

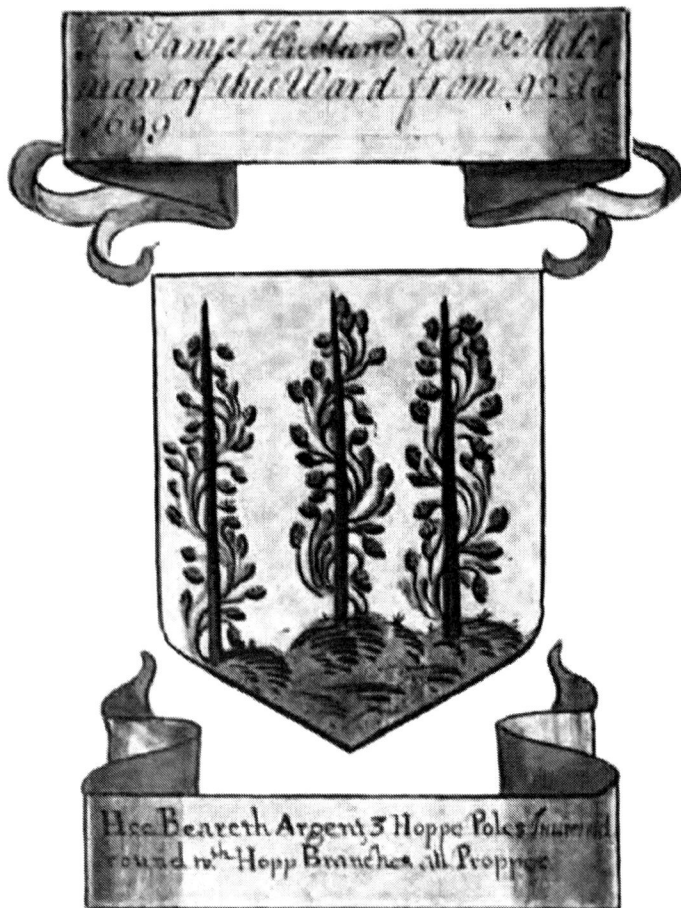

Sr James Houblone Knight & Alderman of this Ward from 9r. of [illegible] 1699

Hee Beareth Argent 3 Hoppe Poles [illegible] round w.th Hopp Branches all Proppge

ARMS OF SIR JAMES HOUBLON.

which he urged is the more required, on account of his
'supineness in matters of this kind; . . . the party made
on the other side being very strong.'[1]   Mr. Pepys com-
plied with the young man's request on this occasion, as
also on a subsequent one of the same nature; but tory
candidates were returned in each case, and James[2] did
not become a member of parliament till he was returned by the City at the general election of 1698.
Luttrell mentions the fact of James Houblon's election
as Alderman of Aldersgate ward in 1691, the vacancy   1691
having been caused by the death of Sir Peter Rich.[2]
He was knighted by the King at the Guildhall feast, in
October following.[3]

Meanwhile Sir John Houblon was for the first time
put forward by the whig party for the office of Lord
Mayor in 1691.   Luttrell writes on the 28th of September
that 'great interest was made on Michaelmas day for the
choice of a Lord Mayor; the Church party' (the Tories)
'put up Raymond and Sir Peter Daniel, and the Whigs,
Sir John Fleet and Sir John Houblon.'[4]   On election
day, although the two whig candidates 'had the majority
plainly on the view, a poll was demanded and granted,
which continued till six this evening, and adjourned till
seven to-morrow morning.'[5]   The books were cast up
at Guildhall on October the 1st, and the majority being
confirmed, the two Whigs were returned (according to
custom) to the Court of Aldermen, and of the two they
chose Sir John Fleet (he being senior to Sir John
Houblon), and he was accordingly declared Lord Mayor
for the year ensuing.

The actual choice of a Lord Mayor rests with the
livery of the City by a majority of hands, and at this
time the livery comprised about seven thousand of the

[1] Rawlinson MS. A. 170, fol. 7.   [2] Luttrell, ii. 571.
[3] *Ibid.*, ii. 603.   1692.   [4] *Ibid.*, ii. 569.
[5] *Ibid.*, ii. 578.

chief citizens, consisting of those individuals who enjoyed the freedom of the City.[1] The names of two aldermen chosen by the livery from among the candidates 'according to seniority,'[2] were then sent up to the council chamber where the reigning Lord Mayor and the Court of Aldermen were sitting, and of the two names submitted to them by the livery they selected one, usually the senior of the two aldermen. At the election by the livery, the names of all the senior aldermen were put up one after another by those supporting their candidature, and as at this time party politics ran high, the election was fought with much spirit. As the office of Lord Mayor was generally filled by one of the two Sheriffs nominated the previous year, the nomination and election of those officials were usually fought much on the same lines. The following year, 1693, Sir John Houblon was again returned by the livery, together with Sir William Ashurst, who being also his senior was selected by the court. When, at last, in 1695 Sir John Houblon became Lord Mayor of London, it would appear that it was partly against his inclination, as will presently be seen by certain correspondence which passed touching his candidature, between the King, then in Flanders, and the Duke of Shrewsbury, Secretary of State. Mean-

1693-4 while he was appointed by commission a Lord of the Admiralty;[3] that department having been put into commission on the accession of William and Mary, with Admiral Russell as Treasurer of the Navy. On the rise of the Whigs to power, and the formation of the Junto ministry, Russell became First Lord of the Admiralty, and was at the same time given command of the fleet. The able financier Charles Montague was made Chancellor of the Exchequer later in the same year.

The appointment of great London merchants to the

---

[1] *New View of London*, 1708, I. xxix. [2] Luttrell, ii. 578.
[3] *Ibid.*, 13 January 1693-4.

Admiralty Board was a new thing, and must have been very welcome both to Sir John Houblon himself and to many others, the success of whose commercial undertakings was intimately bound up in the affairs of the navy.   But apart from commerce, Sir John would have been well known to both Russell and Montague long before their advent to power, for among the Whigs all thought and acted alike on the great questions of the hour.   In their new work and organisation they found in him an able coadjutor, while his high standing among the merchants made him a *persona grata* as an intermediary for dealing with them and their claims.   A letter from the Earl of Nottingham, dated Whitehall,   1693 illustrates this point; for in it he desires that Sir John would 'be at my office to-morrow afternoon at four o'clock precisely,' and 'that you will bring on with you a merchant of the East India Company; a Committee of the Council being appointed to meet here about the affairs of that Company.'[1]

The British fleets of merchantmen laden with precious goods of all kinds were in those days frequently in the greatest peril of capture or destruction, not only from pirates, but from the cupidity and ill-will of the rival nations.   Although many attempts had been made in former reigns to cope with the question of convoys, it was more than ever before impossible for the Admiralty, now at war with France, to keep pace with the vastly increasing commerce, or protect all the merchant vessels sailing to every part of the globe.   So it had come to pass, that but lately a great fleet, laden with goods of immense value, despatched by the Turkey merchants to Smyrna, had been lost or captured by the enemy; a misfortune due to mismanagement with regard to the arrangements made for its convoy.[2]

[1] *H. O. Letter Book* (Secretary's), 1693, 2. 628.
[2] Macaulay, *History of England*, iv. 416 and 468.

1694   From the moment of the formation of the new Commission of the Admiralty in 1694, on which Sir John Houblon had a seat, the mismanagement and corruption which had so long prevailed on the Board—and against which, in time past, poor Pepys so vainly struggled—began to give place to improved conditions, though it would appear that this improvement came about but slowly. Russell and his colleagues worked harmoniously together during the five years in which the former retained office as First Lord.   The business capacity on the new Board of Admiralty was abundantly demonstrated

1695   in the following year, when the English fleet under the command of Russell was forced to remain for many months in the Mediterranean, in order to keep in check the French navy,[1] during which time we are told that, though on an 'inhospitable shore,' the fleet was well supplied with food and stores, and that at no greater cost than when 'mouldy biscuit and nauseous beer' was all 'with which English sailors had wont to be fed.'[2] Great complaints had been made in the House of Commons in 1689 as to the 'ill victualling' of the navy, the Victuallers having even been 'had up in custody of the serjeant-at-arms';[3] and they were then dismissed and others appointed in their place. Sir John Houblon (one of the new Admiralty Lords), was now placed on a fresh Commission of the Victualling Office,[4] and doubtless his large commercial connection with the Peninsula was of great advantage to the fleet while detained in the Mediterranean, while his agents near at hand not only took care that the crews 'had better food and drink than they ever had before,' but that Admiral Russell was enabled to refit his ships with

---

[1] Macaulay, *History of England*, iv. 516.

[2] The commissioners of the Victualling Office 'are to receive proposals and agree for sufficient and wholesome victualling for every Fleet of her Majesty's Ships.' See *New View of London*, 1708, ii. 729.

[3] Kennet, *History of England*, iii. 544.

[4] Luttrell.

expedition and success when lying off Cadiz in the winter months.[1]

His appointment as a Lord of the Admiralty in 1694 was probably the reason that Sir John Houblon was not nominated for the mayoralty that year, as he would otherwise have been in due course; apparently he 'used his influence to be passed over.'[2]   His disinclination to assume the responsibility of the mayoralty, either in 1694 or in the year following, will be the more readily understood when we come to realise the magnitude of another work upon which he was now engaged—a work which was to be the most important of his life, viz. the share which he took in the measures which resulted in the establishment of the Bank of England, and his labours afterwards as its First Governor.   How Sir John came to reconsider his decision of evading the duties of the mayoralty in 1695, we shall find in a correspondence which took place between the King (from the seat of war) and the Duke of Shrewsbury.   In the meantime the office of Mayor in 1694 devolved upon Sir Thomas Lane, a 'weak and contentious person,' during the tenor of whose office the government of the City was by no means wise or dignified.[3]

It will have been observed how the King's necessities as regards money accentuated the influence already exercised by the wealthy citizens of London.   Their growing power was combated with feverish energy by the Tory party and landed interest throughout the country; but in spite of every effort to counteract its effect, and to direct the channel of political influence once again from London burgesses to the great class of landed proprietors who saw it slipping from their grasp,—all efforts failed, and the City and its wealth and intelligence gradually assumed an authority and political weight pro-

[1] Macaulay, *History of England*, iv. 516.
[2] See Coxe, *Private Correspondence of the Duke of Shrewsbury*.
[3] *Ibid.*

portionate to the services it was enabled to render to the State and throne.

The history of the establishment of the Bank of England is of great interest, and reflects honour upon the men whose clear heads conceived principles in advance of their time, and at the same time were possessed of a courage and foresight which permitted them safely to carry through an enterprise of extreme difficulty and risk. As Sir John Houblon had the honour to be chosen its first governor, a slight sketch of the early history of the great Bank will not be considered out of place in these 1694   memoirs.   He was sixty-six years old when, in 1694, he entered upon this, the most arduous period of his life ; and the stress of work then begun was continued for eighteen years.

With the increase of wealth, the necessity for its safe investment had become of paramount importance.   The Goldsmiths' Company—the only bankers—had hitherto been the recipients of money deposits ; but the closing of the Exchequer by Charles II. both ruined many of them and destroyed their credit.   They had been in the habit of making temporary advances of money to the King for state purposes, on his personal security, but their loans were not considered permanent.   It was at the suggestion of 1692   Montague, in 1692, that a public loan was contracted for the raising of a million of money in the open market on the security of certain taxes, in order to carry on the war.   This loan was the origin of the National Debt, and it was at first considered as dangerous to the welfare of the State to increase it further.   It was in 1694, when this and all other sources of revenue had failed, and when the demands upon the Exchequer could not be met, that the society denominated the Governor and Company of the Bank of England was incorporated. This corporation made a loan to the government on the security of the nation itself, provision being made that by paying off the loan in the year 1705, government might—if it so desired—extinguish the Bank's Charter, giving a year's notice to the corporation of its intention to do so. . .

The tallies of previous loans had represented the investment; but what was new in the present plan was the funding principle. Originally it was the practice to borrow on the security of some tax to be set apart as a fund to pay the principal and interest. Funds therefore originally meant the tax appropriated to the discharge of a loan; but as the practice grew, it came to mean, as now, the principal of the loan. The plan of the Bank (based upon that of St. George's Bank of Genoa), by means of which it was now proposed to supply the money required for the war in Holland, was due to William Paterson, a Scotsman, and was suggested by him in 1691 to his city friends. But the idea of a London bank was not a new one; for many years the more enlightened of the merchants had advocated such a scheme. A merchant of the name of Cradock had even put forward such a proposal as early as 1660, while among the great men of the Restoration, Sir William Petty was well known as far in advance of his time for his schemes in this direction; but it was only now adopted by the government on the advice of Montague. By means of the funds with which the Bank supplied him, William III. was able to continue the campaign in the Netherlands without being obliged to call upon the country to the full amount of his necessities. For instance, he obtained a loan from the City for £1,200,000, the yearly interest of which at 8 per cent.—together with £4000 a year which was allowed to the Bank for expenses of management—now cost the taxpayer only £100,000 per annum. The jealousy and distrust with which the scheme of the 'money men' was regarded was nevertheless so great, that its promoters carried it through the House of Lords with the bare majority of twelve ; and all were amazed when in the City itself it met with an instant and immense success.[1]   The fear entertained by many, that the ordinary enterprises of commerce and trade would suffer by great sums of money being diverted into these fresh channels, was proved to be unfounded ;[2] the demand created the supply, and money in plenty was forthcoming so soon as the loan was placed on the market.   The books were opened for

1694   subscriptions on the 21st of June 1694, at Mercers' Hall, when, in the words of Luttrell, some large sums were immediately subscribed.

'The Lords of the Treasury attended personally,' he writes, 'and subscribed £10,000 for the Queen; Sir Robert Howard and his son £18,000, Sir John Houblon £10,000, and so several others.'[3]   After this, subscriptions came pouring in,[4] the success of the scheme was secured, and the conditions upon which the charter was to be granted, were fulfilled.[5]

In the light of present-day business, and of the millions now dealt with in the City of London, the sums of money embarked by the pioneers of modern finance two hundred years ago appear as mean and insignificant. But in those days they were in truth great sums of money ; and the courage which inspired those who ventured their fortunes in this manner was the greater, that the success of their undertaking was dependent upon the chances of war.   Indeed Hamilton, in his *Inquiry on the National Debt* (1818), affirms that

---

[1] Macaulay.

[2] Cunningham, *The Growth of English Industry and Commerce in Modern Times*, p. 392.

[3] Luttrell, ii. 331, 1694.

[4] The original stock raised by subscription (not exceeding £20,000 in one name) was £1,200,000.   See R. Hamilton, *An Inquiry concerning the Rise, Progress, etc., of the National Debt*.   Edinburgh, 1818.

[5] 'The Booke contayning the names, etc. . . . . as shall voluntarily advance y⁰ sume of fifteen hundred thousand pounds *towards the carrying on the War with France*'—is in the Bank of England.

'more difficulty was found in raising the comparatively
moderate sums required in King William's reign than
in obtaining much larger loans in later times,' and this
fact he attributes partly to the inferiority of the national
wealth and the great value of money, and partly to the
'novelty of the system and want of public confidence.'

In an old tract of 1694, a list of the Commissioners
appointed by the King and Queen 'For taking subscriptions for £1,200,000 pursuant to the Act of Parliament' is given. Four of the Houblons were among
the number of these Commissioners. They were
authorised under the Great Seal, and their Majesties
promised, that so soon as the required amount should
be subscribed, they would 'incorporate the subscribers
by the name aforesaid,' viz. 'the Governor and Company
of the Bank of England; and that the whole sum subscribed and paid, should be the capital stock.'[2] By the
abstract of the Bank Charter given in the tract, we find
that provision is made for the 'better ordering of the
corporation, and for a succession of persons to be
governor, deputy-governor, and directors thereof, with
such powers as are hereafter mentioned.' These persons
were to continue in their offices till March 25, 1696,
'unless any of them shall dye,' and their names 'shall
be inserted in our royal charter of incorporation to be
granted as aforesaid, and shall thereby be made and
constituted the first governor, deputy-governor, and
directors of the company.' Subsequently, officers were
to remain in office for the space of one year only. Great
powers were given to the governors and directors as to
the management of the affairs of the Bank. They were
to hold courts of directors, and to summon general

---

[1] R. Hamilton, *An Inquiry concerning the Rise, Progress, etc. of the National Debt.*

[2] The Bank was at first called the Tunnage Bank, because the Act 'made in Parliament had granted to their Majesties several rates and duties upon the tonnage of ships,' etc. 'The Commission for taking Subscriptions, etc.' Tract (Crawford Library) 1694.

courts as often as they saw cause. They were 'direct and manage all affairs of the Corporation in borrowing, receiving monies, and giving securities under the common seal, and in their dealing in bills of exchange, buying or selling bullion, gold, or silver, or selling goods deposited for money lent, and in selling goods being the produce of lands purchased, or in lending any monies · and taking securities for the same ; . . . and generally to act and do in all matters which by the act may be done, which they shall judge necessary for the well ordering and managing the corporation.'[1]   Finally, it was agreed that 'this charter shall be made and sealed without any fine or fee, great or small, to be paid to their Majesties in their Hanaper or elsewhere.'

On the 12th of July Luttrell was able to give the list of directors for the new Bank. They were 'chose by ballotting' from among those subscribers and promoters who had contributed £2000 and upward to the undertaking. The first three names given on the list in the order of election, were those of Sir James Houblon, Sir William Scawen,[2] and Sir John Houblon.[3] It was not till the 27th of July that the Bank Charter was sealed. Meanwhile Sir John Houblon was elected Governor by ballot, and at the same time the Deputy-Governor chosen was Michael Godfrey,[4] who had been one of those most concerned in forwarding the scheme of the Bank. Although Paterson was elected a director he soon retired, withdrawing his money (£2000).[5] The first entry in the court minutes of the Bank records that Sir John

---

[1] 'The Commission for taking Subscriptions, etc.' Tract (Crawford Library) 1694.

[2] He succeeded Sir John Houblon three years later as governor of the Bank.

[3] Luttrell, iii. 242.

[4] He was one of the 'forty substantial men' named for the jury for the trial of Lord Shaftesbury, see p. 227.

[5] It has been suggested that the jealousy of his colleagues caused this retirement; but Paterson's was a creative genius, and it is more likely he wanted both his time and his money for the Darien Scheme now occupying his thoughts. See T. A. Stephens, *A Bibliography of the Bank of England*, 1897, 160, 161.

SEALING OF THE BANK OF ENGLAND CHARTER. 1694.

SIR JOHN HOUBLON.   SIR JOHN SOMERS.   MR. MICHAEL GODFREY
Governor.   *Lord Keeper.*   *Deputy Governor.*

Houblon took the oath as governor required by the charter, 'in company with Michael Godfrey the deputy-governor, and seven of the directors, before the Lord Keeper of the Great Seal (Sir John Somers), at Powis House, on the 27th of July 1694, immediately after the Seal had been affixed by the Lord Keeper to the Bank Charter in their presence.[1]   The minutes further record that the rest of the directors took the required oath at Mercers' Hall before the governor and deputy-governor, some of them on the afternoon of the day on which the Charter was sealed (on which occasion Sir James Houblon was sworn), and others on the following day, (viz. the 28th of July), when Abraham Houblon was of the number who took the oath.[2]

1694

Thus it was that the great Bank of England came into existence, the importance of its birth being perhaps scarcely fully recognised by any one at the time; the new position of the money-owning class giving them political influence, and also strengthening the government of William and Mary; for the 'security of the shareholders was in the good faith of the government,' and became bound up in the stability of the heads of the State.[3]   At the same time, while capital was invested, and the accumulation of money encouraged, the burden incurred by the country was, at the date the loans were incurred, justified by the advantages obtained for the government by the prosecution of the war.   The Bank of England was founded to meet a pressing emergency, but became a permanent institution when it was proved, that—after passing through a period of unprecedented danger and anxiety, during which the courage and constancy of the Bank officials were strained to the utmost—

[1] A fresco in the Royal Exchange represents the First Governor in the act of taking the oath at Powis House.

[2] The above particulars were supplied by the courtesy of the present Directors of the Bank of England.

[3] W. Cunningham, *The Growth of English Industry and Commerce in Modern Times*, p. 391.

the sacrifices of the Whig capitalists in supplying the pressing needs of the army in Flanders were fully compensated by the return obtained for their investment.[1]

The Bank at first sat in Mercers' Chapel, as Luttrell tells us, but at a general court held on September the 28th, just two months after its establishment, Sir John Houblon informed the shareholders that there was a necessity for their removing elsewhere, and therefore he had taken Grocers' Hall for eleven years as its place of business.[2] For the lease, we learn from the Bank minutes, £5500 was paid. The Governor also informed them on this occasion, that 'the Bank was in a flourishing condition, and that the bye-laws were prepared and laid before Sergeant Levinz.'[3] The same day Bank stock was quoted at 101.

Meanwhile the struggle on the Continent was proceeding, William's position having been temporarily strengthened by the funds provided by the Whig capitalists. Moreover, his able opponent Luxembourg was dead, and that great general's successors were no less inferior to him in strategy, than was William himself. The siege of Namur—the occupation of which by Louis XIV. had been so heavy a blow—was begun by the allies on the 2nd of July 1695. It was while engaged in this siege that the correspondence before alluded to, between the King and the Duke of Shrewsbury (Secretary of State), relating to Sir John Houblon, took place. Writing from Whitehall, on the 26th of July, the Duke urged the King to return to England, if possible before the intended dissolution of Parliament, and continued: 'The City being much broke by the imprudence of this present Mayor[4] and

1695

---

[1] For the history of the Bank, see Rogers, *The First Nine Years of the Bank of England*; Postlethwaite, *History of the Public Revenue and State of the Realm*, 1759, iv. 487 ; Macaulay, *History*, vol. iv. ; and T. A. Stephens, *A Bibliography of the Bank of England*, 1897.
[2] Luttrell, iii. 376.
[3] *Ibid.* An eminent London lawyer.
[4] Sir Thomas Lane.

some of the Aldermen, and by the heat of many of the Common Council in a dispute they have depending, it is extremely for your Majesty's interest that a person should succeed the present Mayor upon whose loyalty you may depend, and whose prudence and credit would be able to reconcile those animosities, which the weakness of this man has much contributed to increase. Sir John Houblon is the next in turn, and in all respects the fittest one could choose to act this part; but it is to be apprehended if he thinks his being Mayor inconsistent with his being of the Admiralty, he will use his credit to be passed by, and not be willing for the honour of one year to lose a good constant employment. What we propose is, that your Majesty would allow us to assure him that you think his being Mayor of such importance to your interest in the City, that without removing him from the Admiralty Board, you shall readily excuse his attendance for that year, and think he does you better service being Lord Mayor of London than he could do anywhere else.'[1] The King replied to the above letter on the 11th of August approving Shrewsbury's suggestion as to Sir John, and promising to do his best to return home for the elections. He also begged the Duke to assure Sir John from himself, that in the event of his election as Lord Mayor, 'he shall continue on the board of the Admiralty, and that I will this year excuse his attendance at the board.'[2] Meanwhile the intervention of the Lord Keeper had been requisitioned, and Shrewsbury's next letter to the King informs him that 'Lord Somers[3] has spoken to Sir John Houblon, and as I understand has determined him to obey your Majesty's commands in being Mayor. I hope,' he con-

---

[1] Coxe, *Private Correspondence of the Duke of Shrewsbury*, p. 97.

[2] *Ibid.*, p. 100. The original letters from King William are in the French language, and have been translated into English by Archdeacon Coxe. See Preface, p. v.

[3] See for interesting portrait of this great man, Lord Stanhope, *History of England*, i. 207.

tinues, 'that with his authority, and the assistance of a few others, we shall be able to compose the disorders of the City which at present are many, and cause great heats and dissentions.'[1]

It would appear that, a few months before this time, Sir John Houblon had been visited by a family bereavement, which possibly may have still further militated against his undertaking the duties of the Mayoralty. At an earlier period it will be remembered that all the brothers travelled much, and that one or other of them was frequently in the Peninsula; but now their interests were locally cared for by younger members of the family. Sir John Houblon had several sons, none of whom long survived their father; one of them appears to have been acting as representative of the family interests in Portugal, when he lost his life at Lisbon under very unfortunate circumstances, his death being the consequence of a foolish frolic.

As part of the campaign for the year 1694, it had been arranged that while William carried on the war in the Netherlands, naval operations (which hitherto had been confined to the Channel and Atlantic) should be extended to the Mediterranean, where Louis xiv. had now concentrated a powerful fleet. Two squadrons were to take part in these operations, the one under Berkeley remaining in the Channel, while Admiral Russell sailed for the south. Treason at home[2] disclosed the plan to the court of Versailles, and was the cause of the discomfiture of Berkeley's fleet off the coast of Brittany; but Russell, after long delays owing to contrary winds, at length arrived in the Mediterranean where, as we have already seen, he spent many months. During this period the

---

[1] Coxe, *Correspondence*, p. 101.
[2] 'The truth was, as I heard often in my youth from my father and others who had lived in those times, that the Duke [of Marlborough] trusted the Duchess with the secret, and she her sister, the popish Duchess of Tyrconnel.' See *Private Correspondence of Horace Walpole*, London, 1820.

triumphant progress of the French had spread terror
throughout the Peninsula; but such was the awe with
which the victor of La Hogue was regarded by the
enemy, that no sooner had Russell passed the Straits
with the English fleet, than, unwilling to risk a conflict
with an adversary so dreaded, the French commanders
retired hastily. It was at this moment that, relieved
from the fear which had oppressed both inhabitants of
the country and the English residents, great rejoicings
broke out throughout the Peninsula. At Lisbon (where
there was a large colony of English) they were especially
enthusiastic. Luttrell, writing in August 1694, reports   1694
the arrival of news from that place describing these
rejoicings, and the 'noble feast' which was given by
the English merchants in honour of the envoy Mr.
Methuen,[1] lately arrived. He adds, that unfortunately,
when it was over, 'the young gentlemen were moved
to go a-serenading.' In high spirits and flushed with
wine, the young Englishmen forgot the fiery temperament of the southern races, and an escapade begun in
light-hearted folly ended in deep tragedy. The jealous
Portuguese resented the frolic, and a quarrel ensued,
ending in a fight, in which the Englishmen were probably greatly outnumbered; two of them were killed
and others wounded. 'One of Mr. Methuen's sons,'
writes Luttrell, 'and one Mr. Houblon, were the victims
of this unfortunate affair.'[2]

The Licensing Act, established at the Restoration for
the purpose of control over printing and publishing,
expired in 1695, and as it was not renewed, from that
moment the liberty of the press in this country has
been complete.[3] In consequence of the abolition of

---

[1] Author of the Methuen Treaty with Portugal.
[2] Luttrell, iii. 361.
[3] Liberty of the press was for a time allowed during the Commonwealth,
but it was not long before it was subjected to a stricter censorship than
before.

censorship, in a very short time numerous weekly publications began to appear; all the current political and social news of the day (to the receipt of which the public had until now been treated very sparingly) penetrated into the remotest districts of the country. From these newspapers, much interesting matter is to be extracted. A topic much discussed and of absorbing and growing importance to the community was the degradation of the currency, and the consequent embarrassment it caused. In one of these new journals 95 of events, the writer remarks, in a 'Letter to a friend the 18th of May 1695': 'Guineas continue to be at 29 and 30 shillings; money being so clipp'd it is almost impossible to export any for the payment of our forces in Flanders, or to remit the same by bills of exchange without losing above the fourth part of the sum; for which reason the Bank of England has resolved to settle a bank at Antwerp.'[1] He goes on to say that the directors of the Bank had, on the 16th of May, concluded an advantageous treaty for the King and nation with the Lords of the Treasury, and that it was said they had obtained leave to coin money at Antwerp; and that the deputy-governor of 'this Bank (Mr. Michael Godfrey) and Sir James Houblon were to go to Flanders within a few days.'[2] The same day Luttrell reports the holding of a general court of the Bank, at which these decisions were accepted; 'his Majestie and the Elector of Bavaria having agreed thereto.' He adds, 'they have appointed Sir James Houblon, Sir William Scawen, and Mr. Michael Godfrey deputy-governors to goe thither, to methodize the same.'[3] In the news-letter of the following Saturday, the writer was able to inform his friends 'that the Royal Bank had settled everything

---

[1] *An Historical Account of the Public Transactions of Christendom.* In a letter to a friend in the country. No. 8, Saturday, 18 May 1695.
[2] *Ibid.*
[3] Luttrell, iii. 473, 18 May 1695.

in relation to the new Bank for Antwerp,'[1] while another 'news' writer, boasts of the convenience bound to accrue from the new Bank, 'the design of it appearing extream feasible, and convenient for the paying of the army and other incidents of the war, in the coin of their countries, with much less charge and trouble than in former years.'[2]

But while outside the councils of the Bank the efforts of the directors to meet the requirements of the King in Flanders were accepted as satisfactory, it was very different with regard to some of those subscribers who had embarked their money in Bank stock. It would appear from a report ordered to be taken by the general court in 1697, that the general court on the 16th of May had been a very stormy one. For it was then that these gentlemen learnt the disquieting details as to the great sums of money sent over to Antwerp by the directors. Between the 9th of October 1694 and May 1695 these remittances had amounted to '£690,383, 16s. 4d. sterling.'[3] The agent of the Bank at Antwerp was Monsieur de Coning, who apparently supplied the necessities of the King from time to time through Lord Ranelagh.

All this while the three deputies were waiting for a fair wind and their convoy,[4] but finally set out on the 30th of May. 'The Earl Rivers' (a news-letter reports on the following day) 'and the Lord Cutts, and likewise the directors of the Mint at Antwerp appointed by the Royal Bank of England,—are gone to Flanders.'[5] The promoters of the scheme were disappointed as to its ultimate success, although at the first there seemed a good prospect to the contrary. The historian of the first eventful nine years of the Bank of England finds

1695

---

[1] *Historical Account*, etc., No. 9, 25 May 1695.
[2] *Intelligence, Domestic and Foreign*, No. 4, Friday, 24 May 1695.
[3] See Tract (Crawford Library).
[4] *An Historical Account*, etc., No. 9.
[5] *Intelligence*, etc., No. 6, 31 May.

evidence, in the fluctuations of Bank stock, of the anxiety and stress through which the country was now passing, but sees nothing to account for the 'tendency downwards' during the months of April and May, beyond the 'general uncertainty of a campaign in which William was commanding in person, except it be the rumour that the Bank had determined to establish a branch at Antwerp, where they were to coin money to pay the army in Flanders.'[1]

It is possible that the Bank directors had been obliged in some measure to alter their procedure as to supplying money to the King, owing to the pressure brought to bear on them at the general court. The unsoundness of the policy of a mint at Antwerp would appear to have been immediately felt in financial circles; hence the 'tendency downwards' of Bank stock. But the contemporary tracts, etc., bear strong evidence of the anger and distrust of their subscribers, who, anxious to meet the difficulty and loss of the heavy exchange in the transmission of money abroad, brought about the only measure undertaken by the Bank which was destined to be a failure; nevertheless shortly after the departure of the party for the seat of war, the Bank made a temporary advance of £150,000 to the government on the security of two new taxes.[2]

The three directors went first to Antwerp, where they immediately set about the difficult task which had drawn them thither. Meanwhile Lords Rivers and Cutts, and the other officers who had accompanied them, went straight to join the King before Namur, in the siege of which town he was now engaged.[3] It was more than a fortnight before the Bank directors, having accomplished their mission at Antwerp, appeared before the

[1] Rogers, *First Nine Years of the Bank of England*, pp. 26, 27.
[2] Luttrell, 15 June.
[3] See *The Siege of Namur*, 'by a gentleman attending upon his Majesty.'

King at his headquarters in front of Namur, and it is
to be presumed that they brought with them a sum of
money to meet his immediate requirements. At the
time of their arrival all things were arranged and disposed for an immediate and furious attack upon the
town. There are several interesting accounts of the
siege of Namur from the pens of individuals who
personally assisted at all the operations, and in essential
particulars their accounts agree as to the events that
took place in the storming of the city, as do also those
accounts given by Luttrell and the *London Gazette*, from
letters received from the front. The author of *An
Exact Journal of the Siege of Namur* tells us that 'upon
the 27th of July in the morning, his Majesty having   1695
resolved that an attack should be made upon the first
counterscarp of the town, came into the trenches himself, and after he had given ample and requisite orders,
returned to his quarters.' Having dined in his tent, 'in
the afternoon the King went again into the trenches,
and about five o'clock in the afternoon the attack
began.'[1] The story of the tragic ending of the life of
one of the three Bank deputies may be told by the
other two. 'The Bank of England,' writes Luttrell on
the 25th of July, 'had letters from Sir James Houblon
and Sir William Scawen, signifying that they, together
with Mr. Michael Godfrey, deputy-governor of the
Bank, being invited to dine with the King in his tent,
afterwards waited on him to the trenches to view the
same; when a cannon ball killed Godfrey as he stood
near the King.'[2] 'Mr. Godfrey,' writes the war correspondent of the *London Gazette*, 'who was come from
Antwerp to wait upon the King, standing very near his
Majesty in the trenches, had the misfortune to be killed
by a cannon ball; and Monsieur Eck, Lieut.-Colonel of

---

[1] See *An Exact Journal*, etc. Printed for J. Whitlock, near Stationers'
Hall, 1695.
[2] Luttrell, *Brief Relation*, etc., iii. 503.

the Dutch troop of Guards, had his arm taken off by the same shot.'[1]

Poor Godfrey was only thirty-seven years of age, and, as Luttrell records, was an eminent merchant and much respected. So shocked was the London world that the sensitive fluctuations of Bank stock were affected and fell two per cent. after the receipt of the news,[2] while the term 'being Godfreyed' was the cant phrase for some time after the merchant's tragic death.[3]

The tendency of Bank stock was downwards from the time of the establishment of the mint at Antwerp; and in August following the death of Godfrey, some of the largest shareholders in the Bank lost courage, and it was announced that 'Mr. Charles Duncombe and Lord Godolphin this month sold all their effects in the Bank of England,'[4] those of Duncombe amounting to £80,000. The capture of Namur, however, restored confidence in a great measure, and stock was again nearly at par in September; while the directors were able to declare a dividend of four per cent. on the paid-up capital. But this did not last; for, owing to the failure of the mint at Antwerp—which some ascribed to the jealousy and greed of the Dutch, who had reaped great gain upon the high exchange before its establishment,[5]—the Bank embarked upon another expedient to supply the necessities of the King in Flanders. They borrowed £200,000 of the Bank of Amsterdam at four per cent., and paid the same to William 'without first remitting hence.'[6] From this news resulted the fall of five per cent. between the 27th of September and the 4th of October.[7]

---

[1] *London Gazette*, No. 3099, 25 July 1695.   [2] Luttrell, iii. 505.
[3] *London Gazette*, 29 July 1695.
[4] Sidney, Lord Godolphin, First Commissioner of His Majesty's Treasury. Kennet, *History of England*, iii. 693.
[5] See 'A Brief Account of some of the Encroachments and Depredations of the Dutch in 1695.' By Robert Ferguson, surnamed 'the plotter.' *Dict. Nat. Biog.*   [6] Luttrell, 28 Sept.   [7] *Ibid.*

At this juncture, when the affairs of the Bank must have caused him acute anxiety, Sir John Houblon obeyed the King's behest and was elected Lord Mayor of London.   From what we know of his quiet and 1695 unobtrusive habits and tastes, his unaffected piety, and the already heavy labours in which he was engaged, this compliance probably cost him more than at first sight would be imagined.   For the worldly honours of the great position to which he was called, he would have cared but little ; nor would he have rejoiced in the panegyrics lavished upon him as the holder of so many distinguished posts at one and the same time ; yet there is no doubt that politically his year of office was one deeply important to the City and to the new régime that it had helped to found, as it witnessed the sealing of the interests of the great and rising middle class to those of the King and Queen and their successors.   For during his tenure of the mayoralty Sir John's influence cemented those interests irrevocably, in the pledging of the vast resources of the City of London (as represented by the Bank of England) upon the success of the King's struggle in the Netherlands with the far-reaching ambition of Louis XIV.   Shrewsbury and Lord Somers were happy in their discrimination of character, when they saw in Sir John Houblon the person most fitted to aid in the accomplishment of the ends the King had in view ; but it is to be questioned if any one—beyond, perhaps, the brother who throughout his life was his dearest and closest friend [1]—was fully alive to the true motives of John Houblon's devotion to the spirit of the Revolution and his systematic support of the war.   From his Flemish ancestors he had inherited that love of liberty and progress which subordinated every other consideration to their advancement.   Like them also he would have staked his all, even life itself, in the

[1] Sir James Houblon.

cause of religious freedom. The policy of William III.
in the matter of the war he believed to be sound and far-
reaching, and that his success was of infinite importance;
and so Sir John exerted himself to the utmost in the
way which alone made success possible, viz. the financing
of the war. To him and to the City financiers the
stability of the new government was vital; and in the
sacrifices they made and the risks they ran, they recognised that they had no choice but to carry through
boldly what they had begun. This they accomplished
in the face of the manifest disapproval and jealousy of
their subscribers, whilst the distrust of the public is
shown in the fluctuations of Bank stock, and in the
virulent abuse of tracts and pamphlets. For, while the
governing body sank their personal advantage and that
of the Bank in the effort to cope with the emergency of
the times, the ordinary shareholder saw only the risk to
his own pocket in his sacrifices to enable the King to
carry his work to a successful issue. And we shall
presently see that the outcry against the directors was
such as to shake the friendship and confidence of the
government, as it had already done that of Godolphin.
This base desertion nearly accomplished the ruin of
the Bank, as it occurred at a moment when its enemies
had struck it a blow which shook it to its foundations.

1695 'This morning,' writes Luttrell on the 28th of September 1695, 'Sir John Houblon, one of the Lords of
the Admiralty and Governor of the Bank of England,
was chosen Lord Mayor of this Citty,'[1] and the *Gazette*
informs us that upon the hustings after his election, he
made a speech to the Common Hall, 'full of expressions
of loyalty and duty to his Majesty and his government,
and of zeal and affection for the Citty.'[2] After this 'the
new Lord Mayor, attended by the Aldermen and livery-
men of this Citty (who came down to Westminster in

---

[1] Luttrell, iii. 531.   [2] *London Gazette*, No. 3118.

their barges), was sworn before the Barons of the Exchequer, from whence he returned into the Citty where a splendid entertainment was provided, at which were the Lords of the Council and Judges with divers of the nobility and other persons of quality.'[1]

Soon after this the King made a 'progress' through part of the country; and in this manner he utilised the interval between his return after the fall of Namur, and the assembling of the new Parliament. In the course of this 'progress' he visited some of the more important among the nobility and gentry. According to the *London Gazette*, William started from London on the 28th of October on horseback. Besides being attended by a large retinue, he was escorted on the first day's journey by the City magistracy in their *Formalities*—that is to say, in state. 'The Lord Mayor' (Sir John Houblon), says the *Gazette*, 'and the Aldermen in their scarlet gowns, with the Recorder, Steward, Sheriffs, Town-clerk, and Common-council men, all in their Formalities, attended his Majesty on horseback from the Bar-gates of the City to Colonel Pownall's house, where his Majesty lay.'[2]

The ceremonies attendant on the election of the Lord Mayor, together with the procedure of his office throughout the year, were extremely elaborate and stately. In an old black-letter pamphlet of the date of 1692, we find the order of these proceedings as enacted on these occasions. That part of it which relates to the taking of the oath by the Lord Mayor at Westminster, and the attendances at St. Paul's, we transcribe.

[1] See the *Post Boy*, No. 75, and Luttrell, iii. 543.
[2] *London Gazette*, No. 3128.

The Order of My Lord Mayor, the Aldermen, and the Sheriffs: For their Meeting and Wearing of their Apparel throughout the whole Year. Printed by Samuel Roycroft, Printer to the Honourable City of London, 1692. 35 pages. (Black Letter.)

On the morrow after Simon and Judes-day, for my Lords going to take his Oath at Westminster.

All the Aldermen and the Sheriffs come to my new Lord at eight of the Clock, in their Scarlet Gowns *Velvet Hood.* furred, and their Cloaks born with them, and *Cap of Main-* their Horses, and so ride to the Guild-Hall, *tenance.* and the Batchelors and the Livery of my Lords Company before him.

But the old Lord rideth from his own place to the Hall alone, having no Officers to wait upon him but the *A Velvet Hood* Common Hunt, as a Gentleman Usher, *for both* going, and those Officers that be at liberty, *Mayors.* and the Common Hunt his man (with his own men following him) and so tarrieth at the Hall.

And after they be all come together, they take their Horses, and ride to the Vinetree, and there take Barge to Westminster Bridge.

And after they be landed, the Lord Mayor and the Aldermen put on their Cloaks within the Palace, and go round the Hall, making Courtesie in the Hall, and so go up to the Exchequer to be sworn. Then after the Oath taken in the Exchequer, they come down again, and go first to the King's Bench, and then to the Common Place, and so put off their Cloaks, and go about the King's Tombs in Westminster Abbey, and then take Barge again. And being landed, he rideth to the Guild-Hall to Dinner, and all the Companies of the City with him : And at their coming into the Hall, the new Lord Mayor, with two of the ancient Aldermen, Master Recorder, and the Sheriffs, go up

THE HABIT OF A
LORD MAIOR OF
THE HON.ble CITTY of
LONDON

Exculpta est hac effigies Anno Dni 1657 Mense Marty exeunte.

to my Lords Table to bid them Welcom, and likewise all the other guests there, and from thence to the Lady Mayoress Table, and so come out to the Gentlewomans Table, and to the Judges: And so from thence my said new Lord Mayor goeth into the Chamberlains Office, where he dineth: And the old Lord Mayor at their first coming into the Hall, goeth up to the high Table in the Hustings, and there keepeth the State for that Feast. And after the Hall is almost served of the Second, then the new Lord Mayor goeth with Master Recorder and those Aldermen that dine with him, to bid the old Lord and all the Guests in the Hall Welcom. Then after Dinner goeth to St. Pauls with all the Companies waiting before my Lord.

For going to St. Paul's on All-Saints-day, Christmas-day, Twelfth-day, and Candlemas-day.

All the Aldermen and the Sheriffs come to my Lords place in their Scarlet Gowns furred, their Cloaks and Horses, and from thence ride to the Guild-Hall, my Lords Company and the Batchelors before him, and there hear Evening Prayer: And when Prayer is done, they ride to St. Paul's, and there both the new Lord Mayor and the old put on their Cloaks, and go up to the Quire, and there hear the Sermon: Which done, they go about the Church, and *A Velvet Hood for both. All-Saints-day is the last Day that the old Lord rides, and with the new. Cap of Maintenance.* there put off their Cloaks where they were put on. Then they take their Horses again, and the Aldermen bring my Lord Home; and then they have Spice-Bread and Hippocras, and so take their leave of my Lord.

In spite of the equestrian skill displayed by a late Lord Mayor on a great occasion but a few years ago, it is hardly probable that the horsemanship of the City magnates of these latter days would bear a favourable comparison with that of their precursors in office more than two hundred years ago! We prefer, however, to believe that even then, they were wont to ride upon docile steeds of not too high a courage, suitable to the gravity of deportment, large periwigs, and ample robes of their august cavaliers.

According to the time-honoured custom, still observed in the Lord Mayor's 'Show' of these days, a great pageant was formerly enacted on the day following upon the election of the Lord Mayor. In one among a series of extremely rare pamphlets (copies of which are to be found in the British Museum) called *The Triumphs of London*,[1] Settle the author—who was at once master of the ceremonies and City poet—prints a full account of the pageant performed on the 29th of **1695** October 1695, 'For the entertainment of the Right Honorable Sᵣ John Houblon Kᵗ, Lord Mayor of the City of London, one of the Lords of the Admiralty, Governor of the royal Bank of England. Containing a true description of the several Pageants, etc., etc. . . . all prepared at the proper costs and charges of the Worshipful Company of Grocers.' In his epistle dedicatory the author enlarges, in the laudatory and exaggerated style common at the time, upon the virtues and many honours borne by the new Lord Mayor, whose qualifications for homage he pronounced to be the greater, that 'His Lordship has that innate modesty that he rather studies to deserve encomiums than to hear them.'[2] Sir John Houblon had belonged originally to the Drapers' Company. Since this is one of the twelve great City companies out of whose ranks it was customary to choose the chief magistrate, it is not clear why this transference was made; but, as it had already taken place when he assumed the mayoralty, it is

[1] See Fairholt, *Lord Mayor's Pageants.* Percy Society, 1843, p. 113.
[2] *Ibid.*

probable that it occurred at the time when by Sir John's influence, according to Luttrell, the meetings of the court of directors of the Bank of England were transferred from Mercers' Chapel to Grocers' Hall.   This was in September 1694.[1]   The Grocers,[2] at any rate, not only commemorated his assumption of the mayoralty with great magnificence, but within a few months of that event, elected him Master of their Company.[3]

[1] See Luttrell, *Brief Relation*, iii. 332.

[2] 'The word Grocer was a term at first distinguishing merchants of this society in opposition to inferior retailers.   For that they usually sold in gross quantities by great weights ; and in some of our old books the word signifies merchants, that in their merchandises dealt for the whole of any kind.'   See Ravenhill, 'The Case of the Company of Grocers stated,' 1682.

[3] *Dict. Nat. Biography*, Sir John Houblon, vol. xxvii. 417.

CHAPTER XVI

THE FIRST GOVERNOR

'. . . Tyre, the crowning city, whose merchants are princes, whose
traffickers are the honourable of the earth.'—ISAIAH xxiii. 8.

AN ancient map of London made in 1633, before the
Great Fire, hangs in one of the rooms at Magdalene
College, Cambridge, containing the Pepysian Library. In
this map the scale is large enough to show the elevation
of the more important houses in the city. From it we
find that the original house in Threadneedle Street
belonging to Sir John Houblon possessed three lofty
gables facing the street, the garden extending behind.
When the house was rebuilt after the fire, the plan
was altogether altered. In Hatton's *New View of
London*, we are told that the houses rebuilt by the great
London merchants were numerous and magnificent;
their 'courts, offices, and all necessary apartments
inclosed to themselves,' some with 'noble gates and
frontispieces towards the street,' but that they were
chiefly remarkable as 'ornamental, commodious, and
richly furnished within.' 'For convenience,—and because of the great quantity of ground they are built on,
—they are,' he adds, 'generally situate backward.'[1] A
coloured sketch and plan in the British Museum show
this description to apply exactly to the house of Sir
John Houblon as rebuilt by him. It now stood back
from the street, being approached by a stone-paved

[1] *New View of London*, ii. 627.

SIR JOHN HOUBLON'S HOUSE IN THREADNEEDLE STREET

passage or carriage-way, leading into the open court beyond. The house stood on the opposite side of this court, being approached by a flight of steps, while on each side were ranged buildings comprising stables and offices. Behind the house was a large garden extending for a considerable distance, the space of ground measuring about two hundred and forty feet deep by a hundred feet. On the side facing Threadneedle Street it was somewhat narrower; the plan shows the garden to have been carefully laid out and planted with trees. Close by was the fine old Church of St. Christopher le Stocks with its churchyard.

It was not till the year 1680 that Sir John Houblon 1680 had permitted himself the luxury of a country home. Doubtless the airy London house and garden were deemed sufficient for the requirements of his simple tastes and the well-being of his family. His new property was, like almost all the merchants' country houses at that time, in Essex. The mansion, which is situated in the parish of High Ongar, is now used as a farmhouse; at the time of the purchase it was called the New House, and it still goes by the same name.[1]

The credit of the 'money men,' as they were nick-named outside the City, was not allowed to arrive at its full measure without strong and vigorous opposition. The old ruling class of landowners had suddenly found themselves at disadvantage in political influence, and naturally sought eagerly for occasion to stay the tide of a change so unwelcome. Money was required; it was not desired to dispute that fact, for Parliament was now confronted with the necessity for again providing large sums for the prosecution of the war in the Netherlands. But the effort was now renewed to provide that money from other sources, so as to obviate the necessity for appealing for a fresh loan to the hated owners of

[1] Close Roll, 32 Charles II., Part V., No. 25.

wealth in the City. The plan of a Land Bank of two years before had failed, for it had been obviously based upon unsound and even ridiculous assumptions. But now a new project was brought forward which, it was the confident expectation of the landed interest, would secure the money required for the war.[1] This scheme, which was supported by Parliament and had been subscribed to by the King, failed also; for although the owners of land eagerly desired to borrow money on the security of their land, they were not in a position to lend it. And so the loan, when placed upon the market, met with no response from the public. Only when the government had realised, by the ignominious failure of the Land Bank,[2] the hopelessness of obtaining money elsewhere, did they again turn to the City and the great Bank which had owed its incorporation to the necessities of the State. As we shall presently see, by the countenance and encouragement accorded by the government to the promoters of the Land Bank, they aimed a heavy blow at the institution which had already rendered them such signal service, leading to a crisis which only the presence of mind and resource of the governor and directors of the Bank were able to meet. The first effect of this blow, coming as it did when other circumstances had combined to make it a time of extreme anxiety and difficulty, was to send down the shares of the Bank. The price of Bank

1696 stock fell from 107 on the 31st of January 1695/6, to 83 on the 14th of February following—a significant sign of the stress of the times. The outlook was indeed dark and anxious for those who had staked their all upon the stability of the government of William and the success of the war, in the face of the ignorance and jealousy of an opposition intellectually incapable of appreciating either the great stake at issue, or their efforts to meet it.

[1] See Broadside by Dr. Hugh Chamberlayne, 15 August 1695.
[2] Only £2500 was subscribed beside the £5000 of the King.

And now, not only had that government abandoned them, its friends, but was itself in imminent danger.

The security of William's throne—always an anxiety to the Whig financiers from the many dangers with which it was beset by the plotting of the Jacobites—had received a severe blow by the death of Queen Mary; for it shook the allegiance of a vast number of persons who, seeing in her a legitimate sovereign and heir to her father, had never accorded to her husband more than the respect due to the consort of the Queen. Plots and agitations thickened at home, and the party of King James in France was greatly strengthened and encouraged. But though the French were only too willing to help him to regain his crown (could this end be accomplished without risk to themselves), they were resolute not to move till success became a certainty by a considerable rising on this side the channel; while at the same time the Jacobites at home felt themselves too weak to move until the French should already have crossed the seas.[1] The consequence was, that while each waited for the other, the more reckless and unscrupulous of the party determined to cut short the tension, and, by a bold stroke, to accomplish what fair means hesitated to venture; the result was the attempt to assassinate King William. The discovery of the plot, together with the dismay caused by the threatened French invasion which was to have followed immediately, brought about an immense reaction in William's favour, and resulted, in spite of his general unpopularity, in a decided increase of strength to his throne. Remembering the society formed, a hundred years before, for the protection of Queen Elizabeth after a similar attempt upon her life, a great 'National Association for King William' was enrolled, the orange ribbon of which was seen on every man's hat; and on the 4th of April 1696,

[1] Von Ranke, *History of England*, v. 113.

the House of Commons solemnly 'handed over the roll of the Association' for preservation among the State records.[1]

A general thanksgiving was held throughout the country and in all the City churches on the 16th of April. The City magistracy went in state to St. Mary le Bow,[2] where a thanksgiving sermon was preached before the Lord Mayor, Aldermen, and City Companies, which, containing many encomiums upon, and congratulations to, their Lord Mayor on the 'treble joy' he was supposed to feel on 'the preservation of the Metropolis, Admiralty, and Bank of England, all of which are your Lordship's honourable and next concerns,' was afterwards printed by desire of the Court of Aldermen and dedicated to Sir John Houblon.[3]

Meanwhile King William had been wise enough to shut his eyes to many things for which, had he chosen, he might have impeached various well-known men for high treason, even amongst those about his person. Even before the attempt on his life, however, he sometimes dealt severely with suspected persons, though detective work was occasionally clumsy in those days, and mistakes in identity occurred, as in the following circumstance. A State Paper gives us a letter from T. Fitzpatrick to William Bridgeman, Esq., at his house in Pall Mall, by which it appears that a gentleman wholly innocent of treason had been arrested by order of Secretary Trenchard in August 1693, and 'not only had his house been searched that morning, but he himself committed into the hands of the messengers.' 'I believe,' continues Fitzpatrick, 'if Secretary Trenchard knew that he is an officer of the King of Spain, and served twenty years in Spain, and is now going there in

[1] Von Ranke, *History of England*, v. 122.
[2] The rebuilding of St. Paul's was still in progress.
[3] *Thanksgiving Sermon*, by W. Stephens, B.D. Printed at the Three Pigeons in Cornhill, 1696. 4to.

order to go to the West Indies, and that Sir James
Houblon and several others of the most considerable
merchants of the City are concerned with him for above
£40,000, he would not believe him to be a person likely
to conspire against the government.'[1]   A proclamation
had been issued in 1692 offering a reward of £20 for
the apprehension of persons employed in the printing
and distribution of seditious pamphlets, etc., of which a
large number continually appeared.   A more successful
attempt was soon afterwards made to run to earth the
mischief, and the reward was at length claimed, the
successful applicant being John Bradshaw, the City
Marshal.   With the claim, he presented Sir John
Houblon—the Lord Mayor's—certificate, to the effect
that the culprits had been brought before him, and that
a printing press and many documents were found in
the house searched.[2]

Sir John Houblon's 'triple honours' would have
weighed pretty heavily on him at this time, especially
that of the governorship of the great Bank.   For the
little band of directors, who in the more serious troubles
yet to come remained firm with him in the policy they
had marked out, were beset with the discontent and
irritability of their own shareholders, who, outside their
intimate counsels, rebelled against the conduct of its
affairs.   It was now that, encouraged by the scurvy
treatment accorded to their rival by Parliament, other
enemies of the Bank than those in the Commons were
hopeful of being able to injure or even ruin it.   Besides
holding the original loans for the prosecution of the war,
the subscribers to the Bank were allowed by their
charter to accept money on deposit and lend it out at
interest.[3]   It was this privilege which had specially

[1] Calendar of State Papers, 1693, p. 286.
[2] Treasury Papers, vol. xxxvi., No. 35.
[3] Cunningham, *Growth of English Industry and Commerce in Modern Times*, p. 395.

excited the jealousy of the Goldsmiths, who, as we have seen, had hitherto alone exercised it.   The result was a conspiracy to ruin the new Bank ; a piece of sharp practice unworthy of the great company and its past traditions.   The opportunity presented itself at the critical moment of the renewal of the coinage by Act
1696   of Parliament in 1696.   This measure temporarily disorganised finance, and coin was very scarce.   Its debased condition had long been a matter of extreme difficulty and danger to business, owing to the uncertainty of value and the many disputes arising therefrom. All coin that was not so clipped and worn as to be light, was hoarded by its owners to such an extent that money transactions were extremely difficult, and at length the time had arrived when its renewal was a matter of absolute necessity.   So little were the laws of finance understood by the public, and indeed by public men, that although the vigorous mind of Elizabeth had grasped and acted upon the principle that the intrinsic worth of the coin should equal that of its face or nominal value, the fallacy of an artificial alteration of the standard was still considered an open question.   It was suggested in the reign of Charles 1., when the measure was vigorously and successfully opposed by
1691   Sir Robert Cotton ; [1] it was again bruited in 1691, when a bill was actually in preparation for carrying it into effect.   On this occasion we find by a letter of that date from Sir John Houblon to Sir Henry Caple (now in the British Museum), that he was in consultation with the Tory government upon the question at issue. It is needless to say, that the measure upon which his opinion was invited met with Sir John's emphatic disapproval.   We subjoin the covering letter which he wrote upon this occasion when forwarding his paper

[1] The collector of the Cottonian MSS. at the British Museum.   See for his life, *Dictionary of National Biography*, xii. 311.

upon the subject to Sir Henry.   The paper itself we have not been able to trace :—

'HONNᴰ Sʳ,—I have herewith sent you my thoughts about the   1691 alteration of the coyne, together with Sir Robert Cotton's speech spoken soe many yeares since to King Charles the first in his counsell upon the same subject.   I doubt not but when your liesure will permitt you to peruse the same, you will be satisfied that the bill will never answere the ends designed— not to say pretended; for I am apt to beleeve it hath bine promoted by some who are not of your house, for private interest.

'This is most certaine, that soe often as wee are necessitated to send bullion out of the kingdome, which happens chiefly in tyme of warre when our importations of foreigne goods amounts to more in the value than the exportation of our native comoditys; that then bullion will arise here in price, and be worth more by 2d. to 3d. the ounce than the mint will give, as it hath bine for these three yeares last past.   Now at such a tyme, let parliament alter ye standard and raise it never soe much, yett the bullion will be sould for more than the mint will give, because bullion may be transported and coyne cannot; and therefore let the coyne be lessened in weight never soe much, yett still that light new coyne may be melted downe with advantage, because it will yield more in the bullion than the value amounts to in the new coyne.   And though the Kings of Portugall have within these 50 yeares last passed, lessened their crusade or crowne, from the reall value of 5s.—as then it was—to 2:6 as now it is; (which was done att 5 severall tymes upon pretence of keeping his money in his kingdome); yett still it is brought out of his kingdome, because wee sell our goods there, not accordinge to the denomination of his coyne, but accordinge to the intrinsicall value of the silver there [is] in his coyne.

'Please to pardon this trouble and command as you have occasion.—Sir, your honnors most humble obedient sarvᵗ,

'Jɴᵒ HOUBLON.

'28ᵗʰ Janʸ. 1691.
    'For yᵉ Honnorable
        'Sir HENRY CAPLE these.'

The proposal to alter the standard was dropped in
1691; but it was again brought forward in 1696, when
John Locke was said to have been chiefly instrumental
in dissuading the Junto Government from adopting so
mischievous a measure.   So few were those who had
as yet mastered the principles which are now universally
accepted, that in the division taken upon the vexed
question in the House of Commons, the resolution
rejecting it was carried by eleven votes only.[1]   Nevertheless it was conceived possible by the public that the
alteration might yet be carried out by the government,
and it was partly due to this idea, that after the issue of
the new coin it was still hoarded.   It was two years
after the establishment of the Bank of England that
the financial ability of Montague was brought to bear
upon the important work of the re-coinage, in the carrying through of which he had the assistance of two of
the ablest men of the time, viz. John Locke and Sir
Isaac Newton, the latter of whom was appointed Warden
of the Mint.   In the actual work of the collection of
the abraded money, and its transference to the mint
to be melted up, they had the assistance and co-operation of the Bank of England.   All the old debased and
clipped coin brought in for exchange before a certain
1696   date, viz. the 4th of May, was accepted by the Bank at
its nominal or full value, after which date it ceased to
be current as coin.   In spite of every effort, the coinage
of the new money was at a rate too slow to meet the
demand, and there was a great scarcity of coin.   But
Bank paper was freely issued, the credit of the Bank
being so high that it was accepted without demur
pending the issue of the coin.   At this juncture the
Goldsmiths found their opportunity for embarrassing
the Bank.   They bought up all the paper they could
lay their hands on, and so soon as the old coinage was

[1] Rogers, *First Nine Years of the Bank of England*, p. 47.

withdrawn on the 4th of May, presented it for immediate payment in cash.   It was now that Sir John Houblon devised a plan by which he met the necessity of the moment, and began a masterly series of manœuvres by means of which he extricated the Bank from the difficulties and dangers which beset it from all sides,[1] and having piloted it through the crisis by the exertion of tact and influence, afterwards persuaded the share-holders to make further efforts to supply the pressing needs of the King for the prosecution of the war.

The action of the Goldsmiths with regard to Bank paper led, as was expected, to a panic and a run upon the Bank.   The governor met the crisis by offering to the *bona-fide* applicants for their money, fifteen per cent. of it in new coin, while pledging the Bank to supply the residue so soon and as fast as the mint could supply them.[2]   As to the malicious action of the Goldsmiths, he boldly refused to entertain their application for im-mediate settlement of their demands ; at the same time appealing to the courts for protection.   Pending a de-cision of the legal question—the whole of the resources of the Bank having been absorbed by the State loans[3] —Sir John obtained the money needed to meet the im-mediate demands of the legitimate customers of the Bank, by means of an expedient ; a bold stroke in finance for those days, but justified by the extreme danger of the moment.   He made an assessment upon the capital of the shareholders of twenty per cent. ; and so it was, that with the money thus obtained, the Bank weathered the storm which had threatened to overwhelm it.   On the 11th of June the directors met the pressing necessity of the State (the Land Bank having proved a failure), by bor-

---

[1] Rogers, *First Nine Years of the Bank of England*, pp. 62, 66.
[2] *Ibid.*, p. 63.
[3] The government had failed to perform their part of the original compact by declining to pay the interest on the loans, offering the Bank tallies instead.

rowing of their own subscribers.   They also drew upon the Bank of Amsterdam for £100,000, and were thus able to supply the government with £340,000 ; the whole of which sums they subsequently repaid.[1]   In spite of the serious injury inflicted on it by its support of the Land Bank, we thus find the Bank of England again coming forward to help William's government with funds for the war.   It was now, too, that Exchequer bills were issued for the first time, and found so useful as a means of raising money, that their use was subsequently greatly extended.[2]   Charles Montague was credited with their invention; at any rate his financial genius (leaning on the experience of the City fathers), had recognised the certainty of failure of the Land Bank, and adroitly succeeded in grafting on to the bill for that mad scheme a clause, enabling the government to issue bills which should be negotiable in the form of paper.[3]   The re-coinage was afterwards safely carried through, a work of immense labour and difficulty, in which Montague and his colleagues Locke and Newton were loyally assisted by the 'shrewd and far-seeing men who constituted the first directors of the Bank of England.'[4] But only when the Commons,—some five months after the withdrawal of the old money and in response to the earnest appeal of Montague,—finally abandoned all thought of altering the currency, was the new coin just issued allowed to circulate freely by the public.

During the time in which he was Warden of the Mint, Sir Isaac Newton was probably much in the City,[5] and with him, as also with John Locke, the Bank's governor was doubtless in frequent communication.   It is probable,

---

[1] Rogers, *First Nine Years of the Bank of England*, pp. 65, 93, and Luttrell, 11 June 1696.
[2] Hamilton on the National Debt.
[3] Macaulay, iv. 698.
[4] Rogers, *First Nine Years of the Bank of England*, pp. 45, 68.
[5] He lived in Cambridge, but the coinage was actually carried on in a house at Bristol.

that the great mind of Newton by his wisdom and counsel both supported and encouraged his friends in the Bank during the late crisis of May 1696. It was indeed chiefly owing to the immense difficulties Newton had encountered in a rapid issue of the new coin from the mint which, had led to the dilemma of its scarcity.

But while Montague was giving his whole energies to the financial situation, neither the Secretary of State nor the other great officers who shared with him the government during William's absence abroad, appear to have concerned themselves with the internal working of City affairs.[1] Absorbed in the project of the Land Bank which the government had expected to provide the funds so urgently needed, Shrewsbury had apparently forgotten all about the earlier loans of the Bank of England. But for this, it seems strange to find him writing from Whitehall at this time to the King: 'Some of my acquaintance tell me there is another set of men who will upon exigence show their goodwill.'[2] This was in answer to a letter from William urging that money should be at once raised and sent to him at any cost. 'At present,' he wrote, 'I see no resource which can prevent the army from mutiny or total desertion.'[3] The next day, having decided in his anxiety to send to England, he wrote: 'In the extremity to which we are reduced I have been obliged to send the Earl of Portland to England, that he might represent it to you more particularly.' This referred to the question of the reassembling of Parliament for the voting of supply,—a measure which he strongly deprecated during his absence from England, while he nevertheless admitted that 'rather than perish all must be risked.'[4] The loss of time which had resulted from the fruitless project of

1696

---

[1] For the list of the Lords Justices left in authority by the King, see Kennet, *Complete History of England*, iii. 693. 1706.

[2] Coxe, *Correspondence*, p. 134.

[3] *Ibid.*, July 20/30, p. 129.   [4] *Ibid.*, July 21/31, p. 130.

the Land Bank had indeed placed King William in a position of the greatest embarrassment; for while the government waited for the promised funds it was to produce, his operations at the seat of war were paralysed by lack of means.

The shareholders of the Bank of England were still sore at the assessment upon them of twenty per cent. of their capital, but the directors, upon the urgent appeal of the ministers and the Earl of Portland, undertook to lay the matter before a general court, without the consent of which they could do no more.   So important was the occasion, that the speech of the Governor was carefully considered by the directors[1] before its delivery to the assembled court, on the 15th of August 1696, at Grocers' Hall.   Meanwhile the ministers awaited the result with anxiety. 'If this should not succeed,' the Duke of Shrewsbury wrote to the King, 'God knows what can be done.   Anything must be tried and ventured, rather than lie down and die!'[2]   Lord Macaulay in his history has written a brilliant account of this most momentous time, when the future not only of England but of the powers of Europe appeared, in the success or failure of William III. and his allies, to be trembling in the balance; for William was now in the direst straits.   Once before, at the critical moment before the capture of Namur, the situation had been saved by the timely action of the Bank of England in supplying funds, and now again Lord Macaulay accords to it the credit of having stepped into the breach and enabled the struggle to be carried on which, within a few months, was to end in the Peace of Ryswick.   Macaulay's account of the important meeting in Grocers' Hall of the 15th August we give in his own words.

1696   'On the 15th of August, a great epoch in the history

---

[1] *Records of the Bank.*
[2] Coxe, *Correspondence,* 7 August.

of the Bank, the General Court, was held. In the chair sat Sir John Houblon, the Governor, who was also Lord Mayor of London, and what in these times would be thought strange—a Commissioner of the Admiralty. Sir John, in a speech every word of which had been written and had been carefully considered by the directors, explained the case and implored the assembly to stand by King William. There was at first a little murmuring. "If our notes would do," it was said, "we would be most willing to assist; but £200,000 in hard money at a time like this!" The Governor announced explicitly "that nothing but gold or silver would supply the necessity of the army in Flanders." At length the question was put to the vote, and every hand in the hall was held up for sending the money.'[1]

The following day the Earl of Portland dined with the Lord Mayor, as did also some of the Lords Justices.[2] As the 16th of August was a Sunday, this dinner with the Lord Mayor was probably a private entertainment at Sir John Houblon's own house. The next day Portland hoped to sail for Holland[3] taking with him the money which was to relieve the King of his pressing necessities; but the difficulty of arranging the matter in so short a time was probably the reason he could not start till Tuesday, the 18th of August, on which day 'he set out from Whitehall for Margate' in order to embark for Flanders on the royal yacht *Transport*.[4] Meanwhile the *Centurion* and *Essex*, men-of-war, repaired to Margate to attend him in his passage to Holland. He carried with him bills of exchange for above £200,000, 'the rest to be remitted speedily.'[5]

On the 24th of August the King was able to announce

---

[1] Macaulay, *History of England*, iv. 705. The vote was, however, not unanimous. Macaulay does not mention the large sum supplied by the bank on the 11th of June.
[2] *The Postman*, No. 199.   [3] *Ibid.*
[4] *Ibid.*, No. 200.   [5] *Ibid.*, 20 August 1696.

to Shrewsbury the arrival of Lord Portland with the
money, adding that 'he has fully informed me of what
passed during his journey to England;'[1] he also wrote
of his message of thanks to the Bank, 'it being very
reasonable that they should be rewarded for the good
services they have rendered me on this occasion.'[2] But
while expressing his thanks, the King soon appealed for
a further supply of money; in proffering this request
to the Bank, Shrewsbury found them 'a little restive
because the Treasury are not ready to come to any
account with them as yet,' . . . and complained 'that
they are no longer willing to continue the supply of
money which they have promised, until they have some
certainty what consideration will be had of their past
losses.'[3] So little were the King and his ministers
tolerant of the ordinary procedure of business, that this
no more than ordinary prudence on the part of the Bank
—which had already suffered considerably from the
neglect of their obligations on the part of the government—was received with astonishment and disappointment by those at the seat of war; and Portland wrote
home that 'this is shewing very little confidence, after
being apprised of the King's order to the Treasury.'[4]
Money was, however, forthcoming, and the King was
supplied till the close of the campaign.[5]

Although the Bank had not only been saved from ruin
by its own energy and resource, but had been praised
and honoured for the services it had rendered to the
State, it was not yet in smooth water, principally through
the continued hostility of its enemies, and the ignorant
and mischievous action of the home government. Contemporary tracts and broadsides bear witness to the

---

[1] Coxe, *Correspondence*, p. 137.   [2] *Ibid.*   [3] *Ibid.*, pp. 139, 142.
[4] *Ibid.*, p. 142.   See also von Ranke, *History*, vol. v.
[5] These sums of money supplied by the Bank of England were all temporary loans, distinct from the original and permanent debt of £1,200,000
raised on its incorporation in 1694, and lent to government.

rancour with which it was assailed, as well as to the large amount of officious advice and criticism—no doubt well meant—which was offered to its managers.[1]   In the House of Commons they were subject to the bitterest invective and calumny; but under the strongest provocation they had the good sense and self-control to keep silence, secure in their own rectitude.   At last, when a proposal was made by the government to swamp their stock by a huge addition to their capital, to be provided out of depreciated tallies, their patience suddenly came to an end.   They indignantly refused to entertain any such project, and demanded to be left alone to manage their business in their own way, confident of being able with time to surmount all difficulties, if they were only free from interference.[2]   Confidence, indeed, was already slowly returning, Bank stock continued steadily to rise, and on the 5th of December of 1696 this momentous year Sir John Houblon attended in the House of Commons, and there delivered a statement upon the accounts of the Bank,[3] 'and the debts and credits thereof, which were referred to the committee that inspects the parliamentary funds;' and 'tis said the bank is worth £280,000, their debts paid.'[4]   Finally, in less than a year, the time arrived when the directors considered the moment opportune for increasing their stock with the sanction and approval of Montague,[5] and Luttrell tells us that on the 20th of April 1697, 'Sir John Houblon, Sir William Scawen, and about 30 more, are 1697 appointed Commissioners to take further subscriptions to the Bank of England.'[6]   From this time, with the restored confidence, stock gradually rose from a discount to a premium.   Freed from the pressing troubles which

[1] See collection of tracts, etc., in the Crawford Library at Haigh, Lancashire.

[2] Rogers, *First Nine Years of the Bank of England*, p. 85.

[3] Macaulay, *History of England*, iv. 149, and other evidence.

[4] Luttrell, iv. 149.   [5] Kennet, *History*, iii. 726.

[6] Luttrell, iv. 211.

had surrounded them, their plans and calculations were at length suffered to develop their legitimate fruit of success and prosperity, and thus the careworn veterans of the City were repaid for their pains and sacrifices. Henceforth, in the words of Macaulay: 'On the deep and solid foundation' they had laid, 'was to rise the most gigantic fabric of commercial prosperity that the world has ever seen.'[1]

The danger and stress of this critical year being now over, the Bank directors turned gratefully to their governor, whose cool head and strong will had led them safely through these troublous times. The *haute politique*, which had risked so much and accomplished what it aimed at, in spite of the storm of antagonism, ignorance, and bad faith which had rendered its work so difficult, was in advance of its time, and has yet to receive that full recognition which is its due. But at the same time it must be conceded that, but for the supreme obligation of maintaining the existing government, together with the correlative necessity of meeting, with the point of the sword, the aggressive meddling of Louis XIV. in the affairs of the nation, the policy of the Bank would have been unsound and inexcusable. But as its aim was primarily political and patriotic, for this reason the First Governor and Directors have not been credited, in business circles, with the full measure of what they accomplished. Happily the object of their many sacrifices was at length attained in the Peace of Ryswick, and credit rose by leaps and bounds; the high pressure was over, and the crisis past.

1696   A silver tankard presented to Sir John Houblon after these events by the directors of the Bank, bears witness by the inscription they caused to be engraved upon it, to their high estimate both of the peril the Bank had

[1] Macaulay, *History of England*, iv. 731.

TANKARD PRESENTED TO SIR JOHN HOUBLON BY THE
DIRECTORS OF THE BANK OF ENGLAND, 1696.

incurred, and the valuable services rendered to it by its governor during the crisis. Possibly the lesson of this perilous year was a salutary one, showing that great credit operations on wealth cannot safely be carried through without that wealth being in a form easily realisable;[1] a precaution for the moment not possible for the Bank of England, owing to the peculiar circumstances of its establishment and the political stress through which it had passed. But it was only later that it came fully to be recognised that credit is not capital, though it rests upon it, and facilitates the transference and use of it.[2]

The inscription upon the tankard presented to the governor is as follows:—

'The gift of the Directors of the Bank of England
to Sir John Houblon, Governor, Lord Mayor
of London, in token of his great ability
industry and strict uprightness
at a time of extreme difficulty.
1696.'

This venerable piece of plate is now in America. The fact of its existence was only disclosed in 1893. Having been picked up by an American silversmith in London some years previously and taken to New York, it was there offered for sale, and secured by the Loan Committee of the New York Clearing House, and presented to their chairman, Mr. Frederick D. Tappen (President of the Gallatin National Bank), in token of their appreciation of some very valuable services recently rendered by him. The 'Houblon tankard' was regarded as an appropriate gift, and the circumstances of the two presentations being said to be 'closely parallel,' the American Committee caused it to be engraved

1893

[1] This danger was met by the Bank Acts of 1844.
[2] See Cunningham, *Growth of English Industry and Commerce in Modern Times*, p. 398.

with another inscription identical with the original one, merely substituting the different names, before presenting it to Mr. Tappen. The old tankard, which has thus done double duty in honouring a loyal and able business man, is a large and very massive piece of plate of the ordinary tankard shape of that period, with lid and handle. The original inscription, in bold 'old English' running hand, is on the body of it, while the later one has been engraved on the lid. The hall-marks show it to be authentic, and that it was made in London between March 1695 and June 1696 in the reign of William III.[1] It is a curious coincidence that, in dealing in his history with the great services of Sir Isaac Newton with respect to his work at the mint in 1696, Lord Macaulay makes use of the identical words engraved by the directors of the Bank upon the Houblon tankard, with reference to their governor's services in the late crisis. 'It was,' as the historian expresses it, '*the ability, the industry, and the strict uprightness*' of the great philosopher, which speedily produced a complete revolution throughout the department which was under his direction.[2]

But meanwhile some of the shareholders of the Bank were still fretting under what they considered the 'pernicious management of the governing body, complaining justly enough that it had throughout the past acted not

1696

---

[1] The New York correspondent of the *Standard*, having courteously responded to a request for information as to the latter presentation above alluded to, as also as to how the tankard had been obtained, wrote the above particulars, adding : 'Scores of newspaper cuttings might be sent, so great has the interest been in the affair on this other side of the Atlantic.' (See specially a very interesting account of the crisis of 1696 in connection with the presentation to Sir John Houblon, in the *New York Times*, 26 November 1893.) It may be added that no family record has been found bearing upon this incident in the life of Sir John Houblon, nor do any private papers of his now exist. He left no male descendants, and it can only be supposed that at the death of some one of his daughters' representatives the family effects were sold, including the tankard now in America. At Mr. Tappen's death in 1902 it was presented by his widow to the New York Clearing House Association.

[2] Macaulay, *History of England*, iv. 703.

for their benefit or advantage, but for that of the State. And this the directors themselves freely acknowledged to have been the case; one of them even, in a letter dated the 3rd of September 1697, avowing that they 'could not have answered it to their members, had it been for any less occasion than the preservation of the kingdom.'[1] And so it was, some five months after the handing in of the accounts by Sir John Houblon in the House of Commons,[2] that at a general court of the shareholders they appointed a committee composed of some of their own members to inspect and report upon the accounts and management.   A tract bearing the date the 16th of July 1697, gives the text of the report of this committee, with the names of the eight gentlemen who composed it, together with the comments and criticisms and much good advice by the author of the tract, who signs himself by the initials J. A.   His remarks, which are characterised by much personal animosity to the governing body of the Bank, and are specially pertinent to the coming election of a new court of direction—purport to be an 'Essay claiming to prove that the past losses and discredit did. chiefly proceed from the mismanagement of the directors, and not from publick calamities, as they pretend.'[3]   As to the committee, after finding fault with the management of the business at Antwerp in 1695, and of the sending of the three directors there (of whom Sir James Houblon was one), they recommended a reduction in the remuneration of the said directors, in view of one of them having been killed and the number thus reduced, without the leave of the general court!   They also complain bitterly of the loss entailed upon the corporation by the exchange upon the money remitted to

1697

---

[1] Macaulay, *History of England*, iv. 307.
[2] 5 December 1696.
[3] Tract, p. 5. 'The Committee appointed by a general court the 23rd April 1697 to inspect the accounts of the Bank of England, having considered of the matters to them referred, do make their reports as followeth.'

Antwerp, ignoring that the mission of the deputies was directed with a view to reducing it, and that it had been undertaken upon the vote of a general court.   In the conclusion the committee made sundry recommendations in order ' to avoid a like misfortune for the future,' and propose that the power of the court of direction in lending money or making remittances ' may be limited to a certain sum which they shall not exceed without the consent of the general court first had been obtained.'

It was perhaps natural that some hostility should have been exhibited towards those in whose hands so large a power was vested, as had been given to the court of direction by the Bank Charter.   The directors certainly appear to have acted to the extreme limits of that power ; a responsibility perhaps necessary in view of the great occasion, and of the jealousy which would probably have baulked their patriotic efforts had the general court been consulted.   As is always the case, the privileges of either a special class or individual will be open to criticism or jealousy whenever any excessive preponderance of influence can be traced to it, and we here find evidence of much bitter feeling as to the too ' powerful influence of a certain family' (meaning the Houblons) in the counsels of the direction.   'And for this reason,' the writer proceeds, ' it seems necessary that the members should not chuse any of them or of those concerned in the Antwerp affair, in the forthcoming election on the board of direction.'   In reviewing the qualifications most to be commended, and the contrary, in those eligible in the coming election of directors, the writer of the tract places them in no less than XII. clauses,' in the last of which is the key to the whole contention. ' After all,' he writes, 'let this never be forgotten, not to join too many relations at one time.   To have six in twenty-six, as now there are at least, is a number far too great. This will in a little time make the Bank a family bank, useful to a few persons, as hitherto it has proved serviceable scarce as a Bank to above forty persons, and may become a mear dead weight, and so at pleasure obstruct any designs for good save their own fraternity. Therefore if ever you would have impartial management, and tender the welfare of the Bank, let not many brothers be on the administration at one time, nor many near relations.'[1] The election took place before the tract was issued, but it contains a characteristic and scurrilous postscript on the new governor and deputy-governor, who now relieved the veterans who had borne the heat and burden of the day. From the writer's dissatisfaction, it is at once apparent that no alteration would take place in the management, from the changes now introduced.

By the Bank Charter, the first governor and deputy-governor were to serve two years, after which the election for these posts was to take place yearly. After serving his two years as governor, Sir John Houblon had been again elected in 1696, and in 1697 completed his third year of governorship. Sir William Scawen, who now succeeded him, had from the first been closely identified with the policy and management condemned by a section of the shareholders. Although the most prominent member of the obnoxious family now retired from the position he had filled so ably for three years, he remained on the direction—except for a short interval —till his death, nor did he and his brothers cease to exercise that influence upon the counsels of the Bank which, in spite of the dangers with which it had been attended, had yet been successful, not only in the service it had rendered to the State, but in the financial advantages which had since accrued to the shareholders. The 'six relations' on the board of direction comprised Sir John,

marginal notes: 1697 · 1694-1697

---

[1] Tract, 1697, p. 3, in the Crawford Library, Haigh.

the governor;[1] his brothers, Sir James and Abraham, his nephew Peter Houblon; his brother-in-law, John Lordell, and his cousin, Peter du Cane.[2] Of these, Abraham Houblon was yet to render good service to the Bank. He

1701 was elected deputy-governor in 1701, and was re-elected the following year, at the close of which he was chosen

1704 governor, which post he also held for two years. The Bank's minute-books show that he took an active part in its affairs from the first, and at the expiration of his term of office as governor, the court passed a resolution of thanks to him for his 'care and pains in the affairs of the Bank.'[3]

It would appear that the court of directors not only submitted their accounts to the committee appointed by the general court, but themselves instituted a close inquiry into the accounts received from Flanders in connection with the great loss the Bank had sustained through their remittances during the war. Abraham Houblon was placed on this committee, which was

1696 appointed in 1696.[4] In the general rejoicing at the close of the campaign and the steady rise in Bank stock, it is to be hoped the discontented shareholders found comfort and consolation.[5] The Peace of Ryswick

1697 was signed on the 20th of September 1697, and Louis xiv. acknowledged William iii. as King of England. This event by establishing and strengthening the government of William, and in bringing the war to a successful termination, at the same time confirmed the Bank of

---

[1] There is an excellent life of Sir John Houblon in the *Dictionary of National Biography*, by Mr. Charles Welch, vol. xxvii. p. 417.

[2] Or Du Quesne.

[3] See Bank Minutes.   [4] *Ibid.*

[5] A tract called 'A Discourse concerning Banks' (the copy in the Crawford Library has the following written upon it: '(?) By Sir S. P. Janssen, 1697') argues in favour of limiting the operations of the Bank of England to 'great payments.' We notice that certain private accounts opened in 1694 on the inauguration of the Bank, were closed in 1698. Possibly a change on the lines of the suggestion above noticed may have decided the directorate to reduce the number of their cash accounts. The Houblon family who had banked since 1694 closed their accounts this year.

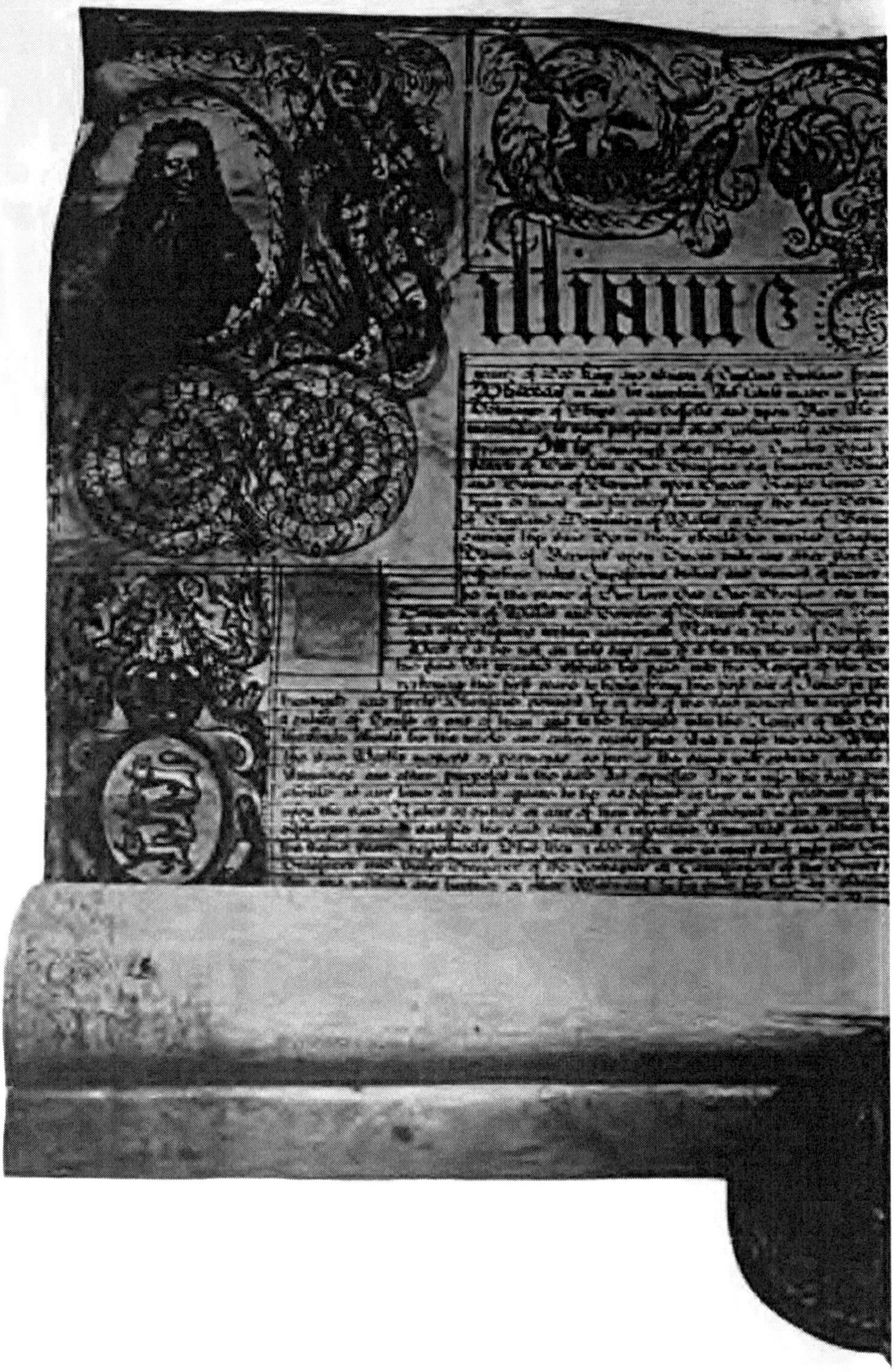

BANK OF ENGLAND, 1694.

England upon sure foundations of credit and honour. The days of adversity and stress were at an end, and Bank stock rose in value, till in the year 1700 it stood as high as 148¼.[1]   1700

The early history of the Bank was, as we have seen, one of apparent reckless adventure.   Unlike the prudent and sound management which afterwards prevailed, this policy was inspired by necessity; but having attained the object for which they had staked all, the directors settled down to the work which finally placed the Bank at the head of the financial council of Europe.[2] The great powers vested in the Bank direction by their charter continued undiminished till 1844, though it had   1844 long been felt that a curtailment of these privileges had become imperative.[3]   Efforts were made at different times with this object, but the Bank continued with unabated power virtually to control the financial world.[4] It remained for perhaps the greatest financier of modern times, Lord Overstone (then Mr. Jones-Loyd), by often-repeated pamphlets, speeches, and evidence given before the House of Commons, both to instigate and inspire the great bill of Sir Robert Peel called the Bank Charter Act (1844).   Thus, while the position of the Bank of England is still one of high authority and weight, it no longer holds in its grasp the control of the world's finance, for it is itself controlled automatically (with regard to its Issue Department) by the store of bullion in the Reserve.[5]

---

[1] Rogers, *First Nine Years of the Bank of England*, Table, p. xxv.
[2] *Ibid.*, p. 164.   [3] *Ibid.*, p. 165.
[4] 'Safe as the Bank' has long been an English proverb!
[5] For the arguments which resulted in the passing of the Bank Acts, see Preface to Lord Overstone's *Evidence before the Select Committee of the House of Commons on the Bank Acts*, 1857.   Longmans, 1858.

CHAPTER XVII

THE BLACK FLAG

'There was the Jolly Roger—the black flag of piracy—flying from her peak !'—STEVENSON : *Treasure Island*.

ALL the Houblons were concerned in commerce with the Peninsula. But while Sir John's name as its chairman was chiefly connected with the company of Portugal merchants (of whom seven bore the name of Houblon), Sir James, his brother, stood in the same position with regard to the other company which traded with Spain. Most of the brothers, and many of the other merchants who belonged to the one company, belonged also to the other.

But while for years the Merchant Adventurers had patiently suffered loss from the dangers of the seas, but little aided by government—which too often ignored their claims, or were not in a position to afford them protection,—the position of the great commercial class had greatly changed when, in the last decade of the seventeenth century, it was possible for the merchants trading to the Peninsula to approach the Board of Trade with a memorial *demanding* convoys for the protection of the fleets they yearly dispatched to the coasts of Portugal.[1] For the increased power and importance of the merchant princes of London since the Revolution was not confined to municipal affairs, nor yet to financial questions. They had now imposed upon the State the necessity of

---

[1] See *Little Directory*, 1677. Introduction to reprint, 1863.

admitting representatives into their councils with regard
to much of the legislation of the country, and especially
in all that appertained to commercial and colonial affairs,
as also of the royal navy.   And this not only during the
rule of the Whig Junto, but even when the Tories held
the reins of power.   Side by side, therefore, with the
names of officers of State representing the great landed
interest, appear those of the City men whom the boroughs
returned to Parliament, or the City of London nominated
to support and advance their views.   Thus on the new
Board of Trade and Plantations they were powerfully
represented, as well as on the new Commission of the
Admiralty that, in consequence of the well-founded
complaints of the merchants, had replaced the one which,
under the Tories Killigrew and Delaval, had suffered
such loss of prestige through the destruction of the
Smyrna fleet.[1]   As we have seen, Sir John Houblon
was elected a City representative on both boards on
their reconstruction.

That the views and interests of the merchants engaged the close attention of the Board of Trade, is
shown by their exhaustive minutes on all sorts of questions affecting them, though it would appear that complaints were frequent as to the said boards not having
access to the Cabinet.

The memorial to which we have alluded is interesting
as illustrative of the character of English trade, as also of
the great dangers attending it from pirates and privateers.   A thousand men were employed on the fleet of
fifty-six merchantmen, which were ready in the autumn
of 1692 to set sail for Portugal.   And for their protec-   1692
tion three men-of-war were deemed sufficient convoy by
their owners, in spite of the crowd of 'Sallee pirates'
and French privateers which they expected to find
hovering about their skirts, ready to 'snap up' any vessel

---

[1] Campbell's *Lives of the Admirals* (*apud* Mahan), p. 192.

lagging behind the rest. We give the text of the petition for the granting of the convoy, signed by Sir John Houblon, the chairman of the company.

'*To the Right Hon*^{ble} *the Lords of the Committee of Trade.*

1692   'The Portugal Merchants do humbly lay before your Lordships what they conceive may be most necessary for the carrying on and securing the Portugal Trade for the approaching season.

'That the Trade of O'Porto and the neighbouring ports of Viana Aveiro and Figuera, will require thirty to fourty sail of small ships, the manning whereof will take up 500 to 600 men.

'That the trade of Lisbon will require 15 to 16 sail at 20 to 25 men, one ship wth the other, wch will be 320 to 400 men.

'That there may be appointed three Fourth Rates[1] for their convoy, to be ready to sail with the said ships from the Downes, on or before the 15th September next. Two wherof may see the ships into Lisbon, and the other to see the Port ships safe over the Bar of O'Porto, and into the other smaller Ports. That during the said ships unloading and reloading in their several Ports, the said three Men of War may be ordered to cruise to and again on the coast of Portugal between the North and South capes; and that in the moneth of January following, two of the said Men of War may call off of the Bar of O'Porto, and the other Frigate to go to Lisbon in order to convoy the said ships back to England, some of them to the Ports of the West, and the rest to London. And the reason why two Men of War is desired outwards for Lisbon, and but one to come back, and but one is desired to O'Porto and two to come back from thence is, Because the estate in woollen goods carried

[1] Men-of-war.

out to Lisbon is double the value of what is brought home from thence. And the estate from O'Porto at return, is twice the value of that which is brought from Lisbon.

'And it is humbly offered that there is a necessity of this fleet going out as neer as can be by the time specified, because the said ships will carry out very large quantities of woollen manufactures and Lead; a great part of which are bought by the Portuguese to supply their West India Trade, which West India Fleet of their's usually sail from Portugal in December and January. And if our goods proper for those places be not early in Portugal (as it happened the last year) they must lye unsold for a whole year longer, which will be a manifest prejudice and a very great loss to the Merchants.

'That it is very necessary the said three frigates, while the ships are reloading, do cruise upon the coast of Portugal between the two Capes as aforesaid, because there is not only 14 to 16 Sail of Sally Men of War at sea (most of which are now upon the coast of Portugal), but also several Privateers of the French, who are both merchant-men and have commissions, who carry very great quantities of goods for Lisbon, part of which goods are afterwards transported to Cadiz; and the ships that carry them, after having unloaden their goods outwards, cruise as Privateers off of the coast of Portugal, when they at that time of the year (as they have done) intercept and take several English and Irish ships with fish, etc., which are forced to trade to and again to Portugal without Convoy.

'All which we humbly submit to your Lordships.

(Signed)   J⁰ HOUBLON, Chairman'
(and thirty-three others).

The document is undated, but in the endorsement

there is a memorandum that it was read 9th August 1692.[1]

Another Board of Trade document shows this fleet and goods to have been quickly followed by another, destined for Spanish ports. It is a report addressed to the Lords of the Privy Council by the merchants, in obedience to their command for information as to the safe arrival of their ships at Bilbao and St. Sebastian. While reporting this, they make the usual request for convoys to ensure their safe return home. 'They have advice,' they say, 'of their ships arrival safe . . . about the 10th of the last month, and that they would be fully laden and ready to returne home by the middle of this month of July. That the said ships will be very richly loaden with Spanish wooll and [considerable monies],[2] and other rich comodityes. Wherefore they humbly pray yor Lo͡pps would be pleased to order a speedy convoy to . fetch home the said ships, suitable to the richness of the fleete and the Danger they will run.' The document is signed by Sir James Houblon, chairman of the Spanish merchants, and thirteen others.[3]

That the question of convoys for merchant fleets was considered in good time in the following year, is proved by a report of the Lords of the Admiralty, dated the 24th of

1694   October 1694, which shows that a committee—probably appointed after the disaster to the Smyrna fleet—had sat and considered the matter. Sir John Houblon's signature, with that of two other Admiralty Lords, is at the foot of

1695   this report.[4] The same affair was considered in 1695 by the Admiralty, when we again find his signature appended to the report.[5] But nevertheless, almost at that very time, the Lords were considering the expedi-

---

[1] Board of Trade, Trade Papers, vol. iv., 1692-1693.
[2] Words nearly obliterated.
[3] Board of Trade, Trade Papers, vol. iv., 26 July 1693.
[4] *Ibid.*, vol. v.   [5] *Ibid.*, vol. xix.

ency of a general embargo.[1] They had also at this period embarked upon a difficult matter, in which Sir John Houblon was keenly interested, and in which he took part—viz. the reform of abuses in the victualling of his Majesty's ships of war.[2]

For their greater security, the merchants trading to the same ports usually dispatched their ships together in fleets of merchantmen. They doubtless paid the King well for the use of the men-of-war placed at their disposal for their protection, but one is inclined to wonder why they did not themselves combine in order to provide vessels for their armed defence; solitary vessels, indeed, usually carried guns. In the Middle Ages, the formation of the Hanses, notably the Hanseatic League of German towns and the Hansa Londinensis of England and Flanders, was for the very purpose of mutual help and protection from the dangers of the seas. But with the decline of the Hanses, and the great development of independent trading on their own initiative by the Merchant Adventurers, dangers increased in proportion as the merchants gained by the freedom from the restrictions which had formerly hampered them. From the earliest times pirates had preyed upon the shipping of all the nations; but chiefly to be feared in the seventeenth century were the wild and lawless peoples of the African coasts.[3] At a later date many pirates infested the West Indies, which at one time were said to have harboured and protected them in great numbers. As will have been observed in the memorial of 1692 embodying the prayer for convoys, the merchants expected to encounter dangers on the Portuguese coasts, not only from the Barbary pirates, but also from the French; for the subjects of

[1] Board of Trade, Trade Papers, vol. vi.
[2] *Ibid.*, vol. vi., 3 July 1695.
[3] Algiers was bombarded by the English as lately as 1816 as a punishment for piracy—*Encyclo. Brit.*, xix. 117.

the Grand Monarque were then encouraged to prey
upon the merchandise of their neighbours whether
friend or foe, while many were granted commissions
empowering them to act as privateers. During the wars
in the Netherlands and till the signing of the Peace of
Ryswick, it was said that the damage done by French
privateers to English commerce was computed at no
less than twelve millions.[1]

Not the least part of the terrors of piracy was the
treatment accorded by these eastern peoples to the
unfortunate seamen who fell into their hands. For
while the goods and vessels were disposed of or appropriated, their crews were sold into slavery. From time
to time funds were raised in this country for the purpose
of the redemption of these unfortunates from captivity,
though it is evident that a large number of captured
seamen and others passed their lives in chains and
slavery. Charles I. tried to cope with this grave matter;
in 1632 he granted letters patent for a general collection
to be made throughout England and Wales, towards
'redeeming the slaves the King's subjects, under the
King of Morocco in Barbary.'[2] By the wording of the
document, it appears that efforts had already been made
in this direction. Three years later, a wiser course was
taken to cope with the evil; the King's first levy of
ship money was used by him to defray the expenses of
the chastisement of pirates.[3] But money continued to
be raised, both in England and France, to buy back
captives,[4] and their redemption was perpetually in the
thoughts of the people and government of this country
—so nearly did their sufferings concern the nation.[5] In

1632

---

[1] Rogers, *First Nine Years of the Bank of England.*
[2] State Papers, Foreign, Barbary States, Morocco, vol. i.
[3] 1635—*Encyclo. Brit.*, xix. p. 117.
[4] See L. Herault, *États barbaresques de Marac, Algers, Tunis, Tripoli,*
etc.
[5] See a 'Relation of the whole proceedings concerning the redemption of
the captives in Argier and Tunis,' 1647.

the British Museum there is a copy of a petition, dated
1661, presented by divers persons who had themselves   1661
suffered captivity 'in most miserable bondage in Algiers
and other places, under the Turks.'[1]   In 1680 matters   1680
were no ways amended, 'for many hundreds of poor
English captives in Algiers were still praying for some
remedy to prevent their increase,'[2] and other documents
among the Trade Papers tell the same tale.[3]   But all
this time the philanthropy of the good people at home
did not extend to any pity for the unfortunate negroes,
large cargoes of whom were yearly shipped on the coasts
of Guinea and elsewhere in Africa, and carried to the
American plantations there to be sold as slaves.

In the last year of King James's reign, Mr. Pepys,   1687
writing from the Admiralty to James Houblon, earnestly
cautioned him, and through him the other merchants, as
to the 'Algierine pirates now in the chanell.'   So bold
were they at this time that they had caused 'such an
interruption to the King's subjects' vessels there, as the
King will find necessary to remedy.'   He goes on to say
that they had even brought into one of our ports in the
West one of their prizes, while a derelict plundered by
them and all her men carried off—had been 'droven'
into another.   After urging James Houblon and 'the
rest of our Streights Traders' to use all the precautions
possible in so 'doubtful a juncture as to peace or warr,'
owing to the methods the King in honour will be forced
to take for preventing or removing them,—he 'fears that
this will leade that heady and faythless people to fly out in
some act of violence or other, that must end in a warr.

---

[1] See British Museum, S. 16, m. 11 (49).
[2] *Ibid.*, T. 100, 76.
[3] A letter from James Houblon to Sir Joseph Williamson, Secretary of
State (S. P. Dom. Chas. II., vol. 380), sends news, just brought him, of Sir
John Narborough, then on a punitive expedition against the Pirate States
(1674-1676).   He had with him the money for redeeming the English
slaves (S. P. Dom. Chas. II. 363, No. 36), and after a fierce fight, killing
six hundred men, he entered Tripoli and delivered the slaves.   See letter.

In which my first wish being, that I may be found mistaken; my next is that our merchants may avoid ye effects of being surprized with it if it should prove true.'[1]

It will be remembered that a ship belonging to old Mr. Houblon was captured in 1669 by Algiers pirates, and brought into the port of Sallee, where she and her cargo were finally bought by a 'Jew of Amsterdam';[2] the ship's company was then dispersed by the pirates, and many of them sold as slaves. We see Sir John Houblon at a later date negotiating the release of a galley-slave named Will Drye, who had formerly been a shipmaster in the employment of the Houblon family. It is possible this man had himself been captured in 1669. In addition to the sum of money paid by Sir John for his redemption from slavery, £40 was contributed towards his purchase out of the 'Captive money' in the Chamber of London,[3] as, a short time before this, the sum of £2000 had been specially raised for this purpose.[4]

It is perhaps not wonderful that the great successes obtained by the pirates of the Barbary States should have inflamed the imaginations of daring English seamen, and tempted them to embark on similar adventures. But such men, once committed to a career of piracy, were forced to continue in it, finding it impossible to abandon the life for fear of punishment.[5]

A famous pirate cruise, late in the seventeenth century, was that of an Englishman named Henry Every, and was carried out in a merchant ship belonging to the Houblon brothers and some others of their company of Spanish merchants. Every's piracies were extraordinarily successful, his men being all bold English seamen.

---

[1] MSS., Magd. Coll., Camb., vol. xiii. pp. 116, 117. Admiralty, 4 June '87.
[2] State Papers, Foreign, Barbary States, Morocco, vol. ii.
[3] Board of Trade, Trade Papers, vol. vi.
[4] State Papers, Foreign, Barbary States, Tripoli, vol. i. No. 453, 5 Jan. 1691-92.
[5] In the *Winwood Memoirs of Affairs of State*, vol. iii. 287, a curious illustration of this fact is to be found.

Not only did they gain great riches during their unlawful cruise in the Indian Ocean, but it was nearly two years before the ship's company broke up and the pirates dispersed; nor was it possible to get in touch with them during all this time, though, long before the end of it, they became famous for their success and daring.

The story begins in November 1693, when the ship *Charles II.*, a 'great merchant-man,' was commissioned in London, with three other similar vessels, by Sir James Houblon and other Spanish merchants. This squadron was designed for the coast of Spain in the first instance, and was afterwards under orders to sail for the Spanish West Indies, where the company had obtained large trading concessions from the King of Spain.[1] The value of the four ships and their cargo was placed by the merchants at £32,000.[2] Among the Board of Trade Papers there is a host of documents bearing upon what followed: the first, in order of time, being a humble petition to the Queen in Council,[3] by the wives of some of the seamen employed on board the ship *Charles II.*, in which they accuse Sir James Houblon and the other merchants of the intent to defraud their husbands of their lawful wages, etc. Jane Maye, wife of the steward of the ship, and several other women whose names are given in the document, proceed to express their feelings very plainly, while calling loudly upon the Queen to redress their wrongs by restoring to them both their wages and their husbands, who, they pleaded, having found themselves 'betrayed,' had gone away with the ship under Henry Every, the mate.[4] This Every, or Avery, was the famous pirate about whose exploits so much was afterwards heard. Only recently, there had

---

[1] See 'Answer of the Owners,' by Sir James Houblon; Board of Trade, Trade Papers, vol. vi.
[2] *Ibid.*
[3] King William was in Flanders.
[4] Board of Trade, Trade Papers, vol. v.

been much trouble among the seamen, both of the navy
and merchant services, due, it was supposed, to the
efforts of the Jacobites to stir up discontent among this
important body of men ; while the late bad administration
of the Admiralty had furnished excuse to many for
uneasiness.   It got about among the seamen's wives
that their husbands 'were to be defrauded of their hard-
earned pay,' and Whitehall was besieged by a crowd of
women clamouring for what was due to their husbands,[1]
and their anxieties were only allayed by the Queen's personal assurances that their alarm was unfounded.   The
Lords of the Council, with the recollection of this recent
tumult in their minds, anxious to appease the wives of
the seamen in the present instance, and impressed with
the apparent hardness of their case, forthwith instructed
the Lords of the Committee on Trade to inquire into
the matter, and a copy of the petition to be sent to Sir
James Houblon, requesting him to furnish a full explanation of the matter in writing 'to this Board.'[2]

The chairman of the important Spanish company of
merchants thus called upon somewhat peremptorily to
give account of the matter, would have required all his
self-possession to meet the situation with dignity.   But
Sir James Houblon possessed a fund of good temper if
not a sense of humour, which, keeping silence till the
last moment, justified himself as to the accusations
against his company, and at the same time turned the
tables upon his female accusers by a counter-charge
against their husbands ; the angry women now learning
the truth, for the first time, as to their escapade.   The
women's petition was presented on the 2nd of August ; the
10th of September is the date of the document signed by
Sir James, which first disclosed the facts.   The Lords met
as arranged, in the Council Chamber at Whitehall, on the

[1] Macaulay, *History*, iv. 422.
[2] Board of Trade, Trade Papers, vol. vi., 6 August 1694.

11th of September, to hear the answer of the owners, the reading of which document was immediately followed by the presentation of a 'memorandum to move her Majesty in Council to order that the ship *Charles II.*, together with all the ship's company, be stopped and seized into safe custody in the Plantations, or wheresoever she shall be met; the ship's company having run away from Corunna in Spain—it is suspected—upon a piratical design.'[1] Indeed, Every had avowed this intention in a letter to the owners, in which he also, with artful mendacity, hinted as to his intention of plying his new trade in the West Indian seas. Thus he succeeded in evading pursuit, and secured to himself undisturbed opportunity for piracy; for, as a matter of fact, he succeeded in mystifying the owners, who, deceived as to the destination of their ship, had flattered themselves with the hope of speedy recapture and the punishment of the culprits. This 'running away' with the ship took place on the 7th of May 1694, so that the pirates had already been four months at sea when the Lords of the Council received the petition of their wives in London.

1694

'Captain' Every—or Bridgeman, as he occasionally called himself—had been mate on board the good ship *Charles*. The captain of the ship did not please him; the mate was probably a better man, in so far as energy and daring were concerned, and he knew it, and so the *fancy* seized him both to evade the irksome authority of his superior, and to give free scope to his longing for adventure. He was a born leader of men, and had no difficulty in persuading nearly the whole of the ship's company to embark with him upon his daring scheme. The ship was partly victualled, and fully equipped with ammunition for her forty guns; and so the opportunity was taken when the captain was ashore, and quietly, at night, the anchors were weighed and the

[1] Board of Trade, Trade Papers, vol. xiii. p. 147.

ship silently slipped away in the darkness, and made sail for the East.

Every rechristened his ship, and she became the embodiment of his idea. His bold plan was according to his *fancy*; and so he named her the *Fancy*—or *Phansy* as it pleased some of his somewhat illiterate crew to spell the word. It is to be questioned, some two years later when the true story of the ship *Charles* was unfolded to the indignant owners, if they saw in her new name the irony which had inspired the change.

During the two years in which he commanded the pirate ship, its captain maintained absolute control and authority over the lawless band of men who had thrown in their lot with his. While some of the crew after a time chose to be put ashore, designing to return home, fresh hands took their place recruited from the vessels they captured. But among those who remained, or those who joined with him at a later date, we neither hear of dissensions, nor yet of their ever disputing the authority of their leader.

The career of the pirate ship was one of unqualified success, while her captain and his men not only gained great spoils, but were wise enough to share them with newcomers into their partnership, without grudging. We possess an account of a great part of the adventurous cruise of this famous ship from the dictation of one of the pirates, whose name was John Dann. When it came to an end, and the ship's company was broken up, Captain Every successfully evaded capture, but some of the more prominent of his men were taken after their return home. One or more turned King's evidence to escape hanging, and John Dann was one of these. The affirmation of Dann was not the first taken down from the lips of one of the pirates at the instance of the Lords Proprietors of Trade; but as it contains the narrative of the ship's earlier adventures, beginning with the 'running away from the groyne,' and ending with her arrival in the West Indies, we propose transcribing it here.

The ship *Charles II.* or *Fancy* was, in the words of Sir James Houblon, a 'stout frigate of forty guns, and an extraordinary sailer.'[1] It will be observed in the narrative of Dann that all the piratical part of the cruise was comprised within the first year; the furthest point of distance in the east to which the pirates attained being the Malacca Straits. No mention is made of piracies during the long return voyage across the Indian Ocean, not even at the 'Babs' (the familiar name for the straits of Bab-el-Mandeb at the entrance to the Red Sea), owing probably to the failure of their supply of powder and shot.

Affidavit by John Dann *re* East India Pirates.

'John Dann attending, as he had been required, acquainted their Lordships that he went out of England with Captain Every, and was along with him all his voiage in the ship *Phansy*, for which he hath obtained his Majesty's pardon. That they went away from the groyn with very small provisions for the Island of Cape Verde; and upon the coast of Guinea, at an island called Princess,[2] they took two Danish ships and plundered them. In them they found forty pound weight of gold dust. They took the men of those ships who were willing along with them, amongst whom was one named Peter Claes. From thence they went about the Cape, and having taken in provisions at Madagascar, they sailed to the Babs, to lye in wait for ships returning out of the Red Sea. There they took the *Gunsway*, a great Moores vessel belonging to the Mogul, and another lesser vessel. The *Gunsway* made a little resistance at

---

[1] Board of Trade, Trade Papers, vol. vi.
[2] In the Gulf of Guinea.

first, but soon gave over ; and after she was taken,
though there were eight hundred persons aboard, all
submitted and let them plunder the ship for three
days together.   After that they went to Rajapore on
the coast of Malabar, and from thence to Mascareen,
where they set about fifty of their men ashore who were
desirous to leave them ; amongst whom was one named
Weaver, who, he has heard, is now in London.   Mascareen is an island in possession of the French, in which
there are two or three towns and about a hundred and
fifty or two hundred French people, to whom the
natives (not being numerous) are slaves.   Whilst they
were cruising about the Babs, there came up to them
these ships following : viz. Captain Thomas Wake in the
Susannah from Boston, a vessel of ninety tons, seven
guns, and seventy men ; which came out from Boston
on pretence of a voyage to Madagascar for slaves (as did
all the rest from other places).   A second, Thomas Tue,
in a sloop of fifty tons, six guns, and sixty men, from
New York.   A third, Joseph Faro, in a ship called the
Portsmouth, Adventurer.   A fourth, William Mayes, in
a Briganteen of six gunns and thirty men, from Rhode
Island.   A fifth . . . a ship called the *Dolphin*, six
guns and sixty men, from Pennsylvania ; which ship they
burnt, and took the men on board theirs.[1]   Mayes and
Faro joined with them in taking the *Gunsway*, and all
Mayes' men had a share with them in the plunder ; but
only five or six of Faro's men.   Wake came to them
three days after, and had taken another Indian ship,
and shared about two hundred pieces of eight a man.'[2]

In continuation, the affirmation of Dann imparts some
information—in response to the inquiries of the Lords
—about 'the seasons and other circumstances, proper to
these pyraticall voyages.'   He said that 'about this

[1] The guns they added to their own armament.
[2] Before His Majesty's Commissioners for Trade and Plantations. Board
of Trade, Trade Papers (Minutes), vol. xcv. No. 231.

time' (July) 'are the westerly *mounsouns*, when the pirates lye and wait for the ships coming out of the Red Sea. But the Straits of Malacca,' he thought, 'the best place to plye for booty; and that if a ship carried with her sufficient powder and shott, with materials for rigging and other necessaries to supply their decays by wear and teare, they might go once a year to Madagascar for victualls, and so subsist many years.'[1]

Ammunition having failed, the pirates were finally forced to turn back from their search for plunder which they were unable to secure ; and so, laden with spoil, the frigate, aided by the monsoon's south-west drift, and having victualled at Madagascar, swept on about the Cape and into the swift-flowing currents of the Atlantic, and from thence northwards to the coasts of Guinea. What was the mission of the pirates at this point of their voyage Dann does not relate, for it had nothing to do with the acts of piracy ; but we find incidentally that they here took on board a cargo of eighty-seven negroes, purposing to sell them as slaves in the West Indian plantations. Having shipped the negroes they struck across the Atlantic to the coasts of Brazil. From thence again they turned northwards, skirting the Barbadoes and other groups of West Indian Islands — to the Bahamas. Here they sailed past the long narrow island of Eleuthera, on the extreme point of which is Royal Island, where the pirates anchored. This long return voyage from the East Indies, of about nine months, unfruitful of spoils, is laconically mentioned by Dann in the words: 'From Mascareen we came to Eleuthera in the Bahamas.'[2]

The *Fancy* arrived at Royal Island in April 1696, and the pirates found themselves at once confronted with 1696 the pressing necessity of the disposal of their slaves and

---

[1] Board of Trade, Trade Papers (Minutes), vol. xcv. No. 231.
[2] *Ibid.*, 1698, vol. lxv. No. 231.

of the valuable treasure they had on board. Their great frigate was indeed equipped with an armament of forty-six guns and upwards of two hundred men all told ; but though formidable to all outward appearance, the pirates knew their weakness, for they had neither powder nor shot, while the West Indian seas were swarming with English and French men-of-war, the naval war between the countries being then in full activity. But Captain Every was no less resourceful than he was bold and reckless. The Island of Providence—the seat of government of the Bahamas—was about twenty leagues from the place of his anchorage, and from thence he entered into communications with the English governor.

In a minute and interesting history of the West Indian Islands, and of their early planting, the author, writing in 1764, gives an account of the government of Colonel Trott. After describing the many confusions and dissensions in Providence prior to his arrival there as governor of the Bahamas, he mentions the fact that **1696** in 1696 he was in the act of building a fort upon the Island, when ' the ship of the famous pirate Avery (*sic*)—which carried forty-six guns and a hundred stout men—arrived in Providence,' and attributed to his diplomatic skill the fact that ' though if he had landed, the governor could not have opposed him with more than seventy men, yet Every and his crew paid for all they called for.'[1] The fact being that ammunition being unobtainable at any price, the breaking up of the ship's company had become inevitable, as well as the disposal of the frigate herself—much to the grief of the pirate crew.[2]

The story is continued by another of Every's men named Middleton, in an affidavit made in London some

[1] *Modern Universal History* (*History of America*), vol. xli. p. 333. London, 1764.
[2] This was in April 1696.

SHIPPING NEGROES OFF THE COAST OF GUINEA.

months later. According to this pirate, Governor Trott received a large bribe as the price of his co-operation in the winding-up of the piratical expedition, consisting of a great sum of money in gold and pieces of eight, together with the ship herself, and all she contained; that she was afterwards put in charge of certain men 'whose incapacity or number were not sufficient to secure her from hurtfull accidents,' and that scarcely had all of value remaining on board been secured by the governor—consisting of a 'great store of Elephant's teeth and other treasure'—than she went ashore, 'it was believed designedly.'[1]

Whatever the circumstances were under which this misfortune to the ship occurred, the indignation and sorrow of her late crew were apparently sincere. But their offers of help to try and secure her (according to Middleton) were rejected, and she accordingly became a complete wreck and a 'sad sight' in the harbour of Providence. 'After this,' the pirate continued,—'the crew of the *Phansy* having broken up, sold their slaves, and divided among them many thousand pounds,—he himself, Dann, and several others, joined Captain Every, who had purchased a sloop, and all went away with him to Ireland about the beginning of June,' the rest of the pirates having preceded them in another small vessel. For his share the captain took £2000, each of his crew receiving to the value of five to six hundred pounds apiece.[2] Two or three only, out of his men, did not return home, but went over to the province of Pennsylvania, where they appear to have induced the governor to refrain from taking proceedings against them, for which lenity he was afterwards severely reprimanded.[3]

[1] Board of Trade, Proprieties, vol. xxv. p. 309 (November 1696).
[2] Board of Trade, Trade Papers (Minutes), vol. xcv. No. 231, 1698.
[3] Board of Trade, Proprieties, vol. ii. No. 521. Letter of John Laurence to Governor Markham.

The first news of the ship's return from the East appears to have reached England in July 1696, when she had already been abandoned as a wreck in the harbour of Providence. A proclamation was nevertheless immediately published in the *Gazette* by order of the Lords Justices of England, 'calling upon all the King's subjects and others to apprehend the said captain and crew, and obtain possession of the ship wherever they may be met with.'[1]   Kennet, in his contemporary history of England, records the issue of this proclamation for the arrest of 'the famous pyrate Every' and his crew, showing that their exploits in the East had been a matter of notoriety while they were yet being enacted.[2]

1696   The affidavit of Philip Middleton was made before Sir John Houblon and the rest of the 'Lords Proprietors' on the 11th of November 1696,[3] and it was at once accepted as true and authentic by the Board. The official account of the affair by the governor of the Bahamas had not yet arrived, nor did the Lords Justices wait for it.   Not only did other accounts from the West Indies and the neighbouring provinces appear to bear out the accusations against Governor Trott, but Governor Markham of Pennsylvania, though himself harbouring some of Every's men, did not hesitate to accuse Trott of the like treason in a letter to Sir John Houblon.[4]

Meanwhile the Lords were besieged by the urgent representations of the angry owners smarting under the heavy loss they had sustained, and still more by the hostile attitude of the East India Company, always eager to punish *interlopers* upon their monopoly of trade in the East, and no less determined to visit upon,

---

[1] Board of Trade, Proprieties, vol. ii. No. 345.
[2] Kennet, *History of England*, iii. 1696.
[3] Board of Trade, Proprieties, vol. ii. No. 687.
[4] Board of Trade, Proprieties, vol. ii. No. 345, B 3.   Sir John was apparently conducting the inquiry of the Lords of the Committee of Trade.

the English governor (whom they believed to have harboured the pirates) the weight of their displeasure.[1] The step between 'interloping' and piracy was not great, inasmuch as in either case it represented a lesser or greater degree of lawlessness ; and indeed the East India Company had no choice but to defend its privileges with vigour. The indignation excited in their august bosoms by the escapade of the ship *Fancy* was born of the very serious complications they anticipated, and which actually followed the piracies committed by Every in the Bab-el-Mandeb Straits.

How was the Great Mogul to distinguish between the Company's proceedings and those of a mendacious pirate? *All* white men were 'English' and 'Sahibs' who spoke English ; and Every and his men, as we have seen, 'plundered a great Moores vessel belonging to the Mogul for three days together,' while her eight hundred men submitted after but slight resistance. The other vessel similarly treated, in fact, turned out to have belonged to Abdul Gophor, a leading merchant of Surat ; and much was the worry and loss which these and subsequent and similar mischiefs caused the great John Company, held responsible by the native princes of India, for the outrages.[2]

So Governor Trott was dismissed from his post by the Home Government, and another governor sent out in his place with full power to examine and report upon his conduct in respect of the pirates. The sequel to the story of the visit of the pirate ship to the Bahamas is not without interest, while an altogether different light was thrown on the situation upon the arrival of Governor Webb at his new post, where he found his predecessor awaiting him *in irons*!

[1] The privilege of trade enjoyed by the East India Company extended along all the coasts of Africa and Asia from the Cape of Good Hope to Japan. See Hamilton on the National Debt.
[2] See Cunningham, *Growth of English Industry and Commerce*, i. 269.

The war with the French was then at its height, and at this time the French had proved far the stronger and more successful of the two belligerents in the West Indies. For while the government of William III. was absorbed in his great struggle on the Continent, the French King had continued to support and encourage continual aggression upon the plantations of the English in America. It was only later that the indomitable pluck and industry of the British settlers resulted in the gradual consolidation of British power in the islands which had been so often temporarily wrested from them by the French. The defence made of his conduct by the friends of Governor Trott was, that in April 1696, 'the said ship *Charles II.* or *Fancey*, Henry Every *alias* Bridgeman, Commander, with 46 guns mounted and 200 men, anchored at Royall Island, Bahama government, 20 leagues from Providence. That a message was sent by the commander to the governor desiring admittance into Providence wanting provisions and repairs. That they stated they were the King's subjects and had been trading to the Guinea coast, that they had done nothing but what they were ready to answer and were willing to surrender themselves to government for.'[1] Whereupon the governor, after consulting with his council, resolved that 'if they could not be admitted to Providence, an English port, the English ship must needs go to Petit Guavez, a French government and the nearest port to Providence.' Furthermore, even 'had the Providence people been stronger than they were to resist them, at that time there was a necessity to suffer them [the pirates], and even to have *invited them in* though knowing them to be pirates (which they did not), because the chiefest Salt Pond[2] had been taken by the French, and the greater

1696

---

[1] Many respectable merchants traded as 'Interlopers' in the East in spite of the East India Company's rights.

[2] They were the source of great profit to the colonists.

part of the inhabitants were away upon that particular, while there were at the time three French vessels lying near by, resolving to take Providence, but were prevented making the attack by the coming in of this great ship.' It was, therefore, 'certainly better to invite a known pirate in to save a place, than by denying them, suffer yᵉ enemy to be master of such an Island fortified.' The governor and people, therefore, 'saw no cause for molesting them or seizing their wealth, even had they known that they had great riches, which the governor knew not till they came a-shoar and aboard some other vessels.' He could not do more then—being rendered suspicious by their 'great plenty of money,'—but oblige them to give bonds (the best security on the island) 'jointly and severally for all their appearances in a year and a day if anything should be laid to their charge.'[1]

'I little expected to have found his justification so great,' writes Governor Webb to Sir James Houblon, 'and only as that the best part of the town do clear him in. I assure you, gentlemen,' he proceeds, 'I could never have proved the tenth part of what he has confessed upon oath.'[2] He concludes by begging that the owners would send him directions as to the sale of the wreck.

After this, the whole subject of piracy and its suppression having been brought prominently forward by Captain Every's famous cruise, and the subsequent scandal in the Bahamas, the Lords Justices with the King's concurrence organised and despatched 'a squadron designed for suppressing the pirates in the East Indies.' And further, we find that the Lords Proprietors received a letter from their Lordships

---

[1] Board of Trade, Proprieties, vol. ii. No. 599.
[2] *Ibid.* See also Sloane MSS., vol. 2902, No. 163; and Board of Trade, Proprieties, vol. ii. No. 475, April, July, and September; also vol. xxv. p. 149, etc.

signifying 'that his Majesty had thought fit that commissioners be appointed to goe with the squadron to the East Indies, to take an account of the money and other effects that shall be taken, in the possession of the said pirates.' And their Excellencies desire further 'that their Lordships do cause a draft of such powers and instructions for the said Commissioners to be prepared and laid before their Excellencies, as their Lordships judge proper for his Majesty's service in that occasion.'[1] The great spoils they expected to lay their hands on through the anticipated captures of pirates were thus wisely protected by their Lordships from possible annexation. As the date is coincident with their piratical troubles, the following entry in Luttrell's *Brief Relation* of current events may refer to the deliberations which finally resulted in this expedition to the Eastern seas: 'Yesterday Coll Kendall, Sir John Houblon, and

1697 other Commissioners of the Admiralty, attended the House of Lords and had six questions put to them, which they are to answer to-morrow.'[2]

Meanwhile Captain Every had disappeared from view; in their affidavits the pirates had been loyal to their leader. Bold and reckless and doubtless cruel, he had been just and liberal to his men, while all plunder had been shared ungrudgingly with each in accordance with a well-considered plan arranged by the pirate republic itself. Under another *alias*, Every had doubtless already embarked on some fresh adventure, while his old friends Dann and Middleton were still throwing dust in the eyes of the Lords Proprietors, or the redoubtable East India Company had launched its thunders against poor Trott! They were not launched in vain, for it does not appear that justice was ever done or

[1] Letter from Mr. Yard *re* pirates. Board of Trade, Trade Papers (Minutes), vol. xcv. No. 231, 1698.
[2] Luttrell, *Brief Relation*, vol. iv. No. 203 (1 April 1697).

compensation made to the deposed governor of the Bahamas.

From the day of the granting of the new Charter to the East India Company in 1693, when their rivals 1693 were practically absorbed into their corporate body, they had been more than ever vigilant in asserting their privileges, persecuting without mercy all interlopers upon the Eastern seas. Hitherto they had been content with defending their rights in the East itself, but latterly the Company had grown bold to exercise them at home, even to the obtaining of orders to restrain merchantmen from leaving the port of London when they had reason to believe they were bound for the East. A flagrant case of this kind roused the whole commercial world to anger; and so great was the indignation of the House of Commons, that it resulted in a partial abrogation of the privileges of the Company, for which misfortune they had only their own intolerance to thank. Sir Josiah Child, their powerful chairman, submitted to the inevitable at home, but his will and great prestige in the East were still for many years strong enough to maintain almost as great a monopoly as before. It is evident that it was not the joint-stock East India Company alone who so jealously guarded its privileges to the exclusion of interlopers. The Spanish and Portuguese merchants, though each and all trading on their own account, enjoyed a monopoly of trade and commerce with the Peninsula by virtue of their charters; but the outcry raised in the Commons forced all for a time to assume a less uncompromising attitude in respect of their rights.[1] This same year we find that by the 'petition of Sir James Houblon and other Spanish merchants,' an embargo had been laid 'by order of Council on certain ships bound for Spain,'

---

[1] 'All of the Companies were in constant feud with interlopers.' See Cunningham, *Growth of Industry and Commerce in Modern Times*, i. 122.

but now the Commissioners of Customs reported to the Lords of the Treasury that the merchants 'no longer object to the removal of the said embargo; and to this they agreed.'[1]

While greatly against their will, the fame of their ship *Charles II.*, under the command of her pirate captain, had been sounded from the Far East only to be echoed back from the West Indies, the brothers Houblon and their friends had borne with what philosophy they could the loss of her and her cargo (she was valued at £14,000), but they had also to deplore the 'overthrow of the whole design' upon which they had engaged her, together with her two sister ships.[2] A severe loss indeed; and Sir James Houblon some-what fretfully complained—'that considering the great privileges obtained from the King of Spain of diving upon all wrecks in all his dominions, and for setting up of magazines in his West Indies, it might have resulted in a great profit.'[3]

The whole story of the piracy of Captain Every is curious and interesting on its own merits. But what enhances its interest still further is the fact that from this romance was evolved another of equal fame. It appears that the expedition designed by the Lords of the Treasury for the suppression of the East Indian pirates, was supplemented by a second one, which had its origin in the West Indian plantations. The government, being unprepared themselves to fit out another expedition, gave leave—on the urgent request of Lord Bellamont, governor of New York—to 'an old mariner' named William Kidd, said to be familiar with the pirates and their haunts (who can say but what he knew them too well!), who undertook, acting under the authority of

[1] Treasury Papers, vol. xxiii. No. 21.
[2] The cost of the adventure of the three ships was £30,000, a very large sum for those days.
[3] Board of Trade, Trade Papers, vol. vi.

the Home Government and under the protection of the British flag, 'to clear the Indian seas of the whole race [of pirates] who prowled between the Cape of Good Hope and the Straits of Malacca.'[1] The cost of the expedition was to be defrayed by private subscription on the basis of an investment, and the money was subsequently subscribed by prominent English gentlemen, including Lords Shrewsbury, Romney, and Oxford, and the Lord Chancellor Somers. Sailing with letters of marque, and carrying a commission under the Great Seal empowering him to seize pirate ships, Captain Kidd found the sport of hunting down and capturing them so congenial a task and so lucrative, that he speedily altered his tactics, and, from a privateer, himself became a pirate!

The consequences of the old seaman's escapade were momentous. For the House of Commons, now hotly Tory, full of ill-will to King William and his ministers, and bent on the reduction of the army, made it an excuse for a violent attack on Lord Somers, the last remaining member in office of the Junto Cabinet. Lord Somers had invested £1000 in the ill-starred expedition of Kidd, and the Commons now accused him of having been cognizant of the Captain's piratical intentions. The crisis was averted by the very absurdity of the accusations brought against the Chancellor, but the violence of the Commons brought dismay to the City. The immense prosperity and commercial activity which had characterised the past three years, in spite of an exhausting war, were now checked; and the fall in Bank stock evidenced the alarm of the financiers. For the City was quick to perceive the bent of opinion as indicated by this explosion, and that the great reaction in the country, weary of the war, and recklessly demanding disarmament, would

---

[1] Macaulay, *History*, iv. 247.

be followed by such measures as would result in the
King and nation being relegated to such a situation
of weakness as would allow of their being treated
as a *quantité négligeable* by the French King, and
thus undo all that had been affected by the heavy
sacrifices of the war.   As a matter of fact, all this came
to pass.

CHAPTER XVIII

AUGUSTA LACRIMANS

'For their merchants : they are Vena Porta ; and if they flourish
not, a kingdom may have good limbs, but will have empty veins
and nourish little.'—BACON : *Of Empire.*

AFTER the Revolution Mr. Pepys had retired entirely
from public life. The suspicion clung to him of being
in sympathy with 'Popery,' and he found it expedient
to live in the closest retirement. He was, indeed, in
consequence of this suspicion, once again committed to
the Tower in the year 1690, and was only liberated by
being bailed for a large sum of money by a few of his
friends, of whom Sir James Houblon was one. The
letter of thanks addressed by him to these friends after
his release bears witness to the gratitude and affection
of the late Secretary to the Admiralty to those who had
delivered him from his painful and alarming position.[1]
Henceforth, surrounded by his books and in close intercourse with his many friends, Pepys spent the remainder
of his life at what the good Mr. Evelyn playfully called his
'paradisian Clapham,' and when he died he was mourned
sincerely by those who had loved and admired this
strange and gifted being, the study of whose personality
—heightened by the transcribing of his diaries—still
exercises the same strong fascination on men as it did

---

[1] He was bailed for £30,000 ; Sir James Houblon, Sir Peter Palavicini,
Mr. Blackborne (secretary to the East India Company), and Mr. Martin,
all powerful London citizens, were the friends who came to his rescue,
Wheatley's *Pepysiana*, p. 58.

more than two hundred years ago. His affection for James Houblon, of whom he wrote many years before as 'the man whom I love mightily,' was warmly reciprocated. 'Dyne with you I cannot,' writes Sir James in the year of the lowest depression of poor Pepys's fortunes, in response to a hospitable invitation; 'but after seven in the evening (which I will spend with you), either by water on the Thames or in your coach at Hide Parke, you shall dispose of me as you please, as you alwayes shall, and of all that I have or within my reach.'[1]

1697 The signing of the Peace of Ryswick, on the 20th of September 1697, for the time brought to an end the long struggle which had been upheld with so much patience by William III. Louis' treasury was exhausted, while behind that of his adversary were still the deep purses of the City magnates. Though the Revolution had been brought about by a general body of opinion in England, William's *welt-politik* was neither generally understood nor appreciated, except indeed by certain of his Whig ministers, and by the princes of commerce who trusted him;[2] and so it came to pass that in less than two years, the fruits of his successes were to be imperilled by the jealousy and short sight of the Tory party, which forced on him the reduction of the army, with its natural consequence of fresh aggressions on the part of King Louis. But meanwhile all rejoiced and 'gave thanks' when the King returned from Holland after the signing of the Peace.

Some ten days before his entry into London, the Earl of Portland and other officers reached Whitehall late at night, bringing the first news of William's speedy return, day and hour depending upon wind and tide. 'If,' in the words of Luttrell, 'the wind permit, his Majesty will make his entry upon horseback Thursday the 4th of

[1] Rawl. MS. A. 170, vol. lviii. The letter is endorsed by Pepys as 'a letter of kindnesse only.'
[2] Lecky, *History of England in the Eighteenth Century*, i. 12, 13.

November, his birthday, that they [the citizens] may be at one charge; the night before which, if he lands in Essex, he will lodge at Copt Hall, the Earl of Dorset's seat, or at Sir James Houblon's, near Epping Forest; but if in Kent, at the Queen's house in Greenwich.'[1] It was thus that the Forest House, lately rebuilt and beautified by Sir James Houblon, was so nearly honoured by William's presence; however, the wind being favourable, the King landed at Margate, and 'lay' that night at the Queen's beautiful house—the present Greenwich Hospital, —then in course of reconstruction.

The return of William III. after the successful termination of the long and tedious negotiations which ended in the Peace of Ryswick, was the signal for immense rejoicing, and his entry into London was one of triumph. The new St. Paul's was now completed, and here he returned thanks publicly before a great crowd for the conclusion of the war. He had had many reverses; he was not a great general; but he had a policy so wide that his island kingdom was but a pawn in it, and he was patient and dogged in working it out to a conclusion. In his struggle with the brilliant Louis he had won, and now William knelt in St. Paul's a much greater man than when he last crossed the Channel; the *Grand Monarque* had bowed to the inevitable and, for the time at least, acknowledged him as King of 1697 Great Britain.

The relief of the country at having reached, as was supposed, a lasting peace through the many troubles of the past years, was profound; except indeed in respect of the Jacobites, whose cause had been discredited and their spirits depressed by the vindictive and short-sighted attitude recently adopted by King James. But the sacrifices of the London citizens were now in a fair way of ample return; the great developments of

---

[1] Luttrell, iv. 294.

commercial and trading interests had brought about a corresponding advance in their influence upon English legislation—an advance necessitated by the well-being of the community; because, as was later remarked by Burke, 'it was not intended that English legislation should be solely one of freeholders, but that they also should have their place in it;[1] and after the Revolution that place became exceedingly great.' At the same time it was evident, that among those who had been hesitating and grudging in their support of the new government, and jealous of the increased power and influence of the City, there were many who were now favourably influenced by a feeling of increasing confidence and security in business matters, which confidence was demonstrated by the steady rise in that Bank stock which had fluctuated so sensitively to the ebb and flow of William's fortunes. With this returning confidence there came about an immense impetus to trade and commerce.

But now that the country had attained—as it imagined—a permanent peace, and enjoyed the certainty of immunity from the dreaded dangers of Popery, the old traditional jealousy of the Dutch, joined to the personal unpopularity of the Dutch King, became more and more a factor in English politics. The

1698 general election of 1698 revealed a surprising reaction in feeling all over the country—except in London, where indeed a clearer insight saw danger in any relaxation of that effort which alone had brought about the present situation. Elsewhere, Tories now replaced the Whigs who before held the majority in the House of Commons, and the consequences of this change at length imposed upon the King so much humiliation, that he seriously contemplated abdicating the throne. The army was reduced to seven thousand men; William was forced to send away his much-loved Dutch guards;

[1] Lecky, *Democracy and Liberty*, I. i. 3.

his gifts of lands to his friends were resumed by the State, and the man who had been hailed as a deliverer and benefactor in the hour of need was not only insulted by the Commons of England, but reduced to impotency in the councils of Europe by his lack of an army! Meanwhile the Whig ministers were one by one forced to resign. The commissioners of the Admiralty—of whom Sir John Houblon was one—were vehemently attacked ; while Charles Montague, the gifted Chancellor of the Exchequer, whose fiscal schemes were scarcely comprehended outside the City which had initiated them, was reviled both for his support of the City itself, and for his independence and self-confident manners. It had long been one of Montague's favourite schemes (in Macaulay's sounding words) 'to elevate the Whig section of that mighty commercial aristocracy which congregated under the arches of the Royal Exchange, and to depress the Tory section,'[1] but now Montague had passed under the condemnation of the Commons, and in his retirement the City, 'whose influence had been felt to the remotest corner of the realm,'[2] was for the time to find its interests neglected and its councils despised. The year 1699 saw Sir John Houblon and his colleagues, with the exception of Admiral Sir George Rooke, ejected from the Admiralty,[3] and for that year we also find that John Houblon was not re-elected a director of the Bank of England, though at the close of it he again took his place at the board, and remained on it till his death in 1712. His fiscal policy had been so closely identified with that of Montague, that we may well believe that, with the fall of the statesman, the policy which Sir John supported found also its condemnation, and the natural result was the exclusion for the time of the exponent of that policy from the councils of the Bank, by the votes of the large section of recalcitrant shareholders.

1699

[1] Macaulay, *History*, v. 62.   [2] *Ibid.*   [3] Luttrell, iv. 520.

It was soon after this temporary retirement from active work that Sir John Houblon was visited by a great sorrow in the death of his brother James. On the 20th of October 1700, Luttrell chronicles the fact 'that Sir James Houblon, Alderman and Member of Parliament for this City is dead.'[1] He was buried at St. Bennet's, Paul's Wharf, on the 31st following, 'about ten at night, in a vault in the middle Ile of that Church.'[2] The reason for the night funeral does not appear, but it seems that they were then not uncommon.[3] Sir James Houblon's two sons survived him, but neither of them married. Both were present at Mr. Pepys's funeral in 1703, and received memorial rings on the occasion according to custom. His old friend bequeathed to Sir James's sons, Wynne and James, 'their father's, mother's, and grandfather's portraits.'[4]

Amongst the commissioners appointed in 1707, under the Seal of Great Britain, 'For managing the Equivalent due to Scotland pursuant to the treaty of Union,' we find the name of James, Houblon the younger.[5] The English commissioners travelled to Edinburgh in July this year to arrange, in conjunction with their Scottish colleagues, matters appertaining to the Union. By a clause in the Act of Union a sum of £400,000, called the Equivalent, was to be paid to Scotland in exchange for her assuming her share of responsibility for a portion of the National Debt. Owing to a large part of the Scottish nation being bitterly hostile to the Union between the two countries, these negotiations were of a very delicate nature. In the possession of the directors of the Bank of England is a very interesting series of extracts from letters written from Scotland, by James,

_1700_

_1703_

_1707_

[1] Luttrell, iv. 701.   [2] Le Neve's *Knights.*
[3] 'He was buried at tenn of clocke at night, it being the hower that mortalls goe to their rest.' See *Autobiography of Sir John Bramston* (14 January 1685), p. 220.
[4] See Appendix to *Diary* of S. Pepys.
[5] *New View of London,* ii. 729.

Houblon (junior) to his brother Wynne, in which he tells the story of his own and his colleagues' work in the Scottish capital. Unknown to the writer, Wynne supplied the directors of the Bank with copies of those portions of his brother's letters which touched upon the business on which he was engaged. Writing on the 16th of September 1707, James, on first hearing of this fact, remarks: 'What I wrote you was to comply wth your desire of knowing what pass'd here, without ever expecting it would be communicated to any body else, especially ye Court of Directors, otherwise I should have done it more fully and also more correctly. However I shall always own ye favour (as I ought to do) of those Gentlemen that declar'd for me with so much Partiality, that they've left me only to wish that what they said was true.' Eulogiums had evidently been sent from Edinburgh on the ability and tact with which this commissioner had done his part as one of the English contingent. To the ignorance of James that any eye but that of his brother Wynne would see his epistles, we owe some amusing and characteristic touches which are to be found interspersed among the dry details of the business he was engaged in. By permission of the present Bank directors we give these letters (verbatim) in an Appendix.[1]

Of Wynne Houblon we know but little, but that he was a friend and occasional correspondent of Strype.[2] Neither brother appears to have survived middle age, and both bequeathed their property to their uncle Abraham.

It is perhaps not strange that the people of this country should have fretted somewhat at a fate which gave them a foreign King with foreign friends and foreign tastes. But the bargain was of their own making.

---

[1] See Appendix B.　　　　[2] Add. MSS. 3853 f. 493.

1707

They had accepted an equivalent in their emancipation from the dangers of absolute monarchy and Popery. It is curious to find that in the matter of policy as we now look for it, the parties were then reversed. While the Whig desired to figure as the strong man armed whose goods were thus in security, it was the Tory who, while hastily putting an end to the war, exposed the country's weakness to danger and insult. As a matter of fact, although the gentlemen of England forgot for a time what was due to themselves and to the man whom they had set on the throne, no sooner did they become aware of their mistake, than they hastened to rectify it, while the sturdy sense of the people reasserted itself under the righteous indignation which greeted the impertinence of Louis XIV.'s acknowledgment of the Prince of Wales as King of England, on the death

1701   of James II.[1] The country awoke as from a dream; once more William was greeted with impassioned loyalty as the saviour of the country, and the bulwark of the faith; and the Commons having voted him 50,000 soldiers and 35,000 seamen, embarked with dogged determination upon another long war.[2]

Louis XIV.—as many others have done to this day—took the attitude of the House of Commons to be a sure index of the indifference of the country to the course of affairs abroad, and its treatment of King William as an abandonment of the principles embodied in his person. But he was soon undeceived. When the reaction came, William was already sick and dying; but he sent Marlborough at the head of an army to represent him, and was at least comforted in that his subjects, who had misunderstood him and his aims, now turned to him once more in confidence and loyalty. He was not, however, to see the end; a fall from his horse on the 20th

[1] September 1701.
[2] Mahan, *Influence of Sea Power*, p. 205.

of February 1702 was too great a shock for his feeble
frame, and he died on the 8th of March following.

The special service in respect of the Peninsula, which
for many years had been rendered to the Board of
Trade and Admiralty departments by Sir James Houblon, dating from the days of Mr. Pepys's secretaryship,
had been closed by his death; but Treasury and Trade
Papers show that Sir John was now frequently called
upon for the help and advice formerly given by his
brother. Corruptions among their agents and public
servants made the authorities at the Admiralty suspicious, while the popular fear of Popery poisoned their
mind against individuals with whom they had business
relations, and we find evidence of these anxieties in 1701,
in respect of the victualling of the ships of war in the
Mediterranean. Documents show Sir John Houblon,
amidst his many labours, quieting the minds and reassur-
ing the Treasury Lords as to certain bills and accounts
being 'just and reasonable,' and the accusations of
'Popish tendencies' against their agents at Cadiz unfounded.[1] This he was able to do through the medium
of his son John, who at that time represented the
interests of his family in the Peninsula.[2]

The substantial result to this country of the long
struggle, called the war of the Spanish Succession, was
the gain of a footing in the Mediterranean by the acquisition of Gibraltar and Port Mahon.[3] Admiral Sir George
Rooke attacked and took Gibraltar on the 4th of August
1704, and it was our friendship with the Portuguese which
enabled him afterwards to relieve the Rock from the
investing squadrons which endeavoured in vain to wrest
it from us again.[4] The people of this country were

---

[1] Treasury Papers, vol. lxxiii. No. 22.

[2] There are many evidences of such difficulties and disputes in the
records of the Public Offices, while the documents relating to those with
which the Houblons were concerned might be worthy of notice but for lack
of space.

[3] Mahan, *Influence of Sea Power*, p. 215.   [4] *Ibid.*, p. 212.

fully aware of the importance of Gibraltar to the consolidation of our growing sea power in the Mediterranean, and great were the rejoicings when the news was received in London of its relief. On the 31st of March

1705 1705, Luttrell tells us in his daily chronicle of events, how that Sir John Houblon was the first to obtain news from his Spanish agent of the raising of the siege by the French and Spaniards,[1] and the same month he records that 'the Lords, by way of ballotting, chose three new Commissioners of Accounts' (of whom Sir John Houblon was one), 'and added them to the bill sent up to them from the Commons.'[2]

Released from the anxiety which had oppressed the country, and the bondage which, prior to the Revolution of 1688, had shut men's mouths, the years following upon it were fruitful in much new thought and speculation of all kinds. As regards trade and commerce in particular, new ideas found expression in various publications, the most important of which were those of John Locke, and with the large majority of thinkers on these questions his views found acceptance. But there were others who advocated theories more in consonance with modern ideas. Public opinion, however, was not yet ready for such views as they advocated, nor would political exigences have allowed of their adoption at the time. The long struggle with France had its object in preventing her obtaining a commercial supremacy in Europe, as well as in the East and in the New World; and the essential elements of the Mercantile System—so called—were based upon this paramount obligation, and continued of necessity so long as the danger lasted. Orders in Council recognised it, and the Methuen Treaty with Portugal was an expression of it.[3] In that their efforts were crowned with success, the exponents of the

---

[1] Luttrell, *Brief Relation*, v. 536.   [2] *Ibid.*, v. 403.
[3] Leslie Stephen, *History of English Thought in the Eighteenth Century*, ii. 299.

old policy should hardly be so scornfully criticised as by many economists of this day, some of whom regard all political economy as crude and empirical before the day of Adam Smith and his *Wealth of Nations*. Neither Great Britain's supremacy on the sea, nor her great colonial Empire, would have been accomplished facts but for the strenuous efforts of the exponents of the mercantile system. But at best the old methods were regarded as designed to meet the exigences of the moment, and, when the right time came, the way was open for Free Trade.

That this was the desideratum of those who looked for better things—even so long ago as 1701—is shown 1701 by a 'remarkable' anonymous tract,[1] entitled *Considerations upon the East India Trade*, published that year, and for which we venture to claim the authorship for Sir John Houblon. The opinions expressed in this pamphlet had been held by the writer many years, and were only now published through the urgent entreaty of his many friends to whom his arguments had always been 'very convincing.'[2] The chief aim of the pamphlet was to meet certain objections which at this time were being very vehemently brought forward against the East India trade by the disciples of the mercantile theory. If, in dealing with the fallacies with which the East India Company was being assailed, the author reasons first as an experienced merchant, in the latter part of his argument it is as a banker that he writes, and with all a banker's authority and information. It is in this portion of his work that we observe a strong resemblance in style and substance to a letter long ago addressed by Sir John Houblon to Sir Henry Caple on the subject of the coinage; both arguments having

[1] See Sir Leslie Stephen, *History of English Thought in the Eighteenth Century*, ii. 299.

[2] '*Considerations upon the East India Trade.* London : Printed for A. and F. Churchill, at the Black Swan in Paternoster Row, MDCCI.' (1701).

reference to the intrinsic values of money and of bullion, before and after being coined into money.[1]   The 'heats and distractions' prevailing in the public councils—for the Tory party was in power, and fiercely hostile to the policy of the Revolution—would sufficiently account for the anonymous publication of this pamphlet, which also allowed of a freer and more pungent treatment of the subject, by one who was so closely identified with Whig principles as Sir John Houblon.   In the words of a distinguished writer: 'The singular acuteness displayed in this tract, may entitle the writer to the credit of having anticipated the doctrines of Adam Smith by just three-quarters of a century, with a clearness very seldom exhibited in any sphere of speculation.   He is not content with the conclusive argument [of Free Trade], but takes the further and more difficult step of thoroughly working out the mode in which Free Trade operates.'[2]   It is, however, remarkable that the dreams of the author, fascinating as they appeared to him, were also regarded by him as impossible under existing conditions political and economical.

The death of his 'dearest friend'[3] prevented the exhaustive treatment of the several trades with which the author had designed to compare that of the East India Company, only the one which relates to the Fishing Trade being completed.[4]   But it is in this connection that he not only anticipates the doctrine of Free Trade, but sketches a busy scene of industry and prosperity under its universal influence as might almost form a chapter in the *Utopia* of Sir Thomas More!   His scheme includes

[1] See Letter, p. 267.
[2] Sir Leslie Stephen, *History of English Thought in the Eighteenth Century*, ii. 299.
[3] The death of Sir James Houblon occurred in October 1700.
[4] 'There is no other way to acquire a satisfactory knowledge of the state, etc., of the manufactures and trade of this kingdom than by treating of each branch separately, . . . every part must be distinctly known, or the whole cannot be well understood.'   See *A Representation Concerning the Knowledge of Commerce*, by Joseph Massie, p. 14.

a free port 'in some convenient place far from where crowded wharfs and keys and dwelling places impede the free exercise of mariners, and untrammelled by their dues and customs and restrictions.'   Here he would 'erect houses and warehouses built for the reception of goods, which at all places may be freely imported hither, and which again may be as freely exported.' [1] 'Such a place,' he pleads, 'would soon be built and peopled.   The interests of merchants would do the thing, and it would be done without any publick Charge.' . . . Here the Dutch would trade, and other nations. For now 'the want of a Free Port, together with the Act of Navigation . . . makes England more dangerous than Rocks and Sands to Holland.' [2]

Another interesting suggestion is made by this writer. In order to cheapen the expense of construction, in such places where, through want of space and other deterrents, high wages prevail, he proposes that the several parts of the thing manufactured which require skill should be completed at a distance, 'already fitted to several scantlings and dimensions as required, and brought hither, when nothing need be left but to lay those several parts together.' [3]   The author thus anticipated modern American methods by not far under two hundred years.

The theories advanced in 1701 were echoed—strangely enough—twelve years later by the Tory government of Lords Harley and St. John, though in a modified form. The proposed commercial treaty with France following upon the Peace of Utrecht was defeated in consequence of the furious antagonism and many terrors of those who were bound by their belief in the mercantile theory.   It   1713

---

[1] A contemporary writes of the Port of London (1906): 'Owing to the high cost of living, and the consequent increase of wages, together with the pressure of taxes and local rates, it seems to be assured that . . . this decline cannot be checked. . . . Meantime the heritage of the past is being thrown away by the *laissez faire* of the present generation.'

[2] *Considerations upon the East India Trade*, p. 125.

[3] *Ibid.*, pp. 120, 121.

was felt that the moment had not arrived when the country's attitude as regards France could be abandoned; nor did it arrive till after the Napoleonic wars, and the long struggle came to an end.   But Free Trade with France, or quasi Free Trade only, as was proposed in 1713, fell very short of the Utopian dream of the author of the *Considerations upon the East India Trade*.   That the promised El Dorado of Cobden has not yet brought us to the golden shores of Free Trade proper is perhaps not wonderful.   It needs co-operation for unity of purpose.   The universal brotherhood of man seems scarcely yet within distance of realisation; but perhaps the aspirations of our author—who, like Cobden, aimed at nothing less than free and open trade with all the world when '*at all places* goods might be freely imported and again as freely exported,'[1]—may yet be realised, if not with all the world, at least within the Empire.   For the rest, the signs of the times may well warn those nations who have profited so greatly by our so-called Free Trade. When the mercantile theory no longer met the exigences of the time, it was abandoned for a better way.   This country is not so conservative that she should not once again meet new conditions with equal wisdom and firmness.

Seventeen years all but two months had passed away since the Charter of the Bank of England was sealed in the presence of its first governor, and he was now an old and wearied man.   But the great Bank still claimed his services, and when he died he was still on the direction.   In the delightful pages of the *Spectator* Addison

1711   describes how, on the 3rd of March 1710/11, he had visited Grocers' Hall, where the officers of the Bank still held their sittings.   The venerable figure of the first governor, with his big spectacles on his nose, and his

---

[1] *Considerations upon the East India Trade*, p. 124.

long, lean face, was doubtless one among those whose busy preoccupation so attracted the essayist. 'In one of my rambles,' he writes, 'or rather speculations, I looked into the great hall where the Bank is kept, and was not a little pleased to see the directors, secretaries and clerks, with all the other members of that wealthy corporation in their several stations.'[1]

We have learnt incidentally of the dim and changing sight of Sir John's advancing years, as also of a cure effected by means of the simple remedies of 'eyebright, sweet marjoram, and betony dry'd'; we are not told whether taken internally or as a salve. Any way, the mild effects of this compound would have been neutralised by the more drastic accompaniment of 'so much of the right sort of Portugal snuff put into the corners of the eyes night and morning, and taken likewise as snuff' to the nose! This treatment, we are assured, cured Sir John Houblon, as well as two other elderly gentlemen, viz. Judge Ayres and Sir Edward Seymour; 'that they could read without spectacles after they had used them many years.'[2]

Of the four Houblons who had shared with Sir John the honour of being among the first twenty-four directors of the Bank of England, he alone now remained. Peter[5] had been long dead, while James[2] had died eleven years since. Abraham, who had done good work at the Bank, had retired from business, and was living at his country seat in Sussex. Only John remained to the last, and finally died 'in harness.' But the Houblon name was not yet to be blotted out from the roll of the Bank servants. Abraham's son Richard became a director in 1713, and **1713** remained for some years on the board of directors;[3] so that with the exception of the few months which elapsed

---

[1] *Spectator*, No. 3, 3 March 1710/11.
[2] See *The Compleat Housewife, or Accomplished Gentlewoman's Companion.* E. Smith, London, 16th edition, 1758.
[3] Till 1719.

between the death of Sir John Houblon and the election of his nephew Sir Richard, the family was represented continuously during the first twenty-five years of the Bank's existence. Long years of hard unremitting work had at last worn out the strong and vigorous frame of the old 'first governor'; while his rule of life, almost ascetic, was persevered in courageously, even to fourscore. He passed away suddenly, on the 10th of January 1711/12, 'very early in the morning, at break of day, after his morning orisons.'[1] . . . On his knees in his chamber, looking out to the east in the grey dawn of the January morning, they found him, cold and lifeless. A little, worn book of prayers, close-written in manuscript and bearing on the cover the initials J. H., has been preserved. It is, perhaps, John Houblon's copy of his good father's Pious Memoirs, and it bears witness to its constant use by its owner. While the Pater Bursae had sought peace and communion with God in the quiet and solitude of the country during the last ten years of his life, his son had remained at his post in the fulfilment of the arduous work in which his had been passed ; but yet, nevertheless, he passed through the gate of death, on his knees, at his morning orisons.

The portrait of its first governor hangs in the committee room of the Bank of England. With a dark, powerful head, almost Spanish in the complexion of the long, rather stern face, it is a dignified and interesting picture of the governor in the prime of life. Although in the rich robes of the mayoralty, the huge sword of the municipality above him, and with the emblems of his civic dignities by his side, the effect is sober and subdued. This picture is by Isaac Whood. A rare mezzotint exists of another portrait by Clostermann, of which all trace has been lost. The original, though well painted, was evidently inartistic, — the thin, shrunken

[1] Luttrell's *Brief Relation.*

Jno Houblon

face and figure being overburdened by the gorgeous municipal robes and immense periwig of the wearer. An earlier picture—painted when Sir John was about forty years old, and which formed part of the family pictures of Mr. James Houblon, his father,—is at Hallingbury.

Although John Houblon lived to see the close of the war for this country, he died before the consummation of the Peace of Utrecht, when England reaped the fruits of all her sacrifices. Nor was he to witness the vast impetus to trade in all its branches which followed. The great Bank he left in peace and prosperity, having been firmly established as the honoured depository of the credit of the State and nation, while its importance and the weight of its authority were such as necessitated its counsels being sought and its convenience consulted in all state measures which might affect it. The well-known tendencies of the corporation, which regarded with suspicion any measure which might lead to a return of the exiled royal family to power, were recognised by Queen Anne after the return of the Tory majority in the Parliament of 1710, when, in the words of Bishop Burnet, 'the Queen's intention to make a change in her ministers began to break out. This gave alarm both at home and abroad; but the Queen to lessen that, said to her subjects here, *in particular to the governor of the Bank of England*, that she should make no other changes.'[1]

1710

Sir John Houblon's funeral elegy was written by Settle, the seventeenth-century City poet. A copy in old brown calf, quarto, with the Houblon arms on the back, is at Hallingbury. It boasts the title *Augusta Lacrimans*, and is a curious specimen of the inflated style of the famous Settle.[2] While devoid of any literary merit, it

[1] *Life and Times of Bishop Burnet.*
[2] E. Settle, *Augusta Lacrimans*, London, MDCCXII.

is interesting to us from a personal point of view, as it contains much incidental information as to the history of the Houblons.[1]

John Houblon was born on the 13th of March 1631/2, and was therefore about twenty-eight when he married in July 1660.   His wife, Marie Jurin, was a member of a Flemish refugee family, and his eldest sister had married a merchant of the same name.   Five sons and six daughters were the issue of his marriage, but two sons only, John and Samuel, survived their father.   The latter, who never married, became an

1719   eminent merchant of large fortune.   In 1719 he was living in Edmonton, for he was in January that year 'discharged from serving the office of Surveyor of the Highways for the said parish, as he is a Justice of

1723   the Peace.'[2]   His will was made in 1723, and he died soon afterwards suddenly, leaving large charitable bequests, amongst which was a donation of £2500 to St. Thomas's Hospital.[3]   His brother John succeeded another brother (who as we have related was killed in Lisbon), as active agent to his family in their Peninsular and Mediterranean commercial affairs.   He died at Port Oporto in Portugal, leaving one daughter.

Two of Sir John Houblon's daughters were married during their father's lifetime : one to a merchant named Denny; the other, Sara, to Richard Mytton of Halston, in Shropshire, Esq., Member of Parliament for Shrewsbury.   They became the ancestors of the famous Squire Mytton of Halston, whose hunting, shooting, and other sporting exploits remain to this day an object of

[1] Sir John was a 'benefactor' to the corporation of the poor of the City of London (*New View of London*, ii. 752-55)—the earliest of the work-houses—his large donations to the funds causing him to be elected a governor.   He was also amongst the earliest subscribers to the 'Queen's House' (Greenwich Hospital); where, according to the custom common at the time, his name as the donor of £100 is still to be seen written upon the south side of the entrance hall of the hospital.

[2] Sessions Book, Edmonton, No. 779 (Sessions held at Hickes Hall).

[3] See *Political State of Great Britain*.

interest and amazement to sportsmen.[1] Their grand-daughter was the mother of Thomas Pennant, the author of *Some Account of London*,[2] in which work we see him lamenting the demolition of the Church of St. Christopher le Stocks in Threadneedle Street, and 'the hard fate of some of his kindred dust [including that of his Houblon ancestors] in the disturbance of their remains.'

Sir John Houblon died at his house in Threadneedle

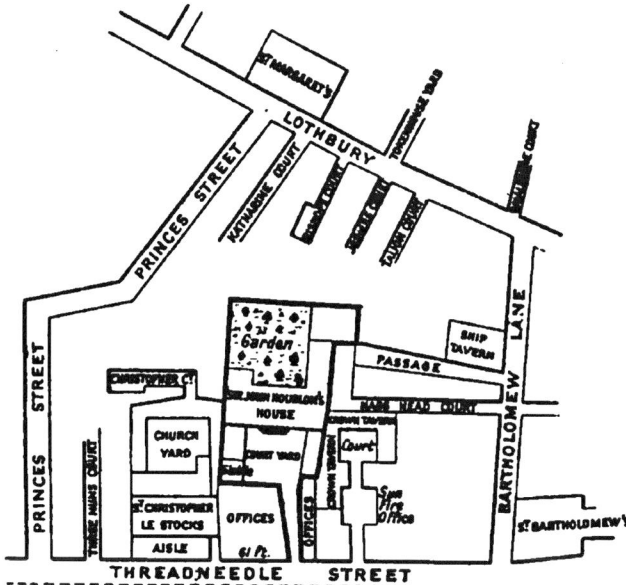

Plan of Sir John Houblon's House and Garden. 1731. (From the Gough Collection in the Bodleian.)
SITE OF THE BANK OF ENGLAND

Street, of which Pennant remarks that it 'stood on the site of the Bank, the noblest monument he could have.'[3] It is indeed in a sense his monument, for he was buried in his parish church of St. Christopher le Stocks close by, which, together with his mansion and garden, are now covered by the huge buildings of the present

[1] See *Memoirs of the Life of the late John Mytton, Esq., of Halston,* etc., by Nimrod.
[2] Thomas Pennant, born 1726, died 1798. *Dictionary of General Biography,* by Cates.
[3] Thomas Pennant, *Some Account of London,* p. 455, 3rd edition, 1793.

Bank of England.   After Lady Houblon's death, which

1732   occurred at Richmond in 1732, the house and garden

1733   were purchased by the corporation of the Bank from
her executors, and the first portion of the building of
Sampson built thereon; subsequently, when the Church
of St. Christopher was destroyed by fire, its site, as
well as that of the old graveyard adjoining, was also
absorbed, and the building enlarged; so that Sir John
and the rest of the dead (who were left undisturbed),
still lie under the great Bank which he helped to found.

Lady Houblon was very old when she died.   Her
daughters continued for many years to live on Richmond Hill, where they had a house.   A group of
almshouses, eleven in number, built and endowed by

1753   them in 1753, still exists, situated on the slope of the
Hill (now covered with houses), about half a mile from
the famous terrace overlooking the valley of the
Thames.   Where change has been busy all around, this
little oasis of the past has remained almost untouched
since the first group of Richmond widows found a refuge
there from the storms of the outer world of poverty
and sorrow.   Though the road to London passes
scarcely fifty yards away, and opposite its brick gateway
the Red Cow Inn plies its trade,—once past the fine
wrought-iron gate crowned by the date 1753 which
leads into the high-walled sanctuary of sleepy peace
within, one can imagine oneself actually in the past,
and conjure up a mental vision of the two little old
ladies, Mistress Rebeckah and Mistress Susanna
Houblon, hooped and powdered, each with a Bible
tucked under her arm, tripping across the quadrangle
between the tall hollyhocks and roses and mignonette,
to 'read a chapter' to the white-capped inmates of the
tiny houses.[1]   Down the steep green lane behind they

---

[1] Each inmate has two rooms, and receives 30s. per month and two tons
of coal per annum.

would have come, and on their own land all the way;
for they owned many goodly acres on Richmond Hill.
But the trustees of the charity have long since turned
the lane to good account, and now it is 'Houblon Road,'
flanked on both sides with dingy brown houses.

Susanna, the last surviving of the sisters, lived for
another twelve years at Richmond. Latterly her niece
Esther, the daughter of Sara Mytton and her husband,
made her home with the old lady. The *St. James's
Evening Post* tells us, on the 25th of August 1765, that   1765
'Mistress Houblon, daughter to Sir John Houblon, who
was Lord Mayor for this City in the year 1696—is
dead: a maiden lady of large fortune.'[1]   Miss Susanna
left £40,000, half of which she bequeathed to her father's
great-great-nephew John, Houblon of Hallingbury, and
half in legacies to the children of her married sisters.
The house and property on Richmond Hill she likewise
left to her great-nephew, subject to the proviso that
Esther Mytton should be allowed to live there undisturbed so long as she should choose to do so; with the
further stipulation that no buildings should be erected,
or alterations made, which might interfere with the
'prospect from her windows'; showing the famous view
from Richmond Hill to have been even then in danger.

[1] *St. James's Evening Post*, No. 5556.

CHAPTER XIX

THE PARTING OF THE WAYS

'And Lot lifted up his eyes and beheld all the plain of Jordan
that it was well watered everywhere . . . and Lot journeyed east.'

As we have related in a former chapter, Mr. Abraham
Houblon was one of the brothers who were elected by
ballot to the board of direction of the Bank of England
in 1694; also that during the years 1761 and 1762 he
served as deputy-governor, and during the subsequent
two years as governor of the Bank. Abraham was
thus the second of his name to fill a position of great
weight and responsibility. He appears to have retired
from participation in the affairs of the Bank some three
years later. In 1702 he was appointed one of the
commissioners of the government victualling department.[1] This appointment was made at an important
time when his business capacities would have been taxed
to the uttermost. The nation's weariness of war had
forced upon William III. vast reductions in the arma-
ments of the country. The disbanding of so many
troops, as well as the dismantling of the navy, were, as
was predicted by the King, closely followed by fresh
troubles upon the Continent : the ambition of Louis XIV.
having been kept in check solely by the powerful hand of
William. The strong reaction in English public opinion
at the death of James II. permitted a reversal of this
policy, and William hastily replaced the forces upon

[1] Luttrell, v. 171 ; and *New View of London*, ii. 729.

their former footing, and in the sudden emergency thus created, the victualling department needed able administration.

When the *New View of London* was published in 1708, Abraham Houblon was on the Commission of Lieutenancy of London. His name is included in the list of members 'which came down in June 1707,' and is given by the author, who thus describes the functions of this important body. 'The Commissioners of Lieutenancy consisteth of the Lord Mayor, Aldermen, and those most powerful and wealthy citizens, formerly called Barons, in whom the military government of London is lodged, as Lord Lieutenants of a County. These make choice of officers of the Train Bands.'[1] Abraham was never an Alderman; but his brothers, Sir James and Sir John, in virtue of their office, as such were included in the Commission of Lieutenancy.[2]

Abraham, who was born on the 23rd of January 1639, survived all his brothers and sisters, and his wife predeceased him in 1703, by twenty years. During the latter part of his life, having retired altogether from business, he lived at Langley, his wife's property in Buckinghamshire. His marriage with Dorothy Hubert had brought him two children, viz. Richard, born in 1672, and Anne, who was born some ten years later. Richard was soon busily employed, like the rest of his family, in commercial matters; and he became a successful merchant of large fortune, apart from what his father bequeathed to him at his death in 1722. When Richard was but little more than twenty-one, we come across his name, together with that of John Harvey, a young man who had lately married Elizabeth, a daughter of Sir James Houblon. Harvey (afterwards Colonel Harvey, of St. Andrew's Hall, Old Beckenham, in

1707

---

[1] *New View of London*, 1708, 1. xl.   [2] *Ibid.*

Norfolk)[1] had fought a duel, Richard Houblon acting as his second. From a State Paper, being a warrant for the reprieve of John Harvey and Richard Houblon of London, gentlemen, if found guilty of manslaughter,[2] we conclude that the result was fatal to their antagonist, also that strong interest was exerted by their friends on behalf of the young men.

1703   Richard Houblon's sister Anne is said to have been very lovely as a young girl, and there is a charming portrait of her painted by Michael Dahl before her marriage, in June 1703, to Henry, eldest son of Sir John Temple, of East Sheen, a brother of the famous Sir William Temple, the friend and adviser of William III. Both were descended from Sir John Temple, one of the Lords Justices in Ireland during the 'troubles' before the Civil Wars. Needless to say, the Temples were all strong Whigs.[3]

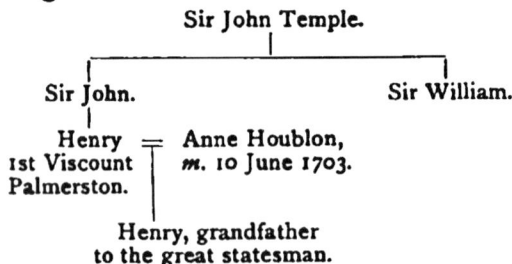

```
                    Sir John Temple.
                          |
         ┌────────────────┴───────────────────┐
     Sir John.                            Sir William.
         |
     Henry  =  Anne Houblon,
  1st Viscount  m. 10 June 1703.
   Palmerston.
         |
     Henry, grandfather
    to the great statesman.
```

Richard Houblon was knighted by King George I. in 1715,[4] and was then described as of Woodford in Essex. But he served as High Sheriff for Herts in 1709,[5] after he had become possessed of Hormead Hall in that county. Later he removed to Langley, the home of his mother's family, where Mr. Abraham Houblon

---

[1] The estate now belongs to Prince F. Duleep Singh.
[2] *H. O. Warrant Book*, vol. vi. p. 498.
[3] See Swift's *Works*, ed. 1883, vi. 416, and *Dictionary of National Biography*, lvi. 15.
[4] *Catalogue of Knights from* 1660-1828, by F. Townsend, Pursuivant of Arms, p. 37.
[5] Robert Clutterbuck, *History of Hertfordshire*, i. p. xxxiv.

ANNE HOUBLON.
m. HENRY, FIRST VISCOUNT PALMERSTON.

had resided till his death in 1722. The same year of the death of his father-in-law, Henry Temple was created Viscount Palmerston. Sir Richard Houblon never married. Besides his business as a merchant, he was deeply interested in the affairs of the Bank of England, of which he became a director in 1713, and continued on the direction till 1719, at which date he retired. Strype gives lists of the officers of the Bank for the years 1718 and 1719, together with those of the South Sea Company at the same period; and we note that the governor and directors were one and the same of both companies.[1] Like everybody else, he invested largely in South Sea stock in the early days of the company; but he seems to have retired from any participation in its affairs before the mad craze of speculation which later led to such dire results in the South Sea Bubble.

Sir Richard was the last of the merchant princes of his name, and already in the latter part of his career the conditions which had brought his father and uncles into touch with the higher politics of the nation had passed away. He appears to have been of a kindly, affectionate disposition, and to have been much loved by the members of his own family, as also of his mother's. So overwhelmed was he by the shock of his father's sudden death in 1722, that we find Lord Palmerston undertaking all letters and business after it occurred. A letter dated the 14th of May, St. James's Square, to the Reverend Jacob₂ Houblon at Bubbingworth,[2] informs him : 'I am desired by my brother Houblon to lett you know that on Fryday night Mr Houblon dyed att Langley, having been well the day before, and not halfe an hours warning of his departure given to any in the family; my brother is now att Langly where I left him

1713
1719
1722

---

[1] 'The Governours and Directors of the South Sea are the same, continuing customarily 3 years.'—Stowe, *Survey of London*, II. iv. 272.

[2] He was a son of Jacob₁, Rector of Moreton (Mr. James Houblon's fifth son), who died 1698.

yesterday, as well as one could expect under so great
an affliction for the loss of so good a father and so extraordinary a friend.' A few days later he again writes:
' I was yesterday att Langly to see my brother, who has
a very melancholy time of it and is alone; and as you
mentioned coming up, I believe your company would
bee very acceptable to him.' He goes on to say that he
has orders from his brother to take care of his 'passage
thither,' or to provide him with the hire of a chariot and
four horses, if he prefers it; meanwhile, if Mr. Houblon
does not go through in a day, a bed in St. James's Square
(at the writer's own house) is at his service, where he
would be heartily welcome. The 'hurry' of getting his
family into mourning and his son's late illness had
prevented their being now at Langley with his brother,
to whom his cousin Jacob would therefore be doubly
welcome.[1] Sir Richard's bad health at the time of his
father's death may partly account for the effects of the
shock upon him.

Above the grave of their father, the brother and
sister erected a large square tomb of brick and stone,
surrounded by iron railings; it is now a bower of roses.
Lady Palmerston tended it with care till her death, and
her husband showed his love for her memory and wishes
twenty years later in his will. To four poor widows
in the parish of Langley he left £4 per annum on condition of keeping the tomb in order. The bequest was
rigidly honoured till after the death of the great statesman — Anne Palmerston's great-grandson — when it
became void by statute of mortmain.

There were a vast number of family and other pictures
collected together at Langley, comprising portraits of
the three families of Hubert of Langley, King, and
Houblon, and among the latter were those family pictures
which had formerly belonged to old Mr. Houblon,

[1] Letter dated 19 May 1722.

besides the portraits of the Pater Bursae himself, and of Sir James and Lady Houblon, which had been in the possession of Mr. Samuel Pepys.[1] A division of these pictures now took place, some of the Houblon portraits being retained by Sir Richard Houblon, and the rest delivered over to his sister, Lady Palmerston, by whom they were removed to her home at East Sheen. Two lists exist in the hand-writing of Lord Palmerston: the one made in 1724, when, as it is to be presumed, Lady Palmerston's share of the Langley portraits was first added to his own collection; and the other, taken two years later, when certain alterations in their arrangement took place. After Lady Palmerston's death, her husband, who was devotedly attached to her, never again resided at East Sheen, but removed to Broad-lands in Hampshire,[2] which beautiful place hereafter became the home of their descendants. To this place Lord Palmerston removed all the pictures, where they still remain.[3]

1724

ARMS OF TEMPLE.

[1] Mr. A. Houblon became possessed of the family pictures (now at Hall-ingbury) through the will of Mr. Peter₆ Houblon, while those which had been in the possession of S. Pepys came to him through Sir James Houblon's sons, both of whom died s. p.

[2] Now the property of the Right Hon. Evelyn Ashley.

[3] Among the portraits included in an 'Account of my Pictures att East Sheene,' made by Lord Palmerston in 1724, are the following: 'Sir Richard Hubert (Lady Palmerston's grandfather); John King, Bishop of London (her great-grandfather); Mrs. Berkeley (she was a daughter of Sir Edw. Berkeley of Stratton, and wife to the Bishop); Lord and Lady Berkeley; Dr. Philip King; Sir John and Lady Temple (the first Lord Palmerston's parents); Sir John and Lady Temple (his grandparents); Lord and Lady Palmerston, by Mr. Dahl (the latter the picture of Anne Houblon prior to her marriage); Lord Portland (the friend of the King) and his wife, by Kneller; Monsieur de Witt, done in Holland; Mr. Peter Houblon; Mr. Isaac Houblon, by Lely; Mr. Harry Houblon, by Wissing; Master Temple, (he died before his father, and his son became the second Viscount, and the father of the statesman); old Mr. Houblon; Mrs. Isaac Houblon (grand-daughter of Henry King, Bishop of Chichester); Mrs. Abraham Houblon (Dorothy King), wife's mother, by Wissing; Mr. Abra. Houblon, by Lely; Mrs. Hubert, by Lely; Lady James Houblon; Lord Palmerston, by Richter; Lady Palmerston and "Bussy."' ₗ This portrait is by Dahl, the dog by

The year 1719 saw a great change in the life of Sir Richard Houblon. Till now he had been in the thick of business, both commercial and of the Bank, while he was also a man of many friends, active and keen in whatever came to his hand. But he now retired from the direction of the Bank, and the same reason that inspired this step doubtless prompted others all pointing towards one object—namely, the reducing all effort, whether mental or physical, to a minimum. We now likewise find a correspondence beginning between him and his cousin, the Reverend Jacob₂ Houblon, showing that the latter had already begun to assist him in many matters relating to his property. Three years subsequently Mr. Abraham Houblon died, but before this event a family council was held, which ultimately found expression in the formation of a Trust, of the objects of which we shall presently hear.

The German King went regularly to Hanover 'to enjoy himself,' which he failed to do in the country of his adoption. Writing in 1719, Sir Richard Houblon announced to his father in the country, one of these expeditions. ' I have noe newes to amuse you with,' he said, 'except that the King goes to Hanover Thursday, and has left these underwritten to governe matters in his absence: Kingston Roxb°, Parker, Canterbury, Kent, Marlb°, Prat, Berkeley, Craggs, Greenwich, Newcastle, Sunderland.' Truly there was safety in numbers of the Lords Justices!

In spite of discontent, matters political had settled down much since the advent of the Hanoverian royal

1719

Wooton. Opposite this full-length picture is one by Allan Ramsay of Queen Caroline, to whom Lady Palmerston was Lady-in-waiting. With reference to the picture of Dr. King, we find his memory still cherished to the third generation. At the foot of his monument in the Cathedral of Chichester is an inscription to the effect that 'The most noble Anne, Viscountess Palmerston, kinswoman of the aforesaid Bishop' (he was her great-uncle), had caused it to be repaired and embellished.

family. The step had been taken, and a sleepy routine —the more pronounced that it was the result of reaction after a great national revolution—had supervened, and political apathy was general. While people were satisfied that in the enjoyment of peace the country's interests were safe, they felt too little concern in the King and his ministers to rouse themselves to either criticise, condemn, or approve; but while all was quiet in politics, it was otherwise with other matters. Having sacrificed their allegiance to their rightful King, because they could not have him without his Church, men now began to criticise in the Church of England what still savoured of 'Rome and Popery.' Under 'Goody Anne, the Church's wet-nurse,'[1] as Horace Walpole irreverently called her, the Church had prospered greatly, and perhaps at the time of her death it was in greater influence and power than at any other period before or since, chiefly through the systematic support of the Queen. But from this time forward, criticism was freely brought to bear on both Church and clergy.

The new freedom to think, speak, and write uncontrolled and uncondemned by theology in power and authority, undoubtedly tended to exaggeration, for the revolt against dogmatic teaching blinded many to the gold of truth, because it had been so long buried in vessels of clay.[2] But, meanwhile, the Church herself, State-supported and State-endowed, retained her privileges unchallenged, except by a wordy warfare.

Deism, or the religion of nature, was another phase of the same spirit of independent criticism and inquiry, and was the direct outcome of the rationalism of the day. This rationalism manifested itself in every direction, in literature, politics, and science, as well as in theology and religion. Many of the best thinkers of the time

---

[1] See *Correspondence of Hon. Horace Walpole*, iv. 558. London, 1820.
[2] See Sir Leslie Stephen, *English Thought in the Eighteenth Century*, ii. 98.

were deists, as well as the most brilliant of the literary
and political circles, both of Whigs and Tories, though
the rank and file of the nation was untouched by the
thought.[1]   Later in the century scepticism increased, and
was to expand into a far more searching speculation into
the deepest questions relating to man and the Deity.
New problems presented themselves to be sifted, studied,
and pondered, and while on the one side men lightly
overthrew the old milestones of their faith, at no period
in the history of thought has a more earnest endeavour
been made than in the common-sense eighteenth century,
to reconcile 'facts and phenomena' with the teachings of
a 'revealed religion,' which had never been questioned
in the past.

While the old thought was changing in this direction, no
less a revolution was going on in another, that, namely,
of the great commercial and industrial concerns of the
country, with the development of which we have tried
to follow the fortunes of the Houblon family.   Trade
and commerce had indeed prospered greatly, but the
merchant of the old school saw many changes coming.
The industrial revolution was already heralding a not far
distant future, and every year saw more clearly where it
would lead.   The old ways, thoughts, and traditions
belonged now to the past, and the domains of commerce
were being freely invaded by new men, who waxed
impatient of the stately methods and solid procedure of
bygone days.[2]

We have told what little is known of Sir Richard
Houblon's life, and it remains but to relate the history
of a plan upon which he had set his heart, and to
which, we believe, his father agreed shortly before his
death.   If he was the last of the merchant princes of
his name, he was not the least original in mind and

[1] Sir Leslie Stephen, *Ford Lecture*, p. 107.
[2] Cunningham, *History of English Industry in the Eighteenth Century*,
p. 362.

SIR RICHARD HOUBLON, KT.

action. Most of the Houblons had possessed some
degree of initiative and independence of thought; they
had not been content as a rule to run in the grooves
they found, simply because they were there, and were
well worn and easy to follow. They were pioneers,
from the time of their first bold break with the fetters of
tradition, in the fair Flanders of the earlier generations,
and they continued to be both progressive and dis-
cerning as to those coming events in human history
which 'cast their shadows before.' Sir Richard Houblon
early recognised the approaching industrial problem.
As one of the old order of business men, he saw that the
position in the future would be untenable, and extricated
himself and his successors in good time. And so it
came to pass that he closed the long line of commercial
Houblons as seventh in direct descent, and carved out
new duties and surroundings for those who were to
follow him.

In agriculture and in its improvement, together with
the life of a country gentleman, Sir Richard recognised
a future of usefulness and honour for coming generations,
and shaped his course accordingly. Besides, a new era
of prosperity had already set in, in respect of agriculture.
A far-reaching and luminous act had been passed in the
early days of the Revolution, having for its object the
increase of the food supply of the country.[1] In that it
resulted in a great revival of the agricultural industry,
and a large increase in the land brought under cultivation, it proved a great success.

All the older merchants had country-houses, and
most had also some land. Within many miles round
London, the villas, residences, farms, and manor-

· [1] 'In 1689 a bounty was given on the export of corn when the price
ranged below 48s., and this was continued, with suspensions, in the four
famine years: 1698, 1709, 1740, 1757. The result was remarkable.' See
W. Cunningham, D.D., *Growth of English Industry and Commerce in
Modern Times*, p. 371.

houses, built or purchased by them, were scattered, and Essex was their favourite haunt. The great gardener, Evelyn, had set the fashion among his many friends for a love of horticulture, while, with clipped alleys and precise walks, a corresponding necessity for order and neatness in the garden arose. New shrubs and fruit-trees were sought with ardour, and while we hear but little as yet of flowers, the vegetable garden had also its beginning and its care. With those individuals who traced a foreign descent, the taste for horticulture was occasionally almost a passion; while the proverbial care bestowed upon the *petite culture* of the United Provinces of the Netherlands had survived in the descendants of the refugees, who even now maintained, after many generations, certain idiosyncrasies, which, however, were not confined to them only.

At the commencement of the eighteenth century the taste for agriculture, which towards the middle became so marked, was but beginning; and to those merchants who, like the Houblon brothers had for many years begun to lay 'field to field' round their country-houses near London, the slovenly, careless, and wasteful processes of English agriculture of those days must have been a continual eyesore. Their efforts to remedy and improve the cultivation of their own land were now leading them more and more to turn their eyes away from town to country, while many of them who had ample means and no need to make money had come to see, in a better development and cultivation of land, a return for capital invested, as well as an occupation both interesting and new to themselves. With the will to purchase, the supply met the demand. Not only did many large estates come into the market, but the yeoman class of small landed proprietors cultivating their own farms—thickly dotted as they were over the country—were both tempted by purchasers' offers, and also frequently willing themselves to become the tenants of those to whom they sold their land, preferring a certain wage to the precarious profit of ownership. Their lives had been hard, and their living uncertain; for the old methods were faulty and wasteful, while the total absence (for the most part) of capital made bad seasons both ruinous to themselves and their property.

The El Dorado of English agriculture had long been over; the wars of the Roses are said to have destroyed it, and it needed strong effort and much capital to root out the weeds which infested both land and the slow-paced thought of country life. Both were found in the class which had already demonstrated its fitness for carrying out well what it should attempt. The owners of capital therefore in London and the big cities, the merchant, the trader, etc., continued to buy land and cultivate it [1] with independence of old systems, and with freedom from the restrictions of poverty which had militated against any such enterprise on the part of the old owners of the soil. Doubtless many mistakes were made and costly experiments wasted; but the new-comers bought their own experience, and if they paid somewhat heavily to gain the knowledge that old ways are not necessarily wrong because they are old, but may occasionally be the outcome of a successful experience, it was no loss to them in the end.

The acquisition of so much land, and the invasion of the counties by this new race of landowners, stirred the sleepy country neighbourhoods to their very depths. Modern political criticism has bombarded these new-comers with much obloquy, and traces to their supposed greed the extinction of the historic yeoman—as if they had not agreed together in a fair bargain! It was nevertheless both a loss to the community at large, and

[1] Lecky, *History of England in the Eighteenth Century*, i. 196.

to the social order in the country, that the yeoman class should disappear, or nearly so. It had in the past formed the link between the so-called rich and the poor of the country-side. The best of them appear to have now drifted to the towns, and found, in the new industrial developments, openings which were destined to make as great a change in the domain of production as their own severance from the land was bringing about in the country. Indeed, so far as our present subject is concerned, it is in this 'general post,' comprising the transference of the town element to the country, while that of the country correspondingly went to meet the demand created by the industrial revolution in the town, that the migration of the Houblon family to a new sphere of existence is illustrative of what was everywhere taking place in the case of scores of other families, both rich and poor.

While taking leave of the commercial Houblons, we may perhaps reflect with some satisfaction, that from the outset of their career in this country, some three hundred and fifty years ago, they were all identified with that integrity and honour which for so long a period characterised the leaders of our commerce, and so justly placed us in the forefront of credit among the nations. For while the majority of the great and the noble amongst our ancestors had come but seldom into contact with other nations—except during the impact brought about by occasional wars,—with the men of commerce it was far otherwise, and from them it was that the character of this people was for a long period taken and received. The title 'nation of shopkeepers' owes its origin to this fact, and it is in itself a tribute to the penetrating enterprise of British commerce, that its great trade has ever been the pioneer which preceded the flag. Nor is it less remarkable, that in the national crises of past centuries, the cause of liberty and religion have ever found their warmest supporters among commercial men.

In recalling the careers of the family whose story we have tried to tell, we cannot but see how much both men and things have changed since their day. When all was at once so much simpler and slower in life and its work, the problems which now beset us on every side were mostly as yet undreamed of. But, for the crystal-clear honesty of purpose and fear of God which characterised the merchant-princes of the Houblon name, and many another like them, we owe a debt of gratitude; for they helped to build up the good name which is still ours.

APPENDIX A

EXTRACTS FROM MR. JAMES HOUBLON'S 'PIOUS MEMOIRS,' 1672-1682

CHILDREN, my joy and my Crown, You see the Earnest pressing of my Love towards you all. Let your old Father charge you to read my Councels. I beseech you neglect them not. If you mind my words and do them, you shall leave a stock behind you, that shall bless God for you.

To his Daughters

Set not your affections upon one Child more than an other, least some of them be discouraged. Have a great care you do not puffe them up with pride of apparell. Be sure you keep them under their degree rather than above. Outward pride puffeth up the heart, and is apt to taint it with other vises besides pride. . . .

When you undertake the matching of any of your Children, beg first the Assistance of God, and see that you match them in familys that fear the Lord and have gotten their estates honestly. So may you expect God's Blessing.

To his Sons

If riches increase, set not your heart upon them, for they are perishing things. But use them to those ends for which they were given, and lay up your treasure in heaven.

Beware of that beastly evill of drinking more than will suffice. This maketh men fools, and draweth after it all other evills.

Refrain from playes, and abhor all those meetings where Satan layes his train. Be diligent in your Callings.

Let your aged Father desire you that you live in love and unity together, so shall you be a bundle of shafts which Satan shall not break.

I have loved you all, therefore so live together that when I am gone men may say, these are the Children of such a Father, see how they love one another!

Where true love is, God is.   For God is the God of love.

The man who is moved by piety hath a pleasure that can never cloy or over-work the mind.   This pleasure is easy and portable; such a one as he cary's about in his bosom without alarming either the eye or the envy of the world.   He is like a traveler puting all his goods into one jewel, the value is the same and the convenience greater.

Be slow to speak, ponder well what you say before you deliver it.   For while it is with you it is your own.   But having spoken, it is anothers.

Be not hasty in any thing you undertake.

Do all things with good deliberation, and in matters of moment first ask Counsel of God, then take advise of them that fear him.

If for our sins God should permit popery to come in, labour by earnest prayers that he would give you his Grace that you may be able to stand in the day of Visitation . . . but say as that good man did : ' I will tread upon Wife and Children rather than forsake my God.'

Whatever losses or sufferings yo may undergo, be sure you hold fast the Jewel of a good Conscience.   Constancy is the crown of religion.   Forsake all your goods, yea your very lives, rather than comply with popery.   If you must needs suffer, choose it rather than sin.   If persecution by God's providence befall you, Remember the holy Martyr who said as he was going to be burnt: ' One stile more and I shall come to my Father's house.'

Be faithful to all trusts that shall be committed to you. Keep a concience clear of all deceit.

Be especially Charitable to the French Church.   I know not any Charity better bestowed or more faithfully managed. Remember them with others.   There your Ancient Father was Babtized, there in a happy day was he married, and in that Congregation were yo all Christen'd.

Children, if there shou'd happen any Troubles or confusions in this Kingdom, be sure you be not drawn to side with any dissenting party. Cleave to him or them which God hath put in Authority.

If it be posible, meddle not with them that are contentious; mind your owne families and callings. Be not too curyous to hear or tell News, for this stealeth away too much of our precious time from better discourse, and the minding of your callings.

APPENDIX B

LETTERS, WRITTEN FROM EDINBURGH IN 1707, BY JAMES, HOUBLON TO HIS BROTHER WYNNE IN LONDON. [*Bank of England.*][1]

Abstract.

BERWICK UPON TWEED, yᵉ 27th *July* 1707.

I write yᵒ Fryday yᵉ 25th from New Castle, wᶜʰ place we left that Afternoon, at 4, we came to Morpeth at 7 being 12 miles, & thence we departed at 6 in yᵉ morning, din'd at Alnwick 14 miles, & Lay att Belford being 12 miles, we Left this Place at 10 a Clock being detain'd by yᵉ Tides flowing in, yᵗ we coud not pass yᵉ Coast sooner, & we got hither by 2 a clock being 12 mile, & now I have given yᵒ an exact Journal of our Progress throughout South Brittain, yesterday we had very rough roads, & our Lodging but Indifferent; we have but 40 mile to Edinburgh, & we intend to persuade our Coachman to drive it thro too morrow, there being no tolerable Lodging by yᵉ Way. This is a miserable place. We found here a letter from yᵉ Post master of Edinbʳ who has taken Lodgings for us there.

EDINBURGH, yᵉ 29th *July* 1707.

I wrote yᵒ, Dear Brother, from Berwick a Sunday where we had Honours done us by yᵉ Govʳ, who set 2 Centinels at our Door all night, order'd yᵉ Gates to be open'd at wᵗ hour we pleas'd, & wⁿ we went out of yᵉ Town 2 Parties of yᵉ Garrison were drawn up in yᵉ Streets, and complimented us wᵗʰ their Muskets, & a Lieutenant at yᵉ Head of 'em Saluted us wᵗʰ great Civility. We left Berwick at ½ an hour after 4 yesterday morn, & got in here by ½ an hour after 8 being 40 miles. We were

[1] Printed by permission of the Governor and Directors of the Bank of England. See p. 316.

much star'd at as we went up ye Town, & coud hardly get out of our Coach for ye throng of People: We have been visited too day by most of ye Comissⁿ of ye Equivalent;[1] & this after-noon waited on ye Lord Chancellour, who has invited us to dinner a Friday, & this night we were handsomly treated at Supper at a Tavern by some of ye Comissⁿ, wch is ye reason I cannot write y^o at Large. I am Lodg'd 4 Stories, & some of us 8 Stories high, here are Houses 16 Stories. Y^e Women all wear Scotch plods on their heads as a vail, & Look like so many Harlequins, & have an Air too of Nuns. Some wear 'em wth a Degagee Air y^t is agreable.

This is no cheap Place as is given out, a Gentleman y^t has Liv'd at Lond^o, says this is ye Dearer. The Scots are uneasy at ye seizing of their Wines after a Transire was granted to send y^m to Lond^o, & also at ye Pressing their Seamen out of Their Ships. These are wrong Steps, and will render matters ye more difficult to us.

I fear ye Post Office wil be Shut being 11 at Night.

Abstract.

EDINB^o. ye 5th Augt 1707.

DEAR BROTHER,—Wee are treated wth all imaginable Civility by our Brother Comissⁿ, & all ye People in ye Gouvernm^t, my Lord Chancelour (who is a fine Gentleman) is particularly obliging to us, wee have twice din'd wth him at his own House, Last night we Supp'd wth my Lord Ross, & Last week wth my Lord Register, besides 2 or 3 other entertainm^{ts}, wch is one very great hardship upon us, not wth Standing ye wine is incompar-able, & y^t I drink Water wth it, to save my self all I can.

I must repeat y^t from ye better sort, & all y^o Friends to ye Union, we have all ye Deference shew'd us y^t is possible, & I may say since we came down, ye affair of ye Equivalent is in a much better Posture, for before nothing was done preparatory to it; ye Comissⁿ at Odds between Themselves, & full of Diffidence ab^t Exchequer-Bills; But we have so manag'd matters, y^t all reasonable People will accept y^m in paym^t; but we have to do wth a Great number y^t are not so, & who are Enemies to ye Gouvernm^t, & therfore 't wil be requisite y^t another Convoy of mony come down from London. The 100,000£ &ca. ariv'd here this noon, & is safe Lodg'd in y^e

[1] See p. 316.

Castle, it gave a very great Alarm to y⁰ People of this Place, &
some are not yet satisfi'd there was Mony in y⁰ Carriages, but
Amunition or Stones, & they're apprehensive they are to carry
back y⁰ Crown, in short a good share of y⁰ Mob are very
Angry, & threw Stones at y⁰ Bank-Officers & Coachmen;
Here are frequently Riots about y⁰ Excise, & some Brewers
have left off Brewing, & y⁰ Mob woud oblige y⁰ rest to put
out their Fires, wᶜʰ is no ill-laid Design to raise a Commotion:
But I find They Stand much in Awe of y⁰ Soldiery; but I
coud wish some of 'em were chang'd for English Troops. The
novelty of paying y⁰ Excise, & y⁰ harshness of some parts of
it to y⁰ Poorer sort, wᵗʰ y⁰ Seising of their Wines, & Pressing
their Seamen all at one Juncture, contributes very much to
sower these People, who were before but too much dispos'd to
be Factious: But I am in hopes, measures wil be taken above,
I mean by my Lord Treasurer &ca. to redress these Matters,
so yᵗ we may Live easy y⁰ Time we are to be here, & to enable
us y⁰ better to succeed in y⁰ Errand we are sent upon.

This comes by Express, my Lord Chancellour having offer'd
us y⁰ Civility to forward our letters.

We were at Kirk a Sunday, & saw Two Stand upon y⁰
Stool of Repentance.

Abstract.

EDINBURGH, 12*th August* 1707.

DEAR BROᴿ.,—Wee hope our next letters will bring an accᵗ of
some progress made in y⁰ Siege of Thoulon, for nothing will
more effectually calm y⁰ Spirits of these people than our
success against y⁰ French, never were greater division in any
Country, & y⁰ Parliamᵗ of Great Brittain will have a great deal
of work to settle matters upon a good foot, y⁰ officers of y⁰
Customs & excise have a very hard task of it, for by their
good will these North Britains would be exempt from both.

Our particular affair of y⁰ Equivalent goes on very well, y⁰
only difficulty I att present apprehend is how to bring about to
secure our leaving this place in October. Indeed all the
Comⁿ who are members of Parliamᵗ seem fully resolved to
be up att y⁰ beginning of y⁰ Sessions, & they are 17 out of 21,
for 4 have not qualified themselves, and 9 being a quorum all
business must stand still, but then on y⁰ other hand 'tis next to
impossible for us to pay the whole equivalent by y⁰ time, nor

will it be allowed (I fear) y^t ye comission should be adjourned while any one has legale demands upon us, how this difficulty will be provided for I cannot Imagine.

Abstract.

EDINBURGH, 26*th* *Aug*^{t} 1707.

DEAR BROTHER,—This day wee began payment to the Affrican Comp^y wch will prove a heavy worke by reason of the many difficulties in peoples titles, some of them have 20 different incumbrances upon em & if the Com^n for the Equivalent should make a wrong payment theyr lyable to make it good, insomuch that wee have paid only 23 Certificates to day Am^o to about £10000, whereof $\frac{2}{3}$ pts in Excheq^r bills, but this will not hold because the takers of bills come most at y^e begining to have the Advantage of being paid before they come in Course Wee having thought it proper to give that preference, & indeed wee Stand in need of all helps to Invite people to Accept of Bills, yesterday the body of Merch^ts mett on purpose & resolved to take none of them, however I am not out of hopes but that wth the £50000 on the Road Wee shall be able to discharge the Affrican Comp^y & for the rest wee shall be better able to deale with them & most of them will be glad to gett bills.

All last Weeke the Councill was taken up to consider of a method for regulating the Coin, & I being one of the Com^tee apointed by the Com^n of the Equivalent to conferr wth their Lord^ps on that subject, had the honour to be gratiously heard by them, & in a good measure to be Instrumentall to putt em by from a project that I thought would be burdensome to the People & very troublesome to the Com^n of the Equivalent, soe that all ended in a proclamation for a free Coynage & for the speedy setting the mint at Worke the Com^n of the Equivalent agreed to advance to the Bank £5000 ste^g upon Condition that they would send into the Mint that summe at least in Curr^t Spetie but all difficultys About the Coyne Arise from the Backwardnesse & ill posture of the Mint who will not be Able when in their Geers to coin above 3 to £4000 a Week the same cause that made the recoyning our money in 1697 soe very dangerous and hurtfull to the Publick.

My Lord Chancellour has been perticulary civill & Obliging & has given us all Imaginable Assistance in our Affaires.

Wee have dined 3 times with him & last Saturday at Leith, at the Invitation of Sr Thomas Burnett who is a great freind of mine, he is Cosin Germain to the Bishop, the head of the family of ab^t £2000 a year—a great Estate in this Country. The going to Leith is the top diversion of this towne & yet 'tis a very small one, but a' Saturday it hapned to be more soe then Ord^y by the coming into the Road of two Dutch men of Warre with about 100 herring Buttes. Wee had a taste of them & I never eat better Pickle Herring. Theres speedily to be a great hunting Match in the highlands, where will meet together about 3000 of the Tories & Papists, the Gouvernment seem to think tis upon some designe, but I beleive they will not dare to Attempt any thing without forreign Assistance & their old freind is not at present in condition to give them any, but these people are soe blind as to be under a full persuasion that ye P. of Wales will be here in less than 6 months. I could not have thought the Populace soe much disaffected to the Union as I find they are, but nothing will sett them to rights soe Effectually as the taking of Tholon of which I hope by next post wee shall have a good Acc^t.

I see Bank stock rises soe I imagine they call in no more 10 PC^{ts} to prevent which nothing will more contribute then our calling for no more money hither, & our leaving a good summe lock'd up in Bills till the Com^n returne from Parliament. I doe not know what our freinds at the Bank think of it, but if they were truely acquainted with the matter they must confesse Wee have done them good service in coming downe, for but a few dayes before wee Arrived the Comm^n were about throwing up all & sending an Expresse to Whitehill not to come forward with the mony & Bills, & what would have been the Consequence of that I leave you to Guesse. You desired mee to give you a perticular Acc^t of our Manadgments here Otherwise I had not said so much of it.

Abstract.

EDINBURGH, ye 16th Sep^t 1707.

What I write y^o was to comply wth your desire of knowing what pass'd here, wth out ever expecting it woud be communicated to any body else, especially ye Court of Directors, otherwise I shoud have done it more fully, & also more

Correctly; however I shall always own y⁰ favour (as I ought to do) of those Genᵗ yᵗ declar'd for me wᵗʰ so much Partiality, yᵗ They've Left me only to wish yᵗ What They said was true.

As to y⁰ Buissness of y⁰ Equivalent, I have Little to add to my Last. We paid yesterday & too day to y⁰ African Compᵃ 8750£ whereof in excheqʳ Bills 3150£, and in all 136300£.

As to Exchequer Bills being at Discᵒ, I remain of Opinion there is more said about it then is done; for on Saturday Last a Merchant came for our Bill on Londᵒ, & brought a part in Specie, and desir'd We woud Change it another time, when He shoud bring us Excheqʳ Bills. We desir'd him to procure Bills then, & accordingly he went in search of 'em, but coud get none, so he paid us his Mony.

Another yesterday desir'd all bills in paymᵗ upon accᵗ his Interest in y⁰ African Compᵃ Stock, & added mony to 'em to make up his Sum for wᶜʰ He took our Bills.

Besides we have for some time given orders to a Person of Repute of this Town, to give any body par for Excheqʳ Bills yᵗ shoud offer 'em upō Discᵒ, as far as some Hundreds of pounds yᵗ we have by us; But to this day, we hear nothing from him: so yᵗ I do think y⁰ Bills are rather more in Credit then They were, & I am of Opinion wⁿ we have finisht y⁰ Gross of our Paymᵗˢ (& then there wil be no more Bills Issu'd) yᵗ They wil be at Par, & possibly better if there be any demand by Exchᵃ for mony at Londᵒ when we have Left this Place; For of abᵗ 64000£ y⁰ Total of wᵗ Issu'd out in Exchequer Bills, we have now taken in abᵗ 41000£. However here are People, who assure us Some Bills have been chang'd at Discᵒ, & this not through a real Want of Reputation in y⁰ Bills; for y⁰ most ignorant know they are mony at Londᵒ, and mony to such who are to pay anything to y⁰ Gouvernmᵗ for y⁰ Land Tax, Excise &ca.: But every one has not opportunities of disposing of their mony yᵗ way, & y⁰ more for yᵗ there are no Bills of 5 & 10£ wᶜʰ woud have greatly promoted their Currency.

Last Week one Murray was taken up for Corresponding wᵗʰ France (where he has Lately been) upon an Information from above.

PARAGRAPH PEDIGREE OF THE
HOUBLON FAMILY

(See also Skeleton Pedigree, page 363)

I. Jehan₁ des Houbelon, gentilhomme of Picardy. Settled at Fives, near Lille, in Flanders, where he died before 1523. Spoken of as 'natif de Fives.' He left a son.

II. Jehan₂ Houbelon. Apprenticed in Lille. By his first wife (a Frenchwoman) he had four children. Admitted bourgeois of Lille, 1523. Was a foreign merchant trading to England. Died in 1555. He married secondly, in 1523, Catherine Bave (bourgeoise), by whom he had three sons and a daughter.

i. Jean₃ Houbelon, eldest son. See below, III.

ii. Pierre₁, second son of first wife. Supposed to have come to England about 1550, and to have settled in Cornwall. Stowe mentions a Peter H. in 1576. A Protestant. Probable ancestor of the Hoblyns of Cornwall. His wife Jehenne ——.

iii. Hubert Houbelon, third son of first marriage. Concerned in a conspiracy and banished from Lille in 1581. Afterwards a *Malcontent* (wars of the Netherlands).

iv. Pasquette.

v. Nicolas₁ Houbelon, merchant, eldest son of second marriage. Born at Lille after 1523. Came with his wife to London before 1550. Made a denizen. As a Merchant

Stranger forwarded protestant literature packed with goods to Lille (1586). Executor to his brother Jean₂ in 1593. Married Marie —— ; she died in 1586. He died *s. p.* in London after 1593.

vi. Regnault Houbelon, merchant of Lille. Born after 1523. Renewed his bourgeoisie in 1550. Married, 1549. There were two sons and a daughter by the marriage, viz.:

i. Pierre Houbelon, son of Regnault of Lille. Born after 1550. He had two sons and a daughter.

1. Antoine, born at Lille, 14 March 1585. Came to London, where a Merchant Stranger. Died *s. p.* Will proved, 17 June 1648. Married Ruth Hanna. She was living in 1636.	2. François, subsequently settled in Cornwall. Died 1618.	3. Margaret, married : 1st —— Taylor 2nd —— Orelieur.

ii. Jehan Houbelon, second son of Regnault. Merchant of Lille. Born after 1550. A bourgeois in 1578. Married Jeanne de Lepierre, by whom he had a daughter :

Catherine Houbelon, sole heir of the catholic branch of the family at Lille. Born in 1589, and married, 20 April 1600, Antoine van Ackère, merchant. (His father, formerly of Ghent, was a prudhomme of Lille.) He died 1646. Catherine died 4 October 1620. Besides a son—a priest—and two daughters—nuns—they had a son, Dénis van Ackère, bourgeois 2 January 1627, who married, 24 March 1626, Catherine du Hot. Their son, Philipe van Ackère, was ancestor of the Comtes van de Cruisse de Waziers. Department de la Somme, France.

vii. Georges Houbelon, sixth son of Jean₂ of Lille. Born after 1523. Renewed bourgeoisie in 1558. A merchant. Died *s. p.*

viii. A daughter. Married, in 1548, François Desquière.

III. Jean₃ Houbelon, eldest son of Jehan₂ of Lille. Born before 1523. A foreign merchant. Joined reformed faith and fled to England (1567) during the Alva persecutions. As a Merchant Stranger in London gave £100 to the City loan to the Queen, 1588. Will proved, May 1593, when he appointed his brother Nicolas₁ and his wife's uncle, Erasme de la Fontaine, his executors.

He married in Lille, Marie, daughter of Nicolas de la Fontaine. By her he had two sons and a daughter, viz. :—

i. Pierre₂ Houbelon. See below, IV.

ii. Nicolas₂, second son of Jean₃ Houbelon and Marie de la Fontaine. Born at Lille. Followed his father to London, where a Merchant Stranger. Executor to his brother Pierre₂, and 'overseer' to his children in 1593. He married, in 1605, Marie Godescal, by whom he had two sons, Nicolas₃ and Jean, and three daughters. Will proved, 18 April 1618. She was living in 1647.

iii. Edeth, daughter of Jean₃ Houbelon and Marie de la Fontaine. Married in London, George Carterith.

IV. Pierre₂ Houbelon, eldest son of Jean₃ and Marie de la Fontaine. Born at Lille, 1557. Followed his father to London. Became a 'distinguished merchant of Elizabeth's time.' A denizen, 2 February 1590. Member of Dyers' Company. Noncupative will, 10 August 1593. Died of plague, and buried at St. Olave's, Southwark, 11 August, aged 36. He married Marie de la Motte, by whom he had four sons and two daughters. Appointed his brother Nicolas₂ 'overseer' to his young children. His wife Marie died (probably of plague), and was buried 7 September 1593. Their children were :—

i. Pierre₃ Houbelon, eldest son of Pierre₂ and Marie de la Motte. A Diacre (minister) of the French Church in Threadneedle Street. He died September 1634, having married Marie, daughter of Jean du Quesne, *l'aisné*, 4 May 1613. They had three sons and two daughters, viz. :—

1. Peter₁ᵥ Houbelon (*le jeune*). Member of the Dyers' Company. A merchant. Captain of the Blue Regiment of Train Bands. Fought in the Civil Wars. Married, 16 April 1632, Marie Mercier. Portrait in armour dated 1651.

2. James Houbelon of Southwark. A merchant.

3. John.

4. Mary. Married, April 1616, Daniel Mercier, merchant.

5. Elizabeth.

ii. Jean Houbelon, second son of Pierre₂ and Marie de la Motte.   Married Marie, daughter of Henri Phélipe of Canterbury.   Died 1625.

iii. ? Justin.   Emigrated to America.

iv. Elizabeth.   Married Jean Durand, merchant.

v. Anne.   Married Jacques Durand, merchant.

vi. James₁ Houblon.   See below, V.

V. James₁ Houblon, youngest child of Pierre₂ and Marie de la Motte.   Born, 2 July 1592, in London.   A Merchant Adventurer.   Member of the City Committee for Affairs of Ireland during Civil Wars.   Styled by S. Pepys (who wrote his epitaph) ' Pater Bursae Londinensis.'   He had ' five sons flourishing merchants.'   He died 20 June 1682, aged 90, having married, 11 November 1620, Marie, daughter of Jean du Quesne, *le jeune*.   She was born 24 October 1602, and died of the plague; buried, 16 September 1646.   They had issue ten sons and three daughters, viz.:—

i. Mary.   Born, 24 October 1621 ; died young.

ii. Peter₄ Houblon, eldest son of James₁ and Mary du Quesne.   Born, 4 July 1623.   Merchant.   Foreman of Inquest, Cordwainers' Company.   He died, 27 January 1691, having married Elizabeth, daughter of Courtois Dingley, by whom he had a son and two daughters, viz. :—

1. Peter₅ Houblon, merchant.   An officer in the London Train Bands ; Colonel in 1690 by appointment of City Lieutenancy.   In 1694 elected one of the original directors of the Bank of England. He bequeathed his grandfather's (Mr. James₁ Houblon) family pictures to his nephew, Sir Richard Houblon.   He died unmarried, 1712.

2. A daughter.

3. A daughter.

iii. Ann, second daughter of James₁ Houblon and Mary du Quesne.   Born, 13 March 1624.   Married, 14 March 1644 : 1st, Jacob Jurin, merchant ; 2nd, Tempest Milner, 7 November 1653.

iv. Sara, third daughter. Born, 18 August 1627. Married, 4 March 1645, James Lordell, merchant and alderman, one of the first directors of the Bank of England in 1694.

v. Sir James₂ Houblon, merchant, second son of James₁ and Mary du Quesne. Chairman of the Spanish Company of Merchants. Alderman of Aldgate Ward, 1691. Knighted by William III., 1691. M.P. for City of London, 1698-1700. One of the original directors of the Bank of England, 1694. A friend of S. Pepys. He died, 20 October 1700, having married, 11 May 1658, Sarah, daughter of Charles Wynne, Esq., by whom he had two sons and two daughters, viz. :—

> 1. Wynne Houblon. Born, 19 December 1659. Merchant. Died unmarried.
>
> 2. James₃ Houblon. Born, 5 March 1665. Merchant. A Commissioner for arranging the Equivalent due to Scotland, Treaty of Union, 1707. Died unmarried.
>
> 3. Catherine. Born, 5 March 1666.
>
> 4. Elizabeth. Born, April 1669. Married John Harvey, Esq., afterwards Colonel Harvey of St. Andrew's Hall, Old Beckenham, Norfolk.

vi. Sir John₄ Houblon, third son of James₁ and Mary du Quesne. Born, 13 March 1631/2. Merchant. Juryman at the trial of Lord Shaftesbury, 1681. Chairman of the Company of Merchants trading to Portugal. Alderman of Cornhill Ward. Sheriff of London, and knighted by William III., 1689. M.P. for Bodmin in three parliaments. First Governor of the Bank of England, 1694-7 ; remained on the direction till his death. A Commissioner of the Admiralty, 1693-9. On Board of Trade. Lord Mayor, 1695. Transferred from the Drapers' to the Grocers' Company. Master of the Grocers' Company, 1695. Commissioner of Accounts, 1705. Died suddenly at his house in Threadneedle Street, 10 January 1711/12. Sir John married, 11 July 1660, Marie, daughter of Isaac Jurin, merchant, by whom he had five sons and six daughters. Lady Houblon died in 1732 at Richmond.

> 1. John. Died unmarried.
> 2. Isaac. Died in Spain.

3. Samuel Houblon. A distinguished merchant. In 1719, J.P. at Edmonton. Died· unmarried in 1723, leaving large charitable bequests.

4. Matthew.

5. Benjamin = Mary Symonds.

6. Mary = Richard Mytton of Halston, Esq., M.P. for Shrewsbury.

7. Other daughters.

(Sir John Houblon's sons left no male descendants.)

vii. Daniel Houblon, fourth son of James₁ and Mary du Quesne. Died early.

viii. Jacob₁ Houblon, fifth son. See below, VI.

ix. Benjamin, sixth son. Born, 1 January 1636; died young.

x. Isaac Houblon, seventh son. Born, 1 July 1638. A merchant. In 1694/5 a director of East India Company. He died, 1700, having married, 1 August 1670, Elizabeth, daughter of Henry King of Sussex, son of the Bishop of Chichester; by her he had—

1. Henry₁, commonly called Harry. He was High Sheriff of Hertfordshire in 1707. Died *s. p.*

2. William. Married Mary ——; died *s. p.*

3. Mary. Married 1st, —— Cook, of Case Horton; 2nd, —— Selwin.

4. Anne. Died unmarried.

xi. Abraham Houblon, eighth son of James₁ and Mary du Quesne. Born, 23 January 1639/40. A merchant. One of the first directors of the Bank of England, 1694; subsequently deputy-governor, 1761-2; and governor, 1763-4. In 1702, a Commissioner in the Victualling Department (Navy). He died at Langley, his wife's property in Buckinghamshire, 11 May 1722, having married, 2 January 1672, Dorothy, only daughter and eventually heir of Sir Richard Hubert, Kt., by whom he had a son and a daughter.

1. Sir Richard Houblon, Kt., only son of Abraham and Dorothy Hubert. A merchant. Born, 19 October 1672. Of Hormead Hall, Hertfordshire, and St. James Place. Knighted by George II., 1715. A director of the Bank of England in 1713-19. Formed a family trust in 1723, in favour of Jacob₃ Houblon, his cousin Charles's only son, and 'the last heir-male of his race'; he died at Langley, November 1724, unmarried, being the last of the merchant princes of his name.

2. Anne Houblon, only daughter of Abraham and Dorothy Hubert. Born, 1682. Married, 10 June 1703, Henry Temple, eldest son of Sir John Temple of East Sheen. First Viscount Palmerston, 1722. She died in 1735, having had a son and two daughters, of whom the former was grandfather of the statesman. Lord Palmerston, who died November 1757, was appointed by his brother-in-law, Sir Richard Houblon, one of the trustees to the family settlement of 1723.

xii. Samuel Houblon, ninth son of James₁. Born, 1 February 1641; died of the plague; buried, 30 August 1646. (His mother died also of plague shortly afterwards.)

xiii. Jeremiah Houblon, tenth son. Born, 10 February 1643; died unmarried.

VI. Jacob₁ Houblon, fifth son of James₁ and Mary du Quesne. Born, 22 December 1634. Fellow of Peterhouse, Cambridge, and M.A., 1657. Instituted, 17 October 1662, to rectory of Moreton, Essex. Died at Moreton, 12 December 1698. He married, 17 July 1662, Elizabeth, daughter and heir of Dr. Thomas Whincop of Elseworth, Cambridgeshire, D.D., by whom he had three sons and five daughters, viz. :—

i. Charles₁ Houblon, eldest son. See below, VII.

ii. Jacob₂ Houblon, second son. Born, 12 February 1666. Clerk. Rector of Bubbingworth, Essex. Made trustee for family settlement by Sir Richard Houblon, 1723, in favour of his nephew, Jacob₃ Houblon, son of Charles. He died unmarried, 1736.

iii. John. A merchant. Died in Portugal.

iv. Anne. Married Dr. Lilly Butler, D.D., rector of St. Anne's, Aldersgate, and Prebendary of Canterbury.

v. Mary. Married John Trimmer.

vi. Elizabeth. Married Thomas Wragge, clerk. Their son was Rector of Great Hallingbury.

VII. Charles₁ Houblon (see vol. ii.), eldest son of Jacob₁ H. and Elizabeth Whincop. Born, 15 October 1664. A merchant trading to Portugal. Purchased

lordship of Bubbingworth Hall, Essex, in 1708.   Died,
20 March 1710/11, having married Mary, daughter and
heir of Daniel Bate, merchant of London and vintner,
and of Barton Court, Abingdon, Berkshire (she died
in 1717), leaving one son, Jacob₈, born a short time
before his father's death.

VIII. Jacob₈ Houblon, only son of Charles₁ and
Mary Bate.   Born, 31 July 1710.   The only heir-male
remaining of his race.   Educated by his uncle and
guardian, the Rev. Jacob₂ Houblon.   On coming of age
he took possession of estates purchased by the trustees
of a family settlement, and in accordance with the will
of Sir Richard Houblon, Kt.

For Jacob₈ Houblon, of Hallingbury Place, Co. Essex,
Esquire, and his descendants, see vol. ii.

DES HOUBELON
(PICARDY).

THE HOUBL

(See also Paragraph

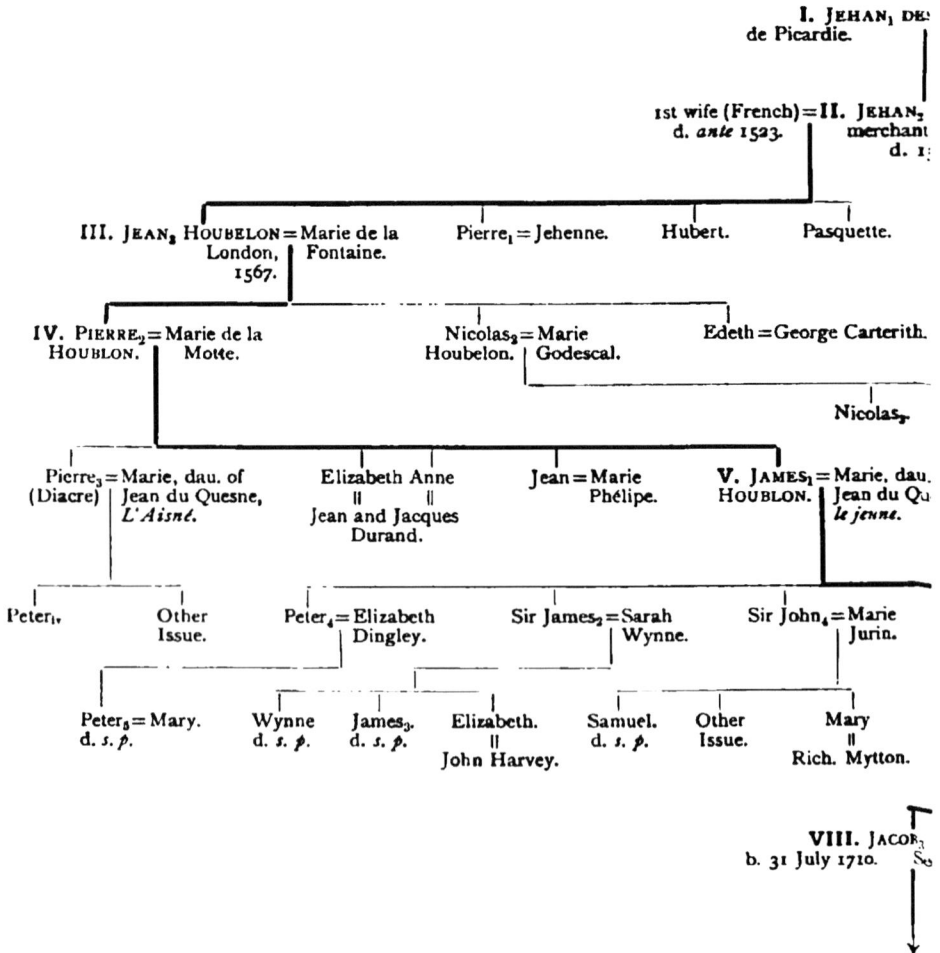

I. JEHAN₁ DE
de Picardie.

1st wife (French) = **II. JEHAN**
d. *ante* 1523. merchant
d. 1

III. JEAN₂ HOUBELON = Marie de la   Pierre₁ = Jehenne.   Hubert.   Pasquette.
London, Fontaine.
1567.

IV. PIERRE₂ = Marie de la   Nicolas₃ = Marie   Edeth = George Carterith.
HOUBLON. Motte.   Houbelon. Godescal.

Nicolas₇

Pierre₃ = Marie, dau. of   Elizabeth Anne   Jean = Marie   **V. JAMES₁** = Marie, dau.
(Diacre) Jean du Quesne,   ‖   ‖   Phélipe.   HOUBLON. Jean du Qu
L'Aisné.   Jean and Jacques   le jeune.
Durand.

Peter₁.   Other   Peter₄ = Elizabeth   Sir James₂ = Sarah   Sir John₄ = Marie
Issue.   Dingley.   Wynne.   Jurin.

Peter₅ = Mary.   Wynne   James₃.   Elizabeth.   Samuel.   Other   Mary
d. *s. p.*   d. *s. p.*   d. *s. p.*   ‖   d. *s. p.*   Issue.   ‖
John Harvey.   Rich. Mytton.

VIII. JACOB
b. 31 July 1710.

HOUBELON (CANTING).

. HOUBELON
d. at Fives, near Lille.
ante 1523.

HOUBELON=Catherine Bave,
of Lille. | 2nd wife, m. 1523.
:55- | d. betw. 1578-80.

Nicolas₁=Marie.　　Regnault=m. 1549.　　Georges,　　A dau. = François
London,　　　　　 of Lille.　　　　　 of Lille.　　　　 Desquière.
1550.

Marie.　　　　 Pierre　　　　 Jehan=Jeanne
　　　　 Houbelon of Lille.　　　 de Lepièrre.

Other Issue.

. of
ɪesne,　　 Anthony=Ruth.　　 Francis.　　 Catherine=Antoine
　　　 London.　 Hama.　　　　　 Houbelon │ van Ackère.
　　　 d. *s. p.*　　　　　　　　 of Lille,
　　　　　　　　　　　　　　 heiress.

VI. JACOB₁=Elizabeth　　 Isaac=Elizabeth　　 Abraham=Dorothy　　 Other
　　　　 Whincop.　　　　 King.　　　　 Hubert.　　 Issue.

VII. CHARLES₁=Mary　 Jacob₂.　 Other　　 William.　 Sir Richard.　 Anne=Henry Temple,
　　　　　 Bate.　 d. *s. p.*　 Issue.　 Henry.　 d. *s. p.*　 │ 1st Viscount
　　　　　　　　　　　　　 Anne.　　　　　　 ↓ Palmerston.
　　　　　　　　　　　　　 d. *s. p.*

ᵢ HOURLON,
ɪee Pedigree, vol. ii.

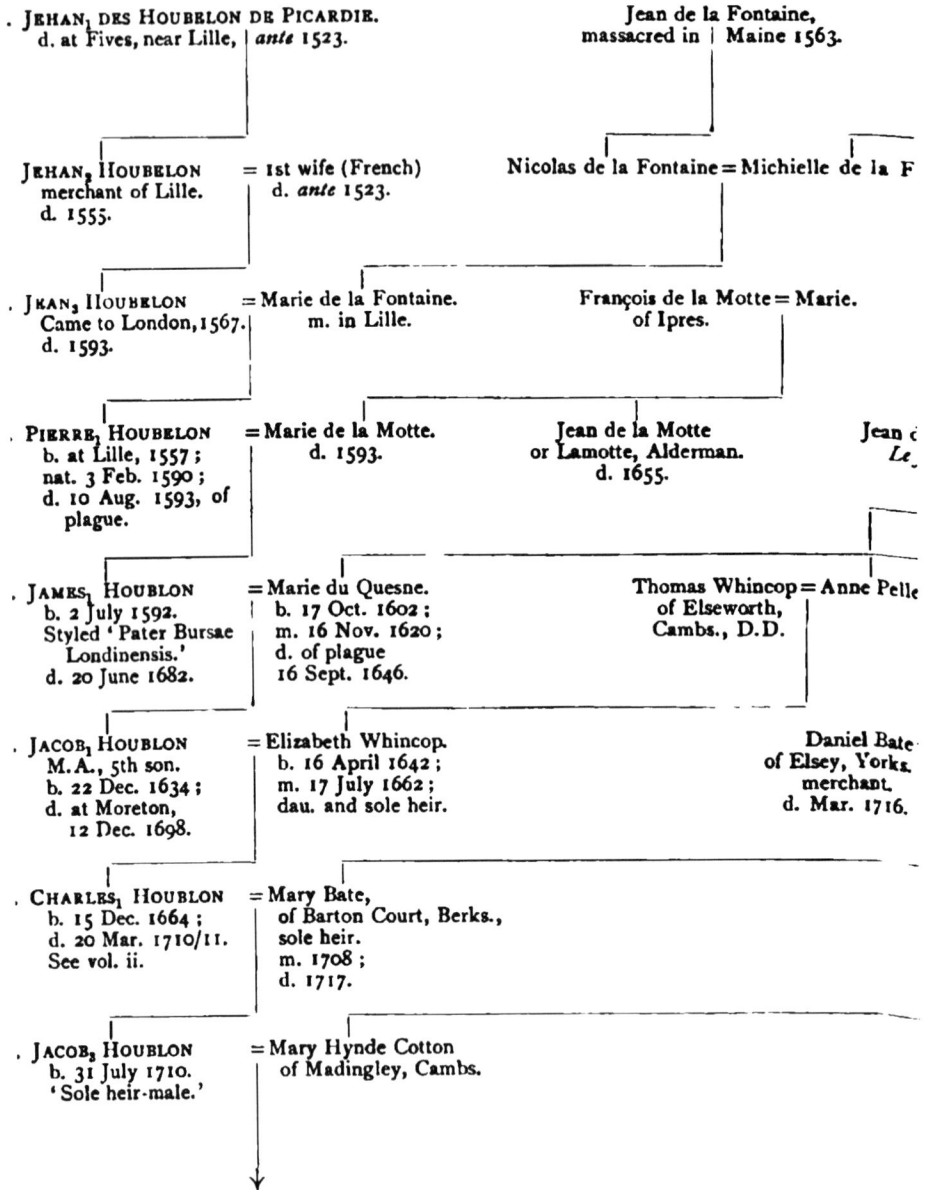

. JEHAN₁ DES HOUBELON DE PICARDIE.
d. at Fives, near Lille, | *ante* 1523.

Jean de la Fontaine,
massacred in | Maine 1563.

JEHAN₂ HOUBELON
merchant of Lille.
d. 1555.

= 1st wife (French)
d. *ante* 1523.

Nicolas de la Fontaine = Michielle de la F

. JEAN₃ HOUBELON
Came to London, 1567.
d. 1593.

= Marie de la Fontaine.
m. in Lille.

François de la Motte = Marie.
of Ipres.

. PIERRE₂ HOUBELON
b. at Lille, 1557;
nat. 3 Feb. 1590;
d. 10 Aug. 1593, of
plague.

= Marie de la Motte.
d. 1593.

Jean de la Motte
or Lamotte, Alderman.
d. 1655.

Jean ¿
L¿

. JAMES₁ HOUBLON
b. 2 July 1592.
Styled 'Pater Bursae
Londinensis.'
d. 20 June 1682.

= Marie du Quesne.
b. 17 Oct. 1602;
m. 16 Nov. 1620;
d. of plague
16 Sept. 1646.

Thomas Whincop = Anne Pelle
of Elseworth,
Cambs., D.D.

. JACOB₁ HOUBLON
M.A., 5th son.
b. 22 Dec. 1634;
d. at Moreton,
12 Dec. 1698.

= Elizabeth Whincop.
b. 16 April 1642;
m. 17 July 1662;
dau. and sole heir.

Daniel Bate
of Elsey, Yorks.
merchant.
d. Mar. 1716.

. CHARLES₁ HOUBLON
b. 15 Dec. 1664;
d. 20 Mar. 1710/11.
See vol. ii.

= Mary Bate,
of Barton Court, Berks.,
sole heir.
m. 1708;
d. 1717.

. JACOB₃ HOUBLON
b. 31 July 1710.
'Sole heir-male.'

= Mary Hynde Cotton
of Madingley, Cambs.

ALLIANCES

Pierre de la Fortérie.

Sir Wm. Cary = Lady Mary Bullen,
Lord   dau. of Earl of Wiltshire
Hunsdon.   and Ormonde (sister to
         Anne Bolyn).

a Fortérie.   Sir Francis Knowles = Lady Katherine Cary.

Jean du Quesne = Marie de la Court   Lady Anne Knowles = Thos. West,
L'Aisné.   (2nd wife).   Lord de la
                                                       Warr.

an du Quesne = Sara de Franqueville.   John Pellet = Lady Anne West.
Le Jeune.   son of
                                    Sir Benj.

Pellet.

3ate = Jane Halcott.
rks. | m. 3 Feb. 1672.
t.
16.

→   See Table of Alliances, vol. ii.

INDEX

LaVergne, TN USA
11 November 2010
204341LV00009B/7/P